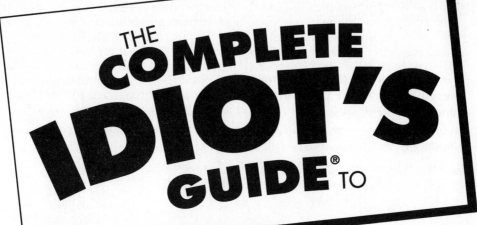

THE COMPLETE IDIOT'S GUIDE® TO

The Roman Empire

by Eric Nelson, Ph.D.

ALPHA

A member of Penguin Group (USA) Inc.

Copyright © 2002 by Eric Nelson

International Standard Book Number: 0-02-864151-5
Library of Congress Catalog Card Number: 2001091102

05   8

Interpretation of the printing code: The rightmost number of the first series of numbers is the year of the book's printing; the rightmost number of the second series of numbers is the number of the book's printing. For example, a printing code of 02-1 shows that the first printing occurred in 2002.

Printed in the United States of America

Publisher
Marie Butler-Knight

Product Manager
Phil Kitchel

Managing Editor
Jennifer Chisholm

Acquisitions Editor
Randy Ladenheim-Gil

Development Editor
Michael Thomas

Production Editor
Katherin Bidwell

Copy Editor
Susan Aufheimer

Illustrator
Chris Sabatino

Cover Designers
Mike Freeland
Kevin Spear

Book Designers
Scott Cook and Amy Adams of DesignLab

Indexer
Amy Lawrence

Layout/Proofreading
Svetlana Dominguez
Lizbeth Patterson

Contents at a Glance

Part 1: All Roads Lead to Rome   **1**

1 Dead Culture, Dead Language, Dead Emperors:
  Why Bother?   3
  *Learn different perspectives for approaching Rome and the
  Romans, and grasp the periods of Roman history and liter-
  ature.*

2 Rome FAQ: Hot Topics in Brief   17
  *Get some quick responses to frequently asked questions
  about Rome and the Romans, and learn where else to look
  in this book for more information.*

3 How Do We Know? Discovering the Romans   31
  *Discover what remains of Rome, as well as some of the
  ways that we know who the Romans were, what they did,
  and what they thought.*

4 Club Mediterrania: Rome in the Context of
  Other Civilizations   43
  *Put early Rome in context by finding out about other
  ancient civilizations that preceded and influenced it.*

5 Seven Hills and One Big Sewer: Rome Becomes a City   57
  *Learn how Rome, under the kings, developed from a group
  of villages at a crossing on the Tiber into a city, and how
  this early formation influenced Roman culture.*

**Part 2: Rome Wasn't Built in a Day: The Roman
Republic (509–27 B.C.E.)**   **73**

6 On Golden Pond: Rome Conquers Italy and the
  Mediterranean   75
  *Follow Rome's conquests of Latium, Italy, and the
  Mediterranean to become a vast empire reaching from
  the Near East to Spain.*

7 Let's Conquer ... Ourselves! The Roman Revolution
  and the End of the Republic   91
  *Learn how Rome's political and cultural forces combined
  to create internal tensions that eventually brought about
  a series of civil wars and ended the Republic.*

8 Rome, Rome on the Range: Romans at Home   105
  *Take a look at Roman culture at its most basic level, the
  family, and how the Romans conceived of themselves as a
  part of this unit. You'll also learn about Roman women
  and slaves.*

9 The Romans Among Themselves 117
Here you'll get a picture of Roman class divisions and how the Romans operated among themselves in politics, the army, and the law courts.

10 The Romans at Large 129
Discover the Romans among other people, and how people outside of Rome belonged to the Roman systems of alliances and citizenship. You'll also enter the world of Roman commerce, business, and work.

11 Literature and Culture of the Republic 139
Follow the rise of Latin literature from the importation of Greek slaves and Latin translations of Greek works to the full development of Latin as a literary language.

12 If They Build It: Roman Engineering 155
Learn how the Romans built for success, and their achievements in constructing roads, buildings, bridges, aqueducts, and machines of war.

Part 3: Empire Without End: Roman Imperial History **171**

13 Easing into Empire 173
See how Augustus and his few intimates transformed the Republic under his Principate into an empire, and how the way he did things set the stage for the dynastic struggles to come.

14 All in the Family: The Julio-Claudian Emperors 185
Learn about the first dynasty of Rome, and follow the careers of some of the most famous and infamous of all the emperors.

15 The (Mostly) Good Emperors: The Flavians to
Marcus Aurelius 199
See how the Flavians reestablished order after Nero's fall, and how a line of adopted emperors established Rome on a more secure basis during the time of its greatest power.

16 The (Mostly) Not-So-Good Emperors: Commodus
to Aurelian 215
Follow the decline and near break-up of Rome in a period of civil unrest, imperial crisis, and barbarian invasions.

17 Divide and (Re)Conquer: Diocletian to Constantine 229
Learn how the emperor Diocletian reestablished order, and how his solutions to rule led to Constantine the Great, who established Constantinople as a new capital and a triumphant Christianity as Rome's state religion.

18 Barbarians at the Gates: The Fall of the Western Empire 243
Discover in what way Rome "fell" in the west, and how the barbarian invasions changed and challenged what survived.

Part 4: Roman Imperial Life and Culture   259

   19 Roman Mass Culture of the Imperial Period   261
       Meet the Roman urban culture that grew during the
       Empire to unite broadly disparate regions and left a
       lasting imprint upon the world.

   20 (Un)Protected Sects: Religions, Tolerance, and
       Persecutions   277
       Investigate the ways in which Rome persecuted threaten-
       ing religious orders and sects in the context of Roman
       attitudes toward religion and personal belief.

   21 *Cogito Ergo Sum*: The Life of the Mind   291
       Discover the literature of the Empire, and the wide variety
       of writers, poets, and theologians who published in both
       Greek and Latin during the Silver Age and Late Antiquity,
       including the development of Christian sacred texts.

   22 That's Entertainment! Public Spectacles   303
       Thrill and chill to the Roman games: chariot racing, the-
       atrical productions of every description, and the macabre
       arena games for which the Romans are especially known.

Part 5: Where Did the Romans Go?   315

   23 And the East Goes On   317
       Follow Rome's legacy in the east through Justinian's at-
       tempt to reclaim the Empire to the sack of Constantinople
       by the Crusades and then the Turks.

   24 Nothing Quiet on the Western Front   331
       Learn how Rome's legacy in the West developed through
       the concept of reinventing the Roman Empire in the west,
       the Crusades, and Latin literature's influence on western
       thought.

Appendixes

   A Timeline   347

   B Finding the Romans on Earth and in Cyberspace   353

   C Lights, Camera, *Actio!* A Short List of Rome and
      Romans in Film   365

   D Glossary   367

      Index   375

Contents

Part 1: All Roads Lead to Rome   **1**

1 Dead Culture, Dead Language, Dead Emperors: Why Bother?   **3**

Some Surprising Facts About Rome and the Romans 4
Rome Was Multicultural 4
The First Universal Declaration of Equal Rights 5
If Latin Is Dead, You're a Talking Zombie 5
Are We Marching into the Future or in Circles? 5
So What Do *You* Mean by "Rome"? 6
Rome the City 6
Rome the State 7
Rome the Empire 8
Rome the Religious Center 8
Rome the Concept 8
Roman History in a Box 8
The Royal Period (ca 800–509 B.C.E.) 9
The Republican Period (ca 509–27 B.C.E.) 9
The Principate of Augustus (27 B.C.E.–C.E. 14) 9
The Imperial Age (Traditionally C.E. 14–476) 10
The Byzantine Period (565–1453) 11
Roman Literature in a Box 11
Early Latin Literature (ca 300–100 B.C.E.) 12
The Golden Age (ca 100 B.C.E.–Death of Augustus
in C.E. 14) 13
The Silver Age (ca 41–180) 13
The Literature of the Late Empire (ca 180–565) 13

2 Rome FAQ: Hot Topics in Brief   **17**

How Did They Do It? Conquering the World 17
It's Their Job 18
Conquering and Cooperation 18
Organization, Organization, Organization 18
Rewards and Punishments 19
Two Thumbs Up! Games and Gladiators 20
The "Games" of Rome 20
Contests of Animals and Humans 20
Human Combat and Spectacle 22
In Chains: Slaves and Slavery 23
Kinds of Slaves 23
Slave Status 23

Where Did They Come From? 24
Becoming Free 24
Some Ironies 25
Almost in Chains? Roman Women 25
Kinds of Women 25
Women's Status 26
Some Ironies 26
Lives of the Rich and Famous:
The Roman Emperors 27
When Did the Emperors Reign? 27
How Did You Get to Be Emperor? 28
What Were Whey Like? 28
Going Over Like a Lead Pipe: Why Did Rome Fall? 28
It's the Water 29
Economies off the Scale: Size Does Matter 29
Global Warming and Dust Bowls 30
The Empire Vandalized: Invasions and Incursions 30

3 How Do We Know? Discovering the Romans   31

Digging In: Ruins, Remains, and Archeological Sites 32
Rome Itself 32
Around Italy 33
*From Britain to Babylon: Remains from the
  Frontiers and Provinces* 34
Gifts of Vesuvius: Pompeii and Herculaneum 34
Under Water: What Goes Down Sometimes Comes Up 36
Words and Texts 37
Official Documents 37
Roman Literature 38
I Was Here: Graffiti and Other Unofficial Remains 39
What Other People Said 39
Early Church Texts 41

**4 Club Mediterrania: Rome in the Context
of Other Civilizations   43**

The Near East 44
Persia 44
Phoenicians 45
Civilizations on the African Continent 45
Egypt 46
Carthage and the Carthaginians 46
Libya and North Africa 47

The Greeks and Greece 48
   The Ancient Greek City-States 48
   The End of the City-State and Alexander's Empire 48
   Magna Graecia 50
Gauls and Other Barbarians 50
   Gauling Developments 50
   Epirus 51
Rome Before the Romans: Ancient Italy 52
   The Etruscans 52
   Northern Italy 53
   Central Italy 54
   The Samnites and Sabines 54
   Southern Italy 54
Location, Location, Location: The Site of the
City of Rome 54

**5 Seven Hills and One Big Sewer:
Rome Becomes a City**   **57**
Virgin Bears *Twins!* Myths of Rome's Founding 58
   The Story of Romulus 58
   The Traditional Story 60
Generals, Slaves, and Entrepreneurs: The Various
Kings of Rome 61
Throw the Bums Out! The Roman Revolution and
the Beginning of the Republic 63
   It Wasn't Murder—It Was Sewerside! *What Probably
   Happened* 64
   Huts on the Hills 64
   Royal Growing Pains 65
   Top to Bottom Social Organization 66
The Aristocratic Republic...67
Trouble in River City: The Conflict of the Orders 68
   Put That in Writing! The Twelve Tables 68
   "You and Whose *Army?" or, "Nothing Secedes Like
   Secession"* 69
   "Dr. No" 70
So ... Wait a Minute Here 71

Part 2: Rome Wasn't Built in a Day: The Roman Republic (509–27 B.C.E.) 73

6 On Golden Pond: Rome Conquers Italy and the Mediterranean 75

You Will Be Assimilated: Rome Conquers Italy
(500–270 B.C.E.) 75
Won't You Be My Neighbor? The Latin League 76
Carving Up the Neighborhood..77
The Gallic Avalanche 78
The Samnites and Central Italy 79
Pyrrhic Losses: Conquering Magna Graecia........................80
Never Out of Africa: Rome Conquers Carthage 81
*Peacemaking and Peacekeeping: The First Punic War
(264–241 B.C.E.)*..82
*Elephant in the Living Room: Hannibal and the Second
Punic War (218–202 B.C.E.)* 83
*Peace Is a Desert: The Third Punic War and the
Destruction of Carthage (151–146 B.C.E.)* 85
Go East Young Man: Rome Conquers Greece and
the East...86
The Illyrian Wars (229–228, 220–219 B.C.E.)....................86
Free to Be Roman: The Macedonian Wars...........................86
Conquering the East 87
The Wild West 88
So Gauling: Settling Northern Italy 88
In Spain, Again 88

7 Let's Conquer ... Ourselves! The Roman Revolution and the End of the Republic 91

King of the Hill 91
Business Boom 92
Trouble at the Bottom 92
He's So Popular: The Gracchae 92
Tiberius Gracchus (d. 133 B.C.E.) 93
Gaius Gracchus (d. 121 B.C.E.) 93
Marius and Sulla 94
Marius and the Birth of the Professional Soldier 94
The Social Wars (90–88 B.C.E.)..95
Call Me "Lucky": The Reign of Sulla 95

Kids These Days: Pompey and Caesar 97
  Gnaius Pompey, The Great (106–48 B.C.E.) 97
  Meet the Players 98
  Julius Caesar (100–44 B.C.E.) 99
Crossing the Rubicon: The Civil War 100
  Everything Old Is New Again 101
  The Ides of March 101
Snakes and Daggers: The Deaths of Anthony
  and Cleopatra..102
  The Second Triumvirate 102
  The End of the Republic 103

8 Rome, Rome on the Range: Romans at Home   105
How the Romans Saw Themselves 105
  Small Farmer, Big Soldier 106
  Discipline and Practicality 106
  Dignity and Authority 106
Public and Private Life 107
  Father Knows Best: The Pater Familias 107
  Education 109
  Women 110
  Urban and Rural 111
Religion 112
  That "Old Time" Religion 112
  Not Everyone's (Got) a Genius 112
  Imports and Others 113
Slaves and Slavery 115

9 The Romans Among Themselves   117
Patricians and Plebs: Social Structure and Divisions 117
  The Patricians 118
  The Plebs 118
  It's Money That Matters: Nobiles *and* Equites 118
  Patrons and the Patronized (Clients) 119
Politics and Political Structure 120
  Roman Assemblies 121
  Roman Magistrates 122
  Getting to the Top: The Cursus Honorum 123
Law 124
  Prosecution and Defense 124
  Going to Court 125
  The Precedent Principle 125

"Roman" Religion 126
Collegia 126
The Army 127
Military Service 128

10 The Romans at Large   129

Some Citizens Are More Equal Than Others 129
Latin Rights *130*
Citizenship in Italy *130*
Citizenship and Rights Abroad *131*
Friends in High Places: Foreign Clients *132*
Follow the Money: Administration and
the Perks of Conquest 132
Bringing Home the Bacon and the Bronze *133*
Got Plastic? *133*
Public-Private Partnerships *134*
It's Who You Know: Lobbyists at Rome *135*
Work, Work, Work 135
Work in the City *135*
Work in the Country *136*
Corporate Farms: Latifundia *136*
Bringing Home the Prosciutto: Trade and Luxury Goods *137*
*So Go Join the Army: The Growth of the Professional
Soldier* *137*

11 Literature and Culture of the Republic   139

Importing Culture: Early "Roman" Literature
and History 140
Liberals at Large: The Scipionic Circle 143
Made in Rome: Cato and Catonism 144
Latin Comes into Its Own: The First Century B.C.E. 145
Marcus Tullius Cicero (Cicero) 145
Pater Patriae *146*
Cicero's Orations *147*
Golden Oldies 148
Marcus Terentius Varro (Varro) *148*
Titus Lucretius Carus (Lucretius) *148*
Gaius Julius Caesar (Caesar) *149*
Gaius Sallustius Crispus (Sallust) *149*
Gaius Valerius Catullus (Catullus) *149*
The Augustan Period 150
Publius Virgilius Maro (Virgil) *150*
Quintus Horatius Flaccus (Horace) *151*

Sextus Propertius (Propertius) 151
Albius Tibullus (Tibullus) 151
Titius Livius (Livy) 151
Publius Ovidius Naso (Ovid) 152

12 If They Build It: Roman Engineering   **155**
The Empire Wore Cement Shoes 156
How All Roads Led to (and from) Rome 157
How Roads Were Built 159
When the Mountain Was High 160
When the Valley Was Low 160
When the River Ran Wide 161
The Open (and Clogged) Road 162
You Can't Lead a City to Water, But ... .163
Getting Water to the City 164
Water, Water, Everywhere 165
I Like to Watch: Theaters and Amphitheaters 166
Urban Planning 167
Building for Victory 168
Roman Camps 168
Siege Equipment 169

Part 3: Empire Without End: Roman Imperial History   **171**

13 Easing into Empire   **173**
Okay, Now What? 174
Octavian = Augustus 174
The Principate: It's the Same, Only Different 175
The Augustan Ages 175
From Actium Until 27 B.C.E. 176
27–19 B.C.E. 177
19 B.C.E.–C.E. 14 177
Augustus's Powers 178
Rome Under Augustus 179
Getting Back to Roman Values 179
In the City 180
On the Borders 180
The Era of Big Government 182
Not Too Successful with Succession 182
Trying to Get Agrippa on It 183
Turning to Tiberius 183
Intriguing or Intrigue? 184

14 All in the Family: The Julio-Claudian Emperors   185

Tiberius (C.E. 14–37) 186
Germanicus and Agrippina 187
Despot or Dilbert? 187
Sejanus 188
Stay Away … and Stay Dead 189
Gaius (Caligula) (C.E. 37–41) 189
Something Lost in the Recovery 190
Schizophrenic Adventures 190
Enough Is Enough 190
Claudius (C.E. 41–54) 191
Will the Real Claudius Please Stand Up? 191
Freedmen and Administration 192
Watch Out for the Wives 193
Nero (C.E. 54–68) 194
Good Beginnings and Mommy Dearest 194
I Gotta Be Me 195
Burn, Baby, Burn 196
Nero on the Tracks 197

**15 The (Mostly) Good Emperors: The Flavians
to Marcus Aurelius   199**

The Year of Living Dangerously 199
Galba (68–69) 200
Otho (69) 200
Vitellius (69) 200
Working Stiffs to Lord and God: The Flavian Dynasty 201
Vespasian (69–79) 202
Titus (79–81) 204
Domitian (81–96) 205
Adopting a Better Succession Policy: The Five
Good Emperors 206
Nerva (96–98) 206
Trajan (98–117) 207
Hadrian (117–138) 209
Antoninus Pius (138–161) 210
Marcus Aurelius (161–180) 211

**16 The (Mostly) Not-So-Good Emperors:
Commodus to Aurelian   215**

A "Good" Hangover: Commodus to the Severi 216
Succession in the Commodus, Again 216
Commodus (180–192) 217

Pertinax (193) *218*

Didius Julianus (March 28–June 1, 193),
Come on Down! *219*

The Severi *220*

Septimius Severus (193–211) *220*

Caracalla (211–217) and Geta (211) *222*

Macrinus (217–218) *223*

Elagabalus (Hierogabalus) (218–222)..............*223*

Alexander Severus (221–235) *224*

Another Day, Another Emperor (235–284) *224*

The Gallic Empire *225*

The Palmyrene Empire *225*

The Illyrian Emperors *226*

17   Divide and (Re)Conquer: Diocletian to
Constantine   229

Diocletian (284–305) *229*

The Dominate *230*

Maximian *231*

Empire in Four-Wheel Drive: The Tetrarchy *231*

Emperor, Reformer, and CEO *232*

Too Many Augusti and Not Enough Caesars *234*

Maxentius and Constantine *235*

Shakedown *235*

The Mulvian Bridge and Maximinus Daza *236*

Showdown *237*

Constantine the Great (324–337) *238*

Moving the Center of the Empire *238*

The Christian Empire *239*

Love and Loss *241*

18   Barbarians at the Gates: The Fall of the
Western Empire   243

"My Three Sons" *244*

Can't Rewind: Julian the Apostate (361–363) *245*

Roman Gothic: Theodosius to Alaric and the
Sack of Rome *246*

Theodosius the Great (379–395) *247*

The Boy Emperors *248*

Women of Influence *249*

Stilicho and Alaric *250*

Barbarians in the Gates: Alaric and the Sack of Rome *251*

The End Is Near 253
Know Your Barbarians 253
Aetius and the End of the Theodosians 255
The Western "Fall" 256
Rimicer (455–472) 256
Okay, This Is Almost It 256
I Said, "Almost" 257

Part 4: Roman Imperial Life and Culture   259

19 Roman Mass Culture of the Imperial Period   261

The Fabric of Empire 262
East Is East and West Is West 262
Major Cities and Capitals 263
Civis Romanus Sum: The Roman Citizen
of the World 264
Have a Little Class 265
The Rich Get Richer 266
The Poor Get Poorer 266
The Middle Gets Squeezed 267
Women 268
Slaves and Freedmen 269
The Army Life 270
Ring Around the Latin Empire 270
Northern Africa 271
Spain 272
Gaul 272
Britain 273
The Germanys 274
Along the Danube 274

20 (Un)Protected Sects: Religions, Tolerance,
and Persecutions   277

Family, Public, and Personal Religious Practice ...278
One Nation Under God(s) 278
Following One's Bliss 279
Protected Sects: Religious Philosophy and Mystery
Religions 280
Think It Through (Our Way) 281
Stop Making Sense and Just Sense: Mystery Religions ...282
The Cult of Isis 282
The Cult of Mithras 283

Unprotected Sects: Druids, Jews, and Christians 284
Druidism 284
Judaism 285
Christianity 286
Christian Persecutions 287
Christian Versus Christian 289

21 *Cogito Ergo Sum:* The Life of the Mind   291

The Silver Age of Latin Literature 291
Poetry and Epic 292
History and Biography 292
Novel and Satire..293
How To, and Bet You Didn't Know 294
Philosophy, Rhetoric, and Letters 294
Technical Subjects 294
Medicine and Science 295
Antiquarians and Encyclopedists 295
It's Greek to Everyone 296
Rise of the Romance Novel 296
The Second Sophistic 296
Early Christian Writers 297
From Marcus Aurelius Until the Fall of Rome 298
Some Roman Greek Authors 299
Authors of Pagan Pride 299
Christian Literature of the Later Empire 300
*Writers at the Passing of the Greco-Roman Tradition
   in the Latin West* 301

22 That's Entertainment! Public Spectacles   303

They Liked to Watch 303
History of the Games 304
The Circus 305
How the Races Were Done 306
The Drivers 307
The Crowds 307
Gladiators 307
Who Were the Gladiators? 309
Specialists 309
Dwarfs, Amazones, and Amateurs 311
The Greatest Show on Earth 312
A Day at the Games...312
The End of the Games 314
Why? 314

Part 5: Where Did the Romans Go? — 315

23 And the East Goes On — 317

Nova Roma (Constantinople) 318
  Byzantine Beginnings 318
  Justinian (518–565) 320
  How the West Was Won—And Lost for Good 322
Byzantine History: It's Called "Byzantine" for a
Reason 323
  C.E. *610–711: Fighting to Keep Place* 323
  Breaks Me Up: Icons and Iconoclasts (717–867) 324
  Power and Splendor (867–1200) 325
  *With Friends Like You … the Crusades and Conquest
    (1200–1453)* 326
  Falling Star: The Influence of Byzantium 327

24 Nothing Quiet on the Western Front — 331

Rome After the Fall 331
  The Papal Tiger 332
  Like a Rock: Pope Gregory the Great 333
  If I Had a Hammer: Clovis to Charles Martel 334
The Empire Strikes Back 335
  Great *Big Caesar's Ghost! Charles the Great
    (Charlemagne)* 336
  The Carolingian Renaissance 337
  The Holy Roman Empire 339
  Onward Christian Soldier 339
The New Romans 341
  Reichs and Rulers 341
  American Romans 342
Et Tu Brute: You're a Roman, Too 343
  Back to Globalization 344
  The Living Latin Language 344
  An American's Reflection 344

Appendixes

A Timeline   347

B Finding the Romans on Earth and in
   Cyberspace   353

C Lights, Camera, *Actio!* A Short List of Rome
   and Romans in Film   365

D Glossary   367

   Index   375

Foreword

Those familiar with Latin literature of the second century C.E. will of course know the *Attic Nights* written by Aulus Gellius. It was during the wintry nights in Attica (hence the title) that Aulus contemplated the writing of this multivolume collection of notes he culled from the host of books he read, all of which were designed to entertain and educate his children.

Few people, however, know of his brother, Marcus Gellius, or his book titled *Spartan Afternoons*, in which he catalogued the foolish behavior and idiotic sayings of contemporary Romans at home and abroad. Although the book was ultimately condemned on moral grounds by the emperor Marcus Aurelius and all copies of the work were burned in the Roman Forum (together with the unfortunate Gellius), a few quotations from the work survive to give us an idea about its content that will help explain why *The Complete Idiot's Guide to the Roman Empire* is essential reading.

By the second century C.E., the Romans had their own classics: Plautus, Ennius, Cicero, Caesar, Catullus, Virgil, Ovid, *et cetera*. A Roman simply was not considered educated unless he knew not only Roman literature, but also Roman history, rhetoric, religion, and law, *inter alia*. It was for this reason that Marcus Gellius focused on the stories of famous *illiterati* and their utterly useless lives.

One such person featured in his book was Quintus Gluteus Maximus. His ignorance of Roman culture and resulting inability to string together a coherent thought were so profound and so complete that he once uttered the following infamous statement in a meeting of the senate: *Caesar quidem, si hodie viveret, in sepulchro versaretur* ("If Caesar were alive today he would be spinning in his grave"). Because of this statement, plus other fatuous observations and unmistakable evidences of stupidity, he quickly became the butt of many jokes. His own parents were said to have remarked, "Quintus is the biggest ass we have ever known. Why did he have to be *our* son?"

Then, as today, ignorance of Roman culture was a serious social liability. Now, thanks to Professor Eric Nelson of Pacific Lutheran University, there is hope! Here, in one valuable tome, the culturally disadvantaged will find in 24 chapters, numerous sidebars, and 4 appendixes enough information about the Romans—their cities, customs, literature, history, architecture, legal structure, and more—to fend off any and all accusations of idiocy. Gone are the days when the historically inept fear to appear in public lest a question regarding the ancient Romans comes up in conversation. Once you read this book, no one will ever call you a Gluteus Maximus!

Professor Nelson carefully and thoroughly leads even the most hapless reader through a chronological reconstruction of the culture of one of the most influential peoples of all times. The vast amount of material covered is well organized and easily grasped and, better yet, his clear and engaging account of ancient Rome will keep you reading into the wee hours of the morning, whether you live or sojourn in Athens, Sparta, or Poughkeepsie.

—James J. Clauss

James J. Clauss, Professor of Classics at the University of Washington, is the author of *The Best of the Argonauts* (University of California Press, 1993), co-editor of *Medea: Essays on Medea in Myth, Literature, Philosophy, and Art* (Princeton University Press, 1997), and author of numerous articles and reviews on Greek and Latin literature and history.

Introduction

In our fast-forward world, you'd think that the ancient past would be too obscure, too remote, and too foreign to be of relevance. Nowadays the *present* seems obsolete. And yet, ancient civilizations captivate us. Why?

Well, in part, we are drawn by similarities and differences between these cultures and our own. It's really interesting to see how other people lived, worked, fought, and loved. Ancient civilizations often confront us with differences so stark that they shock, delight, and appall us. As remote as some aspects of these civilizations are, isn't it engaging that they were still *people?* Both similarities and differences speak to the human condition, and what it means to live as a member of the human race.

In addition, we sometimes look to ancient civilizations for models. We like patterns, and in a complicated world, it would be helpful to find models for solving (or avoiding) some of our own problems and to predict what might happen next. Humans have been at the work of being humans for a long time. Perhaps someone already figured out one of our problems, or tried similar solutions to them.

Finally, we sometimes look back to better understand how things got the way they are. Sometimes we just don't know; other times it becomes clear that our understanding has been blunted by stereotypes, generalizations, and inaccurate ideas. As we look closer, generalizations begin to yield to a more complicated picture than the one we began with. Sometimes that original picture changes a lot, and sometimes it stays pretty much the same, but inquiry always produces a more accurate, insightful, and satisfying understanding.

You may hear people object, what can the past offer us anyway? History is written by the conquerors; the same people have been in charge of the same things since the Bronze Age. Such stereotypes and generalizations deserve to go in the trash bin of history along with the many others that elicited such remarks in the first place. Fortunately for all of us, it's much more complicated, much more interesting, and much more important than that.

Whether we like it or not, what we have *now*, what we know *now*, and who we are *now* all have pasts, and those pasts *matter*. That's largely why I wrote this book, and I hope that this perspective shows. Institutions, ideas, and ways of looking at the world have just as much of a genealogy as people do. But unlike our physical characteristics, which we can see, we are often unaware that we have also inherited broad assumptions about time, purpose, organization, cultural habits, and ourselves. As long as we see things from one perspective, it's no wonder that some things seem obvious and some things so strange.

Hopefully, the process of education (that's from the Latin *educare,* "to raise up") takes us out of our own perspective, not necessarily to change it but to mature it. In the best case, education shows us where our perspectives come from and how they relate and interrelate with others. In any case, we can understand a great deal about where we are and where we're going from appreciating where we've been and how we got here. If you're interested in where you are and how you got here, a good part of the answer would inevitably involve the Romans.

I'm not saying that we are bound by history. We all know the saying that goes (usually in a droning monotone) something like this: "Those who do not understand the mistakes of the past are doomed to repeat them." You might be surprised to discover that I don't *precisely* agree. Our problems are very much our own. The past does not provide us with ready answers to them, at least if you think of the past as a list of quick answers in the back of the "Current Problems" textbook.

Nevertheless, when you study the past in depth you come to the realization that, although the specifics change, people have been coping with the same kinds of problems for a very long time. Family tensions, political and social problems, environmental issues, economic policy, moral dilemmas—if we're wondering about or laughing about or struggling with something now, it's a fair bet that others have been in the same boat in the past. Now, that boat may have had *oars* and no Global Positioning System, but the question of "Where in the heck are we and where are we going?" has remained the same.

Ancient cultures fascinate and entertain us for many reasons, and understanding them benefits us in many ways. When we see how past peoples met common challenges and where their past connects with our present, ancient civilizations become both fascinating and relevant. I'll do my best in this book to give you an accurate picture of the Romans, and make learning about this influential ancient people both worthwhile and entertaining.

What You'll Learn in This Book

This book helps you to conquer Rome by dividing Roman history, culture, and legacy into five parts. Although the parts follow a rough chronological order, they overlap a bit as they refer back and forth.

Part 1, "All Roads Lead to Rome," gives you necessary background for studying the Romans by laying out major periods of history and setting the stage in the Mediterranean for Rome's rise. It also provides thumbnail answers to some "frequently asked questions" and directs you to more information elsewhere in the book.

Part 2, "Rome Wasn't Built in a Day: The Roman Republic (509–27 B.C.E.)," takes you through the rise of Rome in the fifth century B.C.E. to the end of the Roman Republic in 27 B.C.E. It helps you to understand how Rome was successful in conquering Italy and the Mediterranean, and why the Republic fell apart. In addition, you meet some of Rome's great personalities and writers and follow Latin literature from its lowest beginnings to its highest achievements.

Part 3, "Empire Without End: Roman Imperial History," begins with the Principate of Augustus and takes you to the fall of the western Empire. This section helps you understand how the Roman Empire developed, how it nearly came apart several times, and how emperors ruled this vast conglomeration of cities, regions, tribes, and kingdoms.

Part 4, "Roman Imperial Life and Culture," takes you back over the period of the Empire from a cultural and literary perspective. It also covers the rise of Christianity and the subject of Roman games and spectacles.

Part 5, "Where Did the Romans Go?" provides an overview of the Romans' legacy. In the east, we'll follow Roman history through Byzantium to both the Renaissance and Imperial Russia. In the west, we'll watch the papacy and Frankish kings reinvent the "old" Rome with an empire that continues to influence Europe today. This part also shows you some of the ways in which Rome influenced thinkers from the Renaissance to the formation of the American State.

Addendum

You'll find lots of additional information and insight in the sidebars that appear throughout the chapters. These provide examples for, clarifications of, and definitions of things that you read in the main text. Here's what they mean:

Lend Me Your Ears!

The Romans had a lot to say about themselves. This sidebar allows you to read them in their own (translated) words.

When in Rome

This sidebar provides definitions, examples, and explanations for jargon, Latin terms, and Roman ways of doing things.

Great Caesar's Ghost!

It's amazing where the Romans crop up. These sidebars contain surprising instances of Roman influence on our world.

Veto!

This sidebar provides cautions and context to common generalizations, misused terms, and other misunderstandings.

Roamin' the Romans

The Romans left ruins, remains, and hard-scape wherever they went. This sidebar points out where travelers can find Roman remains in various countries.

Acknowledgements

No one accomplishes anything of scope without the help and support of many untold individuals. The same is true of this book, so allow me to make a few of those who brought it about known to you. This book was the suggestion of my friend and colleague, Don Ryan, who gave invaluable advice and direction in its process. My heartfelt thanks go as well to my editors Randy Ladenheim-Gil and Mike Thomas, who patiently navigated this project with me through some rough waters and provided valuable direction. I am especially grateful to Professor Rochelle Snee, my friend, mentor, and colleague, who knows more about the ancient world than Homer himself could have kept straight. I have relied on and respected her comprehensive expertise since my student days; she did heroic work to help me bring you a book that is both comprehensive *and* accurate. Finally, I cannot adequately acknowledge the debt of love and gratitude that I owe my wife, Susan, whose encouragement, direction, and insight not only made this book a reality, but whose love, patience, and assistance more than proves Virgil's declaration: *amor omnia vicit.*

et nos cedamus amori. April 29, 2001

Trademarks

Part 1

All Roads Lead to Rome

People have been fascinated by Rome and the Romans from the founding of the city to the last credits of the movie Gladiator. *But just what do you mean by those terms "Rome" and "Romans"? Before answering, take a look through the following chapters: You'll get some background for understanding Rome from a variety of viewpoints in history and culture.*

Does your approach to the Romans need to be a bit like veni, vidi, vici *(Julius Caesar's "I came, I saw, I conquered")? This part has quick overviews of Roman history and literature and quick responses to frequently asked questions, such as who the gladiators were and why Rome "fell."*

Chapter 1

Dead Culture, Dead Language, Dead Emperors: Why Bother?

In This Chapter

➤ Why learn about Rome and the Romans?

➤ Where Rome stands in history and culture

➤ The meaning of "Rome"

➤ Roman history and literature in broad terms

Whether you love them or hate them, there's no getting around the Romans.

No other civilization has left such an imprint on the laws, lives, borders, religion, literature, politics, art, architecture, and popular imagination of the west. This is not to deny the influence of other cultures. But Rome established a framework of ideals, infrastructure, politics, military tactics, economics, communications, and education that girded together the west from Roman times to the present. In either metaphorical or concrete terms, much of what has traveled from point A to point B in the west has done so along a Roman road.

It's easy to romanticize or demonize ancient cultures. The more you know, however, the more complicated easy judgments become. While the Romans were insightful, ambitious, pragmatic, and influential, they could also be cruel, rigid, bloodthirsty, stifling, overly garish, and still a bit drab. I'll try to present a balanced picture in this book.

Here are some terms and abbreviations you'll need to get started:

➤ B.C.E.: Before the common era. The time period represented by the abbreviation B.C., which stands for Before Christ.

➤ C.E.: Of the common era. Indicates the same time as the abbreviation A.D., which stands for the Latin *anno domini nostri jesu christi* (the year of our lord, Jesus Christ). In this book, if you see a date without a designation of B.C.E. or C.E., assume it's C.E.

➤ ca: From the Latin *circa*, "about." This term is used for approximate dates. For example, ca C.E. 49 means "sometime around the year 49 of the common era."

Lend Me Your Ears

What the god Jupiter had to say about the Romans:

His ego nec metas rerum nec tempora pono: imperium sine fine dedi.

"For these people [the Romans] I place no boundaries of space or time: I have given them empire without end."

—Virgil's *Aeneid*, Book I, lines 278–279 (composed between 30 and 19 B.C.E.)

Some Surprising Facts About Rome and the Romans

Beginning in the Renaissance, and especially in the late eighteenth and nineteenth centuries, the west has romanticized classical Greek culture into both a radical alternative to Roman culture and into the true source of Western culture. You'll sometimes find Roman civilization portrayed as a kind of cultural pilot biscuit (a tasteless but hearty cracker) whose only value was to serve up a tasty selection of Greek cultural hors d'ouvres to modern taste buds. But there's a lot to learn about and from the Romans. You might find some facets of the Roman story remarkably contemporary in application and impact. The following are a few examples.

Rome Was Multicultural

Rome emerged from a mixture of local cultures and ended as an empire ruled by emperors from Italy, Africa, the Middle East, and northern Europe. The Romans had to bring people diverse in ethnic background, religion, and culture into an overarching system in which they shared some common identity and purpose. We might not like some of the ways that the Romans addressed this tension, but it's often surprising to see just how diverse their empire became.

The First Universal Declaration of Equal Rights

The abstraction of civil rights is one of the Romans' most important achievements. As Rome grew, it developed different formal and informal relationships with neighboring cities, states, territories, peoples, and empires. And as these became, in turn, "Roman," the concept of who was a Roman, and what it meant to be Roman, evolved. As a result, the Romans faced abstract and practical problems of civic identity—the scope of which hasn't been seen until our present day. Eventually, through the *Constitutio Antoniniana* in C.E. 212, all Roman citizens regardless of birth, economic status, or ethnic background, had equal civic status.

If Latin Is Dead, You're a Talking Zombie

The geographic and cultural extent of Rome's influence remains evident in the impact of its language, Latin, upon modern languages. True, classical Latin isn't typically spoken (although spoken Latin is on somewhat of a comeback), but neither is Middle or Elizabethan English. But what about Italian? Spanish? French? Portuguese? Romanian? All these languages grew directly out of Latin. And English? Well, although English is a Germanic language, it was heavily influenced by Latin through French (both through conquest and through French-educated authors like Chaucer) and by the Latin of the Catholic Church. If you're speaking English *now,* many of the words you're using derive from Latin roots.

Great Caesar's Ghost!

Words such as "romantic" and "romanticize" do come from "Roman," but were developed from late medieval literature written in common dialects that evolved from Latin. The Old French term for these dialects was *romans*—hence, the Romance languages. While official documents were written in Latin, works for popular consumption were written in romans and tended to be (check the supermarket) "romantic" in nature.

Are We Marching into the Future or in Circles?

Most ancient cultures believed time was circular: History operated, like the seasons, within cycles that were recognizable but unalterable. The Romans saw time as linear. They believed that one had control over (and responsibility for) the future by the choices one made. It was a different attitude from that which you see in the literature of the ancient Greeks. Much of Greek literature confronts how to live well within what is essentially a "no-win" scenario. The Romans didn't believe in the no-win scenario. Jupiter had given them, in the words of the poet Virgil, *imperium sine fine,* "empire without end," and all the possibilities and responsibilities that implied. We are, in many ways, inheritors of that essentially optimistic outlook.

Great Caesar's Ghost!

You can easily see how a common Latin tongue grew into the Romance languages if you look at certain Latin words. Take *bonus* (good), for example: The Italian (*buono*), French (*bon*), and Spanish (*bueno*) derivatives are clear. With some background, you can also see how English words like "sinister" go back to Latin in different ways: *sinister* in Latin is "left" (compare the Italian *sinistra*), but it also means "unlucky" or "ill-omened." Other Latin phrases, such as *per se* or *pro bono*, have found their way directly into English.

So What Do *You* Mean by "Rome"?

Let's start with the name itself. What do you think of when someone refers to "Rome"? The Italian city? An empire? A religious institution? Images of chariot races or battles from movies? Crowds wandering about in togas? Christians being fed to lions? Debauched banquets? Obviously, the name carries a lot of baggage. When you see the word "Rome," what the name means depends on the context in which it appears.

Let's take a look at some of the meanings "Rome" can have.

Rome the City

Of course, Rome is both a modern and an ancient city. As far as modern Rome goes, there is an incredible depth to the city, which swirls with visible reminders from (and this is important) every era of its past.

But Rome isn't just about the medallions and scars of an influential veteran of history, it's about the experience of living here and now against the backdrop of there and then. That's what gives the city a profound depth, a sharp poignancy, and (at times) a rich absurdity. An angry child takes a stand on an ancient stone in the forum and, gesturing like an orator, demands his *gelato;* traffic swirls around piazzas like a never-ending chariot race; and, amid the din and dust, a tired Roman washes his hands and neck at an ancient fountain and lovingly caresses the carved face from which the water trickles.

So go to Rome in the here and now, savor the complexity and contradictions, marvel at the majesty and madness, and throw a few coins in Trevi Fountain for me.

Rome new, old, and older. Sit by the Renaissance fountain with a cold gelato *and contemplate the Pantheon—an inspiration to both past and present.*

We often think of the Romans as people of a land, like the Egyptians. But they were the citizens of a single city, the people who lived in and around its walls. As they expanded their influence, they became much more than the city; at their core the Romans remained a conservative people centered on the traditions and values of this one place. It's amazing to think that an ancient Latin city, no larger than a couple of modern cruise ships, could become so powerful and influential.

Rome the State

The people of ancient Rome established a framework of laws, treaties, and conventions among themselves and with those whom they conquered and governed. Over time, some outsiders became Roman citizens, and people from other towns and cities could be "Roman" in the same way that people born in Rome were. Others enjoyed various privileges, depending on their city's relationship with Rome. In any case, the political, cultural, and legal system that bound these people together, but which nevertheless remained centered on the city of Rome, is sometimes what is meant by "Rome."

Veto!

You'll see the term "Roman Empire" used loosely to refer to the Roman imperialistic state. But the "Empire," or "Imperial Age," is also a specific period in Roman history, namely, when emperors ruled Rome. This differs from the "Republic" and the "Principate." So look carefully at whether the term is being used in the context of Romans governing the conquered or the Romans governing themselves!

Rome the Empire

Over time, the city of Rome, its citizens, and their allies conquered and controlled (to various degrees) an enormous expanse of tribal lands, cities, and kingdoms. Some of these were under direct Roman control; others were loosely controlled by alliances backed by the threat of force or installed leaders friendly to the Romans. The ways that Rome controlled and dominated these areas changed over time, and the term "Rome" at times refers to what might be thought of as the Roman sphere of influence. This control was not always exercised from the city of Rome itself; at times the city of Rome was secondary to Constantinople, Milan, Ravenna, and even Alexandria as the geographical source of "Rome's" directive power.

Roamin' the Romans

If you're in Washington, D.C., there are plenty of Romanesque things to see. But as you wander around the neoclassical architecture, reflect a moment on the fact that American government features a "Senate" and not a Parliament, located on the "Capitol" hill. In such ways did the American founders borrow not only Roman political institutions but also from Roman political geography in forming their own "Republic."

Rome the Religious Center

You will sometimes hear the term "Rome" used with reference to the Vatican. The Vatican is a Roman Catholic state established on the outskirts of Rome during the chaos of the fall of the western Roman Empire by the bishops of Rome, or popes. "Rome," in this context, sometimes refers more to the Holy See, the power of institutional and ecclesiastical authority vested in and proceeding from the Popes. The Holy See, and consequently the Vatican, grew through the Middle Ages into a powerful and influential religious and political institution.

Rome the Concept

People have, over time, referred to Rome or the Romans when advancing or attacking ideas about power, authority, governance, and moral order. Western history is littered with rulers and authors who longed for a "new Rome" in one form or another. Spanish conquistadors argued about whether they were, in fact, following a Roman model or escaping from it in conquering the New World. Political theorists, such as John Adams and Thomas Jefferson, argued for versions of the American constitution using dueling references to Rome and famous Romans. In these contexts, "Rome" is less about a city or ancient people than it is a term that symbolizes a bundle of political, moral, and cultural ideas.

Roman History in a Box

In this book, we'll investigate all these aspects of Rome and the Romans. To start, however, it helps to have a scholar's basic framework of the periods of Roman history and literature. So let's get a handle on what these periods are called and (broadly) what happened during them. Historical and literary periods don't precisely overlap, so I've included a rough outline of each. From these outlines, we'll go into more depth in the following chapters.

The Royal Period (ca 800–509 B.C.E.)

The Royal period refers to the time when kings ruled Rome—that is, from whenever Rome became a ruled city, sometime between 800 and 700 B.C.E., to when the Etruscan kings were deposed, ca 509 B.C.E. Rome was never again ruled by a king although Senators accused Julius Caesar of trying to do so before they assassinated him. During this period, Rome grew from established settlements on the Tibur River (traditionally 753 B.C.E.) into one of the most powerful cities in central Italy. The Royal and very early Republic is sometimes referred to as the Archaic period.

The Republican Period (ca 509–27 B.C.E.)

The Republican period begins with the establishment of the Roman Republic (traditionally 509 B.C.E.), which followed the overthrow of the kings. Not much is known about the early Republic although it's clear that internal and external strife were constant problems. Nevertheless, Rome started with its troublesome neighbors and went on to conquer what would today be northern and southern Italy, all of north Africa, Egypt, Spain, France, most of Britain, Switzerland, Austria, the Balkans, Romania, Bulgaria, Greece, Turkey, Ar-menia, and most of the Middle East.

Intense civil unrest marked the final century of the Republic. Beginning in 133 B.C.E., there were a series of civil disturbances and wars between competing factions and generals: the Gracchus brothers and the Senate, the generals Marius and Sulla, Julius Caesar and Pompey the Great, and finally Octavian and Antony. This last conflict, fought in the aftermath of Julius Caesar's assassination, brought about the collapse of the Republic. Octavian, Caesar's adopted son, was victorious over Antony and Cleopatra at Actium in 31 B.C.E. His return to Rome in 27 B.C.E. is the traditional end of the Republic.

The Principate of Augustus (27 B.C.E.–C.E. 14)

The Principate is technically the period between the Republic and the Dominate of Diocletian (C.E. 284) when Rome's ruler was known as the *princeps*. Generally, however, it refers to the transitional rule of Augustus between Republic and Empire. Octavian, victorious over Anthony and Cleopatra in 31 B.C.E. claimed to restore the Republic, and in some ways he did. But otherwise, Octavian reorganized the Roman state so that he maintained a delicate balance between old ways and authoritarian rule until his death in C.E. 14. Octavian was awarded the name Augustus ("reverent and solemn") and the title *Princeps* ("first among his peers"). His successors adopted this title from which the period gets its name. Under Augustus, Rome, both as a city and as an empire, flourished in a period of relative peace and stability.

The Imperial Age (Traditionally C.E. 14–476)

The Imperial Age or Empire period begins with the death of Augustus. During the Empire, successions of emperors—both good and bad—ruled over the vast Roman dominions until the Emperor Diocletian split the Empire into two parts in 284. Constantine the Great reunited the Empire and moved the capital to Constantinople (modern-day Istanbul) in 330 and made Christianity the official Roman religion.

From this point, continuing pressure from Goths, Attila the Hun, the Vandals, economic and social stagnation, and other factors combined to send the crumbling west teetering toward the Dark Ages. The traditional end date for the fall of the western Empire was set by Edward Gibbon in 1776 in his monumental work, *The Decline and Fall of the Roman Empire.* He established the date as 476 when Germanic mercenaries deposed Romulus Augustulus and made their leader, Odoacer, emperor. Even though he was recognized by the eastern Emperor Zeno, Odoacer marks the point at which the western Roman Empire slides over the line from being a remnant of the Roman Imperial system into becoming a patchwork of Germanic kingdoms.

> **Great Caesar's Ghost!**
>
> Two terms for political authorities come from this period as a result of Augustus's nebulous position. The first is Augustus's title of *Imperator* (commander) from which we get "Emperor." The second is his title of *Princeps* ("First Citizen") from which we get "Prince."

> **Roamin' the Romans**
>
> If you travel to northern Italy, be sure to visit Ravenna, the Ostrogoth capital where western emperors lived since Honorius (395–423) and where Theodoric is buried. Justinian's forces took the city in 540. His archbishops Maximian and Agnellus built or refurbished the churches of San Vitale, St. Apollinare in Classe, and St. Apollinare Nuovo. These churches and their world-famous mosaics remain as reminders of Justinian's attempt to reunite the Roman Empire and to elevate Ravenna above Rome as the new capital of the west.

The eastern half of the Empire tried to reestablish control under the Emperor Justinian (532–565). His efforts failed, and with his death the eastern Empire turned to soldier on alone for another thousand years.

The Byzantine Period (565–1453)

People don't often think of the Byzantine culture as "Roman." Greek, not Latin, was the language of the realm and the Orthodox Church developed apart from the Latin Roman Catholic Church. Nevertheless, the culture we know as Byzantine was the continuation of the eastern Roman Empire and saw itself in that light. Citizens called themselves *Romaioi* (Romans) and recognized their emperor as the legitimate Roman emperor in the "New Rome," Constantinople.

When in Rome

Byzantium refers to the civilization that developed from the eastern Empire after the death of the emperor Justinian (C.E. 565).

Constantinople was first sacked in 1204 by its Latin Christian brothers in the Crusades and then taken by the Muslims in 1453. Refugees and migrants from *Byzantium* brought Greek literature and learning with them to Italian cities such as Venice and Florence and helped to fuel the emerging Italian Renaissance.

Great Caesar's Ghost!

The city of Byzantium was founded by Greeks around 667 B.C.E. Torn back and forth between Greeks and Persians in the classical period, the city remained Greek until captured by the Romans in C.E. 196. Constantine refounded the city as "New Rome" in 330, but it quickly became known as "Constantine's city," or Constantinopole. The modern name, Istanbul, reportedly comes from the Greek *eis tēn polin*, which means "to the city." This was apparently the common answer to a question, "So, where ya' headed?" asked of Greeks traveling along the provincial roads for over a thousand years.

Roman Literature in a Box

Latin literature was slow out of the blocks in comparison to other cultures such as the Greeks. Homer's *Iliad* and *Odyssey*, for example, were composed sometime around 750 B.C.E., just about the same time as the traditional date of the founding of Rome. Classical Greek literature hit its high point roughly between 450–350 B.C.E. during the time when the Roman Republic was tottering about on its first marching legs. It wasn't until the mid-third century (300–200) B.C.E. that the Romans began to cultivate a literature of their own.

Periods in Roman History...

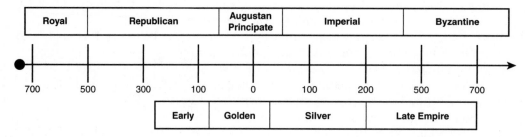

A comparative timeline of Roman history and literature.

There are several reasons for the late start. First, the Romans were a practical people focused on action. They saw themselves as hard-working, hard-fighting, practical, salt-of-the-earth farmers who had little time for literature and other idle-headed activities. Romans, in the public sphere, served the state through war or politics. Anything that distracted from those tasks was suspect. The strength of this attitude shows up in great authors like Cicero and the historian Sallust, who still felt compelled to defend the value of literature in relation to one's public life and value.

Maturity is also a factor. A culture needs time to develop its own literature. There have to be enough people with a common language and culture, a shared appreciation of literary forms, and a sufficient level of literacy. The rapidly expanding Roman state did not assemble these until the third century B.C.E. The Romans were too busy conquering Italy, Greece, and Carthage to put things down on paper. Once they started, however, they made up for lost time. And although the Romans imitated the Greeks at the beginning, their literature quickly took on a stamp and character that, like everything else they did, were very much their own.

Early Latin Literature (ca 300–100 B.C.E.)

Early Latin literature is characterized by two things: experimentation with and adaptation of Greek forms to the Latin language and the emergence of a Roman perspective. The first writers and educators of this period were Greeks from southern Italy, who were brought to Rome as slaves of conquest. Soon, however, the Greek literary forms of epic, comedy, tragedy, and history were in the hands of Latin authors, and philosophy and rhetoric began to develop a distinctive Roman approach.

The Golden Age (ca 100 B.C.E.–Death of Augustus in C.E. 14)

Turmoil marked the last century of the Republic. Civil unrest and civil wars erupted from a social and cultural system struggling to maintain control over its dominions and its own power. Amid the turmoil, Roman literature not only survived but seems to have risen to the challenge of its times (to fashion a more comprehensive role and identity for Rome and the Romans in the world) in a way that the Roman political system did not. Latin poetry, history, philosophy, and rhetoric were transformed by authors such as Catullus, Caesar, Lucretius, and Cicero. These authors synthesized Latin and Greek forms into a profound, powerful, and uniquely Roman literature. Their works are neither isolationist nor naively imitative in tone or technique but reveal a level of cultural confidence and sophistication in which authors master and combine elements of both Greek and Latin styles to their own satisfaction. This synthesis reached its zenith under Augustus. His reign ushered in a period of peace and stability that produced some of the West's finest literature from authors such as Virgil, Horace, Livy, and Ovid.

The Silver Age (ca 41–180)

After a bumpy start in imperial succession under Tiberius and Gaius (Caligula), Latin literature entered a period distinguished particularly by the quantity of literature. The literature is wonderful for its quality as well, but against the likes of Virgil and Horace, this later phase is known as the Silver Age. Authors from this period include Petronius (novel), Lucan (epic), Martial (epigram), Tacitus (history), Suetonius (biography), and Juvenal (satire). Most of the modern popular images of Imperial Rome come from these authors.

The Silver Age was ended by another imperial succession crisis brought on by the death of the emperor Marcus Aurelius, who was himself an author of an influential work, the *Meditations*.

Great Caesar's Ghost!

Robert Grave's popular book (and the PBS series) *I, Claudius* was developed from the work of the Roman author Tacitus (ca 56–117). Tacitus was an aristocratic Roman who served under the Roman emperors. He wrote dark and incriminating histories of the Imperial Age that show great insight into character and the effects of power. His writings, however, are also marred by his own biases.

The Literature of the Late Empire (ca 180–565)

During this period, Greco-Roman education and literacy was still strong. Latin literature, however, began to show the strains of both the west's decline and the turbulence of the struggles between Christian and pagan traditions. By the time the

Greco-Roman world had lost the upper hand, however, both eastern and western traditions had been indelibly stamped with its literature, rhetoric, and thought. One can see where sacred and secular combine to remarkable effect in the writings of St. Augustine of Hippo (354–430) and Boethius (480–524).

Meanwhile, literature in Greek, both sacred and secular, remained more viable in the eastern Empire and continued into the next millennium under the Byzantine umbrella.

Great Caesar's Ghost!

The Emperor Marcus Aurelius reflects the divergent cultural forces at work in the later Roman Empire. Born to wealthy Spanish parents in Rome, he was educated by, among others, the African rhetorician Fronto, the Greek rhetorician Herodes Atticus, and the Roman Junius Rusticus. Although a man of peace, as emperor he spent most of his time on the German and Parthian borders defending the Empire. It was during one of these campaigns that he wrote—in Greek—his reflections on the Stoic principles he admired and tried to live by. These reflections, called "Things for himself" (*Ta eis heauton*), became known as the *Meditations*.

Well, you've accomplished a lot already in this odyssey through Roman history and civilization! Besides thinking about some of the different aspects of "Rome" that we'll be encountering, you've had a chance to look over a roadmap of Roman history and culture and learn a bit about some reasons for taking the trip. But before we hit the road, let's go to Chapter 2, "Rome FAQ: Hot Topics in Brief," for some of the perennial highlights for Roman explorers like you.

The Least You Need to Know

➤ To understand how our world got to be as it is today, you have to know something about the Romans.

➤ Rome was a multicultural civilization that developed abstract concepts of civil and human rights and held a philosophically unusual view of time.

➤ "Rome" can mean many things—a city, a state, an empire, a religious center, a concept.

➤ Roman history divides primarily into the "Republic" and the "Empire," with the "Principate" of Augustus providing the transition between the two.

➤ Roman literature developed long after Greek literature, and although it was highly influenced by the Greeks, it quickly took on a character of its own.

Chapter 2

Rome FAQ: Hot Topics in Brief

In This Chapter

➤ Four good reasons for Roman conquest

➤ A quick stab at Roman games and spectacles

➤ Roman slaves and slavery

➤ Looking at women and women's lives

➤ Theories for why Rome fell

Okay. You have a basic understanding of Roman history and literature. What now? Since we're covering a broad range of times and topics, this book is primarily organized chronologically. But, you know, sometimes you don't *want* to wade around in three periods of Roman history to find a quick, basic answer to something you're interested in. This chapter helps out by providing brief overviews of Roman topics that people most frequently want to know about.

How Did They Do It? Conquering the World

What are the Romans most famous for? In a word, conquest. The Romans had a gift for conquering people. Without it, we wouldn't be reading about their other qualities and contributions to history. In fact, it is largely Roman skills in winning and maintaining an empire that made the rest possible. Their ability to martial forces and materials, to execute a campaign, to adapt to circumstances, and, above all, to persevere is profoundly impressive. Frighteningly impressive.

It's Their Job

The Romans saw themselves as destined by fate and the gods to conquer and rule. Their literature, architecture, and art make it clear that they believed Roman rule of the world was the natural order of things. They seemed to realize that this role had limitations (they didn't think that Romans were best at *everything*), but accepted them as the necessary burdens of those who were responsible for carrying out the practical duties of governance.

Lend Me Your Ears

"Others will hammer out bronzes so gracefully that you would think that their statues breathed, and bring out the living features of a face from stone. They will plead cases better, better trace out the wanderings of the heavens with a compass, and name the rising stars. But you, Roman, remember, these are your skills: to govern the peoples with power and to establish the habit of peace; to be sparing of the vanquished and to crush the arrogant in war."

—Virgil's *Aeneid* 6.847–853

Conquering and Cooperation

The Romans not only conquered well, they also successfully integrated conquered peoples into their system. Being a part of the Roman world had distinct advantages that conquered peoples (especially the elite) came to value. In fact, some of Rome's problems stemmed not from people wanting to escape but from people wanting more rights within the system that they served.

Organization, Organization, Organization

The Romans were incredibly organized, disciplined, and determined. In war, as long as they had space and time, and especially in the area of siege warfare, they were without equal. Because of their tendency to be deliberate, the Romans were sometimes surprised or caught off guard by quicker and more mobile enemies. But Roman organization and tenacity generally triumphed.

Roamin' the Romans

You can visit the spectacular site of a Roman siege at Masada along the Dead Sea. King Herod fortified the site, perched high upon the cliffs, in the first century B.C.E., and Jewish insurgents took refuge there against the Romans after the fall of Jerusalem in C.E. 69. After waiting at the bottom of the cliffs for two years, the Romans began piling dirt until they built a ramp from which to march into the stronghold in 73—but not before some of the insurgents may have killed themselves (and their families) to avoid capture.

Rewards and Punishments

The Roman system of punishments and rewards could be summed up with something like this: "Use some reason in making mandatory compliance bearable, and use terror to make noncompliance unimaginable. Provide examples when necessary." This applied to both discipline of the military and treatment of enemies.

The rewards for settling with the Romans were often a degree of local autonomy and integration within the Roman orbit. The potential for rewards tapered off quickly as an enemy resisted and then passed into horrific punishments. All right of negotiated surrender for terms ended when the first battering ram hit the wall or gate of the town. After that, Roman reprisals could be so incredibly harsh and far-reaching that everyone thought twice before crossing that line.

Great Caesar's Ghost!

The word decimate came from the rarely used Roman military punishment of *Decimatio* in which every tenth man of a unit was selected to die. In what was a gruesome and savage twist to group punishment, the selected men had to be beaten or stoned to death by the comrades spared in the lottery. The brutal practice, though seldom used, imprinted our language with words for a terrible, random, and deadly thinning of group members.

Two Thumbs Up! Games and Gladiators

Roman games and spectacles are one of the major areas of interest about the Romans to the modern audience. These public entertainment venues grew in size, depravity, and popularity during the last century of the Republic and first century of the Empire. Modern readers focus on the arena games because of the jaw-dropping horror and fascination that they evoke. The Romans' penchant for the grand scale played into this area—they even flooded the Colosseum to create naval battles. It's sobering to contemplate what these events may have to say about Roman mass culture, since they occurred by popular demand.

To be sure, the arena games were big events and had many spectators. But their fans in no way represented a majority; the popularity of the arena paled in comparison to the Romans' love of chariot racing. Whether you compare the number of race tracks to arenas or the size of the crowds at those venues, racing wins by several lengths. The Colosseum, for example, held around 45,000 people. The Circus Maximus held *250,000.*

Veto!

The most famous Roman entertainment venue is the Colosseum, built in Rome under the emperor Vespasian in C.E. 72. It held around 45,000 spectators. Nearly destroyed as a rock quarry in the Middle Ages, the Colosseum was protected during the sixteenth and seventeenth centuries as a place of Christian martyrdom. Lots of blood was spilled in the Colosseum but not, however, in Christian persecutions.

The "Games" of Rome

Roman games, or *ludi*, originated in festivals and holidays that included public entertainment, much like county fairs. This entertainment began with races and theatrical events and grew, over time, to include arena spectacles of death and carnage. The Romans seemed to have a fascination with death and combat. It's important to keep in mind, however, that the executions and gladiatorial combat were only a part of the public venue. Many Romans deplored the games of the arena and considered them to be a sad and barbaric commentary on both their culture and human nature in general.

Contests of Animals and Humans

The Romans imported thousands upon thousands of animals for their games. Some were killed in mass hunts; others were paired against each other in experimental battles (to see what happened if you pitted an ox against a bear, for example). Lions and tigers were imported in huge numbers and used for killing both other animals and people. Sometimes armed men were pitted against the cats, but most of the time unarmed (and often bound) criminals were thrown into the arenas or other enclosures with them.

Lend Me Your Ears

"What fun is it for a civilized person to watch either a helpless man being torn apart by a powerful animal, or some magnificent beast stabbed over and over with a spear? Even if this was something to behold, you've seen it often enough already, and I, who was watching there, saw nothing new. The last day was for the elephants. The huge crowd was genuinely impressed, but didn't really enjoy it very much. In fact, there was a kind of sympathy for the elephants, and an impression that there was some connection between that large animal and humans."

—From Cicero's *Letters to His Friends*, 2.1

Mosaics from the Villa Romana at Piazza Armerina, Sicily show animals, such as this elephant, being loaded in Africa for transport to Rome.

Roamin' the Romans

If you visit Sicily, head north from Gela to Piazza Armerina. There you'll find a wonderfully preserved third-century Roman villa alive with floor mosaics. Many of the mosaics feature scenes of animals being imported from Africa just a short sail away.

Human Combat and Spectacle

The arena games also featured human combat. At one end of the spectrum were serial executions in which an armed criminal fought (and killed) an unarmed criminal. The winner was disarmed and the next (armed) opponent brought out. This scenario was repeated until all had been killed in some manner. At the other end of the spectrum were highly trained gladiators who often fought to the death. The gladiators were slaves owned and trained by the owner of a gladiator school. Some of them developed huge popular followings just like present-day World Wrestling Federation stars. A very, very few eventually won their freedom.

Human combat or punishments sometimes took on the absurd and theatrical. The emperor Nero put aristocratic women in the arena to fight each other. The emperor Domitian pitted women against dwarfs. Commodus (the evil emperor of the movie *Gladiator*) put cripples in the arena to fight each other and finished them off himself. Theatrical performances took on deadly twists of realism: Some arena productions included plays with real murders, and in one "performance," a man was burned alive to reenact the funeral pyre of Hercules (must have been a one-night-only showing).

Veto!

When a gladiator or other contestant was beaten but still alive, it was up to the gladiator owner or emperor to decide his fate. The crowd joined in like a game show audience, shouting, waving handkerchiefs, and signaling thumbs up or down for whether they wished to have the contestant finished off or spared. But where we use the "thumbs up" sign to signal "good job" or "yes," the Roman thumbs up (*police verso*) probably signified *Jugula!* ("Cut his throat!")—the last thing the contestant wanted to see.

In Chains: Slaves and Slavery

Slavery pervaded the ancient world, and Rome was no exception. Slaves were involved in every aspect of daily life, at every level of society, in every kind of economic activity. Philosophers and moralists debated on how to treat or conceptualize them, but slaves were so integral to ancient cultures that, for the most part, they were assumed to be a natural part of things.

Kinds of Slaves

Though there were no grades of slaves, some slaves had it better than others. In general, the closer the slave was to some kind of personal or business relationship with the owner, the better his chances for decent treatment and eventual freedom. The slaves who had it the worst were those who worked the mines. Such slaves were no more than interchangeable parts to be worked to death and replaced. Other terrible conditions were found on the large plantations and in the gladiatorial schools, where slaves were trained to kill or be killed for entertainment.

Great Caesar's Ghost!

The movie *Spartacus* is a romanticized tale of a famous slave revolt. There were a number of slave rebellions that began after Rome imported huge numbers of slaves into Italy for mass labor. Spartacus was a Thracian gladiator in a school at Naples. The rebellion he led there produced an army of 90,000, which defeated the Romans several times. The Roman general Crassus finally captured Spartacus's army in 71 B.C.E. In reprisal, over 6,000 captives were crucified along the main road leading from Rome to the rebellion's origin, although Spartacus's body was never found.

Slave Status

Slaves had no status, legal or otherwise. Their bodies and their children were the property of their masters. The Empire period was a time of small improvements in the treatment of slaves. The emperors gave slaves some legal protections, such as protection from being arbitrarily killed by their masters or from being forcibly castrated for profit. Still, draconian laws, such as the killing of every slave (men, women, children) owned by a master if he was murdered by one them, were enforced.

Over time, however, the large number of freed slaves (freedmen) in the empire and a dwindling number of slaves from conquest had a positive influence on slave treatment. Also, philosophical systems, such as Epicureanism and Stoicism, and the teachings of Christianity helped change some attitudes about how slaves were to be treated.

Lend Me Your Ears

"'They are slaves,' you say. Well, they are your fellow slaves when you consider that fortune has the same power over both them and you …. Please, keep it in mind that the man whom you call your slave was born like you, has the same sky above him as you, breathes as you do, lives and dies as you do! Treat your slave kindly and courteously. Allow him to share your conversations, plans, and company."

—Seneca, excerpts from *Epistula Moralis*, 47, written ca 60

Where Did They Come From?

Slaves came from a variety of sources. People could fall into debt and eventually be sold into slavery. Infants and children who were unwanted or could not be cared for by their families were also sold as slaves (children of slaves were already slaves). Conquered peoples were major sources: Aemilius Paulus sold 150,000 slaves after the battle of Pydna (168 B.C.E.), and Julius Caesar eventually contributed about a million slaves to the Roman economy from his campaigns in Gaul (58–51 B.C.E.). There was also a thriving business throughout the Mediterranean in kidnapping both children and adults and selling them into slavery.

Becoming Free

Roman slaves, in contrast to the slaves of other cultures, could become free in several ways. Since they were property with value, their freedom could be purchased by someone else or by themselves with money they earned. Masters sometimes freed slaves as a gesture of good will, often in their wills. Masters also set slaves free for economic advantages, either to work with or under the former master as freedmen or because an old or sick slave had become too burdensome for upkeep.

Some Ironies

Although slaves had the legal status of a chair, slaves of wealthy owners were in a position to become successful if they were freed. Freedmen could not vote or run for office, but through their connections they became a wealthy and powerful class during the Empire. Emancipation catapulted them from someone you ordered around to someone who ordered you around—far too quickly for many. "Real" Romans (as other citizens sometimes saw themselves) often resented these newcomers. They complained that freedmen took jobs real Romans needed, corrupted traditional Roman values with foreign ways, bought up the Empire, and talked funny.

Roamin' the Romans

If you visit Turkey, visit the ancient city of Ephesus. As you wander around the agora (market), reflect on the magnificent Gate of Mazeus and Mythridates. It was built by a freedman of Augustus, who had enough money as a recent freedman to build this in thanks to his former master.

Almost in Chains? Roman Women

In the study of ancient culture, the lives of women have often been defined and measured as a subset of the lives of men. When we ask how much power, personal autonomy, or cultural value women had, this is often gauged, not only against how much men had, but by the standards and values that created the measurement in the first place. This can keep women from being studied—and valued—on their own terms. Fortunately, a great deal of scholarship in recent years has yielded a fuller picture of Roman women's lives both in terms of their relationship to men and in terms of themselves.

Kinds of Women

When talking in general about Roman women, things break down by time periods and by classes. Whether a women was a slave, poor but free, or came from a wealthier class made a great deal of difference. It also made a difference, at least for the women of the middle and upper classes, which period you're talking about. Rome's conquests meant that men were often away for long periods of time and might not come back at all. Women were left in charge of seeing that things got done. After the conquest of Carthage, the enormous wealth brought back to Italy allowed middle- and upper-class women to run things with a great deal more independence and power.

Great Caesar's Ghost!

Latin words for different kinds of women have found their way into English in ways that still carry some of their original meaning. Here are four examples:

➤ **Matrona:** the married female head of the house, from whom we get the dignified words "matron" and "matronly"

➤ **Virgo:** a young woman, who was to be both virgin and virginal

➤ **Ancilla:** a female house slave, whose supportive but minor role is conveyed to us in the word "ancillary"

➤ **Soror:** a sister, from whom we get "sorority"

Women's Status

While Roman women were viewed as inferior to men on men's terms, their status was complex. Women and men mixed with each other in the home and society at all levels in ways that would have been unthinkable to some other cultures of the time.

In addition, although laws originally made a daughter the property of her father and a wife the property of her husband, other laws and customs developed over time that provided some loopholes. These opportunities were available primarily to the upper classes. Middle-class women, about whom we know comparatively little, are praised on gravestones for their traditional domestic and family-raising duties, and it seems that these domestic and maternal roles remained at the heart of a woman's cultural identity.

Some Ironies

Roman women's lives are much more relevant to the present than you might think. Contemporary women and men will find much to sympathize with and to learn from them. Not only do we have very personal insights into women's and men's lives from Syria to Britain, but modern readers will recognize many current issues. Expanding roles for women, cultural backlashes, tensions between culturally defined roles and present realities, and differences between women of different socioeconomic classes make Roman women a worthwhile study for all.

Lives of the Rich and Famous: The Roman Emperors

The Roman emperors' lives and actions have been a source of fascination since their own time. The entire authority of the Roman state was vested in the figure of the emperor, and almost every aspect of Roman public and private life hung on his decisions. The emperor oversaw foreign and domestic affairs, urban and regional planning, civil and legal administration, economic policy, cultural events, and military campaigns. Foreign representatives, city councils, administrators, and citizens (like St. Paul) could appeal directly to his judgement, and many did. Paul's appeal (recorded in the book of *Acts* in the New Testament) landed him in Rome where, according to tradition, he wrote several epistles before he was executed.

Veto!

The prevalent picture of the emperors as degenerate and power-mad autocrats comes primarily from the Roman historian Tacitus, the biographer Suetonius, and early Christian writers. This reputation is partly warranted, but the picture is often simplistic. Many emperors were talented and intelligent governors, administrators, and legislators, and their accomplishments were often minimized or glossed over by later hostile critics.

Military, civil, legal, and symbolic power combined to make the emperors some of the most powerful rulers to walk the planet. With so much power, it's no wonder that some emperors thought themselves divine. The combination of power, responsibility, and pressure proved too much for some, but many handled it remarkably well. Nevertheless, this power was always subject to the capriciousness of individuals with egos the size of Rome itself, and they were often manipulated by those close to them, upon whom they depended for advice and information.

When Did the Emperors Reign?

The Roman state was originally a Republic. This Republic ended in 31 B.C.E. when Octavian, the adopted son of the assassinated Julius Caesar, defeated Marc Antony and Cleopatra. He changed his name to Augustus, and until C.E. 14 governed Rome as a kind of "first citizen," or *princeps*. (See Chapter 1, "Dead Culture, Dead Language, Dead Emperors: Why Bother?" for more on the Roman Republic.)

Augustus kept alive many of the civil forms of the Republic (magistrates, for example, continued to be elected and the senate continued to meet and debate) and in fact claimed to have "restored" the Republic back to the Roman people. Nevertheless, Augustus maintained firm control of the state's essential legislative and military powers. After Augustus' death in C.E. 14, his position was handed on, first to successors in his family, then to others. The successors to Augustus were known in different contexts as *Caesar* (Caesar), *Dominus* (Lord), and *Imperator* (Commander), but we know them as the Emperors.

When in Rome

The **Praetorian Guard** evolved from the bodyguards that protected a general. Augustus established several units from his own troops, and they became the later emperors' personal elite force.

Great Caesar's Ghost!

The emperor Vespasian, an earthy and practical man, was the first to introduce public pay toilets to Rome. He was ridiculed by the upper crust. They gave the toilets his name (akin to what happened to Col. John Crapper, the inventor of the modern toilet) and the name stuck. It may have been meant as ridicule, but any traveler to Rome can still think fondly of the emperor when asking where to find a *vespasiano*.

How Did You Get to Be Emperor?

Well, that isn't easy to summarize. Emperors were supposed to be declared and recognized by the people and the Senate. Each emperor indicated who was to be his successor, but after his death, it was the imperial family, imperial guards, and the legions who finalized the decision. When these groups disagreed, the issue was settled by force or palace intrigue. The low point came when the *Praetorian Guard* auctioned the post to the highest bidder. (See Chapter 16, "The [Mostly] Not-So-Good Emperors: Commodus to Aurelian," for the case of Didius Julianus.)

What Were Whey Like?

Roman emperors are a study in both character and caricature. There were the notorious emperors like Gaius (Caligula), Nero, Commodus, and Heliogabalus, whose cruel megalomanias became legendary. But there were also hard and practical men like Vespasian and Severus; educated men like Claudius and Marcus Aurelius; and men like the fabulously wealthy Didius Julianus. Julianus purchased the emperorship from the Praetorian Guard at the urging of his wife (who wanted him to amount to something) and was assassinated within a few weeks. Each emperor is worth looking into and any generalization of them omits much.

Going Over Like a Lead Pipe: Why Did Rome Fall?

Just as people want to know why and how Rome became a great empire, they want to know the end of the story. When one empire conquers another, it's easy to identify why one succeeds and the other fails, but when a great empire drifts into anarchy and a dark age, one wants to know what happened. Were there fatal flaws in the Roman Empire? Was there something from within the system, or were the Romans conquered by outside forces they couldn't defeat? Did the culture that thought it could manipulate the future make the wrong choices and fail the possibilities of their divine mandate, or did their empire simply run a natural course of growth, maturity, decline, and fall?

The simple answer is "Yes." But let's rephrase things a bit. It would probably be more instructive to ask why and how things lasted as long as they did. Rome wasn't built in a day, and it didn't fall in a day, either. In fact, the application of the word "fall" to any particular date in Roman history is arbitrary. No Roman of the time would have recognized 476 as the date when Rome "fell." But let's go on with some of the main popular theories.

Veto!

The Romans themselves identified moral decay as a cause of the collapse of their empire, but it's best that we don't. Romans started saying this from at least the second century B.C.E. (That's 600 years of "When I was a boy, Rome was *Rome!*") Rome's last centuries contained, besides decadence, moral and ethical advancements over earlier periods. Interestingly, many Romans blamed their decline on the fact that traditions and values had been corrupted by the conversion of the empire to Christianity.

It's the Water

The use of lead in water pipes and other utensils is often cited as a reason for Rome's decline. According to the lead pipe theory, the Roman aristocracy was poisoned by its own affluence because it was able to afford lead plumbing and cooking utensils. Lead leaching into the water resulted in a kind of Roman "brain (down the) drain." This theory, which has the advantage of a certain ironic justice, isn't supported by chemical analysis of the skeletal evidence, comparative analysis with other cultures, or common sense.

Economies off the Scale: Size Does Matter

Many economic factors contributed to the weakening of the Empire. The western half was larger, harder and more costly to defend, and yet produced little revenue from commerce or conquest. This put a terrible tax burden on the agrarian base and further depressed its economy. The eastern half of the Empire was wealthier, more compact, and more vital, but it did not have the wealth or vitality to keep the vast dominions of the West afloat. Cultural traditions that stifled innovation, shortages of manual labor, and a system that encouraged waste and corruption also contributed to Rome's decline.

Global Warming and Dust Bowls

Global climate changes, ecological effects brought on by resource management, and a degrading of soil productivity have sometimes been identified as underlying causes of Rome's fall. While there is evidence for all these things taking place, evidence that any of them individually or in combination contributed significantly to Rome's decline has yet to be shown.

The Empire Vandalized: Invasions and Incursions

Overwhelming invasions by barbarians and Rome's use of unreliable barbarian armies and mercenaries to defend against them have been cited as decisive in Rome's fall. This, too, is an oversimplification. Rome had successfully (well, mostly successfully) defended the western borders for centuries and continued to do so in the east. Moreover, the barbarian armies, like all armies, were effective in defending the frontiers when they had good leadership. The reasons Rome came to depend upon foreign armies, and why Germanic kings gained enough power to overthrow the western emperors, have underlying causes that lie in the Roman Empire, not with invading or migrating barbarians.

I hope that this chapter *hasn't* answered all your questions—only whetted your appetite and interest for more. And there is more—the Romans left a vast amount of information about themselves (at least in comparison with other ancient cultures). But where does what we know about the Romans come from? That's what the Chapter 3, "How Do We Know? Discovering the Romans," covers.

The Least You Need to Know

➤ The Romans used a combination of military organization, practical politics, and ruthless terrorizing in their conquests.

➤ Roman public spectacles were often gruesome executions on a grand scale.

➤ The office of emperor was individually determined; therefore emperors and their reigns have to be studied individually.

➤ Not only isn't there a simple answer to Rome's decline, but there wasn't really a "fall."

Chapter 3

How Do We Know? Discovering the Romans

In This Chapter

➤ Evidence for Roman civilization and culture

➤ Where the important archeological evidence comes from

➤ Where the important textual evidence comes from

When reading what someone tells you about an ancient culture, especially about what the people were like and what they thought, it's always a good idea to ask the question, "How do we know?" Information comes from a variety of sources: the physical remains of what that culture left behind, evidence of how that culture influenced subsequent or surrounding cultures, and written texts from or about that culture. Added to this mix comes a hearty dose of (hopefully educated) imagination and careful analysis.

The Romans left behind practically everything, and in practically every possible form. Thousands of archeological remains litter the Mediterranean landscape from the Middle East to Scotland, from North Africa to the Danube. Pompeii and Herculaneum have been preserved as time capsules of the first century C.E. Rome's presence, customs, and language made a profound and discernable impact upon surrounding and conquered peoples. Finally, we have hundreds of thousands of public and private texts from over a thousand years.

Digging In: Ruins, Remains, and Archeological Sites

The Romans were famous builders and engineers, and the remains that they left us show that, when possible, they built to last. Many of these remains (such as roads, buildings, bridges, and aqueducts) are still in use today, or were up to recent times. Many of these constructions were either preserved during the Middle Ages through conversion to other uses or lost because their building stone was used for other projects. Other remote locations remain remarkably preserved.

Veto!

People have an urge to romanticize ancient cultures as utopian (that is, an ideal and perfected society) in direct proportion to the scarcity of texts we possess by them. This has happened at different times with the Egyptians, Etruscans, and Minoans of Bronze Age Crete. Without textual evidence, keep a big salt shaker at hand when reading about the character, religion, or ethics of ancient cultures, and always ask, "How do we know?"

Rome Itself

As you can imagine, you can't walk anywhere in Rome without stepping on several layers of Roman archeological remains. It's often frustrating for the people who actually live there: They can't do anything above or below ground without having to stop and carefully consider what is being lost and found. A prime example of this is the ongoing construction of Rome's subway system, which seems to be as eternal as the city itself.

What is so remarkable about Rome is being able to see Roman history represented from beginning to present in its archeological remains. The Romans were conscious, even in early times and especially in the case of the Forum, of preserving their legacy, and other Roman buildings were preserved by being converted into other uses. The result is a visible record of history, quite literally, in the making.

This dramatic mixture of ancient to modern interconnection swirls around you wherever you look. When you go down to the Tiber you can see the still functional *Cloaca Maxima* (big sewer) that the Etruscan kings built in the sixth century B.C.E. to create the Forum. Head out of the train station and you enter the magnificent Baths of Diocletian, which were transformed into a Church by Michelangelo in the sixteenth century as a fitting last word to this persecutor of Christians. Take a walk past the remains of the Theater of Marcellus, upon whose clear foundations grow modern apartments and offices in the curved shape of the seating area. It's not seamless history, but the stitching, as in a quilt, brings an added appreciation.

Around Italy

There are, of course, Roman ruins throughout Italy. If you have a car, you can follow the ancient Roman roads through the countryside. Most of the time modern roads have been paved over or been put alongside the ancient ones, but there are some places where people continue to use the ancient stone roadways for local access! Depending on your driving skills and adrenaline addiction, traveling by car makes for a thrilling—or chilling—way to explore the geography of the past.

Great Caesar's Ghost!

Public baths were one of the most important of public spaces and included bathing facilities, libraries, eating spaces, and both indoor and outdoor exercise and leisure areas. The great public baths built in Rome by the Emperor Caracula (C.E. 211–217) have been transformed in recent years into a splendid venue for opera and musical performances by such entertainers as "The Three Tenors."

Roamin' the Romans

The Museo Civico in Gubbio preserves 7 of 14 bronze tablets discovered in C.E. 1444. These tablets, the largest of which is about 3 by 2 feet, were written at different times between 400 and 90 B.C.E. in the Osco-Umbrian dialect of the area. They contain religious associations, customs, and rituals and provide a wonderful illustration of how culturally and linguistically diverse Roman Italy remained even in areas often thought of as completely "Romanized."

When you explore Italy, however, remember that what you're seeing is often not Roman in the sense of the city of Rome. Italy has (and had) its own distinct cultures and subcultures, and people were proud of regional differences even as they became part of the Roman world. So as you drive into Tuscany, you'll see Roman ruins with a distinctly Etruscan flair as well as the pre-Roman Etruscan remains at Cerveteri; as you drive into Umbria, you'll see the "Roman" ruins change with the landscape and the people. Visit Gubbio and see tablets written in the native dialect of rugged ancient people of this area. Drive south from Rome to Naples and into Magna Graecia and Campania, where the ancient ruins of Paestum remind you of the Greek foundations upon which cities like Naples, Tarento, and Syracuse rest.

From Britain to Babylon: Remains from the Frontiers and Provinces

The border areas of the Roman Empire were not only areas of great conflict and Roman defensive works, but areas of intensive cultural and economic exchange. Ruins from these areas contain both Roman military forts (which housed troops stationed along the border) and fortifications (the defensive walls and towers protecting borders, towns, and forts), as well as a vibrant array of towns and settlements that thrived along the borders during different periods.

The most famous of these frontier archeological sites is Hadrian's Wall, which roughly divides England from Scotland. The 73-mile wall not only featured Roman garrisons and guard stations, but military and civilian settlements along its path. You can also find spectacular remains in other far-flung areas such as Volubilis (in Morocco), Leptis Magna (in Libya), Zeugma (in Syria), and Aquincum (in Hungary).

Gifts of Vesuvius: Pompeii and Herculaneum

In C.E. 79, Vesuvius, a rumbling volcanic mountain just south of Naples, roared to life and blew half of its contents onto the countryside. In the sudden eruption, two towns and many of their inhabitants were covered and preserved for later discovery. Initially looted for treasures and art, Pompeii has become a well-trod tourist destination and the focus of such popular media as *The Last Days of Pompeii*. But the eruption of Vesuvius was a real-life drama and disaster film of its own.

The eruption of Vesuvius occasioned the first recorded eyewitness account of a volcanic eruption, given by Pliny the Younger. His uncle, Pliny the Elder, died after sailing to rescue some friends who lived closer to the mountain. At least 3,600 people died in the eruption, which began at about noon on the 24th of August, C.E. 79. The volcano spewed four to five feet of ash and pumice onto Pompeii in the first several hours of the eruption. The ash did not kill the inhabitants. In fact, many were walking around on top of the ash when they were killed and covered by surges of volcanic gasses and debris shortly after the same surges had destroyed Herculaneum. A heavy ash fall covered the town and its inhabitants.

In Herculaneum, many residents had already left when the material from the volcanic eruption began cascading down the slopes toward the town, reaching it in about four minutes. It's not clear whether remaining residents saw the surge coming or were already taking cover, but several hundred people were under the piers along the water when they were killed instantly as the volcanic gasses and mud flows boiled over and poured into the town. The flow hit with the force of an atomic weapon and carried parts of the town for several miles, but subsequent flows buried Herculaneum until almost no part of the town showed above the surface.

In Pompeii, the ash fall preserved far more of the buildings, leaving even signs and interior painting intact. In Herculaneum, the mud and volcanic debris collapsed buildings and destroyed more of the architecture but sealed and preserved artifacts inside the buildings. This has enabled the recovery of important organic items, like papyrus rolls containing personal and literary works of the time.

People and animals were also covered. As bodies decayed, they left empty impressions in the hardened rock. These forms, when filled in with plaster (like bronze poured into a mold), yield fascinating and terrifying sculptures. A man clutches his money purse. A pregnant woman clutches her stomach. A dog writhes in the agony of asphyxiation. Hordes of hopeful fugitives remain trapped under a pier.

Notwithstanding the initial looting, Pompeii and Herculaneum have provided an incredible treasure-trove of artifacts and information and give us a remarkably comprehensive look into Roman life in the first century C.E. Besides the archeological finds, the towns have been used as a touchstone for dating and studying artistic styles, architecture, urban planning, social and civic organization, economics, and private life.

Great Caesar's Ghost!

I live in Washington state. We got a first-hand view of a modern Vesuvius when Mt. St. Helens blew its top in May of 1981. The force of the blast leveled thousands of acres of forest and covered several states with ash. The mud flow obliterated the Spirit Lake Lodge (including a modern Pliny, the obstinate innkeeper Harry Truman, who refused to leave) and washed a good portion of the mountain down the Cowlitz river looking like a cataclysmic milk shake.

Veto!

Pompeii has often been depicted as a typical Roman town (a kind of Roman Mayberry), but it was a great deal more complicated that that. Both Pompeii and Herculaneum had their own cultures, styles, and traditions. Pompeii offers us a precious glimpse into the past, but it was typically Roman only in the way that Seattle would be typically American if it were covered by the eruption of Mt. Rainier.

Lend Me Your Ears

"On August twenty-fourth at about one o'clock, my mother pointed out a cloud to him [Pliny the Elder] that was very unusual both for its size and for its appearance. He had just taken a cold bath and was warming up by lying about in the sun after breakfast while reading a bit. He called for his slippers and went up the hill from which the wonder could best be seen. A cloud was rising up out of a mountain (this was only later recognized to be Vesuvius because it was hard to tell from such a distance from which mountain the cloud was coming at the time) which was closest in form and shape to an umbrella pine tree. For it rose up on a kind of very tall trunk and poured outward at the top like in branches. It was sometimes bright white, and sometimes dark and spotted, depending on whether it had brought up ash or earth."

—Pliny the Younger, *Letter* 6.16, written to the historian Tacitus, ca C.E. 110

Roamin' the Romans

When in Turkey, be sure to visit Bodrum (ancient Halicarnassus), where there is a fine museum dedicated to underwater archeology. Much more than Roman artifacts are there, of course, but you'll get an overview of the role that seafaring and merchant trade played throughout ancient history.

Under Water: What Goes Down Sometimes Comes Up

The Mediterranean is littered with shipwrecks, and the sunken treasure that they have provided includes more than objects of art and gold. They also tell us a great deal about trade, travel, and technology.

Freshwater lakes have also yielded some remarkable finds. Two well-preserved vessels from the early empire were excavated between 1929 and 1932 at the bottom of Lake Nemi, not far outside of Rome. Excavators drained the lake (using, in part, the old Roman aqueduct) down to the ships, which were placed in a museum designed for their preservation and study. Unfortunately, the Nazis burned it all as they abandoned Italy. Drawings, some photographs, and other material remain. Efforts are underway to rebuild full-scale working replicas of the original ships.

Words and Texts

We have a great deal of textual evidence from and about the Romans. Both Greek and Roman culture were highly literate, which means that people ranging from private individuals to state officials created a variety of written documents.

On the public and state level, there is a great deal of literature that recorded what happened and when, described decrees and laws, and proclaimed the purpose or origin of buildings and public monuments. Other public texts, like the signs that adorn the walls of Pompeii, give us an idea of the kinds of public discourse that took place in a bustling Roman town.

Literature of all kinds, much of it highly introspective and self-analytic, circulated in the public sphere. Moreover, a great deal of personal material has been recovered, which gives us a look into the lives of individuals—evidence often sorely lacking in the study of ancient cultures.

Official Documents

Official texts were often preserved in what was literally a "hard copy"—stone or bronze. Treaties, dedications, proclamations, and official documents such as the Twelve Tables (see the following list) were inscribed to ensure their permanence. Other official records were kept in less secure ways, and most were lost in the sack of Rome by the Gauls in 390 B.C.E. The most important official public documents for the study of Roman history and culture are …

➤ **Lapis Niger:** Also called the Black Stone, this is the only original document of Roman history that we possess, and the oldest monument in the Roman Forum. The Lapis Niger is a fragmented stone pyramid dating to the period of the Kings (sixth century B.C.E.) with inscriptions concerning ritual law and practice.

➤ **Twelve Tables:** These were law codes originally written on wood and later inscribed in bronze (see Chapter 5, "Seven Hills and One Big Sewer: Rome Becomes a City," for more on them). Although we do not possess the originals, we have a good idea of what they contained. Early Roman historians had access to them, and Roman schoolchildren of the first century B.C.E. were forced to memorize them much as has been done at times in the United States with the Constitution and Bill of Rights.

➤ **Fasti:** These were originally public lists of days on which legal and public business could be held. They were kept by magistrates and priests. Over time, these lists came to include yearly records of public concern such as magistrates, treaties, triumphs, and portents. These records were used by early Roman historians for chronological and historical information. The Fasti are more accurate for dates after about 300 B.C.E., but overall they are pretty accurate. Augustus had information combined from several fasti and set up the *Fasti Capitolini* (also known as the Regia Inscription), which covered the period from Romulus to about 12 B.C.E. You can see fragments of this inscription in Capitoline Museum in Rome.

➤ **Annales Maximi:** These were yearly records kept by the *Pontifex Maximus*, or chief priest. These were kept since the time of the kings, but like many other records, perished in the Gallic sack of 390 B.C.E. Various other lists were brought back together to restore the record in about 133 B.C.E.

Veto!

We possess few original documents from the Romans. Much of what we know about official records, such as the Twelve Tables, comes from quotations by other authors or fragments of inscriptions that are themselves copies. A few original documents of personal nature, such as papyrus fragments, graffiti, and signs, have been preserved in archeological finds, and there are many epitaphs with personalized inscriptions. But we possess no "first edition" works of Roman literature. These works were passed on through copies and preserved in libraries and monasteries.

Veto!

Oral sources are not necessarily suspect simply because they are passed on by word of mouth rather than in written documents. Many cultures, ancient as well as modern, preserve details of their history in traditional oral forms that are remarkably accurate and comprehensive.

Roman Literature

The Romans left an incredible amount of literature, and we'll cover the specifics in Chapter 11, "Literature and Culture of the Republic," and Chapter 21, "*Cogito Ergo Sum:* The Life of the Mind." There is poetry, history, philosophy, biography, satire, ethnography—even a cookbook! Overall, however, the Romans loved to talk about themselves, both in self-adulation and self-criticism. They were also quite conscious of preserving their legacy and their traditions. Consequently, we have lots of material about almost all aspects of Roman life—once the Romans began to record them. Unfortunately, they didn't start to pursue literature until the end of the second century B.C.E., so much of what we know about the early Romans comes from later sources and oral tradition.

I Was Here: Graffiti and Other Unofficial Remains

It may surprise you, but the scribbles and scratches that you find on bathroom walls and alleyways has a long and honorable history as far as cultural historians are concerned. We learn a great deal that you might never think of from such writings. For example, since most people (like myself) tend to (mis)spell things phonetically, misspelled graffiti can tell us how Latin was pronounced in different times and in different places. Graffiti can also give us an insight into the composition of neighborhoods, social issues and attitudes, and facets of culture that were originally meant for public viewing but rarely, if ever, seen.

Lend Me Your Ears

Here are a few examples of graffiti found at Pompeii.

➤ Town rivalries: *puteolanis felicia omnibus Nucerinis felicia et uncum Pompeianis Petecusanis*, meaning "Happiness to the people of Puzzuoli! Happiness to everyone of Nuceria! And the meat hook for the Pompeians and Pithecusians";

➤ I was here: *Lucius pinxit*, meaning "Lucius wrote (painted) this";

➤ "It's a dirty job," but: *pecunia non olet*, meaning "Money don't stink."

What Other People Said

It's always helpful, when studying a culture, to have the perspectives of both insiders and outsiders. There are other writers who wrote in other languages (mostly Greek) about the Romans and events in which Rome was involved. Most of these authors were "Romanized" either as captives in war or by acculturation, and they often sought to explain Roman successes and the new world order to their audiences. Four of the most influential were …

➤ **Polybius** (ca 220–120 B.C.E.). Polybius was an influential Greek who was taken to Rome after the battle of Pydna (168 B.C.E.). There he became the tutor of a powerful Roman, Scipio Aemelianus. Eventually he oversaw part of the reorganization of Greece after the destruction of Corinth in 146 B.C.E. and wrote a history about Rome's domination of the Mediterranean. In it he includes a famous analysis of the Roman constitution as being a superior mix of the elements of monarchy (the Roman consuls), aristocracy (the Roman senate), and democracy (the Roman assemblies).

➤ **Flavius Josephus** (ca C.E. 37–100). Josephus was a Jewish statesman, soldier, and Pharisee during the Jewish rebellion of 68. He became an attendant of the emperors Vespasian and Titus and was present at the fall of Jerusalem in 70. He returned to Rome and became a citizen. There he wrote several works which include his perspective on Rome and the Romans. The first was "The History of the Jewish War Against the Romans," which was originally written in Aramaic for Jews in Mesopotamia but then translated into Greek. His other works were written in Greek and included a history of the Jews from Creation to 66 B.C.E., an autobiography, and two essays against Apion of Alexandria, an anti-Semitic scholar.

➤ **Plutarch** (ca C.E. 46–120). Plutarch was a prolific Greek writer, moralist, and lecturer who lived in central Greece. He appears to have traveled the empire on several occasions. His works are too many to describe here, but they include the biographical "Parallel Lives," in which the lives of 23 famous Greeks are told alongside that of an equal number of famous Romans with a brief comparison after each pair.

➤ **Cassius Dio** (ca C.E. 150–235). Dio was from Nicea in Bythinia (modern Turkey). He became consul in Rome and governor of Africa and Dalmatia. Although a Roman citizen and a powerful one, Dio is included here because he spent 22 years writing a comprehensive Roman history in Greek. Part of it survives, including the only surviving account of Claudius's invasion of Britain.

Relief showing the spoils of Jerusalem in Emperor Titus's triumphal parade. From the arch of Titus in Rome.

Roamin' the Romans

When in the Forum in Rome, walk through the Arch of Titus. Titus, the son of Vespasian, took over the siege of Jerusalem when his father left for Rome to become emperor in C.E. 69. Titus, accompanied by historian Josephus, stayed and conquered Jerusalem in 70. He then became emperor after Vespasian died. You can see Titus's triumphal parade carved into the arch, including a scene of the menorah from the temple in Jerusalem being carried as part of the spoils.

Early Church Texts

The story of the early Christian church is inexorably bound up with the Romans. Romans, such as the centurian whose daughter Jesus heals, Pontius Pilate, and the Roman emperor whom St. Paul appeals to in the book of Acts in the New Testament, play a pivotal role in church texts from the beginning. In addition, the Roman empire and the role that Rome played in the designs of the gods, God, or fate continued to be an issue in the struggle between pagan and Christian world views until about the sixth century C.E. We'll take a closer look at these texts and the transition of the Roman empire from pagan to Christian in Chapter 17, "Divide and (Re)Conquer: Diocletian to Constantine," Chapter 20, "(Un)Protected Sects: Religions, Tolerance, and Persecutions," and Chapter 21. Here, however, are two major writers to know:

➤ **St. Augustine** (C.E. 354–430). The son of a pagan father and Christian mother, he was a highly educated teacher who converted to Christianity after a long intellectual and spiritual struggle. He eventually became the bishop of Hippo in Africa. Augustine's works, such as his *Confessions* and *City of God,* are among the most influential of early Christian literature and give us an illuminating perspective on this period in Roman history and culture.

➤ **Eusebius** (ca C.E. 265–340). Eusebius was the bishop of Caesarea in Palestine. Among his many works (written in Greek) is his "Ecclesiastical History," which describes early Christianity's struggle within the Roman Empire until the conversion of the Emperor Constantine to Christianity in 314.

All right. The last chapter presented you with an overall framework for Roman history and literature. This chapter has given you an idea of how we know what we know about the Romans. You've read about some of the kinds of evidence that we have, and where this evidence comes from. Next, let's give you some background. Rome was, in every way, the new kid on the block among the great civilizations that sprang up around the Mediterranean Basin. To understand and appreciate how Rome grew and developed, you need some perspective on what else was going on leading up to Rome's rise.

The Least You Need to Know

➤ The Romans left an enormous amount of archeological evidence about their culture.

➤ Excavations at Pompeii and Herculaneum have provided an incredible treasure-trove of artifacts and information to give us a remarkably comprehensive look into Roman life in the first century C.E.

➤ Roman textual evidence includes official documents, literature, and even graffiti.

➤ Texts about the Romans come from Roman, Greek, and Jewish authors.

Chapter 4

Club Mediterrania: Rome in the Context of Other Civilizations

In This Chapter

➤ Civilizations around the ancient Mediterranean

➤ Who's a barbarian?

➤ The many peoples of ancient Italy

➤ Rome at the crossroads of cultures

When Rome began to develop, it was a relative newcomer on the outskirts of a Mediterranean neighborhood with a history. To the east, there were the much older civilizations of Mesopotamia and Egypt. To the south, Greek colonies in southern Italy and Sicily were so numerous and so developed that the area got the name Magna Gracia (the Big Greece). Further south along north Africa, the Phoenician city of Carthage and its trading empire spread from Libya around the coast all the way to present-day southern France. There, more Greek colonies dotted the turbulent landscape of the west. Behind them, and along and over the Alps, Gauls, Goths, Celts, and other tribes ranged and roamed. And central Italy itself—*mamma mia!*—was an antipasti buffet of Etruscans, Latins, Oscans, and other native peoples.

Let's take a look at what the different areas around the Mediterranean were like as Rome grew and developed, and what role they played as the Mediterranean became, for the Romans, *mare nostrum*—our pond.

Mediterranean cultures at about the time of the Roman revolution, ca 500 B.C.E.

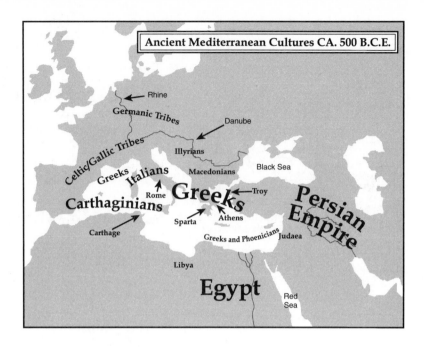

The Near East

The Near East

The cultures of the Near East developed in Mesopotamia (between the Tigris and Euphrates rivers) during the early Bronze Age (back to roughly 5000 B.C.E.). We don't have room to recap them all, but civilizations such as the Sumerians, Accadians, Babylonians, and Hittites go here. Let's start in about the eighth century B.C.E. (800–700 B.C.E.) and work our way up to the time of Rome's revolution from the kings.

Persia

The Persians were an Aryan people who migrated into what is now Iran sometime before 800 B.C.E. They established a great empire in the wake of the Assyrians and Babylonians beginning under Cyrus the Great (ca 550 B.C.E.). Cyrus conquered Lydia (western Turkey) and the Greek city-states (Ionia) along the eastern Aegean. His successors conquered Egypt, pushed east into modern India, and gained a foothold in Europe. The Persians attempted to conquer Greece and made it as far as the Isthmus of Corinth, where the combined

Veto!

Converting centuries to years is a bit counterintuitive. It seems like the fifth century, for example, should include the years 500–599. But remember that, because we start from zero, the fifth century is 400–499. If you think of the century number name as being the *end* of the century, it's sometimes easier to keep straight. For example, the fifteenth century includes the hundred years leading *up to* 1500 (1400–1499).

forces of the Greeks turned them back and eventually forced them back across the Aegean.

The Persian Empire remained one of the major forces in the eastern Mediterranean until conquered by Alexander the Great about 330 B.C.E. After his death, Persia was ruled by the Greek Seleucid dynasty and then by the Parthians (a native people from northern Persia). The Romans were able to conquer the Seleucids in western Asia Minor but not the Parthians.

Phoenicians

The Phoenicians probably came from the Persian Gulf and settled up and down the eastern Mediterranean. Their primary cities were Sidon, Tyre, and Biblos. The Phoenicians were great traders and seafarers. They may be the origin of the mysterious Phaiacians, who finally brought Odysseus home to Ithaca in Homer's *Odyssey*. The Phoenicians founded the city of Carthage as a colony around 800 B.C.E. Carthage grew into a trading empire of its own. The Phoenicians' most influential import was the alphabet.

Great Caesar's Ghost!

More than just goods travel from one culture to another. Phoenician traders used a writing system in which pictorial symbols represented syllables of spoken language. The Greeks modified the symbols to represent individual phonetic sounds of their language. In Italy, the Etruscans modified the system and passed it on to the Romans. These writing systems came to be known by the first two symbols of the Phoenician script: *aleph* (ox) and *beth* (house)—the alphabet.

Civilizations on the African Continent

The vast African continent borders the Mediterranean to the south, and different peoples had began to settle along north Africa in remote antiquity. The African continent west of Egypt was a mixture of indigenous tribes and settlements of Greeks and Phoenicians.

Egypt is most often included with the cultures of Mesopotamia and the Near East, civilizations with whom it shares a rough chronology. Some scholars in the last century tended to treat Egypt as another early European outpost. More recently, books such as Martin Bernal's *Black Athena* have made the case for Egypt being recognized as an African civilization. Even though subsequent investigation has not sustained many of Bernal's sweeping claims, scholars have come again to see Egypt more like the Greeks and Romans did: as a distinct, and distinctly ancient, culture.

Egypt

During the time of Rome's birth and rise to power, Egypt was viewed as the rich old granddaddy of civilizations. By the time Greeks and Romans arrived, Egyptian higher culture was already 2,000 years old, isolated, and ingrained. Conquests by the Persians and later by Alexander the Great never really had all that much impact on it. Even the Ptolemaic dynasty, which ruled over Egypt for 300 years (from 323 B.C.E. until Cleopatra's suicide in 30 B.C.E.), never really changed it. The Emperor Augustus took Egypt as his personal possession, and he and subsequent emperors used the riches of the province to stabilize the Roman empire's finances until they had drained most of it.

Carthage and the Carthaginians

The Phoenicians established trading colonies and ports wherever they went, sort of like the Hudson's Bay Company did in North America. In about 800 B.C.E., Phoenician settlers established the colony of Carthage in present-day Tunisia. The city's position just south of Sicily gave it a powerful position to exploit trade routes to the west. It grew quickly through trade and colonization throughout the western Mediterranean, and by the third century B.C.E., it was one of the Mediterranean's richest cities.

The Carthaginians were never in the mood for a land empire; they preferred to establish an empire of trade and of the sea, much as the Genovese and Venetians were to do in the late Middle Ages. They jealously guarded their trade routes and fought the Greeks and Etruscans for control of Sicily. A combined force of Etruscans and Greeks defeated them in 480 B.C.E., and they were forced to the western part of the island.

The Carthaginians were at first allies of Rome. The two cities made treaties in 509 and 348 B.C.E., and *Punic* fleets helped the Romans defeat Pyrrhus in 280 B.C.E. As Roman power grew, however, the Mediterranean shrank and the two powers came into conflict. The Romans and Carthaginians fought three wars: the First Punic War (264–241 B.C.E.), in which the Carthaginians lost Sicily; the Second Punic War (218–210 B.C.E.), in which Hannibal invaded Italy and very nearly destroyed Rome; and the Third Punic War (149–156 B.C.E.), which Rome provoked to finish off its weakened rival. Rome destroyed Carthage completely and made its territory into the province of Africa.

When in Rome

Punic is derived from the Latin *Punici,* which the Romans called the Carthaginians. The word comes from their origin as Phoenicians. Classicists and historians therefore refer to the Roman wars with Carthage as the Punic, not Carthaginian, Wars.

Libya and North Africa

All of north Africa was known pretty much as Libya. Greek and Phoenician settlements dominated the north coasts west of Egypt, and Phoenicians appear to have sailed down the Atlantic Coast as far as Sierra Leone. Behind the coastlands, the most prominent people with whom the Romans came into contact were the Numidians and the Moors.

Numidia was the region south and west of Carthage, populated by nomadic Berber tribes. The tribes had a loose coalition under a king. They were famous for their horsemanship; Hannibal used Numidian cavalry with great success against the Romans. Later, the Romans fought the Numidian king Jugurtha from 111–104 B.C.E. Numidia was bordered in the south by the Sahara and to the west by what came to be called Mauretania, the land of the Moors.

Mauretania stretched from Numidia around the Straight of Gibraltar. The people were a mixture of African and Berber tribes with Phoenician settlements and were ruled by tribal chieftains. Some of the chieftains from this area played a part in the war with Jugurtha and in the later Roman Civil War; under Roman rule, it provided important cavalry units for Roman armies.

The Greeks and Greece

It would be hard to overestimate the influence that the Greeks had on the Roman world both directly and indirectly. Greek colonies existed in every corner of the Mediterranean, and after Alexander the Great, Greek became the lingua franca of the ancient world. Greek culture also served as a model from which the Romans developed Latin literature, philosophy, and rhetoric.

The Ancient Greek City-States

When Rome was nothing more than a collection of small mud huts along the Tiber, Greek culture was emerging from a long dark age after the fall of Mycenean Culture (the Bronze Age Greek civilization) about 1200 B.C.E. After three or four centuries of dislocation, migration, and new settlements, the Greeks began to develop the Phoenician alphabet, and a long fermentation of oral literature sprang, fully formed, onto the page (or papyrus roll) with Homer's *Iliad* and *Odyssey*. These works were written down about the same time as the traditional date of the founding of Rome by Romulus and Remus, ca 756 B.C.E.

From the eighth through fifth centuries B.C.E., the Greeks got rid of their monarchies and established *poleis,* or city-states. Cities and their surrounding territories were organized, governed, and defended by citizens. Aristocracies generally controlled the city-state, but some places, such as Athens, developed more broadly based governance in which the general citizenry, or *demos,* had more control.

The Persians tried to conquer Greece in the early fifth century, and the Greek city-states cooperated to drive them from Greece. This conflict is called the Persian War (490–480 B.C.E.). Two states emerged as the most influential: Sparta, located in the Peloponnesus, and Athens, located in central Greece. These two city-states represented very different ideals in the fifth century. Sparta was a conservative, traditional, and land-based power; Athens was a radical, innovative, and sea-based empire.

These states and their allies went to war at the end of the fifth century. This conflict is called the Peloponnesian War (430–404 B.C.E.). Sparta was eventually victorious, but not before Athens blossomed (in part through the tribute it extracted from its "allies") into the city of literature, drama, science, culture, philosophy, art, and architecture that students have been studying ever since. We often think of the Golden Age of Greece as being one in which men in white frocks strolled about marble buildings pulling their beards while musing about poetry and philosophy, but this period was, in fact, about as turbulent and unstable as it could be. In Chinese proverbial terms, it really was "interesting times."

The End of the City-State and Alexander's Empire

In the fourth century, Athens regained some of its footing, but the age of the city-state was on the decline. Only two possibilities for larger order existed: cooperative federation of the city-states under some larger body or conquest of the rest by one. Between the fractious city-states, Greek federations lasted about as long as modern Italian governments (not very long), so the conquest of the rest by one became the possibility that was eventually realized.

A Macedonian king, whom many of the Greeks (at the time) would have considered a barbarian, brought this conquest about. Philip II (king from 359–336 B.C.E.) unified Macedonia, created a professional army, and conquered the rest of Greece. He brought the Greeks together for a combined attack on the Persian Empire. (There's nothing like a good war against a common enemy to bring fractious people together.) Unfortunately, Philip was assassinated on the eve of this expedition.

Philip's 20-year-old son, Alexander, took his father's place. After putting down some of the disorder that erupted in Greece, Alexander went on to conquer Persia, Egypt, and all the territory over to the Hindu Kush mountain range. A ruthless and brilliant general, Alexander never lived to try to make something permanent of his conquest. He died at the age of 33.

Great Caesar's Ghost!

Several Romans tried on Alexander the Great's mantle as a god-like and youthful conqueror. The famous general Gaius Pompeius Magnus (Pompey the Great) was given the name Magnus in emulation of Alexander because of his youth and his great victories in the East. Julius Caesar defeated Pompey for control of Rome. Caesar was in part marketing himself as Alexander by using the trappings of royalty while making sweeping plans for eastern conquests (like Alexander's) at the time of his assassination.

After Alexander's death, his generals divided up the regions of his empire. The general Ptolemy governed Egypt and founded the Ptolemaic dynasty (this period of Egyptian history is known as Ptolemaic). The general Seleucus eventually controlled the east and founded the Seleucid dynasty that ruled over that area. The general Cassander controlled Macedonia, but descendants of Antigonus finally came to rule it in an Antigonid dynasty. Greece and Macedonia were thereafter in turmoil as Macedonians struggled for power, Greek city-states jockeyed for position, and other Greek areas (such as Aetolia) formed powerful leagues. The Romans eventually put a stop to the commotion.

Magna Graecia

On the other side of the Mediterranean, things were a bit calmer, but only a bit. Southern Italy and Sicily had been colonized by the Greeks since the eighth century B.C.E., and powerful city-states such as Neapolis (Naples), Tarentum (Tarento), and Syracusa (Syracuse) were well established by the time Rome began to develop into a city and regional power. Like their mainland counterparts, however, the Greek city-states of Magna Graecia never could cooperate effectively and thus were unable to resist Roman expansion. Only Tarentum put up an effective fight, and that was, in part, by calling in help from Epirus.

When in Rome

Barbarian is originally a Greek word, and probably comes from emulating how non-Greek speakers sounded ("bar-bar-bar-bar"). To the Greeks, it would, have applied to everyone who did not speak Greek (including the Romans!). Romans used the term to apply to tribal peoples whom they considered less civilized than cultures, such as the Greeks and Etruscans.

Gauls and Other Barbarians

The *barbarian* tribes that lived in the far north of Italy and beyond the Alps played a major role in Rome's history and development. As far as Rome expanded, the people along its northern border, whether that was in northern Italy or along the Danube, were both a menace and a source of wealth, conquest, manpower, and vitality. Across the Adriatic, Illyrians and the kingdom of Epirus were also to play a vital role in Rome's expansion, and during the period of the Empire, in providing both the troops and the emperors who held the Empire together in a period of crisis.

Gauling Developments

For the Romans, Gaul was the lands that lay just before and beyond the Alps to the Rhine and west to the ocean. *Gauls* began migrating over the Alps from the north and settled the far northern region of Italy in the sixth century B.C.E. The Romans called the Gallic lands on their side of the Alps *Gallia Cicalpina* (Cicalpine Gaul). The rest was *Gallia Transalpina* (Transalpine Gaul). Transalpine Gaul was conquered by Julius Caesar. It was organized by Augustus into *Gallia Narbonensis* (basically Provence), and the farther reaches of Gaul were called *Gallia Comata* (or Long-haired Gaul).

When in Rome

The term "**Gaul**" is a catchall term for the Celtic and Germanic tribes that fought and migrated their way back and forth over Europe for centuries. In other places, you will find some of these people differentiated as Celts, Germans, or by their specific tribal names.

Great Caesar's Ghost!

As the Romans encountered various Gallic tribes, they Latinized their names. Many of these names remain with us today. Here's a few:

➤ The *Belgae* were the war-like Celtic and Germanic tribes living in what is today northeast France. Caesar fought and subdued the Belgians in 57 B.C.E.

➤ The *Alemanni* was a Germanic tribe who gave the Romans trouble up and down the Rhine and into present-day Switzerland. The French name for the Germans, *Allemands,* comes from their name.

➤ The *Germani,* according to the historian Tacitus, was the name of a particular Germanic tribe and the various tribes adopted this name as the one that would represent them as a whole while fighting together against the Romans.

The Gauls were fierce warriors and were always a threat to the stability of Roman conquests. Though their tribes were too uncooperative and disorganized to maintain gains when they made them. Besides, the tribes were more concerned with plunder and with finding land to settle on than with creating an empire. Gallic forces twice sacked Rome (in 390 B.C.E. and C.E. 455), but they didn't try to rule Rome. They went back to their own lands after they had enough pillage and ransom.

Epirus

Epirus was the wild region of northwest Greece that lay across the Adriatic Sea from southern Italy. The area was famous for its pirates, and I mention it because Alexander of Molossia, Alexander the Great's uncle, unified the area. Alexander came to the aid of Tarentum against Rome in 333 B.C.E. and conquered most of

Roamin' the Romans

If you're in France and visit Narbonne, you're in the ancient Gallic capital *Narbo.* This Celtic and Iberian capital was settled by the Romans as a colony (*colonia Narbo*) in 118 B.C.E. After Caesar's conquest of Gaul it became the capital of the Roman *Gallia Narbonensis* and the most Roman of the Gallic provinces.

When in Rome

The cost of a "**pyrrhic victory**" is so great that it brings eventual defeat. In other words, you win the battle but (because of the cost of the battle) lose the war.

southern Italy. This set a precedent for a later Molossian king, Pyrrhus, to again become involved in southern Italy on the side of Tarentum. Pyrrhus won several *pyrrhic victories* against Rome between 280 and 275 B.C.E., but given his huge losses, he was forced by the Romans and Carthaginians to withdraw from Italy.

Rome Before the Romans: Ancient Italy

Ancient Italy was a wild and rugged place, made up of many peoples with their own ethnic identities. Latium, the area from which Romans considered "their" people to come, was a relatively small portion of central Italy. From Rome, the civilized part of Italy was confined mostly to the west coast. Directly to the south, Greek colonies and settlements spread down through Italy and Sicily; directly to the north, the Etruscans controlled the territory up to the present-day Italian Riviera. These cultures also controlled the fertile valleys stretching up into the hinterland. From there, things got rough.

The Etruscans

The Etruscans were the most developed of the early Italic peoples, and their domination of Rome during the period of the kings left a lasting mark upon the city. The Etruscans organized the early Roman army and political and religious institutions, and these basic frameworks held. They also left an indelible mark upon the foundations of Roman religion, myth, and family life.

The Etruscan necropolis (city of the dead) at Cerveteri.

There has been controversy about the origin of the Etruscans since ancient days. The Greek historian Herodotus (ca 450 B.C.E.) claimed that the Etruscans were migrants from Lydia (Turkey). Herodotus came from a city in this area (Halicarnassus, modern Bodrum), and you would think he'd know. However, the historian Dionysus (ca 25 B.C.E.), who came from the same city, claimed that the Etruscans were of native Italian origin.

The best guess is that sometime in the eighth century B.C.E., a group of immigrants from Asia Minor arrived on the shores of northwest Italy, but instead of maintaining a separate cultural identity, they combined with the native Villanovan peoples of the area and became the Etruscans.

Either way, by the sixth century B.C.E., there was a powerful group of Etruscan cities, modeled on the Greek city-state, in north central Italy. The Etruscans used the rich resources of Etruria to become powerful and rich. They were fine craftsmen, ingenious architects and builders, and wonderful workers in bronze and gold. Their art, left primarily in their lavish tomb paintings, is some of the finest of the ancient world.

> **Roamin' the Romans**
>
> Modern word "Tuscany" comes from a Latin name for the Etruscans, Tursci. You can find Etruscan remains all over this area of Italy, but be sure to visit the tombs at Tarquinia and Cerveteri. Famous Etruscan artifacts can be found at Tarquinia, the Villa Julia in Rome, and the Vatican Museum.

Each city was governed by an aristocracy and maintained its own autonomy and independence. Like the Greek city-states, their lack of ability to cooperate under a central authority enabled the Gauls, Greeks, and Samnites to check their expansion, and allowed Rome eventually to divide and conquer them by 350 B.C.E.

For as vibrant and as important a culture as the Etruscans were, we possess little of their written language. Etruscan remained a spoken language into the time of the Roman Empire, and the Emperor Claudius was able to collect enough original material to write 20 books of Etruscan history. All this, including the original materials, is lost. All that remains of them are the pictures and creations of a vibrant, passionate, and artistic people, and the traditions the Romans adopted and passed on.

Northern Italy

Northern Italy, in addition to the Etruscans, was composed of three Italic peoples who were intermixed with invading Gauls who had settled there. These were the Ligurians, who lived in northwest Italy. Their chief city was Genoa. In the central area lived the Raeti, and in the northeast, the Veneti.

Central Italy

Central Italy was a mixture of people. In the east coast lived the Piceni. These people were connected ethnically to the peoples across the Adriatic in Illyria. On the west coast were the Latins, of whom the Romans were only a part. There were many prosperous Latin towns, such as Ardea, Alba Longa, Tiber, Praeneste, and Lanuvium. All these places figure prominently in early Roman history and lore.

The Samnites and Sabines

Living up and down the central spine of Italy were groups of rugged pastoral peoples with whom Rome came frequently into conflict throughout its early history. These were tribes like the Umbrians, Volsci, Aequi, Marsi, Samnites, and Sabines. The Sabines feature prominently in Rome's early mythological history, and Rome's early development and expansion are full of conflicts with the others.

Southern Italy

Along with the Greek population of Magna Gracia, the Samnites, the Oscans, and the Iapygians inhabited southern Italy. The Oscans lived in the southwest; the Iapygians were the Italic peoples living around the heel of the "boot" of Italy. Over on the island of Sicily, besides the inhabitants of Greek and Phoenician background, there were native Sicels. These people had migrated, probably from Africa, long before the Greek colonists arrived. Sicels could be found in parts of southwest Italy as well.

Location, Location, Location: The Site of the City of Rome

The site of the city of Rome was central to this mixture of peoples and resources in many ways. In respect to Latium, it occupied a central place in a rich and prosperous area, a building site rich in materials such as wood and stone, and a strategic position for commerce and defense. The resources and manpower that Latium could muster proved to be a deep well from which Rome drew strength after it conquered and united the area.

In respect to Italy, Rome occupied a central location that was both strategically and economically advantageous. Rome grew at the first easy inland crossing of the Tiber river, which made it a crossroads for commerce and travel going both north to south and east to west. In addition, there was an important salt route along the Tiber valley. But despite this strategic location, Rome lacked the kind of harbor from which it could develop into a major seaport. While this was of some disadvantage, it made Rome difficult to invade by sea; and the Tiber, its valley, and the hills of Rome made the city difficult to attack by land. On the other hand, once Rome conquered the areas around itself and built roads out from the city, Rome's location allowed Roman armies quick and ready mobility throughout Italy.

In respect to the Mediterranean basin, Rome occupied the center of Italy, which in turn dangled down into the center of the Mediterranean Sea. This gave it a central location from which to control both east and west.

Rome's strategic advantage thus worked outward in concentric circles. The city location itself was rich in natural resources and good for defense. It was, however, also central to commerce and communication for a resource- and population-rich region of a centrally located resource- and population-rich land, in the resource- and population-rich Mediterranean basin. Given such a natural advantage, if a people could somehow work their way out from this central spot, they might be able to impose control on it all. The Romans did just that.

The Least You Need to Know

➤ During the rise of Rome there were many ancient cultures in various stages of development around the Mediterranean.

➤ The Greeks and Phoenicians were the primary colonists of the Mediterranean.

➤ There were many peoples in ancient Italy. Etruscans controlled the northwest, Greek settlements controlled the south, and the Latins were between. Various other tribes occupied the central spine of Italy running north–south.

➤ The Etruscans had the most influence on early Roman development and culture.

➤ The city of Rome's strategic position within Italy, and Italy's strategic position within the Mediterranean, gave Rome a natural base from which to establish an empire over all the Mediterranean and the surrounding regions.

Chapter 5

Seven Hills and One Big Sewer: Rome Becomes a City

In This Chapter

➤ Traditional and more accurate accounts of Rome's beginning

➤ The Roman kings

➤ Rome's revolution from the kings

➤ Early plebeian and patrician struggles

➤ The first stages of Roman government

So how did a group of villages along the marshy Tibur River grow, not only into a unified city, but also into a people with the wherewithal to conquer most of the known world? To ask it in simpler terms: How did Rome become "Rome" and the Romans become "the Romans"?

A good place to start is by asking the Romans themselves. As all people do, the Romans had a variety of traditional stories that both reminded them of where they came from and explained how they developed into a particular group of people. In American terms, they had their own versions of the story of Columbus, Thanksgiving, and George Washington and the cherry tree.

These kinds of stories are based partly in history and mostly in imagination. Nevertheless, they tell us a great deal about how the Romans saw themselves. When we put them together with archeological and other historical information, we get a fairly good idea of how Rome became a city and how the Romans became a people.

Virgin Bears *Twins!* Myths of Rome's Founding

Just as Rome grew from various cultures, stories about its beginning came from a variety of sources. These traditions came from the different ethnic groups that lived in and around Rome's environs, and they were stitched together by later writers into a (more or less) coherent story.

Lend Me Your Ears

"Things that happened before the city's conception or founding are passed on more as poetic embellishments than sound history, and I don't intend to support or refute them. It's a convention of antiquity to make the founding of cities seem more important by adding divine intervention. Besides, if any people deserve to claim gods in their beginnings, the Roman people have won that right by conquest. So when Rome claims that Mars is its patron and father, everyone accepts this claim without question like they accept Rome's rule."

—Livy, from his preface to *The History of Rome from the Founding of the City,* written about 25 B.C.E.

The Story of Romulus

Almost all places in the ancient world had an eponymous founder—some mythic man or woman for whom the place or city was named. These figures are almost never historical, although in the nebulous mixture of ancient history and myth, it's better never to say never.

Romus (Rome guy) or Romulus (little Rome guy) was Rome's eponymous founder. There was a variety of traditions about him, which came from the different communities that made up the ancient city. All these traditions had their problems, and most of them ended up contributing something to the final version.

Here are a few of the versions:

➤ **A Latin story:** A young *vestal virgin,* Rhea Silvia, is impregnated by the god Mars and gives birth to twins, Romulus and Remus. The twins are left by the river to die, but they are suckled by a she-wolf until a herdsman, Faustulus, discovers and raises them. Later, when Romulus breaks ground for a city on the Palatine hill, Remus does the same on the Aventine hill. The brothers quarrel over the new cities and Romulus kills Remus. The problem with this story is that it fails to take into account popularly held traditions contained in competing versions.

When in Rome

Vestal virgins were an ancient line of priestesses of the goddess of the hearth, Vesta. A vestal entered service at about 6 to 10 years old, and served for 30 years. After 30 years, a vestal was free to marry, though few did. Vestals oversaw a number of rituals and objects thought vital to the preservation of the Roman State. Vestals had rights (such as owning property and having wills) and privileges (such as box seats in the Coliseum) that other women didn't have. On the other hand, if vestals were caught being unvirginal, they were buried alive in an underground chamber.

➤ **A Greek story:** Greeks, who also lived in the area, linked their own local heroes to the site of Rome. One obscure tradition claimed that a king, Evander, ruled over the village of Pallantium (a.k.a. Rome's Pallatine hill). Evander's name means "good guy," which gives you an indication of how historical *he* really was. This Greek tradition doesn't really say anything about Rome or explain why it didn't end up being called "Evanderville."

➤ **Another Greek story:** This one connects the Greek hero Odysseus with the city. In Homer's *Odyssey*, Odysseus stops for awhile at the island of the enchantress Circe. The story goes that they had a son, Romus, who traveled to Italy and founded the city of Rome. The problem with this story is that it's, well, lame. Homer never mentions that Odysseus and Circe had any children. The ancients didn't buy it either and it never became popular.

➤ **An Etruscan story:** The Etruscans were unwilling to let the Greek heroes claim responsibility for establishing Rome. Their tradition connected Rome's beginning to the Trojan hero, Aeneas. Aeneas was the son of a Trojan hero, Anchises, and the goddess Venus (Greek Aphrodite). There was already a Greek tradition that Aeneas founded cities around the Mediterranean after he fled Troy's destruction. Under Etruscan and Latin influence, Aeneas eventually reached the site of Rome. There he had a son, Romus, after whom he named his city.

However, by the time this story became popular, the Greco-Roman world had already dated the fall of Troy to about 1184 B.C.E., and the founding of Rome to somewhere around 800 B.C.E. This story, then, presented a problem: Aeneas would have been about 370 years old when he founded Rome.

The Traditional Story

In any case, these stories were woven together by the first century B.C.E. in the following manner:

Roamin' the Romans

Roman literature included traditions from and about cities around Rome and Italy. The result is that you can find many of the places referred to in famous works, such as the *Aeneid* by Virgil, on the map today. Such places include the ancient region of the Latins, Laium (modern Lazio) to which Aeneas comes, and the town of Lavinium (modern Lanuvio), which Aeneas founds.

➤ The Trojan hero Aeneas escapes the destruction of Troy and, with a band of Trojan exiles, eventually arrives in Italy. Here he meets opposition from the Latins but finds an ally in a king, Evander, who lived in Pallantium. After winning the right to stay in Italy in battle, Aeneas weds a local royal princess, Lavinia, and founds the city of Lavinium.

➤ Aeneas's son, Ascanius (also known as Iulus), leaves and establishes the city of Alba Longa.

➤ One of Ascanius's descendents, King Numitor, is driven out by his evil younger brother Amulius. Amulius makes Numitor's daughter, Rhea Silvia, a vestal virgin in order to make sure that there are no rightful heirs to the throne.

➤ Alas! The god Mars sleeps with Rhea, and the twins Romulus and Remus are born. The evil king orders his servants to take the boys and throw them into the river. But the river is high and mucky, so the attendants leave them in the basket by the side of the reed marsh.

➤ Divine providence intervenes. The basket doesn't sink, but floats as the river rises to another shore. A she-wolf finds the infants there and suckles them until they are found by the shepherd Faustulus. He raises Romulus and Remus until they discover their true identity. The brothers decide to establish their own city on the site of the Palatine hill.

➤ Romulus and Remus (and their respective followers) quarrel over who gets to name and rule the city. Romulus kills Remus and becomes king.

Veto!

Quarrels between brothers feature prominently in the traditional stories of various cultures (think Cain and Abel) as do twins. The twin brothers Romulus and Remus are not historical but "doublets," that is, different versions of the same name. The story of their quarrel probably accounts for how one of two ancient names for the city became dominant.

The Romans believed that, in addition to founding the city, Romulus was responsible for several important elements in Rome's development. He established, for example, a group of 100 *patres* (fathers or elders) which laid the foundation for the patrician class and the senate.

Romulus added to Rome's manpower by making the Capitoline hill a place of asylum for fugitives, but without women to go with them, Rome's future still was in doubt. The Romans raided a Sabine festival and carried off the young women to Rome. This is known as the *Rape of the Sabines*. As the story goes, the Romans were able to convince the girls to stay of their own volition before their families showed up for an Italic reenactment of the Trojan War. The Sabines captured the city, but the girls persuaded the two groups to merge and rule together. The story as told by Livy is implausible but may reflect the mixed ethnic nature of Rome's early beginnings.

Veto!

"Rape" in mythology sometimes means "kidnapping" (from the Latin *raptus*, "snatched up"). Other times (such as the story of Lucretia), "rape" means "rape."

Generals, Slaves, and Entrepreneurs: The Various Kings of Rome

Roman tradition held that there were a series of kings after Romulus. Each of these introduced traditional "Roman" customs and fought various neighbors to establish Rome as the chief city in the region. Some may—or may not—be historical figures, but as the Roman historian Livy said before beginning his account of the kings, "It is now generally accepted (*Iam primum satis constat*)" that they were as follows:

1. **Romulus** (traditionally 753–715 B.C.E.). You already know him from our earlier discussions so we don't need to elaborate here.

2. **Titus Tatius** (traditionally 753–715 B.C.E.). A compatriot of Romulus, Titus was the leader of the Sabines. Tradition credits him with enlarging the city and founding several religious cults.

3. **Numa Pompilius** (traditionally 715–673 B.C.E.). Numa was the founder of religious temples and offices, such as the vestal virgins and the *pontifex maximus* (the chief priest in Rome). Numa's name, like that of his predecessor Titus Tatius, has also been also connected to the Sabine cultural element in early Rome.

4. **Tullus Hostilius** (traditionally 673–642 B.C.E.). Tullus was thought to have established Rome's senate house, the *Curia Hostilia,* and to have conquered the rival city of Alba Longa (the one founded by Aeneas's son Ascanius).

5. **Ancus Marcius** (traditionally 642–617 B.C.E.). Ancus was thought to be responsible for enlarging Rome's territorial control into regions previously controlled by the Etruscans to the north and west to the port city of Ostia.

6. **Tarquinius Priscus**, or Tarquin the Elder (traditionally 616–579 B.C.E.). According to tradition, Tarquin and his wife, Tanaquil, came to Rome from Etruria with ambitions to go to the top. They brought Etruscan customs, culture, and builders with them and worked hard to succeed. Once king, Tarquin undertook many of the earliest public works projects in Rome, such as the temples on the Capitoline and the public sewer, the Cloaca Maxima. He also fought a number of wars against neighboring cities. Tarquin, a successful and arrogant newcomer, made a number of enemies among the other royal clans, including the sons of Ancus Marcius, who conspired to have him killed.

7. **Servius Tullius** (traditionally 578–535 B.C.E.). Servius was said to have been a slave in Tarquin's house, and he became king after Tarquin was murdered. He is traditionally remembered as a mild and kind ruler (in comparison to the aristocratic and cruel Tarquins), and he is believed to have instituted the census and Rome's ancient assembly, the *Curia Centuriata.* Rome's ancient fortification wall (still called the Servian Wall) was also attributed to him. Servius's daughter, Tullia, married the son of Tarquin the Elder, Lucius Tarquinius.

8. **Lucius Tarquinius Superbus**, or Tarquin the Proud (traditionally 535–509 B.C.E.). I-Just-Can't-Wait-to-Be-Queen Tullia urged Lucius to assassinate her father, and his henchmen assassinated

Roamin' the Romans

In Rome, you'll find remains of the Servian Wall, the ancient fortification wall ascribed to Servius Tullius. This wall (which was not built by Servius) was well within Rome's city limits even by the third century B.C.E. (much like Wall Street in New York City).

Servius in the city. They left his body in the street, and in a demonstration of solidarity, Tullia drove her chariot over her father's body, which was now just a royal road bump on the way to ultimate power. Tarquin the Proud was the last king of Rome. He was driven out by Roman aristocrats for his arrogant ways and the actions of his son, Sextus, who raped Lucretia, the wife of Sextus's cousin Lucius Tarquinius Collatinus (see the story of Lucretia in the following section).

A section of the Servian Wall in Rome.

Throw the Bums Out! The Roman Revolution and the Beginning of the Republic

According to legend, Tarquin the Proud enjoyed a brief tenure as king. His tyrannical rule angered the other Roman nobles until an act of outrage committed by his son, Sextus, brought about a rebellion.

Sextus and a group of young Roman nobles were out on the battlefront. One night the young bucks were comparing the virtues of their wives. Each one praised his own, so they decided to return to Rome and spy on their wives to see what each one was doing while her husband was away. Of them all, only Lucretia, the wife of Sextus's cousin Lucius Tarquinius Collatinus, was hard at work taking care of her household rather than partying it up like the other wives. Sextus was filled with desire for Lucretia.

Later, Sextus returned to Collatinus's home where Lucretia entertained him properly as a guest. Late that night, he entered her room and tried to force himself on her at sword point. When she refused, he threatened to first rape her, kill a slave and lay them side by side and make it look like she had been sleeping with the servants while her husband was away. With that, Lucretia relented, but told her husband (when he returned) what had happened. Refusing to be comforted by the fact that she had been

Great Caesar's Ghost!

Our word "republic" comes from the Romans' term for their new state, in which all had a share of power (instead of a kingdom, ruled by a king). They called it, in Latin, the *Res Publica*. It's hard to translate: *res* is a very broad word. You could translate it as "the public thingy," but it means something like "the public concern" or "public affair(s)."

Great Caesar's Ghost!

Authors no less than Chaucer and Shakespeare have retold the story of Lucretia, and the *Rape of the Sabines* is the basis for the musical *Seven Brides for Seven Brothers!*

forced, Lucretia displayed that good ol' Roman sensibility for setting the proper example by promptly killing herself so she would not provide an excuse for other women to act improperly.

This outrage inspired Lucius Junius Brutus, another nephew of Tarquin the Proud, to start a rebellion against the Tarquins and drive them from power. Brutus was both brave and crafty. The Tarquins had been in a habit of killing off potential rivals, and Brutus's brother had been killed in this way. Brutus, however, had avoided suspicion by acting like an idiot. After the rebellion, Brutus became one of Rome's first consuls and carried on the example of stern discipline by putting his own sons to death for trying to restore the Tarquins to power.

It Wasn't Murder—It Was Sewerside! What Probably Happened

"Great story," I hear you saying. "But what *really* happened?" Well, to tell you the truth, the traditional stories appear to be roughly corroborated by archeological evidence, at least in outline.

Huts on the Hills

The site of Rome, a marshy crossing along the Tibur River, was settled sometime between 1000–900 B.C.E. by a people known to us by their archeological remains as Villanovan. They immigrated from the north bringing with them an ability to work iron and an Indo-European language. They lived in round huts, and it is probably from this kind of ancient dwelling that the temple of the goddess Vesta (as in the vestal virgins) got its circular shape.

Over the next couple hundred years, the growth of the Etruscan civilization, the immigration of Greeks into southern Italy, and the growth of Italic settlements in central Italy helped to create a variety of trade routes that intersected at Rome and made the site more important.

64

Villages began to spring up on the hills that rose out of the marshes at the point where the various routes crossed each other and the river. These villages were settled by various ethnic peoples: Latins, Oscans, Sabines, Greeks, and Etruscans. We can tell roughly how large the settlements were by the remains of ancient cemeteries from this time. Burials were always located *outside* of the village/city limits, and burials can be found along the base of the foothills and marshes between the settlements.

As population and commercial activity grew, the villages formed some kind of cooperative union. This is probably reflected in the names and stories of the Romans' traditional history, which show a mixture of Sabine and Latin (Roman) elements. Rome was by no means an important place at this time—other cities such as Alba Longa, which was a religious and political center of a federation of Latin towns, were more developed and more powerful. The "Romans" probably had a "king" (*rex*) who was elected and advised by a band of elders, the *patres*. The *patres* were the ancient precursor of the patrician class and the senate. But in order to evolve into a real city, Rome needed to become a geographically unified place, it needed public spaces for markets and businesses, and it needed to become politically significant in the region. But those annoying marshes kept Rome's villages isolated.

Roamin' the Romans

When roaming the Roman world, you'll notice that the temples of the goddess Vesta, the goddess of the hearth, are round. This shape probably goes back to the ancient round dwellings, such as we find with the Villanovan culture in Rome, which, quite literally, were centered on the hearth.

Royal Growing Pains

The Etruscans, whose commercial and cultural power was extending down past Rome into central Italy, probably brought Rome into being as a city and center of power. The growing trade between the federation of Etruscan cities, the Greeks, and Phoenicians was transforming Rome into a boom town. The story of entrepreneurial Etruscans moving in and becoming a governing class, as told about the Tarquins, may be mostly true.

About 600 B.C.E., the Etruscans brought in the skills and knowledge to drain the marshes by means of a great sewer, or *Cloaca Maxima,* which means "really big sewer" (although a student once identified it on a test as the emperor Hadrian's wife). Over this newly created area, the kings erected royal buildings (such as the *regia* and house of the vestals) and places for public assembly (the *comitium*), and they began the construction of temples that were worthy of a regional center of power.

The Cloaca Maxima *is tastefully (perhaps the wrong word here, all things considered) built into the Tibur's modern retaining wall.*

When in Rome

The **Latin League** was a confederation of Latin cities neighboring Rome; each member held equal rights in the coalition. Rome conquered the Latins, broke up the League, and federated individual towns with itself.

Rome's expansion did not come without cost. The Romans fought constantly with their Latin neighbors to enlarge and protect their city's growing sphere of influence. In particular, Rome conquered the powerful cities of Veii and Alba Longa. Alba was the political and religious center of the *Latin League* (see Chapter 6, "On Golden Pond: Rome Conquers Italy and the Mediterranean," for more on the Latin League). Rome's ambitions to take Alba's place led it to destroy the Alba and moved most of its important families to Rome. Some of these families, which included the ancestral family of Julius Caesar, became influential players in Roman history and culture.

By the beginning of the Republic (that is, by about 509 B.C.E.), Rome was among the most powerful of the cities in the region, and it controlled roughly 350 square miles of territory.

Top to Bottom Social Organization

Social organization was hierarchical. At the top of the social pyramid was the king, or *rex,* and his royal family, priests, and attendants. Next in line was the senate (*senatus*) made up of aristocratic representatives (*patres*) of the noble families. The senate advised the king on matters of law and state, mustered the army, and governed the clans. The senators and patricians enjoyed an enormous amount of social, economic, religious, and legal advantage over the common people (the *populus*).

The kings also organized the people into an assembly, the *comitia centuriata,* by property classes. Divisions in classes were made according to how much military equipment one could afford. Those who could afford a horse were at one end, and those who could afford only a stick or slingshot were at the other. This organization made a place for the growing importance of the foot soldier to the Roman army of the time.

The creation of the *comitia centuriata,* even weighted as it was in the aristocrat's favor, may actually have been intended by the kings to help preserve their own power. For, despite the fact that the kings were Etruscan, Rome remained a "Roman" city. There were tensions between the noble Roman families and Etruscan royalty. The new assembly gave the king a forum to appeal directly to the infantry. This population was growing, and it was not only becoming increasingly important in military affairs, but it came from the lower orders—many of whom were from outside the city.

Judging from later tensions between plebeians and patricians, many in the lower orders felt oppressed by the nobility. By basing the class divisions on property, the assembly also began to give this growing propertied class a foothold in the political process independent of their birth. These considerations may help to explain why Rome's pending revolution was a revolution of, by, and for the aristocrats. If so, it also helps explain why, after the overthrow of the kings, patricians and plebeians spent nearly as much of their time fighting each other as they did foreign enemies.

The Aristocratic Republic

Sometime in the late sixth century B.C.E., traditionally 509 B.C.E., the aristocrats drove out the Etruscan kings and formed a new government and constitution that put them in complete control. They abolished the office of the king but kept some of the royal religious offices such as the *potifex maximus* and vestals (revolution against the king is one thing, but revolution against the gods is quite another). The senate was retained, and to replace the king, they created two annually elected officers, called consuls.

Originally, the consuls had to be of patrician birth although plebeians were eventually allowed (in theory, though not much in practice) to become consuls. The consuls had the king's power of supreme authority in war and in law (including the power of execution). This power, called *imperium,* was gradually extended to other Roman magistrates in other capacities, but the consuls retained the executive authority over the Roman State until the end of the Republic.

Great Caesar's Ghost!

The name of the Romans' chief priest, the *pontifex maximus,* was later adopted by the Latin church for the Bishop of Rome, that *is,* the Pope. If you look at inscriptions or documents, you'll still find the Pope referred to in this way, often by the abbreviation *pont. max.*

When in Rome

When looking at things Roman, you might spot the fasces—bundles of wooden rods bound around a double axe with a red ribbon. Fasces were symbols of command authority, or **imperium,** which included punishment (rods) and execution (the axe). Mussolini, who hoped to establish a new Roman Empire, chose this symbol to express his political philosophy. He called his party fascist (but he apparently forgot the bit about being subject to the law).

The people were divided into two classes, patricians (nobles) and plebeians (commoners). Patricians could hold offices, become senators, priests, consuls and the like. Plebeians could, well, serve in the army (which they did a lot), go into debt (which they did while serving in the unpaid army), and work off the debt as indentured labor for the patricians between battles. If they couldn't pay their debts, they lost their land and their freedom.

Trouble in River City: The Conflict of the Orders

Archeological evidence indicates that Rome went into a steep economic decline in the period immediately following the expulsion of the Etruscan kings. Tradition also indicates that there were continual battles: The Etruscans tried to retake Rome, cities and towns that had been subservient rebelled or attacked, and internal factions within the noble class fought for power.

In addition, the next 200 years saw a long struggle by the commoners to obtain legal and political rights in spite of the aristocrats. This sometimes brutal and bloody struggle is called the Conflict of the Orders. Although the Romans eventually resolved this conflict, the manner in which they resolved it lay at the roots of the Roman Republic's eventual disintegration into civil war.

Put That in Writing! The Twelve Tables

Things were especially bad for the plebs who were under the aristocrats' control in the battlefield, under their jurisdiction at home, and dependent upon them as keepers of legal and religious traditions. But as Rome's fortunes began to stabilize again, by around 450 B.C.E., the social unrest generated by these pressures began to bring changes to Roman society and culture.

One artifact of these changes was the Romans' longest surviving legal documents, the Twelve Tables. Sometime around 450 B.C.E., a board of 10 men was entrusted with drawing up the basic legal traditions and publishing them on wood (later bronze) tablets in the forum. Before the Twelve Tables, laws were a matter of legal and religious tradition, and these traditions were promulgated by the aristocrats. The laws, even as published, still favored the rich and powerful, but the mere fact that they were written down indicates the popular pressure that was exerted to have them recorded and codified.

Roamin' the Romans

Here are three laws from the Twelve Tables:

➤ IV. 2: If a father gives up his son for sale three times, the son shall be free.

➤ VIII. 1: If anyone has sung or composed a song against another person that was causing slander or insult ... he shall be clubbed to death.

➤ (Unknown number): There are eight kinds of punishment: fine, fetters, flogging, retaliation in kind, civil disgrace, banishment, slavery, and death.

Many of these laws became obsolete, but portions of them remained in effect until the Emperor Justinian's reform of the Roman legal codes in C.E. 530, 1,100 years later.

"You and Whose Army?" or, "Nothing Secedes Like Secession"

The plebeians were beginning to make inroads into the Roman upper classes at the time of the Twelve Tables. A few years before, for example, it had been made legal for plebeians to marry patricians. But don't imagine that this was some kind of warm-hearted acknowledgement for "wrong side of the tracks" marriages; it reflected the fact that some plebeian families had enough power and prestige to be acceptable to the noble class.

Roman tradition has it that the plebeians also succeeded in forcing the nobles to give them more power by seceding—that is, by withdrawing into their own portion of the city and refusing to fight in the army. By so doing, they left the aristocrats and their loyalists to fend for themselves. Such a maneuver, when done on the eve of a pending attack, could be p-r-e-t-t-y effective. ("Go ahead and die for *your* city, don't let *us* stop you!") The aristocrats pleaded for patriotism, tried force, but eventually had to deal.

The plebs created their own political institutions to safeguard their interests. They formed an assembly, the *comitia tribunis* (tribal assembly), and elected representatives, called tribunes (*tribuni plebis*). The plebeian assembly, besides electing the tribunes, discussed and decided collective action on behalf of the plebs. It also elected its own financial officers (called *aediles*) and established its own record keeping system and office. It was, for many years, a virtual, but not officially recognized, part of the political and cultural landscape.

"Dr. No"

A tribune's job was to protect the people and to stop any abuses against them by the magistrates or others. He accomplished this through his power of *intercessio* (literally, "getting in the way"), and by means of a *veto* ("I forbid" in Latin). While tribunes interceded for specific individuals, they exercised their veto over other assemblies (including the senate) and magistrates. If they thought something was against the interests of the common people, the tribunes could intercede, and the matter—regardless of the number of votes or who was doing it—could not proceed.

Tribunes had no legal place in legal and political traditions, and so the senate didn't recognize their powers at first. The plebs, however, gave tribunes the condition of being "inviolate," which basically means, "touch him and we all touch you." This status gave the tribunes the backing they needed to intervene where they saw fit.

Gradually, however, the plebs and their institutions became recognized as parts of the Roman social and political system. By 287 B.C.E., plebeians were not only allowed to hold any office, but one of the two consuls was required to be plebeian. The plebeian assembly was also granted the official recognition that it needed to pass legislation at this time.

Government of the Roman Republic.

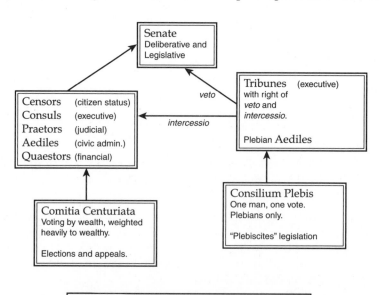

The Roman Republican Government in Brief

So ... Wait a Minute Here

You might notice some problems with this arrangement. It seems, doesn't it, that there are really *two* separate legislative bodies (plebeian and senatorial) that don't have to come to agreement before a piece of legislation becomes law. Imagine the United States House and Senate each being able to pass legislation without coming to conference! Well, you're *right*. And doesn't it seem problematic to give a relatively minor official the ability to veto everything in the state without provision of an override? Well, you're right there, too. Still, the system worked remarkably well.

One reason this system worked for so long was that the upper crust of the plebeian families actually had more in common with their patrician rivals than with the other "common" people. As long as this was true, plebeian and patrician sides of the aisle were basically two facets of the same political and economic elite, and they exercised power in the service of their common interests (which, I must add, were not always different from those of the people). To students of political science, this may seem shockingly contemporary. Such are the lessons of history.

Nevertheless, despite these internal struggles, Rome continued to conquer Italy, Carthage and north Africa, Greece, the Mediterranean, Egypt, Palestine, most of Western Europe, and parts of Britain. These conquests brought new peoples, problems, ideas, and opportunities into the Romans' complex and sometimes contradictory way of handling their expanding empire.

The Least You Need to Know

➤ Roman traditions about the past are roughly accurate but mostly entertaining.

➤ Both traditional and archeological evidence show that several cultures were influential in Rome's beginnings.

➤ The Etruscan kings made Rome into a powerful city through public works projects and military and political organization.

➤ The period after the kings was marked by social, political, and economic struggle between the Roman orders.

➤ The plebeians created their own assembly and officials to protect their interests. There was an uneasy balance of power between these institutions and those of the senate.

Part 2

Rome Wasn't Built in a Day: The Roman Republic (509–27 B.C.E.)

After the overthrow of the kings, Rome entered a period of history in which it was governed by elected magistrates, assemblies, and the Senate. This period is known as the "Republic" (from the Latin Res Publica) and ends in the establishment of the Principate under the first emperor, Augustus.

Although the Republic had a shaky start, it soon entered a period of incredible expansion and development. In a struggle for dominance, the Romans began to exert control over their immediate neighbors, then their neighbors, and then their neighbors, until not just Italy but the whole Mediterranean became a part of Rome's neighborhood. Rome went from a mid-sized Latin city to the center of an enormous empire. Roman civil engineering paved the way for this development, and Latin literature rocketed from primitive beginnings to the rhetorical highs of Cicero and the sublime poetry of Virgil and Horace. How did that happen? Well, read on!

Chapter 6

On Golden Pond: Rome Conquers Italy and the Mediterranean

In This Chapter

➤ Struggles after the fall of the kings

➤ Rome establishes a powerful base in central Italy

➤ Expansion into central and southern Italy

➤ The Punic Wars with Carthage

➤ Roman conquests in the East and West

You can divide the roughly 500 years of the Roman Republic into three general sections:

1. 500–270 B.C.E.: Rome conquers Italy
2. 270–133 B.C.E.: Rome conquers the Mediterranean
3. 133–20 B.C.E.: Rome conquers everything else (including itself)

We'll save number three for Chapter 7, "Let's Conquer … Ourselves! The Roman Revolution and the End of the Republic." Right now—quick march!—we've got a lot of territory to cover.

You Will Be Assimilated: Rome Conquers Italy (500–270 B.C.E.)

The early Roman Republic had trouble with all its neighbors before all its neighbors had trouble with Rome. Etruscans, Gauls, and neighboring tribes made attempts on

Roman territory while Rome struggled with new political and social order. Often on the verge of defeat or internal collapse, Rome gained its feet and overcame both internal and external threats. As it did, Rome established itself as the chief power in central Italy and laid down the foundations for a great empire. Then it went on the offense and conquered the whole Italian peninsula. This, in turn, brought Rome into conflict with Greece and Carthage who also had major interests in southern Italy.

After the Tarquins were thrown out of Rome (see Chapter 5, "Seven Hills and One Big Sewer: Rome Becomes a City"), the leader of the Etruscan confederation, Lars Porsenna, attacked the city. Archeological evidence indicates that the Etruscans did reoccupy Rome for a time, but Roman tradition says that a number of heroic Romans kept them at bay. Here are a few of them, who became models for Roman valor:

➤ **Horatius Cocles.** Horatius single-handedly blocked Porsenna's forces while the Romans were dismantling the wooden bridge over the Tiber, the *Pons Sublicius*. The sight of one man challenging and threatening their entire army stunned the Etruscans. They hesitated long enough to allow the bridge to be disassembled. Horatius then plunged, fully armed, into the Tiber and swam back to the cheering Romans.

➤ **Mucius Scaevola.** Mucius sneaked into the Etruscan camp and attempted to assassinate Porsenna. To show the Etruscan just what kind of people he was dealing with, Mucius stuck his hand in a fire and impassively let it burn. Porsenna was so impressed at his bravery that he let him go. According to Roman lore, this is how Mucius got the name Scaevola, which means "left-handed."

➤ **Cloelia.** During the war, the Romans were forced to give hostages to the Etruscans. Among them was a young girl, Cloelia. Cloelia bravely escaped and swam the Tiber back to Rome. The Romans, who were the a-deal-is-a-deal kind of people, sent her back. Porsenna admired her courage and let her and some of the other hostages go.

Whether the Etruscans got into the city again or didn't, the Latin and Greek cities south of Rome were not about to let Etruscans reoccupy the territory. They attacked and defeated Porsenna's son, Arruns, and broke the Etruscan hold over Latium. Rome was once again free.

Won't You Be My Neighbor? The Latin League

Peace didn't last long. Rome had been a powerful city and wanted to stay that way. The Latins, however, didn't want the same Rome under new management. Rome and the Latins went to war, which ended in 493 B.C.E. with an important treaty called the *foedus Cassianum*. Rome and the Latin League (the coalition of Latin cities) contributed equally to the common defense, shared some citizen rights, and equally divided the spoils of conquest (that is, Rome got half and the Latin League got half). This put Rome on a footing equal to the whole League and allowed Rome alone to summon the entire allied force.

The Latins, alarmed by continued Roman expansion after the First Samnite War (see "The Samnites and Central Italy" later in this chapter), revolted. Rome defeated the Latins in 338 B.C.E and broke up the Latin League. In place of the league, it made Latin cities *municipiae* and established *colonae* among them. These strategies proved to be crucial for Rome's future success and strength.

Great Caesar's Ghost!

Two of Rome's successful strategies for ruling their conquests, *municipiae* and *colonae*, have come down to us in the words "municipality" and "colony."

Rome's arrangements with the individual Latin states required service to Rome but also gave the Latins rights and privileges as Roman citizens. Latin cities became *municipiae* (municipalities), from the Latin *munera*, which means "burden" (in this case, the burdens of citizenship). Several *municipiae* were completely incorporated into the Roman state, and although they maintained limited local autonomy, they received full Roman citizenship, including the right to vote and hold office (*civitas*). Other cities retained "Latin" status: more autonomy but without voting privileges (*civitas sine suffragio*).

Municipiae had to defer to Rome in foreign policy and supply troops when called. Municipal citizens could intermarry and hold contracts with Romans but not among themselves. These arrangements tied the Latins' social and economic status, power, and identity to Rome. The Romans used this model as they conquered the rest of their empire and as they established colonies.

Colonae, or colonies, were new settlements established with surplus population. Ancient states had established colonies for centuries, but the Romans made a studied policy of it after 338 B.C.E. As they conquered territory, they established colonies in important strategic and economic locations. The status of these colonies mirrored the status of *municipae:* Their citizens received full Roman rights. "Roman" colonies were small defensive outposts in difficult locations. "Latin" colonies were large enough to be viable on their own and had the status of other Latin *municipiae*. Both Romans and Latins could belong to either kind of colony.

Carving Up the Neighborhood

Etruscan power declined in the period after losing Rome leaving the entire region unstable. Rome faced constant threat from neighbors competing for territory: the Volsci in the south, the Aequi in the east, and the Etruscan city of Veii about 12 miles to the north.

Great Caesar's Ghost!

The Roman hero of this period was Cincinnatus. With a Roman army pinned down by the Aequi, the senate called upon Cincinnatus to save them. They found him plowing in his small field, and made him dictator (emergency commander). Cincinnatus put down the plow, led an army, defeated the Aequi, returned to his farm, and picked up the plow again. He became a symbol for the Roman ideals of military service, frugality, and simplicity.

When in Rome

Rome actively sought to keep potential enemies from forming united opposition by exploiting rivalries and by keeping relationships with Rome individual and separate. In this way opposition was kept fragmented and isolated. This strategy was called *divida et impera,* or "divide and rule."

The Hinerci were a people sandwiched between the Aequi and Volsci. The Romans followed a policy of *divida et impera* (divide and rule) and formed an alliance with the Hinerci against the other two. This kept the Aequi and Volsci from uniting during the years of fierce fighting between Rome and these tribes. To the north, Rome eventually conquered Veii by tunneling under its walls in 396 B.C.E. This was a great victory for Rome, and the first in a long line of successful military operations.

The Gallic Avalanche

Gallic tribes, under the pressures of population growth and the invasions of Germanic peoples from the north, had poured over the Alps in search of pasture and plunder since the sixth century B.C.E. In 390 B.C.E., a Gallic army reached the river Allia (about 10 miles north of Rome) and met the Roman force. The Romans were used to fighting with spears in a disciplined and organized phalanx. But the Gauls, fierce warriors with big swords, just ran or rode up on them from every side! The Romans were completely routed.

Back in Rome, people fled the city. A few remained on the Capitoline hill, and tradition says that the old noble men remained in their halls in silent dignity. The Gauls, when they entered to plunder the halls, thought that the men were marvelous statues—until one pulled a Roman's beard—then they killed them all. The Gauls tried to capture the Capitoline, but geese kept as sacred to the goddess Juno started to honk as the Gauls crept up the hill and thwarted the attack. Finally, after plundering the city and being paid a huge ransom, the Gauls left and headed back to the north where they had other fish to fry.

The defeat badly weakened Rome. This is when the Aequi and Volsci began to attack, the Latins began to revolt, and things looked pretty bleak for Rome's future. But the Romans rebuilt their city defenses, defeated their enemies, recaptured their territory, settled the affairs with the Latins, and went on to bigger things.

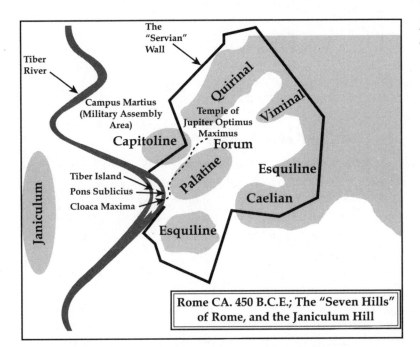

Rome and Italy, ca 450 B.C.E.

The Samnites and Central Italy

Rome's next major conflict was with the Samnites, the fierce mountain tribes of south-central Italy. These tribes lived in a loose federation of highland villages and towns. Roman and Latin colonies had encroached on their territory at the same time as the Samnites themselves were expanding and brought on a series of conflicts called the Samnite Wars.

The first Samnite War (343–341 B.C.E.) was fought for control around the city of Capua and ended in a treaty that left intact the Romans' alliance with Capua (just north of Naples) and the Samnites' holdings in central Italy.

The second Samnite War (327–303 B.C.E.) was fought to a draw. The Romans suffered a great defeat (although how great has been questioned by historians) at Caudine Forks in 321 B.C.E. The Samnites lured a Roman army into a narrow pass, captured it, and forced the Roman soldiers to surrender shamefully. Rome refused the terms of surrender and renewed the war.

Although the Samnites lost none of their territory, Rome gained in many ways. It learned how to make its fighting forces more flexible and maneuverable, and under the leadership of Appius Claudius Caecus, the Romans built the *Via Appia* (the famous Appian Way) from Rome to Capua. This road proved so important that they built roads to other parts of their emerging empire. The Roman "interstate highway system" became an important component in keeping the empire defensible, unified, and economically viable.

Roamin' the Romans

From the city of Rome, you can still follow the ancient stones of the *Via Appia Antiqua* past Roman tomb monuments. The road was named for Appius Claudius Caecus, The Blind, the most influential Roman of this period. Appius instituted many important and popular social reforms (such as land redistribution) that kept Rome internally strong, built the first great Roman aqueduct (the *aqua Appia*), and proposed the road for troop movements to Capua that still bears his name.

The third Samnite War (298–290 B.C.E.) was fought against Rome by the Samnites, Etruscans, and Gauls to try to stop Rome's continued expansion and control over Italy. By this time, Rome's strength was too great. The Samnites surrendered in 290 B.C.E. and were assimilated into the status of Roman allies. When the Gauls and Etruscans settled a few years later, Rome had all but the very southern portion of Italy under its rule.

Pyrrhic Losses: Conquering Magna Graecia

The Samnites were also fighting with the great Greek city of Tarentum. Tarentum depended on Greek mercenary forces, such as those under Alexander of Epirus in 334 B.C.E. Alexander negotiated a treaty with the Romans, in which the Romans agreed neither to help the Samnites nor send ships into the bay of Tarentum. Nevertheless, Rome's defeat of the Samnites and the colonies that they established there involved them in the affairs of Magna Graecia (Greek colonies including Tarentum, Sybaris, Crotona, Heraclea, and Neapolis). Eventually, Tarentum attacked the Romans and called in King Pyrrhus of Epirus to help.

Pyrrhus had ambitions to be another *Alexander the Great*. He arrived in Italy in 280 B.C.E. with 25,000 mercenary forces and 20 war elephants purchased from India. He won his battles, but at a high cost. The Samnites joined him, but the larger revolt of Roman allies that he counted on never materialized. He attacked Sicily where he again bogged down after initial success against the Carthaginians, who protected their trading settlements and the Greek cities on the island.

When in Rome

Alexander the Great (356–323 B.C.E.) was the greatest commander of antiquity. The son of Philip II of Macedon, who conquered Greece in 356 B.C.E., Alexander conquered Egypt and Asia Minor all the way to the steps of the Himalayas before he died at the age of 33.

Pyrrhus finally returned to Epirus in 274 B.C.E. where he again rescued defeat from the jaws of victory. After winning Macedon and most of Greece, he was killed when a woman threw a pot out of a second story window in the city of Argos and hit him on the head. That had to hurt—in more ways than one.

Tarentum, now on its own, surrendered to a Roman siege in 272 B.C.E. With it, the Romans captured a great deal of booty, the fertile lands and trade routes of the south, control of all Italy, and Livius Andronicus. It was Andronicus, a Greek slave, who introduced the Romans to Greek drama and epic by translating the *Odyssey* into Latin. We'll talk more about him in Chapter 8, "Rome, Rome on the Range: Romans at Home," but let's just note that this began the cultural and literary process by which, as the Roman poet Horace put it, "captive Greece captured its captor."

Never Out of Africa: Rome Conquers Carthage

Carthage was founded about 800 B.C.E on the north African coast (in modern Tunisia) by Phoenician colonists. It grew into a great commercial and naval power (kind of like the Hudson's Bay Company) with settlements all over the western Mediterranean (including Spain and the islands of Sicily, Sardenia, and Corsica). From the birth of the Republic (509 B.C.E.) through the invasion of Italy by Pyrrhus (280 B.C.E.), Carthage and Rome were allies. Each had common interests against the Etruscans and the Greeks and separate spheres of influence. This situation ended when Rome had southern Italy firmly in its grasp. The two great states were now in a position where the Mediterranean was just not going to be big enough for both of them. This led to the Punic Wars.

Rome and Italy,
ca 270 B.C.E.

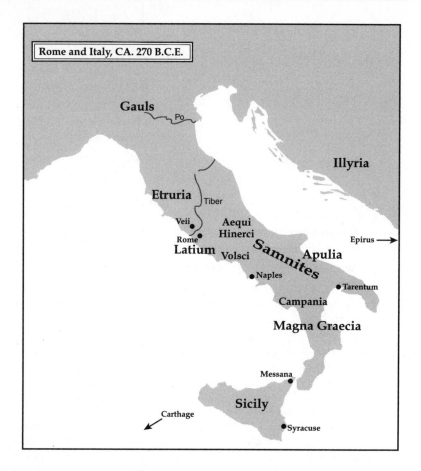

Peacemaking and Peacekeeping: The First Punic War (264–241 B.C.E.)

The first Punic War was fought over Sicily. Mercenaries from Magna Graecia, the Mammertines, had been fighting there on behalf of Syracuse (the most powerful city in Sicily). There was a falling out over pay, and the Mammertines captured the Sicilian city of Messana (modern Messina). When Syracuse attacked the rebels, the Mammertines called on both Carthage and Rome for help.

Sicily was a rich and strategically situated island, and Rome was interested in having a piece of the pie. When both Rome and Carthage showed up to help the Mammertines, both Syracuse and the Mammertines soon became irrelevant. Rome wanted into Sicily, and Carthage wanted the Romans out. So, for the next 20 years, Rome and Carthage fought each other over Sicily. Eventually the Romans won and made Sicily the first Roman province in 241 B.C.E. A few years later they forced the Carthaginians out of Sardinia and made that island a province as well. Carthage, like the proverbial elephant, never forgot the insult.

Great Caesar's Ghost!

The Romans were not sailors. At first they had a terrible time against the Carthaginians, but eventually found a way to make sea warfare more like land warfare. They outfitted ships with big landing ramps with a huge spike called a *corvus* (the "crow") at the end. When they let down the gangway—smack!—the spike stuck in the other ship. Then, instead of being able to run around like a berserk Gaul, the enemy ship had to sit there while the Romans ran across and attacked. This was one of the innovations that allowed them to defeat the Carthaginian fleet in 241 B.C.E.

Elephant in the Living Room: Hannibal and the Second Punic War (218–202 B.C.E.)

When an empire takes a big hit, loose pieces start to shake and fall off. Carthaginian territories in Spain began to rebel after the loss of Sicily and Sardinia. The great Carthaginian general Hamilcar Barcawas was in charge of getting things back in order. Hamilcar carried a deep grudge against Rome. According to tradition, he brought his young son, Hannibal, with him and made him vow an undying oath of hatred against the Romans. Eventually, Hannibal inherited a loyal, well-trained, and well-armed army to carry out his vow.

The Romans and Carthaginians had an uneasy border in Spain along the Ebro River, and the flashpoint was the town of Saguntum. Hannibal conquered Saguntum, but there is some disagreement as to whether he meant this as a provocation. In any case, hotter heads prevailed, and hostilities began.

The Carthaginian (remember that Carthage had been a naval power) found himself in a strange situation. He had the better army but the Romans controlled the sea. Hannibal's only chance was to make Rome recall all its forces where its navy couldn't help it, and that place was Italy. But the only way to get to Italy without going along the coast was over the Alps.

The Romans, who considered the Alps their northern defense wall, sent one army to cut off Hannibal at the Rhone river and another to Sicily from where they could invade Africa and attack Carthage. But the first army arrived too late at the Rhone. Hannibal was already across and headed up the Alps. Rome, shocked and alarmed, began to scramble for a Plan B.

We don't know Hannibal's exact route, but the crossing is the stuff of legend. Attacked by Gauls and facing incredible challenges of logistics and terrain, Hannibal lost at least a third of his entire army. Still, he, 26,000 infantry, 4,000 cavalry, and 20 of 60 elephants made their way down the Alps into Italy in 218 B.C.E. There, Gauls who were already at war with Rome flocked to him, and he began to head south.

Even with the Gauls, Hannibal did not have the forces or support to attack Rome itself. His strategy was to try to break apart the Roman system from within. If he defeated Roman forces in Italy, allies in Italy might abandon Rome or revolt. If so, the reserves that gave Rome its stamina would be drained away. Moreover, because Rome had to call in troops from the borders of its empire to defend Italy, hostile forces in other places would begin to encroach and further weaken the overall system. Hannibal's plan was very nearly successful.

Hannibal won victories over the Romans in northern Italy at the Ticinus and Trebia rivers in 218 B.C.E. The Romans tried to cut him off from central Italy, but he surprised them and took an unguarded route into Etruria. He then ambushed a Roman army of 36,000 under the leadership of Gaius Flaminius at Lake Trasemine in 217 B.C.E. and destroyed it. Instead of marching on Rome, however, he headed into central and southern Italy.

Great Caesar's Ghost!

Quintus Fabius's strategy of delay and harassment have come down to us in the expression "Fabian tactics."

Rome elected the conservative Quintus Fabius to the office of dictator that year. Fabius adopted a very un-Roman strategy: He would not engage Hannibal head-to-head but rather keep his forces on high ground where Hannibal's cavalry had no advantage. This did not endear Fabius to Romans who were eager for a fight, and especially to those who had interests in the regions that Hannibal was pillaging. They nicknamed Fabius "Cunctator" (Delayer). When Fabius's term was over, they elected consuls (the chief magistrates and commanders) who would lead forces against Hannibal.

The ensuing battle at Cannae was a disaster—for the Romans. Hannibal, in a brilliant display of tactics, pinned the full Roman army against a river and annihilated it. Over 70,000 Romans, including the consul and many important Romans, lost their lives. The Romans went to code blue, drafting boys above 16 and even slaves into the legions. The Samnites, cities in southern Italy, and Syracuse sided with Hannibal. Philip V of Macedon (northern Greece), who wanted the Romans to stay on their own side of the Adriatic, (see "The Illyrian Wars [229–228, 220–219 B.C.E.]" later in this chapter), allied with Carthage. The Roman system was breaking apart at the seams.

But most alliances held, and the persistent Romans began to win back their interests in Spain, Sicily, and Illyria (the territory across the Adriatic from Italy). The Latins groaned under enormous burdens of taxation and military drafts, but eventually, after 15 years, the tide began to turn. Hannibal's one army couldn't protect his gains. He summoned help from his brother's army in Spain, but the Romans, led by a young and brilliant general, Scipio, cut it off and defeated it at the Metaurus River in 207 B.C.E. Scipio was then elected consul and sent with an army to north Africa, which forced Carthage to recall Hannibal. There, at the battle of Zama (modern Naraggara), Scipio defeated Hannibal in 202 B.C.E. Rome became master of the western Mediterranean, and Scipio received the title "Africanus," the "Conqueror of Africa."

The Roman system of alliances, which had grown from judicious settlements with the Italians, had held against great odds. Rome was able to call on resources, built up through these alliances, and deploy them with persistence and skill. Fabius's intelligent tactics had given the Romans a chance to mobilize them yet again.

Peace Is a Desert: The Third Punic War and the Destruction of Carthage (151–146 B.C.E.)

After the battle of Zama, Hannibal himself brought the Romans' terms of surrender to Carthage and proposed acceptance. Terms were harsh: Carthage lost all its holdings outside Africa and had to recognize the independence of Numidia (which allied with Rome). Carthage paid an enormous yearly indemnity to Rome, and agreed not to wage war anywhere outside Africa and not within Africa without Roman permission.

Despite these terms, Carthage quickly recovered as a major economic power. Hannibal proved as good a civic administrator as a general. This didn't go down well at Rome, so Rome demanded Hannibal be surrendered as a war criminal. He fled to the east where the Romans continued to try to track him down as they conquered and expanded there. Hounded by the Romans until the end, Hannibal took poison to avoid capture in 182 B.C.E.

Carthaginian economic strength continued to be a source of envy and worry to Rome. To complete their domination, the Romans manufactured a crisis with the help of its ally Numidia, who goaded Carthage into attacking it in 151 B.C.E. so Rome could declare war. Carthage held out heroically but eventually surrendered in 146 B.C.E. The city was destroyed, its inhabitants sold into slavery, and its lands made into the Roman province of Africa. That same year Rome also destroyed the Greek city of Corinth.

Great Caesar's Ghost

Politicians sometimes keep repeating certain phrases as "sound bites" to capture the public imagination. They can look back to Cato the Elder who, to keep hammering home his conviction that Rome should eliminate Carthage altogether, worked *Carthago delenda est* ("Carthage has to be destroyed!") into every speech and party conversation whether it pertained or not.

Go East Young Man: Rome Conquers Greece and the East

In Chapter 4, "Club Mediterrania: Rome in the Context of Other Civilizations," we described how Alexander the Great's empire was carved up by his generals into the *Hellenistic* dynasties of the Antigonids (of Macedon), Ptolemies (of Egypt), and Seleucids (of Asia Minor). These kingdoms fought a seesaw battle of cutthroat among themselves for dominance. Along the fault lines, a number of Greek city-states, islands, and leagues held on to a measure of independence by playing one dynasty against another. As Rome entered the picture, these smaller players tried to do the same thing with Rome. The conquest of Carthage had made Roman nobles and middle class citizens rich in goods, land, and slaves, and the rich Hellenistic kingdoms promised other opportunities for expansion and glory.

The Illyrian Wars (229–228, 220–219 B.C.E.)

The Illyrian Wars set the stage for Roman involvement in Greece. The Greek cities of Magna Graecia had always suffered from piracy, and the Illyrians, who lived across the Adriatic from Italy (modern Yugoslavia), were particularly good at it. The Romans negotiating with the Illyrian queen, Teuta, and when that didn't work, they conquered part of her kingdom and gave it to a Greek adventurer by the name of Demetrius of Pharos. When Demetrius turned out to be a loose cannon and began to conquer his neighbors, the Romans expelled him and set up their own Roman garrison at Dyrrachium. Demetrius fled to king Philip V of Macedon and urged him to attack the Romans before it was too late. Philip V did form a brief alliance with Hannibal after Rome's defeat at Cannae, but he backed off and made peace with Rome in 206 B.C.E. when things went badly for Carthage.

When in Rome

The term **Hellenistic** refers to Greek civilization and culture throughout the Mediterranean and Asia Minor after the death of Alexander the Great in 323 B.C.E. to the Roman conquest of Egypt in 31 B.C.E.

Free to Be Roman: The Macedonian Wars

Philip V turned his attention to defeating the Ptolemies of Egypt. His successes threatened the independence of the island of Rhodes. Rhodes appealed to Rome and claimed that Philip was conspiring with Antiochus III of Syria to divide up Egypt. This would have made Philip far too powerful for Rome's tastes. They invaded Macedonia in 200 B.C.E. but had trouble until a gifted general and diplomat, Gaius Flaminius, took over the effort. Flaminius spoke fluent Greek and was well-liked by the other Greeks. He defeated Philip at Cynoscephalae in 197 B.C.E.

In 196 B.C.E. at the Isthmean Games (in Corinth), Flaminius declared in the name of Rome that all Greek city-states were to be free and independent. Pandemonium broke out. Greek cities minted coins with his image, and in some cities he was, like Alexander, worshipped as a god. Freedom for Greece, however, served Roman interests. It kept the Greeks fragmented while the Roman declaration made any unifier think twice. Unfortunately, the Greeks, whom Flaminius admired, proved incapable of managing their affairs, and Greece dissolved into chaos and anarchy. Eventually the Romans imposed a terrible order.

Trouble with Philip V's son, Perseus, brought the Romans back in 171 B.C.E. After the general Aemilius Paullus defeated Perseus at Pydna in 168 B.C.E., the Romans broke Macedonia up into four separate republics. The war spoils and Macedon's yearly *tribute* to Rome was so great that all Romans were exempted from direct taxes. The Macedonians rebelled in 149 B.C.E. under the yoke. Rome crushed them and made the once great state of Macedon into a Roman province, Macedonia.

In Greece, the Romans traded anarchy for oppression. They plundered and depopulated whole areas, selling at one point 150,000 captives as slaves. They helped local despots to terrorize their people, and when they found some of Perseus's papers with the names of leading Achaean citizens, they deported them to Greece (including the historian Polybius) and kept them imprisoned for years. Finally, in response to yet another Greek uprising, the consul Lucius Mummius sacked Corinth in 146 B.C.E., plundered its treasures, razed it to the ground, and killed its citizens or sold them into slavery. The city-states of Greece were placed under Roman-approved authorities. Eventually the emperor Augustus separated Greece from Macedonia and made it the province of Achaia in 27 B.C.E.

Conquering the East

The Seleucid king, Antiochus III, the Great of Syria, had taken advantage of Philip's troubles with the Romans. He conquered the eastern Mediterranean from Europe to Egypt. The city of Pergamum (western Turkey) appealed to Rome for assistance against Antiochus, and Flaminius (the general who defeated Philip V) went to have a talk with Antiochus. Antiochus was not impressed.

> ### When in Rome
>
> **Tribute** (*tributum*) was the yearly assessment of taxes. Provinces and conquered peoples also paid installments as a part of treaties to cover the costs of conquest (yes, conquered people paid for their own subjugation).

> ### Roamin' the Romans
>
> Pergamum became a powerful and wealthy city, renowned for its medical school, sculpture, town planning, library, and the famous Altar of Zeus. You can visit the site of Pergamum in Turkey, and you can see the amazing high-relief sculpture of the "Pergamum Altar" in Berlin.

It was about that time that Hannibal, on the run from Carthage, showed up in at Antiochus' court in Syria. He advised Antiochus to cooperate with the other Greeks against Rome, but Antiochus attacked Greece instead in 192 B.C.E. This brought the Romans in, big-time. The Romans combined with Macedon, Carthage, and Greece to drive Antiochus back to Syria where the Romans pursued and defeated him at the battle of Magnesia in 190 B.C.E. Antiochus made a final peace in 188, and died plundering a temple in 187 B.C.E. The Romans carved a huge slice out of his empire for their ally, the city of Pergamum, who had originally appealed to them for help. Pergamum returned the favor in 133 B.C.E. when King Attalus III of Pergamum willed his kingdom to the Roman people, and Pergamum became a possession of Rome.

The Wild West

Besides Rome's conquest of the eastern Mediterranean, there was conquest going on in the west. It's hard to imagine that the Romans were able to fight wars on so many fronts. Gauls in northern Italy, who had joined Hannibal, remained an unpredictable and dangerously unstable force on the northern border. Meanwhile, Rome had inherited Spain from Carthage, but with a very messy probate: Spain's rugged terrain and rugged people proved difficult to subdue.

So Gauling: Settling Northern Italy

After the Second Punic War, the Romans reconquered, colonized, and imposed order on the Gauls in northern Italy between 197 and 170 B.C.E. They settled colonies from Aquilia on the Adriatic to the Italian Riviera, and relocated troublesome people like the Ligurians from their homelands to places where they could be better controlled. The Romans also went on a road-building boom to unify the area and better connect it with Rome. Colonies, economic development, and infrastructure accomplished what armies could not, and northern Italy became peaceful, stable, and Romanized.

In Spain, Again

Rome took over Carthaginian holdings in Spain, which was rich in resources and manpower. They had trouble, however, subjugating the Spaniards, who were adept at guerilla warfare in the mountainous Spanish terrain. In 197 B.C.E., the Romans divided Spain into *Hispania Citerior* (Nearer) and *Ulterior* (Farther) and tried to impose taxes on the tribes that would pay for Spain's administration. This went badly until Cato the Elder (195 B.C.E.) and Tiberius Sempronius Gracchus (180–178 B.C.E.), two Roman governors, set up fairer and more equitable terms and conditions.

Later, Roman governors provoked the Spanish into rebellions. The tribes achieved successes against the Romans under a charismatic leader, Viriathus (141 B.C.E.), and at the city of Numantia (137 B.C.E.), the Romans shamelessly broke treaties made in good faith with both. Traitors to Spain, bribed by Rome, slit Viriathus's throat and shipped his people off to a colony. Numantia was besieged, starved into surrender, and burned in 133 B.C.E.

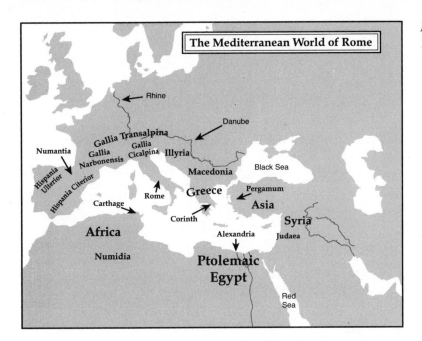

Roman conquests in 133 B.C.E.

The year 133 B.C.E. marks Rome's completed conquest. Rome's dominions extended from Syria in the east to the Atlantic ocean (with Spain), and from the Alps to the north down across the sea into Africa. It was a conquest marked initially by foresight, cooperation, and restraint, and later by brutal subjugation, exploitation, and dishonesty. The allure of unimaginable power, wealth, and glory through conquest and political dominance at Rome was strong, too strong not to have some terrible effects on Rome's treatment of other nations and on Rome internally in the years to come.

The Least You Need to Know

➤ Rome's success depended largely upon relationships formed with states and colonies in early conquests of central Italy.

➤ Rome's conquest of southern Italy led to conflicts with the Carthaginians and the Macedonians, who also had interests there.

➤ Rome's ability to recover and fight on multiple fronts allowed Rome to defeat Carthage while still maintaining and expanding its empire.

➤ Rome destroyed Carthage and Corinth in the same year (146 B.C.E.) and in 133 B.C.E., possessed Spain and the Pergamum empire.

Chapter 7

Let's Conquer ... Ourselves! The Roman Revolution and the End of the Republic

In This Chapter

➤ The breakdown of the Republic

➤ The Gracchae, *optimates,* and *populares*

➤ Marius and Sulla

➤ Caesar and Pompey

➤ Octavian (Augustus) and Antony and Cleopatra

In this chapter, we'll follow the implosion of the Roman Republic as individual political and military power came to dominate the internal and external affairs of Rome. The story of the last century of the Republic is one of competition between factions of nobles. It begins with the Gracchae and the senate, proceeds to individual commanders with their own armies (Marius and Sulla, Pompey and Caesar), and ends in the destruction of the state (Antony and Octavian).

King of the Hill

As of 146 B.C.E., with Rome's defeat of Corinth and Carthage, no other power remained to challenge Rome's dominance. The bounty of conquest funneled into the hands of the few who controlled the Roman state. War tribute flowed to Rome, and hundreds of thousands of slaves were imported to work in *latifundia*, huge private or corporate farms (see Chapter 10, "The Romans at Large," for more on the latifundia). Many Romans became fabulously rich, and the spoils of conquests created a thriving upper class, especially in importing, banking, and financing.

Business Boom

Two economic classes in particular became economically influential and powerful. One class was the *equites*, or "cavalrymen"—wealthy Romans who were not senators. The name comes from the top property classifications the *comitia centuriata* (the general assembly during the Republic). Senators, who were also in this property classification, could not legally engage in business outside of real estate and farming. The *Equites* therefore came to refer to wealthy men who chose commerce over politics, or businessmen who became wealthy enough to enter the top brackets. This growing "business class" became quite powerful after the Punic Wars. Another influential economic group was the *publicani*—members of the Equestrian Order who formed companies (*societates*) to bid on and administer public contracts, the collection of taxes in the provinces, and other public works.

Trouble at the Bottom

The continual wars, however, had taken a toll on Italy, and after 146 B.C.E., there were no more rich conquests. Costly wars in Spain and Gaul and slave rebellions at home offered no return. The Italian allies, who had served Rome so faithfully, wanted a bigger share of Roman rights. Small farmers, from whom the soldiers came, were dislocated by economic change and by continual military service. Many lost or abandoned their farms and migrated to the cities in search of work. Military recruitment began to plummet, partly because the number of small landowners was declining, and partly because dangerous military service against slaves or Spanish tribes offered no reward.

The nobility, however, were not inclined to give up their enormous share nor change the political structures that allowed them to keep it. They did, however, learn to utilize the manpower of the lower classes in their armies and the plebs' political power to advance their own interests in the popular assemblies.

He's So Popular: The Gracchae

Gaius and Tiberius Gracchus were brothers from a distinguished noble family. Their father, Tiberius Sempronius Gracchus, was the fair-minded governor of Spain (179 B.C.E.). (For more about Spain in this era, see Chapter 6, "On Golden Pond: Rome Conquers Italy and the Mediterranean.") The brothers were raised by their famous mother, Cornelia, who was the daughter of Scipio Africanus (conqueror of Hannibal). Tiberius was married to the daughter of Appius Claudius, the leading senator of the day. In other words, these two guys were connected.

Gaius and Tiberius addressed the urgent problems of their day in ways that exploited a fatal flaw in the Roman political system: the presence of two separate legislative bodies (plebeian and senatorial) that didn't have to come to agreement before a piece of legislation became law. Gaius and Tiberius took their causes to the plebeian assembly and passed legislation there in direct opposition to the senate. They showed that there was, through the popular assembly, another avenue to power besides through the senate. The senate's violent backlash would set forces in motion that eventually tore the Republic apart.

Tiberius Gracchus (d. 133 B.C.E.)

Tiberius was elected tribune in 133 B.C.E. He proposed to enforce an old law limiting the amount of public land controlled by one citizen. He wanted to distribute the remaining land to landless Romans and set up a commission to oversee the redistribution. When the senate refused funds, Tiberius gave the donation of Attalus III's kingdom (Pergamum) to the Roman people (133 B.C.E.). (For more about Pergamum, see Chapter 6.) The senate bribed another tribune to veto the legislation. When Tiberius got the tribune deposed, things got ugly. A mob led by senators killed Tiberius during the next election.

Gaius Gracchus (d. 121 B.C.E.)

Gaius was tribune in 123 B.C.E. He won over the equites by protecting their economic and judicial interests; he won over the urban poor by proposing public works projects, a ceiling on grain prices, and military reforms; he won over the landless farmers when he proposed a new colony at Carthage. When he went off to Africa to set up the new colony, his enemies in the senate used another tribune to undercut Gaius by offering even more sweeping and radical proposals (which they never intended to fulfill). When Gaius returned, he attempted to broaden his base by proposing to give the vote to the Italian allies. This enraged the urban poor, who felt threatened, and there were riots.

Veto!

The Gracchi are sometimes portrayed as radical champions of the common people. This is far too simplistic. Tiberius's proposals, for example, had already been made in the senate by Appius Claudius.

When in Rome

The **senatus consultum ultimum** allowed the consul to take any steps he saw fit for protecting the Republic.

Optimates favored the ultimate power of the senate and pursued their ambitions by traditional means. **Populares** promoted their interests through the popular assembly, and protected (when it suited their interests) the rights of the tribunes such as *intercessio* and *veto*.

Gaius unsuccessfully tried for election two more times. Riots continued, mostly provoked by the senators. The senate eventually imposed martial law under a *senatus consultum ultimum*. The consul, Opimius, had offered a reward for Gaius's head: its weight in gold. Senators and their supporters attacked and killed about 250 of Gaius's followers. Gaius was cornered and ordered his slave to kill him. About 3,000 of the Gracchae's supporters were later executed.

The Gracchae became hallowed martyrs. Statues were set up to them, the places they died became shrines, and no politician would dare speak ill of them. Their causes and strategies were taken up (not always genuinely) by other ambitious Roman aristocrats in pursuit of power, which resulted in the rough division of Roman politics into *optimates* and *populares*.

Veto!

Optimates and *populares* in no way represented what we might think of as political parties or ideologies. These terms apply more to how individuals pursued their aims at a particular time. If rejected or beaten in the senate, a politician might seek to accomplish what he wanted through the popular assembly and friendly tribunes. If so, he could be labeled a *popularis* by his political enemies in the senate and by supporters in the popular assembly.

Marius and Sulla

The careers of Gaius Marius (157–86 B.C.E.) and Lucius Sulla (138–78 B.C.E.) would add the explosive power of personal armies to the volatile mixture of politics at Rome. The interdependent relationship between a general, who relied on his army for spoils abroad and for votes at home, and his army, who relied on the general to take care of them at home, would prove devastating to any political opposition.

Marius and the Birth of the Professional Soldier

Marius was ambitious—a brilliant general and an opportunistic politician. As a member of a nonnoble family, he became a *novus homo* and consul seven times by winning immense popularity in successive victories against the Numidian rebel Jugurtha in Africa, against the Gauls in northern Italy (between 105 and 101 B.C.E.), and against an enormous slave revolt in Sicily (104–99 B.C.E.), which erupted when a promise to free slaves who were held illegally was cancelled. It was for the Jugurthine campaign that Marius opened enrollment in the army to everyone. This filled the army with dispossessed men who became professional soldiers and who became more loyal to their general than to the state.

The Romans elected Marius consul five times successively in his absence. This was illegal (one had to declare for election in Rome and wait 10 years before consular reelection), but apparently the Gallic threat and Marius's popularity took prominence. Upon returning to Rome, however, Marius fared badly because politically he was still an outsider. He became embroiled in a political fiasco and, as consul in 98, was compelled by senate decree to use force against his political associates. This left him hated and distrusted by both sides.

The Social Wars (90–88 B.C.E.)

In 90 B.C.E., the allies erupted into revolt when a tribune who proposed giving the vote to them was assassinated. The Marsi, Samnites, and others set up their own confederation. For two years Italians who had fought together for two centuries waged a bitter civil war. Rome won, in part, through the passage of laws giving the allies what they wanted if they laid down their arms. In the end, Italy was devastated and exhausted, but men from the river Po in the north to the toe of Italy in the south became full citizens of Rome. Rome did, however, distribute allies's votes so that they had less clout than they should have.

Call Me "Lucky": The Reign of Sulla

Lucius Cornelius Sulla "Felix" (Lucky) was an ambitious optimate who came up under Marius. He distinguished himself in the Jugurthine and Social Wars. Since Marius's political prestige had been weakened, the optimates ventured to appoint Sulla commander against the eastern potentate, Mithridates. Both Marius and Sulla wanted this command, which promised riches, popularity, and power. When a Marian tribune proposed to take

When in Rome

A **novus homo** was a man who became consul for the first time in his family's history and thus "ennobled" his family. Only Cato the Elder, Marius, and Cicero achieved this distinction in the last two centuries. All came from the equestrian class.

Great Caesar's Ghost!

The Romans' war with Jugurtha, in which Marius and Sulla started their careers, is the subject of a famous history by the Roman historian Sallust (86–35 B.C.E.), *Bellum Jugurthinum*. Sallust identifies this period as the beginning of the end for the Roman Republic.

the command from Sulla and give it to Marius, riots broke out from which Sulla had to hide in Marius's own house and escape out the back. But instead of getting out of Italy, Sulla merely got out of town, got his army, and came back. A Roman had attacked Rome.

Sulla's forces burned the city and murdered their political enemies. Marius escaped to Africa by the skin of his teeth. Sulla settled affairs in the senate and left for the war with Mithridates. As soon as he was gone, one of the consuls, Lucius Cinna, recalled Marius. Marius brought his army, starved Rome into surrender, and went on his own bloody vendetta. He was elected consul for the seventh time but fell ill and died within a few days of taking office. Rome functioned under Cinna until his death in 83 B.C.E.

Sulla concluded a treaty with Mithridates and returned from the east in 83 B.C.E. with a well-trained army. His opponents in Rome tried to martial forces to stop him, but only the Samnites, at the famous battle of the Colline Gate, came close to turning the tide against him. Six thousand Samnite prisoners were tortured to death as Sulla, appointed dictator, calmly spoke over their screams to the frightened senate. In the following period, Sulla organized a reign of terror, known as the *proscriptions*. When that didn't bring enough money, he extorted tribute from some towns, destroyed others and sold their inhabitants as slaves, and turned Samnium into a wasteland. These atrocities left deep and bitter antipathies between Romans of the next generations.

When in Rome

Proscriptions were published lists of names. A man on the list was declared a public outlaw and could be hunted down and killed for a reward. His sons lost their citizenship, and his property was confiscated and given to Sulla's friends or sold to pay his veterans. Many of the proscribed were guilty of nothing more than being rich.

As dictator, Sulla also reformed the constitution to strengthen the power of the senate and curb the tribunes and popular assembly. He also reformed the Roman judicial system (one of his few reforms to survive). To avoid another Marius, Sulla put the senate in control of armies. He restricted governors to fighting only in their provinces. If a commander's jurisdiction needed to exceed provincial boundaries, Sulla made provisions for the senate to appoint a general of their own choosing to an "extraordinary command."

Sulla resigned the dictatorship in 80 B.C.E. and retired to write his memoirs. He died two years later, never to see that instead of creating stability he had only built up coals that would feed the flames of destruction. Marian exiles and Spaniards under the leadership of Marius's general Sertorius set up a government in exile in Spain. Sulla's veterans, who settled on confiscated land, had no knack for farming. They soon became a debt-ridden, disenchanted, and dangerous element in Roman politics. In addition, the resentment and discontent of the groups he subjugated and disenfranchised was manipulated by the next generation until the whole deadly brew erupted into another civil war. Sulla's reforms were quickly overturned after his death, while the means he used for achieving them proved catastrophic.

Kids These Days: Pompey and Caesar

Pompey and Caesar were about as different as could be. Pompey fought under Sulla; Caesar's aunt was married to Marius. Pompey was careful and deliberate, Caesar daring and decisive. Pompey was neither particularly original nor good on his feet in public; Caesar was both. Pompey became the champion of the senatorial *optimates,* Caesar of the *populares.* Pompey wanted to be the most important and powerful Roman of his day, and Caesar … well, that was the problem: In that respect, they were both the same.

Gnaius Pompey, The Great (106–48 B.C.E.)

A very young Gnaius Pompeius distinguished himself under Sulla, who sarcastically nicknamed named him "Magnus" and the name stuck. After Sulla's death and still too young to stand for election, Pompey was given an extraordinary command against Sertorius in Spain, which he won (though some claimed Sulla had already done the lion's share). He became consul in 70 with Crassus and helped to restore the tribune powers that Sulla had taken away. He was then given an extraordinary command to clear the Mediterranean of pirates. He accomplished this by a progressive dragnet moving West to East across the entire sea in just three months. He was then appointed to another extraordinary command against Mithridates.

Pompey defeated Mithridates and went on to conquer Syria, Judaea, and Mesopotamia. His settlement of these lands was extremely influential and farsighted. He founded new cities and encouraged or restored others with privileges. He settled pirates on territory and gave them an alternative to piracy. He was influential on Judaism by choosing Hyrcanus, who was supported by the Pharasees, over his brother Aristobulus, who was supported by the Sadducees, for the throne of Judaea. In short, Pompey's achievements between his Mediterranean and eastern commands brought great wealth to Rome, safety to Mediterranean travel and commerce, and stability to the anarchy of the east.

When Pompey returned to Italy in 62 B.C.E., there was great anxiety about what he would do with his army. To everyone's surprise, he disbanded it and made his way to Rome. He expected to be treated like a conquering hero and to win easy ratification of his settlements in the east and benefits for his veterans. But Pompey had made enemies in the senate, in particular among some members of the powerful Metelli family, whose toes he had stepped on as he pursued his extraordinary commands in the provinces where Metelli held posts. They and others in the senate insulted the Pompey, stymied his proposals, and eventually forced him into cooperation with Caesar and Crassus.

When in Rome

Standards are the banners and/or emblems carried before the troops. It was Marius who introduced the silver eagle as the standard of the legion.

Lend Me Your Ears

"Good Romans, this very day you yourselves have seen the state, your way of life, your goods, fortunes, your wives and children, and even this very seat of most famous rule, our most blessed and beautiful city, snatched by the highest divine providence from fire, sword, and very nearly from the jaws of fate by my devotion, efforts, plans, and personal danger, and you behold it preserved and restored to you."

—Cicero, *Against Catiline* 3.1

Meet the Players

There are three other major players in the years leading up to the civil war between Pompey and Caesar:

➤ **Marcus Licinius Crassus** (?–53 B.C.E.). Crassus was a partisan of Sulla's and became the wealthiest man in Rome. He defeated the rebel Spartacus, and as consul with Pompey in 70 B.C.E., restored much of the tribunes' powers. Crassus joined his rivals, Pompey and Caesar, in 60 B.C.E. in order to secure their individual aims (the first triumvirate). Crassus received a potentially lucrative campaign against the Parthians (in Persia), which ended in disaster. The Parthians killed Crassus and captured his *standards* at Carrhae in 53 B.C.E.

➤ **Marcus Tullius Cicero** (106–43 B.C.E.). Cicero, the influential orator, became consul in 63 B.C.E. He foiled a plot by Catiline and others to take over the state, an event of which he never tired of talking. He wanted to forge a working alliance of the different political factions but was unable to moderate between Caesar and Pompey. Banished and then recalled to Rome, Cicero came back into prominence after Caesar's death. He attacked Antony in a series of speeches, and was executed by Antony's agents in 43 B.C.E. when Antony, Octavian, and Lepidus formed the second triumvirate.

➤ **Marcus Porcius Cato** (95–46 B.C.E.). Cato was the great-grandson of Carthage-must-be-destroyed Cato the Censor. A rigid and uncompromising (one might add pigheaded—no pun on Porcius) moralist, he became influential as the "conscience of Rome" and a determined opponent of Caesar. After a last reading of Plato's *Phaedo*, a discussion surrounding Socrates' suicide, Cato killed himself in Utica (near Carthage) to avoid being captured by Caesar's forces.

Julius Caesar (100–44 B.C.E.)

Gaius Julius Caesar was from an ancient aristo-cratic family that was supposedly relocated to Rome from Alba Longa when Rome destroyed that town in the fifth century B.C.E. Ambitious, quick-witted, and self-assured, Caesar possessed a natural talent for decisive action. After surviving Sulla's proscriptions, Caesar rose quickly as a *popularis* maintaining his identity as a Marian. He borrowed and spent enormous sums of money on public games at Aedile in 65 B.C.E. He developed a reputa-tion for generosity and magnanimity, and his popular appeal helped him achieve the post of Pontifex Maximus (chief priest) in 63 B.C.E. He was sent to Spain as governor in 61 B.C.E.

Rome was in turmoil and gridlock in 60 B.C.E. Although Cicero was still talking about the *concor-dia ordinis* (his concept of harmony between the various political and economic factions and par-ties), there was neither harmony nor order. Cato and other optimates had denied Pompey's requests for his eastern settlements and veterans' benefits; Cato and other optimates had blocked legislation favorable to Crassus and other equites; Cato and other optimates blocked Caesar's request, from Spain, to stand for the consulship *in abstentia*. Caesar surprised the optimates, returned to Rome, and ran successfully for consul.

Caesar, as consul, met with Crassus and Pompey, and the three informally agreed to work together. This cooperative agreement is known as the first triumvirate. Pompey and Crassus wanted their leg-islation, and Caesar wanted a command in Gaul. The optimates resisted every attempt, but eventu-ally all three men got what they wanted. In addi-tion, Caesar passed legislation distributing land to needy Romans, laws restricting the ability of provincial governors to abuse their authority, and instituted an ancient form of C-SPAN, the *Acta Diurna*. The *Acta* was a daily bulletin of the texts of laws and the essence of the debates in the senate and popular assembly. This was posted in the forum and distributed to Italy and the provinces.

Veto!

The "first triumvirate" is techni-cally a misnomer of later history because it was an unofficial arrangement. A triumvirate was an official board of three, such as was later formed by Octavian, Antony, and Lepidus.

Great Caesar's Ghost!

One of Caesar's most lasting achievements was to reform the Roman calendar from a 355-day lunar to a 365-day solar calen-dar. Caesar's birth month was re-named Julius (July) in his honor, and the next month later be-came August after his successor, Augustus. Pope Gregory XIII re-vised the "Julian" calendar in 1582 by adding ten days to make up for lost time and promoted moving year "0" from the birth of Rome to the birth of Jesus.

Roamin' the Romans

Although the site of the battle of Alesia is a matter of some dispute, it is generally agreed to be at the French town of Alise-Sainte-Reine in Burgundy.

Caesar expanded Roman conquests in Gaul to the Rhine river and crossed over the channel to Britain. These conquests were hard fought, involving the Helvatians of Switzerland, king Ariovistus of Germany, the Belgians of northern Gaul, and the Veneti of Brittany. He returned to northern Italy in 56 B.C.E. to renew a strained triumvirate with Pompey and Crassus, who stood for consuls in 56 B.C.E. Caesar returned to Gaul and accomplished two remarkable feats: He crossed over into Britain and established a Roman presence there (55 B.C.E.), and returned to Gaul where he (barely) won the decisive battle at the siege of Alesia (52 B.C.E.). This incredible battle, in which Caesar had to construct one set of defenses to keep a Gallic army in Alesia and another line of defenses to keep out an enormous army of Gallic reinforcements, broke the Gauls' struggle for independence and determined the future of Europe.

Crossing the Rubicon: The Civil War

Back in Rome, however, another crisis was erupting. Crassus was killed by the Parthians in Asia Minor, leaving Pompey and Caesar to compete for preeminence. Pompey, in Rome, drifted toward the optimates, and the two men, rivals but never enemies, became polarized by factions as Rome descended into mob rule by political gangs. A political battle to deprive either Caesar or Pompey (or both) of their command authority eventually led to a *senatus consultum ultimum* (the senate's martial law decree) against Caesar in 49 B.C.E. Caesar's tribunes, Marcus Antonius (Mark Antony) and Quintus Cassius, tried to veto the legislation but were censored and fled for their lives. Caesar was stationed at Ravenna in northern Italy with only one legion. There he marshalled his troops on the northern bank of the Rubicon river, which separated his province from Italy. "The die is cast," he said, and led them across.

Caesar's swift attack stunned the forces of Pompey. The Republicans fled Rome, and Caesar met with little opposition as he raced down the eastern coast in an effort to cut the Pompeians off from leaving Italy. He was too late: Pompey fled with loyalists to Greece to martial a great army, and Caesar returned to Rome. There he pardoned enemies, increased the senate with Italians outside of Rome, reduced debts, granted citizenship to his loyal northern Italian Gauls, and in a grand gesture, recalled those exiled by both Pompey and Sulla. He then won victories over Pompeian loyalists in Spain and, in another surprise move, sailed seven legions into Greece in the dead of winter to attack Pompey.

In Greece, Pompey already had assembled twice Caesar's infantry and seven times his cavalry, but the careful and deliberate general was caught off balance by Caesar's swift deployment. Instead of pinning Caesar in Greece and invading Italy, Pompey pursued Caesar into Greece to stamp him out. At Pharsalus in 48 B.C.E., Caesar's confidence in his well-trained and experienced army proved better founded than Pompey's confidence in overwhelming force: Caesar routed the Republicans. Pompey fled farther east where he still had veterans and connections, but was stabbed and killed by a Roman when he got off the boat in Egypt.

Ptolemy XIII was fighting for the throne of Egypt against his sister, Cleopatra. Ptolemy's advisors cut off Pompey's head and brined it for Caesar when he arrived, hoping to curry a bit of favor. Caesar was not amused. He placed Cleopatra (with whom he became, shall we say, familiar) on the throne, and after almost being over-run by Ptolemy's army and the mobs of Alexandria, restored order to Egypt and the eastern provinces. He then returned to Rome in 47 B.C.E. where more unrest, economic plight, disgruntled legions, and campaigns in Africa and Spain awaited him.

After settling Africa and Spain, Caesar set about transforming Rome into the capital of an integrated world state, and himself into the sole ruler of that world.

Everything Old Is New Again

Caesar reorganized Italy, set out colonies into the provinces, reformed legal and civil administration throughout the Roman empire, and embarked upon a massive building program of public works. In particular, he transformed both eastern and western provinces into viable regions, and reformed the currency so that there could be economic cohesion.

The new Rome needed central authority and decision making and to keep military power away from the hands of provincial governors. Caesar did this by being appointed *dictator perpetuus* (dictator for life) in 44 B.C.E. This gave him the power of a king, which seems to be how he envisioned his role in the new world order. He began to act and dress in a regal manner, issued coins with his likeness, and sat on a golden throne. It seemed that the Etruscan monarchy had returned, and a king was the one thing that the Roman nobility could not abide.

The Ides of March

Many senators, even Caesar's former friends, feared that his power and popularity were leading to a monarchy. Over 60 of them conspired to assassinate him. Caesar was about to embark on a sweeping military campaign in the east, and success there would render him even more powerful. Three days before he left, on March 15, 44 B.C.E , Caesar met the senators next door to the Theater of Pompey. Senators crowded around and stabbed him repeatedly. Ironically, Caesar died at the foot of the statue of his political and military rival, Pompey. Nevertheless, Caesar's successes had

Veto!

The famous quote, *et tu, Brute?* (and also you, Brutus?) comes from Shakespeare (*Julius Caesar*, Act III, scene 1), not Caesar. According to the biographer Suetonius (*Life of Caesar*), Caesar said, in Greek, *kai su teknon* ("and you too, my son).

not only shown the way forward, but also left behind a huge and mobilized army with which to complete the task.

The city of Rome did not welcome being freed from the tyrant as the conspirators hoped. In fact, by the time the senators met to annul Caesar's acts, they were convinced by Caesar's colleague Mark Antony and the howling mobs outside to ratify them instead. Antony secured Caesar's legislation and brokered an amnesty for the conspirators. He also took possession of Caesar's personal papers and will. The next day he read the will (which included Brutus as a minor heir) and displayed Caesar's bloody toga with a wax image of Caesar's corpse. The mob went wild, rampaged through the city, and burned the senate house along with Caesar's body. The conspirators decided it was a good idea to get out of town.

Snakes and Daggers: The Deaths of Anthony and Cleopatra

It appeared for a time that Mark Antony would take Caesar's place. But Caesar's heir, his 18-year-old grandnephew Gaius Octavianus Thurnius, became the final victor in the quest for preeminent *gloria, dignitas,* and *auctoritas.* Octavian's power grew upon the power of Caesar's name, and was encouraged by senators, like Cicero, who saw him as a disposable counterbalance to Antony. But by guile, deceit, skillful maneuvering, and his cachet as Gaius Iulius Caesar Octavianus, Octavian became "Augustus," the first Roman emperor, in 27 B.C.E.

The Second Triumvirate

Antony moved quickly to dominate the state, but was undermined on several fronts. Octavian capitalized on his status as Caesar's heir to undermine Antony's authority with Caesar's troops. Cicero blasted Antony in speech and in print. He, and other senators who sympathized with the conspirators, forced Antony out of Rome. When Antony attacked Brutus at Mutina, the senate, at Cicero's request, sent the young Octavian with an army to help Brutus. Antony was forced to abandon his attack, and the senate, feeling momentum shifting its way, declared Antony a public enemy in 43 B.C.E.

Thinking that Octavian was now disposable, the senate snubbed him, which only forced Octavian back toward Antony, who was conspiring with Caesar's aging governor of Spain, Lepidus. When Antony and Lepidus combined forces and marched into northern Italy, they found Octavian waiting for them. Caesar's troops were not about to attack Caesar's heir, so the three formed a triumvirate with absolute power for five years.

The triumvirate was legalized by a friendly tribune in the popular assembly and embarked on another round of ruthless proscriptions. Among the victims was Antony's enemy, Cicero, whose tongue and right hand were nailed to the rostrum in Rome. The triumvirs packed the senate with their clients, and the newly constituted senate declared Caesar to be among the gods of the Roman state.

The triumvirate quickly devolved into binary opposition. Antony and Octavian sidelined Lepidus by giving him a forced appointment in Africa, and then attacked and defeated Brutus and Cassius at Philippi (northern Greece) in 42 B.C.E. Octavian and Antony then began to maneuver against each other. Direct confrontation was avoided with the Pact of Brundesium in 40 B.C.E., in which Antony took the rich east and left Octavian the troubled west. Antony married Octavian's sister, Octavia, to seal the bargain. The two negotiated a treaty at Misenum (modern Miseno, near Naples) in 39 B.C.E. with Pompeius, the son of Pompey the great, who controlled Sicily and Sardinia and was blocking grain importation to Rome.

The End of the Republic

Antony and Octavian began to consolidate power in their respective hemispheres. Antony's armies reconquered Armenia and Mesopotamia, where he sought to recreate Alexander's empire with Cleopatra. Antony married Cleopatra in 37 B.C.E. (this was not a legally recognized marriage—he remained married to Octavia at the time), which served both rulers' ambitions and set the stage for a great campaign against the Parthians. Octavian consolidated power in the west by military and political maneuvering. He improved his connections with the nobility by divorcing his wife, Scribonia (on the day that she bore him a daughter, Julia) and marrying the noble Livia Drusilla. Livia was divorced for this purpose by her husband, Tiberius Claudius Nero, even though she had one son by him (Tiberius Claudius Nero, the future emperor Tiberius) and was pregnant with another (Tiberius Claudius Drusus).

Although Octavian was no Caesar, his brilliant general, Agrippa, was able to put down rebellions in Gaul and, together with Antony and Lepidus, defeat Pompey for good in 36 B.C.E. Octavian used the power of his position as Caesar's heir to take the credit for these victories and became recognized as the savior of the west. As Octavian's power and popularity grew, he waged a fierce propaganda war against Antony and Cleopatra, portraying Cleopatra as a threat to Rome and Antony as her puppet. Antony became more dependent upon Cleopatra's resources and finally broke off his ties with Octavian by divorcing his loyal wife, Octavia, in 35 B.C.E.

The Romans' fears were heightened in 34 B.C.E., when Antony recognized Cleopatra and her children as rulers of Egypt and his conquests in the east, and came to a head in 32 B.C.E. Octavian illegally seized Antony's will (which may have been a forgery) and read it to the horrified senate and people. It not only recognized Antony's donations to Cleopatra but also recognized her son, Caesarion (Little Caesar), as Caesar's true heir and asked that Antony be buried beside Cleopatra in Alexandria. Playing upon popular sentiment, Octavian stripped Antony of his right to command and declared war upon Cleopatra.

Antony and Cleopatra assembled a huge force and waited for Octavian at Actium in Greece. Their combined force was larger than Octavian's, but Antony's troops were disheartened, his ships large and cumbersome, and his crews poorly trained. In a short sea battle off Actium in 31 B.C.E., Antony's ships were being beaten when he saw Cleopatra's ships sailing away. He sailed after her leaving his troops without leadership, and they surrendered to Octavian. Antony and Cleopatra fled to Alexandria. When Octavian's army in 30 B.C.E. defeated their troops there, both committed suicide and left Octavian not only the kingdom of Egypt and all its riches, but also the whole of the Roman Empire.

Great Caesar's Ghost!

Antony killed himself with a sword. Cleopatra is reported to have killed herself with the bite of an asp, the sacred messenger of the Egyptian sun god Ra, smuggled in to her in a basket of fruit.

The Least You Need to Know

➤ The period from 146 B.C.E. is marked by internal Roman strife inflamed by expansion, inequality of civic and economic privileges, and the acquisition of enormous power and wealth by ambitious Roman nobles.

➤ Roman nobles, such as the Gracchae, learned to pursue their personal ambitions through the popular assembly, often against opposition in the senate.

➤ The creation of professional and personal armies, especially in the provinces, allowed Roman nobles to bring military force into political disputes.

➤ The last century of the Republic was marked by competition among pairs of generals for preeminent power over the state: Marius against Sulla, Julius Caesar against Pompey the Great, and Octavian against Antony and Cleopatra.

Chapter 8

Rome, Rome on the Range: Romans at Home

> **In This Chapter**
>
> ➤ The Romans' self-image
>
> ➤ Roman family structure and the *pater familias*
>
> ➤ Education
>
> ➤ Women and slaves of the household
>
> ➤ Roman household gods

We've covered a lot of Roman history, from villagers on the Tibur to masters of the Mediterranean. But who were the Romans, how did they see themselves, and how did others see them? In this chapter, we'll take a general look at the Roman family. We'll examine the internal framework of the Romans' self-image and the structure of the *familia*, upon which Roman social and political organization grew.

How the Romans Saw Themselves

In short, the Romans saw themselves as hard-working, hard-fighting, salt-of-the-earth small farmers; a practical, disciplined, and pious people of old-time religion who had little use for the vagaries of philosophy, the fineries of luxury, or the uncertainty of instability. Even as Roman culture evolved, the Romans retained at the core of their identity a heartland picture of themselves, a kind of "American Gothic" with a sword.

Small Farmer, Big Soldier

Romans, even the patricians (the noble class) of the senate, began as farmers. Consequently, land ownership and the self-reliance it brought were core Roman values. Even as industry and commercial activity grew and flourished, the intrinsic value of land possession remained at the heart of what it meant to be Roman. Senators, for example, were excluded from commerce and restricted to earning a living from their land holdings. This exclusion essentially created the class of equites (men who belonged to the upper property classes but were not senators) although senators did find ways to exploit these other resources.

The Romans were proud of being citizen-soldiers, and they had to do a lot of fighting. Today, when professional militaries are the norm, it's hard to imagine civilians being on call to fight. Imagine receiving a group e-mail to pick up your sword, abandon your cubicle, assemble in the conference room, and march off to meet an invasion of another company who wants to take over the cafeteria! Romans prized the picture of themselves as tough, resolute, and ready warriors. Even as campaigns grew longer and farther from home, the minuteman ideal of Cincinnatus, the dictator who was called from his plow to save the state and who went right back to it after winning the victory, remained an icon.

Discipline and Practicality

In keeping with the farmer-soldier ideal, the Romans prized the discipline, practical bent, and devotion to duty necessary to work a constant battle with the land. The self-sufficiency, stern nature, unflagging persistence, and resolute ability to soldier on even after catastrophe were all fundamental elements of Rome's self-image and national ideal.

Romans were generally conservative and suspicious of innovation and new-fangled ideas. When things went bad, they were quick to react against whatever was perceived as "un-Roman." The pursuit of theory and abstract ideas was hindered by the monumental *mos maiorum* (ancestral custom, traditional values, or "the way we've always done it") dragging behind as heavily as a sea anchor. The *mos maiorum* had brought them this far; if there were problems, it was probably because too many Romans had taken to soft beds, foreign religions, Greek philosophy, or some other gobbledygook. One thing was certain, however: the *mos maiorum* was never wrong.

Dignity and Authority

Romans worthy of respect within their community had to have both *dignitas* (an honorable reputation) and *auctoritas* (the power to direct others based on prestige). To attain them, they had to possess *virtus*. *Virtus* was composed of a set of values and traits that a true man (*vir*) ought to possess. He had to have the proper respect and loyalty to divine, communal, and paternal authority, which Romans called *pietas*.

106

He had to be true to his word and to his pledges, that is, to have *fides*. His bearing had to show *gravitas*, which meant that he was grounded, realistic, and solid, unmoved by emotion, personal desires, or disaster. Finally, his actions had to show *constantia*, which meant that no matter what, you just kept going as long as it was right to go.

Great Caesar's Ghost!

As you can probably tell from the Latin words, many of the traits that the Romans admired are still with us today: dignity, authority, virtue, virility, piety, fidelity, gravity, and constancy.

Public and Private Life

The distinction between public and private life was less clear for the ancient Romans than it is for us. Today, we live mostly as individuals who have both a direct relationship to a state as citizens and a sharply demarcated personal realm over which we have discretion and control. Romans were primarily members of extended groups to whom they were expected to give complete loyalty and proper obedience. These groups exercised nearly complete control over an individual's identity, status, and private occupations.

First and , Romans belonged to a family (*familia*) under the authority of the family head, or *pater familias*. The family included more than blood relations: It included slaves, freedmen, all household members, and property—the entire extended family and household system. In early Rome, several generations might live, work, and eat together on the farm. Later, as Roman society grew larger and more complex, relatives would move into their own households but remain connected under the authority of the *pater familias* as if they were still under one roof.

Traditionally, related families made up a *gens* (clan). In early times, these clans were self-governing within their own clan territory under the authority of a clan leader. *Gentes* cooperated together to form the state (*civitas*), and the clan leaders were probably the ones who elected the first kings. The importance of the *gens* waned by the early Republic.

In none of these groupings did a person exist individually in the same way that we do today. Romans emphasized the submission of the individual to the group and to the recognition of the group head's absolute authority and *potestas* (power), whether it be the *pater familias* of the family, the *patres* (patricians) of the senate, or the magistrates who exercised the power of command (*imperium*) for the *patria*, or homeland.

Father Knows Best: The Pater Familias

Have you noticed the repetition of "patr" or "pater" in the terms for authoritarian figures or the state? There's a reason for that: Roman social and political order was based on the ancient paradigm of the *pater familias*, the male patriarch or head of the household in its broad sense.

Great Caesar's Ghost!

Some names for Roman members of the household:

- ➤ *Pater:* father; *mater:* mother

- ➤ *Parens:* parent

- ➤ *Infans:* infant, baby

- ➤ *Filius:* son; *filia:* daughter

- ➤ *Puer:* boy; *puella:* girl

- ➤ *Vir:* husband; *uxor:* wife

- ➤ *Adulescens:* young man; *virgo:* young woman

- ➤ *Senex:* elderly man; *matrona:* mature (and married) woman

- ➤ *Servus:* male slave; *serva:* female slave

- ➤ *Coccus:* cook; *ancilla:* maid

All members of the *familia,* regardless of age or where they lived, were subject to his *patria potestas,* or paternal power. The *pater* was judge, jury, priest, and autocrat. He could punish, execute, or otherwise dispose of any person or material belonging to his *familia* at his judgment and discretion. Other members or property brought in by marriage, adoption, purchase, or conquest were also under his *potestas.* He was the only individual in the entire extended structure of the *familia* who had what we would call an individual and independent status before law and the state.

Veto!

The *pater familias's* power was absolute but within a cultural context. A *pater* was responsible for the welfare of the entire family, including its standing with the gods. He was expected to consult and cooperate with important family members, including the *mater familias* (usually his wife). Nevertheless, final choices and the power to act remained his.

Romans were ingrained with respect and reverence for the *pater,* and Roman parents saw instilling it in their sons as one of their most important tasks. These sensibilities, which had their roots directly in the Roman *familia,* left a visible imprint on Roman society, culture, and history as a whole. As Rome grew, analogous patterns of authority were replicated outward, to relationships between clients (*clientes*) and patrons (*patroni*), populus and magistrates, soldiers and commanders, and Rome and other "client" states. When Cicero and Augustus were given the title *pater patriae* (father of the state) in the late Republic, it was much more than a window-dressing platitude.

When in Rome

A **client** was a person of inferior standing who entered into a relationship with a **patron,** a person of superior standing. Patron and client were bound to support and protect each other's interests and to look out for each other.

Education

Early education took place in the home and depended largely upon class. In general, children were taught whatever their parents thought appropriate until about the age of seven. At that point, girls went with the women and boys accompanied their fathers to learn to work, fight, and live as a Roman citizen. At 15, the boy put on his *toga virilis* (the toga of a man) with great fanfare and was deemed a young adult.

Aristocratic families furthered their sons' education for preparation for military and civic service and advancement. They sent their sons to live with and learn the ropes from important friends, who further trained and educated them. Young men began to serve in the military at about age 17. There they worked their way up the ranks under the guidance of commanders. Once they reached an age and suitable character, men, under the training and care of old friends of the family, began their political careers and public life.

As Rome grew, and particularly when it conquered Greece, the aristocratic education expanded upon the Roman model. In addition to the ways in which Roman men learned and apprenticed, noble Romans adopted elements of Greek culture and education. Those who could afford them bought Greek slaves as tutors to educate their children. Other Romans sent their children to schools that had been set up by enterprising Greeks. Most of this education was in Greek language and literature, but by the second century, there were schools in Latin as well. As they progressed, young Romans might study rhetoric and philosophy under a teacher at Rome or even be sent to study with the famous philosophers and rhetoricians in one of the schools at Athens. All this study was intended to give him the means to speak and to conduct himself as an effective Roman man in politics and public affairs.

Women

It's difficult to know much about the actual lives of
Roman women until later in Rome's history—that is,
after about the third century B.C.E. The Roman woman
was, like all members of the *familia*, under the jurisdiction of her *pater familias* unless he transferred her
"into the hand" of her husband in a form of marriage
called *conventio in manum.* If he did, her husband had
the same kind of *potestas* over her as her *pater familias*
did before.

Women were expected to be the nurturing and binding element in the Roman family, as hard working and
serious in their roles as the men, and as devoted to the
good of the whole. They were, however, always cast in
the supportive role compared to men at whatever level
they were or in whatever activity they were engaged.

Still, it's clear that Roman women, from early on, exercised influence and were visible in ways that many
other cultures would have considered unthinkable.
Tradition featured heroines who were active and influential (within Roman sensibilities), not just passive
and submissive, and women who were important to
the state and community, not just to the household
and their husband. A part of these attitudes may have
come to Rome through the influence of Etruscan culture, in which women (at least those of the aristocracy) appear to have had a status accorded elsewhere
only to men.

Additional elements that came to be important in
maintaining a degree of female independence were
Roman laws and customs on marriage and divorce.
While divorce doesn't appear early on, one form of
Roman marriage (*sine manu*) listed in the Twelve
Tables (450 B.C.E.) permitted the woman to remain free
of her husband's possession if she remained away from
his house for three nights per year. She was, however,
still under the *potestas* of her father. This form of marriage became extremely common in the later Republic
and was the subject of criticism by social conservatives
and those who thought that family values needed
strengthening by making marriages more binding (on
women). Under Augustus, a woman gained her legal independence if she had produced three children (or produced a document saying she had).

After Rome conquered the Mediterranean, some Roman aristocrats began to give their daughters a higher degree of education. The influx of wealth into Italy and the lengthy absences of men on military campaigns helped to create a class of women who exercised power and a degree of freedom and independence. The mothers, daughters, and wives of nearly all the influential and important Roman men of the last century of the Republic were active, educated, and influential. These women influenced public policy through their association with leading figures and, occasionally, through direct public action and demonstration. A remarkable example is Hortensia, the daughter of the famous Roman orator Hortentius. In 42 B.C.E., in opposition to a tax imposed on wealthy women, Hortensia broke precedent when she mounted the Rostra in the Forum, delivered an oration on a matter of public policy, and won her point. She was, however, the first and last to do this.

Girls were married early (at about 14 to 15 years old) and often to a much older man. Ideally, the wife was to remain faithful, work hard for the family, teach children their virtues, and produce sons. Such a woman, given that she married initially to an older man and soldier, might have spent a good deal of the time as head of her household while her husband was away fighting and might have been widowed once or twice.

Among the upper classes, divorce became fairly common in the late Republic as marriages became a part of political and social networking. During this time, upper-class Roman women began to display a great deal more sexual freedom. Concerns about morality and declining birthrates brought legislation that attempted to restrict what women could wear in public and exacted penalties for adultery, being single, and being childless. Like most moralistic legislation passed by people who have the privilege of moral hypocrisy, it failed to have an effect.

Urban and Rural

The Romans' picture of themselves was firmly rooted in the ideal of a small rural community. Rome was the "town" to which the small farmers went to trade and to conduct public business. Wealthy families might live in the city most of the time where the *pater familias* and other men conducted business and politics; their land holdings were worked by slaves and tenement farmers, and they visited these holdings from time to time.

As Rome grew, the Romans became progressively urbanized and the city became increasingly the center of power. Land ownership consolidated as Roman farmers lost their land to debts and taxes during the campaigns against Carthage or conquests abroad. The soldiers and dispossessed migrated to the cities, where a vast urban proletariat became a restless and hungry force to be reckoned with by politicians.

Nevertheless, the Roman psyche remained essentially rural complete with a deep suspicion of the city slicker, the foreigner, and the itinerant worker (unskilled or professional). The picture of the small farmer working a piece of land in the country continued to be promoted and idealized by poets and public policy well past its time.

Religion

Roman religion had several layers. The Romans had family practices and beliefs that originated from time immemorial and community practices that were shared by the peoples of Italy. They also, at another level, adopted customs and beliefs from other influential cultures such as the Etruscans and the Greeks. As Rome grew, some foreign cults found a home as well. Finally, there was Roman state religious practice, which developed to encompass all these and to represent Rome as a whole.

Great Caesar's Ghost!

Boundaries and thresholds have always held a special place in beliefs and rituals. The traditional practice of carrying the bride over the threshold comes from the Roman wedding ceremony. The bride smeared Janus's threshold with wolf fat and was lifted over the threshold into her new community.

That "Old Time" Religion

The oldest Roman religious practice persevered in the home and, like the household culture, influenced many aspects of Roman culture. The home itself and the land on which it depended were sacred spaces, and within this universe, gods and spirits existed for its benefit and protection. Every morning and evening the family, including slaves, gathered and the *pater familias* led prayers to these spirits and to the ancestors on the family's behalf.

If you started in the field and walked toward the house you passed through the family gods' various terrain. Coming through the fields you were in the domain of the Lares, guardian spirits of the home's fields and farm. As you entered the door, you passed Janus, a two-faced god who represented and guarded the entrance of the home. Inside, there were the Penates, household spirits who blessed and guarded the food and the home. When you reached the symbolic center of the house—the hearth that provided light, food, and warmth—you reached the goddess Vesta. Vesta's hearth and sacred objects (a table, salt, cake) were tended by the women of the family. New additions to the family such as children and brides were presented to her for blessing and acceptance.

Not Everyone's (Got) a Genius

Ancestor worship was an important part of family tradition and religion. Roman ancestors were as much a part of the family as any living member, and their approval was sought just as members sought to live up to their example. Families kept busts (statue portraits) and death masks of illustrious members and paraded them at funerals and special ceremonies. Family oral traditions about their deeds, recounted at funerals, became an important source for the first Roman historians.

Great Caesar's Ghost!

Just as the hierarchy of the household served as a model for Roman civic authority, its religious structure was projected onto the city and land of Rome. The gates of Janus, through which the ancient armies marched in and out, stood open at an entrance to the Forum. These gates were closed only in times of peace. At the center of the Forum was the Temple of Vesta, with its female attendants, which contained the sacred hearth-fire of Rome. Thus the larger community of Rome came in many ways to resemble the clannish families from which it developed.

The ancestors represented the line of the family *genius,* the spirit of the family that was present physically and symbolically in the *pater familias.* His *genius* was revered as a unique and distinguishing connection to the gods, to tradition, and to legitimacy. It was both his (that is, he wasn't "possessed" by some ancestral spirit) and yet passed to the next *pater familias* as a kind of guardian angel and guiding spirit. It appears that the *mater familias* had a similar spirit that was worshipped after death—the *iuno.*

Imports and Others

As Rome developed into a regional power, it also developed into a religious center. Etruscan and Italic gods were taken into the city and were later understood as rough equivalents with the Greek gods. The high god of Rome was Jove/Jupiter, who became the divine *pater familias:* the highest authority, bringer of victory, and guarantor of justice. Next were Mars, who became the guardian of Roman war and defense of the city, and Quirinus, a Roman/Sabine god without a Greek or Etruscan

Roamin' the Romans

You'll find busts of Romans in museums all over the world. Their fondness for portrait sculpture went back to portraits and death masks of ancestors. In the late Republic, wealthy Romans began to have marble portraits done of themselves (many more frankly realistic than you might imagine paying for) and sculpture became big business. You could, for instance, have your head done and select from a variety of pre-made bodies to put it on!

counterpart. Juno, the *mater familias* wife of Jove, became prominent as well. Gradually, a pantheon of gods and goddesses had official temples and sacrifices in the city.

113

A bust of a Roman matron from the Glyptotech in Munich, Germany.

Here's a partial list of corresponding Latin and Greek gods:

Latin	Greek	Identity
Jupiter/Jove	Zeus	Rule, power, justice
Juno	Hera	Women
Mars	Ares	War
Minerva	Athena	Wisdom, strategy, skill
Diana	Artemis	Goddess of the wild
Apollo	Apollo	Divine wisdom, knowledge
Vulcan	Hephaistus	Fire, metallurgy
Vesta	Hestia	Hearth and home
Venus	Aphrodite	Love and attraction
Cupid	Eros	Desire
Dis	Hades	The dead
Mercury	Hermes	Boundaries, commerce
Hercules	Herakles	Hero and son of Zeus

Other than those, the Romans were quite suspicious of foreign religions, especially any that seemed emotional and charismatic. Even as Romans began to engage in foreign religious practices (especially in times of stress and uncertainty), officially Rome was very much a NIMBY (not in my back yard) culture. The city did, in 205 B.C.E., take in the "Great Mother" (*magna mater*) cult while in crisis and on orders from the Sibylline Oracles but didn't officially recognize another god until Julius Caesar. The senate forbade the worship of Bacchus in 186 B.C.E. and periodically condemned followers of other religions and philosophies.

It wasn't that Rome believed its gods were exclusive (many Romans had stopped believing in the traditional state gods long before the end of the Republic); it was that foreign religions threatened stability and the nobility's lock on the power and influence of the traditional priesthood. Besides, they weren't *Roman*. Still, official warnings and decrees were to no avail: Romans practiced their family religions *and* others that they found appealing and fulfilling, such as the worship of the Egyptian goddess, Isis.

Roamin' the Romans

When you visit Pompeii, you can see some of the household shrines, still beautifully preserved, around which Romans would have engaged in their family worship, as well as temples of Isis.

Slaves and Slavery

Romans of any worth kept slaves at home and on any other holdings. Slaves in the early Republic were children sold into slavery (quite common), people who had fallen into slavery by debt (also quite common), people kidnapped and sold into slavery, or people captured during conquest. The last became a huge source of slaves.

Slaves worked beside their masters in the house, on the farm, and as personal attendants (such as hairdressers) and accompanied children to school or their masters to the baths. A slave might be allowed to have a form of slave marriage, the *contubernium*, but it was not a legal marriage. Partners could be separated and any children were the property of the slave's owner. Slaves could earn money on the side doing other work; with this money they could sometimes save enough to buy their freedom. If they did, they became freedmen and usually clients of their former owners.

In the home, household slaves held different positions and were organized under the supervision of a foreman. Having several slaves to attend you in public was a mark of prestige and status. Some slaves became trusted and valued members of the family, but Roman laws, history, and literature show that even these slaves lived in the condition of the family dog that gets petted when its owners are pleased and kicked when they are not.

Horrible beatings and tortures for slaves were legal and common. Roman literature, for example, portrays upper-class women violently taking out their bad hair days on their slave hairdressers, and dinners upon the slave cooks. Sex (consensual or not) with slaves was common enough, and obstinate or runaway slaves were branded, tortured, crucified, or thrown to the beasts. It isn't until the Empire (C.E. 14–476) that castrating male slaves for profit or killing your slave just because you felt like it was made illegal.

Lend Me Your Ears

As I said earlier, slaves had the legal status of a chair, or should I say, a hoe? Here are two writers giving advice on good farm practice:

"Concerning implements by which one cultivates the soil: Some people divide cultivation implements into three sets: implements with the power of speech, namely, slaves; implements without the power of speech, namely oxen and such; and implements without sound, such as carts, etc."

—Varro (116–27 B.C.E.), *On Farm Affairs*, 1.17.1

"When your oxen get old, sell them ... do the same with old plows, old tools, and old or sick slaves."

—Cato the Elder (234–149 B.C.E.), *On Agricultural Production*, 2

The Least You Need to Know

➤ The Roman household was patriarchal under the absolute rule of the *pater familias*.

➤ Roman family values and structure were the basis for state authority and structure.

➤ Roman upper-class women began to develop an increasing amount of personal freedom and power in the late Republic.

➤ Household and farm slaves made up an integral part of the *familia*. They had no status that protected them from cruel or capricious treatment.

The Romans Among Themselves

Now that we've taken a look at the family, let's look outside the family to *apud Romanos* (among the Romans). Roman citizens distinguished themselves by social class and wealth. As Rome grew, the picture became more complex as different kinds of citizens and foreign clients were added to the mix. We'll take a look at that mix in the next chapter. For now, let's concentrate on Roman relations with others whom they recognized as Roman.

Patricians and Plebs: Social Structure and Divisions

Romans were extremely class conscious. Some classes were determined by birth (the patricians and plebs) and others, such as the equites, by wealth. But class distinctions became a bit hard to define. Wealth brought political power, and during the middle Republic, a class of *nobiles* (nobles) was created from patrician and plebeian families who had previously held political office. This class became as exclusionary as those conveyed by birth: In the last two centuries of the Republic, only Cato, Marius, and Cicero (see Chapter 7, "Let's Conquer … Ourselves! The Roman Revolution and the End of the Republic") became "new men" and "ennobled" their families.

The Patricians

The patricians (*patricii*) were formed in the period of the monarchy (roughly 700–509 B.C.E.) from clan leaders of Roman and Etruscan families. These *patres* made up the king's advisors and became the foundation of the early senate. They were also the men from whom the priests were chosen.

Patricians guarded their prestige and privileges jealously. In the early Republic (509–450 B.C.E.), patricians used their religious and political privileges to limit the plebeians' power and sought to restrict their social mobility by forbidding marriage between plebeian and patrician families. Plebeian families had made inroads into patrician circles early on. Intermarriage with plebeians was allowed in 455 B.C.E., and over time, wealthy patricians and plebeians came to have more in common with each other than either did with the less fortunate of their own class.

Many patrician families fell onto hard times in the later Republic and died out. Only about 15 remained by Augustus's time (27 B.C.E.–C.E. 14), and he began a practice of creating new patricians by decree.

The Plebs

No one really knows where the class of *plebs* came from originally. They may have been non-Roman families in the early royal period, or they may have been simply the horde (plebs means, "the many") under the aristocrats. In either case, by the time of the Republic there were already wealthy and powerful plebeians and plebeian families. The so-called "Conflict of the Orders" resulted from an attempt by the patricians to squeeze the plebeians out of access to political and religious power after the monarchy fell. The plebeians fought back and, through their secession, the formation of the *consilium plebis* and its legislation, came to have political rights commensurate with the patricians by 287 B.C.E. By then the wealthy were pretty much a class of their own as far as politics was concerned.

It's Money That Matters: Nobiles *and* Equites

By the third century B.C.E., two powerful classes were emerging that depended on wealth, one technically confined to a political realm, the other technically confined to the world of business.

The first was the class of *nobiles,* men whose families had been elected to the magistracies for at least three consecutive generations. *Nobiles* came exclusively from the upper classes as it depended upon wealth and prestige to maintain a family's ability to produce magistrates and consuls. Moreover, men of such status expected to be engaged in a full-time and unpaid pursuit of civic duties and public service. For this reason, they were restricted to earning their living from land, the only proper way for a Roman noble to maintain wealth.

When in Rome

"Into this mess came another greater terror: Latin cavalrymen galloped in with the news that the Volsci were coming with an invasion force to besiege the city. The news—and this is how much the tension had divided one city into two parts—affected the patricians and plebes, when each heard them, very differently. The plebeians were thrilled: They said that divine vengeance for the arrogance of the patricians was at hand. Each man encouraged the other not to enlist for service. Better to perish all together than alone, they said; let the patricians fight, let *them* take up some weapons so that the same people who got the rewards of war also got the dangers."

—Livy, *The History of Rome*, 2.24

The *equites* were a class from the property rank of cavalryman in the *comitia centuriata*. After the second Punic War (218–202 B.C.E.), equestrian status was given to all free citizens who met the property qualification. The *equites* became Rome's business class doing the public contracts, banking, and tax collecting.

As Rome expanded, the *equites* became wealthy and powerful but were often pitted against the senatorial class. Senators made up the magistrates under whom the *equites* did business in the provinces and who were in a position to pressure them and demand kickbacks. Moreover, the senatorial class made up the juries in which corrupt officials were prosecuted and tended to protect their own. Finally, wealthy *equites* who wanted to enter politics found, for the most part, the ranks of the *nobiles* closed against them getting into high offices. This led to a certain amount of class hostility, which the emperors later exploited by finding qualified men among the *equites* who would be more loyal to them than the senate would be.

Patrons and the Patronized (Clients)

Romans also developed hierarchical relationships with *clientes,* or clients. Clients were persons of inferior standing who entered into a mutual relationship with a person of higher standing. The latter

When in Rome

Fides means "faith" or "trust" and indicates living according to one's responsibilities, agreements, and pledges.

became their *patronus,* or patron. Each was obligated to look out for the other's interests. Clients received economic benefits and social protection; patrons expected to receive loyal assistance (such as labor, military support, votes) in return. It was a breach of *fides* for either side to abuse or neglect this relationship.

Patrons sought power and influence by extending and expanding their base of clients. As Rome grew, this kind of relationship was replicated between Rome and conquered states, between powerful Romans and foreign peoples, and between military commanders and their soldiers. The patron/client relationship helps to explain, for example, how commanders such as Pompey the Great (from Rome), could raise entire armies abroad (see Chapter 7).

Great Caesar's Ghost!

Romans in the city made their morning *salutatio* (greeting) a ritual of social prestige and etiquette. Every morning from about 6 to 8 A.M., groups of clients visited the homes of their patrons. For this they received a small basket of food or some money. After the *salutatio,* patrons headed to the Forum. Equites began business; others engaged in the unpaid public service that was their responsibility and privilege. Romans of all classes knocked off work around 2 to 3 P.M. and headed to the public baths to relax, work out, and socialize. Dinner was about five-ish. Invitations to dinner were a mark of social prestige or a reward for a good client from his patron; some people made the morning *salutatio* and getting a dinner invitation somewhat of an occupation in and of itself.

Politics and Political Structure

You learned a little bit about Roman governance in Chapter 5, "Seven Hills and One Big Sewer: Rome Becomes a City." Let's put it together here. Before we do, however, remember that no matter what the structure was, the Romans still operated like Romans: They deferred to authority, preserved precedent, and operated within their family and patron-client bonds. Their leaders, no matter who they were, strove for similar values as well: They sought to increase their *auctoritas* and *dignitas* and to win *gloria* for themselves, their family, and Rome.

Roman Assemblies

There were four Roman political bodies coming from different periods of Roman history and serving various functions:

1. *Comitia curiata* (**ward assembly**). This was the oldest assembly of the Romans dating from the time of the kings. All citizens who could bear arms were members, but they were organized into *curiae* (wards), which seem to have originated in the early settlements of Rome. Each *curia* voted as a block. Its major duties included witnessing and approving the king and (later) other magistrates (such as consuls and praetors) who had *imperium* (the power of command). The assembly ceased to function for all practical purposes in the early Republic, though it continued to perform ceremonial functions and to grant *imperium*.

2. *Comitia centuriata* (**centuriate assembly**). This assembly was created by the kings, organized originally by fighting units of 100 men (hence, a "centuriate" organization). It developed into the general assembly in the Republic, electing magistrates and hearing appeals. The centuries were organized according to property classification, and the classes voted as a block. Unfortunately for the lower classes, the voting was such that if the two richest property classes voted in agreement (which they often did), the vote was decided.

3. *Concilium plebis* (**plebeian assembly**). This was the assembly that the plebs set up for themselves as a part of their succession in the "Conflict of the Orders." Only plebeians participated although patricians often influenced it through its ties with the wealthy plebeians and the tribunes. Occasionally, a patrician had himself adopted by a pleb to become eligible. The *comitia plebis* operated on the principle of "one man, one vote." It passed legislation, called *plebescita* (plebiscites), and elected officials (aediles) and their powerful representatives, the tribunes. The validity of plebiscites waxed and waned through the Republic depending on the strength of the senatorial party and the cohesion of the *nobiles*.

4. *Senatus* (**Senate**). The Senate was originally made up of the *patres,* the aristocratic clan leaders who advised the king and from among whom the king was elected. By the time of the Republic, the number of senators was fixed at 300 at which it remained until Sulla (80 B.C.E.) (see Chapter 7 for more about Sulla). The Senate was Rome's deliberated body: It formed policy, approved legislation passed in the assembly, passed decrees, ratified treaties, and appointed magistrates to provinces or to promagisterial duties. It could also, through the final decree of the senate (*senatus consultum ultimum*), impose a condition of martial law. During the last half of the Republic, a few powerful and influential families dominated the senate and the office of consul. This was, in part, what forced other nobles and aristocrats to turn to the popular assemblies and to violence in an attempt to advance their own ambitions.

Roamin' the Romans

Wherever you are in the Roman world, when you find a forum (public square and market-place), you've found the heart of the political city. There were several fora in Rome, but the Forum Romanum was the most important. It was the political, commercial, religious, and social hub of the city. The *comitia tributa* joined the Forum in 145 B.C.E., and the construction of basilicas to house public business and law courts began soon after. Other important public buildings included the *Curia* (Senate House) and *Rostra* (speaker's platform).

Roman Magistrates

Most Roman magistrates were elected by the assemblies and served for a term of one year. Some officials, like dictator, pro-praetors, and pro-consuls, were appointed and could have flexible terms. Most, if not all, had age minimums after 180 B.C.E. although in the later Republic such minimums were overlooked for young men such as Pompey the Great. Here's a list, beginning at the bottom of the political pecking order:

1. **Quaestors** were public finance and record officials (roughly a Purser or Treasurer). They had to be at least 25 years old.

2. **Aediles** were in charge of urban affairs including weights and measurements, public works, public games, and public safety (a bit like a county Auditor). They had to be at least 36 years old.

3. **Praetors** were second to consuls. They were primarily judicial officials (judges) and could have the power of *imperium*. They had to be at least 39 years old.

4. **Consuls** were the chief executive officials of Rome. They commanded the army, handled national and foreign affairs, and possessed *imperium*. The American President is modeled on this office. Consuls were supposed to be at least 42 years old. Romans passed different laws on their ability to be reelected; at first there was a required 10-year span between elections and then, in 150 B.C.E., a ban on reelection. As Marius, Sulla, Pompey, and Caesar all demonstrate, this ban didn't hold.

5. **Censors** were elected every four or five years. They did not have *imperium* but had other powers that made them eventually one of the most influential officials. They possessed the power of enrolling citizens in the proper tax and military rolls and acted as auditors of public expenditures. They could also remove members of the senate for immoral behavior.

6. **Dictators** (a supreme commander) were nominated by a consul and approved by the senate for a set period of time. The dictator was the chief official under a state of emergency and military law. He had complete control of all civil and military affairs.

7. **Pro-praetors and pro-consuls** were *ad hoc* praetors and consuls who were appointed by the senate to act in the place of a praetor or consul for a specific assignment. These offices became a common way for Rome to meet the military and administrative needs of its growing empire.

Government of the Roman Republic

Cursus Honorum

- - - - - ➤ Consuls   (Executive)

Praetors   (Judicial)

Aediles   (Urban Affairs, Public Works)

Quaestors (Finance and Records) ◄—

Senate (300 Members for Life)
- Appoint and determine *provincia*
- Debate and Recommend Policy
- Ratify Treaties and *acta*
- Declare Martial Law (*senatus consultum ultimum*)
- Approve Dictator (Nominated by Consul)

Censor
- Audit State
- Determine Citizenship
- Cull or Appoint Senators

Elects

Tribunes
- Protect
- Veto

Consilium Plebis (Plebian Only, 1 Man = 1 Vote)
- Pass Legislation (Plebiscites)
- Elect Plebian Magistrates (Tribunes, Plebian Aediles)

Elects

Comitia Curiata
- Grant *Imperium*

Comitia Centuriata (Property Classes)
- Pass Legislation
- Elect Magistrates
- Hear Appeals

The basics of Roman Republican Government.

Getting to the Top: The Cursus Honorum

Young aristocrats sought to follow a career path from quaestor to consul that was, in fact, called the "path of offices," or the *cursus honorum*. After 180 B.C.E., minimum ages and a two-year interval between offices were legalized. The final stages of this path became monopolized, as we've said, by an increasingly smaller number of families over time even as the rewards—and costs—of achieving office grew. This led, in campaigning, to wildly competing expenditures and campaign practices. Romans passed a series of campaign laws (none of which worked) to cut back on them. It also led ambitious Romans, when blocked, to exploit the tribal assemblies and to bring their clients, political gangs, and (finally) armies onto the political landscape (see Chapter 7).

Law

Roman law, *ius,* and the handling of laws, *leges,* are one of the Romans' most enduring achievements. Important developments in Roman legal history took place during the Republic; these were refined during the Empire and finally codified and published under the emperor Justinian in C.E. 540. Justinian's *Corpus Iuris Civilis* (The Body of Civil Law) encompassed over a thousand years of Roman legal history and remains an integral part of western European law. The Romans divided their law into public and private. Public law applied to affairs of the state, private to the affairs of individuals. We'll concern ourselves with private law here.

Veto!

Whereas western European and international law is indebted to the Romans, United States law is not; it depends more on the traditions of Anglo-Saxon law passed down from Britain.

Before the Twelve Tables (450 B.C.E.), law was in the hands of the aristocratic patricians and priests (also patricians) who oversaw the rigid formulas that had to be precisely followed and witnessed before their authority. Legal questions concerning the rigid interpretation of what was said in the formulas was theirs as well. But after the publication of the Twelve Tables, affairs began to change. Roman interactions among themselves and with other people became more complex. Judges were required to gauge intent and to render decisions based on the case and measured against a partially recorded tradition. Over time, the judgments and proclamations of these judges became a body of tradition in and of itself.

Prosecution and Defense

The state did not bring either civil or criminal cases; there was no "*the state vs.* _____." All prosecutions were brought by private individuals; plaintiffs personally brought defendants before presiding magistrates (sometimes defendants who were dodging court had to be physically dragged!) to prosecute their case. Plaintiffs were required to speak for themselves unless they were women or children. Prosecutors could, however, bring in secondary speakers. Defendants could defend themselves and/or have others speak in their defense—hopefully people whose *dignitas* and *auctoritas* the jurors recognized. Having patrons or talented clients was an asset. Cicero came to prominence representing clients both Roman and foreign.

Going to Court

Court was a different affair back then. At first, criminal trials were held before the assembly under a praetor. Later, standing juries (*quaestiones perpetuae*) were set up under a praetor or an appointed judge (*iudex*). In civil cases, trials took place before a private judge (*unus iudex*) or, in major cases, before a jury of 100 (*centumviri*) presided over by a magistrate or learned jurist.

Plaintiffs brought their cases and defendants before the presiding magistrate. In civil cases, the magistrate would question the participants and might elicit a resolution to the case or determine that there was no grounds for trial. If there were grounds, he determined the exact nature of the charges and the legal question to be considered and sent his instructions to a judge (*iudex*) or a jury (in important cases) for consideration.

The Precedent Principle

The rendering of opinions by the magistrates referring cases to trial, the proclamations of the praetors, and the decisions of the judges were law. But by the third century B.C.E., such decisions had begun to acquire a tradition of their own. Influential Romans, such as the first plebeian *pontifex maximus* (high priest of Rome), began giving legal advice to bolster their political support. Opinions of jurists became a part of the mix as well: In 204 B.C.E., Aelius Catus published a legal commentary on the law of the Twelve Tables as it had developed. Romans, in keeping with their tendency to base the future upon the past, looked to precedent (literally, what "goes on before") against which new decisions could be made, and from which decisions could be applied to new situations.

Lend Me Your Ears

The poet Horace was saved from an unwanted tag-along in the Forum:

"By chance we met someone who had a suit against him. 'And where are you going, you wretch?' he cried and turned to me. 'Can you be a witness for me?' he asked. I assented and he snatched him off to court, thank god."

—Horace, *Satires* 1.9

Veto!

Romans may have valued precedent, but they were not legally bound by it. Neither civil nor criminal law was codified; decisions were at the sole discretion of judge and/or jury.

"Roman" Religion

Romans worshipped a number of gods, or versions of gods, that came from the Etruscans, Italians, Celts, and others who made up the peoples of Italy and Rome. There were, however, gods that the Romans chiefly came to view as their own.

The first was Jupiter, *Optimus Maximus* (The Best and the Greatest), whose great temple was first built by the Etruscan kings on the Capitoline hill. It was to this temple that Roman generals proceeded on the Sacred Way in a triumph to present their spoils and to give thanks for victory. Next was the god of war, Mars, originally a woodland deity who protected farm and field. Vesta, Janus, and Venus were also venerated as deities with whom Rome and the Romans had a special relationship.

Roman religious practice consisted of sacrifices, rituals, and prayer formulas that had to be performed in exactly the right way. One inadvertent mistake spoiled the effect; prayers were ruined and everything had to be started over. By the end of the Republic, most Romans had little personal religious attachment to state religion but remained supportive of their state religious practice and identification.

Veto!

Roman priesthoods and their *collegia* were much more secular than sacred in nature. Julius Caesar, for example, was elected as *Pontifex Maximus* but was hardly a figure of religious sincerity, publicly or privately!

Collegia

The Romans had boards (*collegia*) of priests (*pontifices*), augurs (*augures*), and other religious officials (such as the vestals) to oversee, perform, and organize Rome's religious rites. Some of these (such as the *pontifex maximus*) were elected, but most were appointed.

The priests originated in the time of the kings to oversee the state cults and to determine the calendar for sacred and secular days. Augurs were responsible for figuring out what the gods wanted. They did this by interpreting omens from sacrifices and from *auspices*, the observance of birds. The Romans were a tremendously superstitious people, and a bad omen could ruin one's day, career, or military campaign. No public event could take place without favorable omens. Sometimes, factions manipulated the omens for political effect. Caesar's optimate colleague of 59 B.C.E., Bibulus, attempted to thwart Caesar's efforts to pass legislation by setting all dates on which the assembly could meet as holidays.

The chief priests in the Roman state were the …

1. *Pontifex maximus.* The high priest of Rome, the head of Roman state religion, and the head of the college of pontiffs. He appointed and oversaw the vestal virgins. Julius Caesar, all emperors, and finally the popes had this position and title.

2. *Rex sacrorum*. The king of sacred matters. The early Romans established this position after they booted out the kings. *Rex sacrorum* was for those really important religious rituals in which one *needed* a king but didn't have one because they weren't around anymore.

3. *Flamen dialis*. The priest of Jupiter. Flamens were priests devoted to individual gods. The *flamen dialis* was the greatest of these and a figure surrounded by a host of taboos. He could not, for instance, eat beans, touch a goat, ride a horse, or have his hair cut by a slave! These restrictions, however, were very unusual.

The Army

The Latins, the Romans among them, adapted the Greek and Etruscan fighting unit of the phalanx to their own needs in the sixth and fifth centuries B.C.E. Men originally were divided (according to the *comitia centuriata*) by what armor they could afford. During the fourth century, after the Gauls sacked Rome and the Latins revolted, Rome reorganized its military formation to be more flexible. It organized into forces that reflected both age and experience while taking ability to afford arms into account. The Roman army continued to adapt organization, tactics, equipment, and strategy as it met new challenges and new foes. It learned a great deal from the Sabines and Hannibal (see Chapter 6, "On Golden Pond: Rome Conquers Italy and the Mediterranean"), and by the time it came into conflict with Greece in the Macedonian Wars of the second century B.C.E., Roman military tactics far outstripped those of its Greek ancestors.

In very general terms, the early Roman fighting unit of the Republic was the maniple, originally a band of 60 men. Maniples of various grades and with various functions were organized into the largest military unit, the legion. At the front was a maniple of *hastati*, younger soldiers well-armed with a sword, rectangular shield, and two throwing javelins. About 20 *leves* (light-armed men with spears) assisted the *hastati*. Behind them was a maniple of *principes,* veteran fighters, who, with more *leves,* reinforced the *hastati* as the backbone of the force. After the *principes* came several maniples of *triarii* and other more inexperienced groups of fighters. These were called in if the enemy broke the *principes*.

Originally the legion was made up of about 15 maniples of *hastati* and *principes* each and about 45 of the rest. This brought the strength of the early legions to around 5,000 men not counting cavalry (after about the third century, Romans depended upon allies for their cavalry units). The numbers of men assigned to a maniple gradually increased through the second century B.C.E., and under Marius, the maniple gave way to a new organizational unit of about 600 men, called a cohort (*cohors*), made up of three maniples.

Military Service

Army service was a part of every Roman citizen's life. In what capacity you served depended on your property class, your experience, and your connections. The Punic Wars with Hannibal took a dreadful toll on soldiers both Roman and Italian. Campaigns increased in number and duration. After 200 B.C.E., men might be gone for several years at a stretch; many lost homes and land in the meantime. When they did, they dropped off the service rolls because they no longer owned property. Rome settled some of them on conquered territory, but many migrated to the cities, for Rome was becoming a much more urbanized culture.

Romans had to depend more and more upon allies to make up their legions. Marius took the growing numbers of dispossessed and began the era of paid professional soldiers. These soldiers, however, still looked forward to pieces of land upon discharge on which they could settle, farm, and remain Romans of Roman ideal. By the time of Sulla (138–78 B.C.E.), however, it became clear that professional soldiers had little taste for hard farm life; they had grown accustomed to the life of mercenaries. It was hard enough for real farmers to compete in the age of slave farms and *latifundia* (corporate farms, which are discussed in Chapter 10, "The Romans at Large"). Soldiers fell into debt, lost their land, and began the dangerous cycle once more.

The Least You Need to Know

➤ Birth and wealth determined Roman class structures.

➤ Roman legal history began with the Twelve Tables.

➤ Roman law was under the complete discretion of judges, but precedent and tradition guided decisions.

➤ Roman state religion was overseen by a variety of *collegia,* or religious boards. The high priest of Rome was called the *pontifex maximus.*

➤ The Romans adapted the Greek phalanx into a more tactical structure; participation in the army depended upon property qualification, status, and experience.

Chapter 10

The Romans at Large

> **In This Chapter**
>
> ➤ Roman citizenship beyond Rome
>
> ➤ Roman administration of *provinciae* and client states
>
> ➤ Roman economics and work

The Romans, who were after all a people made up of several ethnic groups and extended clans, soon began to incorporate others into their political and civic structure.
This was a part of the Romans' genius for rule and government—finding flexible and
practical ways to meet new challenges by working from old structures. In this chapter,
we'll explore how relationships with Latins, Italians, Colonists, and subject peoples
developed and functioned in the Late Republic. We'll also take a look at how Roman
economics and trade worked and affected what different people did.

Some Citizens Are More Equal Than Others

Originally, being a Roman citizen meant that you were a citizen of the city-state of
Rome itself. Both parents had to be Roman, or if one parent was not, the foreign parent had to come from a city-state with which there was an agreement of *conubium* (re-
ciprocal marriage rights). In special cases, individuals and their whole *familia* might be
granted citizen status by an act of the people. Tradition has it that several of Rome's
important patrician families became "Roman" in this way.

Roman citizens had both rights (*iura*) and responsibilities (*munera*). A citizen had voting rights (*suffragium*) in the assemblies to which he could belong and was eligible for offices (*honores*) depending on his ability to be elected or appointed. He was also afforded the protections of Roman traditions, could form contracts, have a recognized marriage, and pursue legal redress through Roman courts. His primary *munera* meant compulsory military service for the state but came to include the paying of taxes and other social and public obligations expected of citizens to the larger community.

You'll notice that I've used "he" above—and it's true that only men could exercise most of these rights. Although Roman women could not vote, run for political office, or be in the military, they were covered by the protections of citizenship and responsible for whatever other civic roles their status and property classification dictated. Independent women governed their own affairs, paid taxes, and concluded contracts. Cicero's wife, Terentia, for example, was much more successful handling her own estates than her husband was at handling his. (They were divorced when she refused to keep subsidizing him.) In the later Republic, upper-class woman achieved prominence and became active in ways that were unimaginable to other cultures. The notorious Sempronia helped to foil the conspiracy of Catiline for Cicero, Hortensia gave a successful public oration against pending legislation, and Octavia raised money, troops, and political support for her husband Antony. Other evidence, both literary and epigraphic, shows that women of that period held status not much bettered until last century.

Latin Rights

As Rome conquered the surrounding Latin city-states it extended facets of its citizenship to them through treaties between 380 and 250 B.C.E. Latin cities became either *municipia sine suffragio* or *cum suffragio;* the former were without voting rights but had social privileges, and the latter had full rights. This extension of rights to the Latins became known as the *ius Latium* (Latin rights) and was eventually bestowed on selected colonies and municipalities. Both statuses required the subject states to provide soldiers as their *munera*. Full citizenship, which meant being able to vote and run for office, was naturally accompanied by less local autonomy.

In addition, Rome established colonies within Italy with Latin rights. The earliest of these settlements, too small to be their own state and close to Rome, maintained full citizenship. Later, other small military colonies were also given the same privileges. The colonies, along with the Latins and the allies, came to full citizenship after the Social War (90–88 B.C.E.). For more on the extension of citizenship, see Chapter 7, "Let's Conquer … Ourselves! The Roman Revolution and the End of the Republic."

Citizenship in Italy

There were, of course, many other people besides colonists and Latins. The Etruscans, Sabines, and Greeks remained autonomous and self-governing peoples, but were placed under Roman protection (or subjugation) by treaty (*foedus*). These *socii*, or allies, were generally restrained from making foreign policy decisions apart from

Rome. They had commercial and social rights with Rome (as spelled out by their individual treaties), but generally were inferior to those people with Latin rights. Nevertheless, they were still required to provide troops for Rome when requested.

As Rome came to dominate the Italian peninsula, the allies bore an increasing amount of the burden of sustaining Rome's conquests. Under Roman abuses, the allies began to agitate for either autonomy or Latin rights. This brought trouble during the time of the Gracchae (see Chapter 7) and erupted into the Social War, which ended with Rome's extension of rights to all Italy by 89 B.C.E. With this extension, there was a shift in the concept of citizenship; Rome was now more than a city—it was becoming a *patria* with a capital and numerous municipal centers to which one might belong and be a "Roman." Rome's model of civic organization and urbanization spread throughout Italy and helped to Romanize the entire peninsula.

Citizenship and Rights Abroad

Roman citizens enjoyed considerable privileges and protections abroad. Rome considered an attack upon citizens as an attack upon the *dignitas* of the state. Abuses of power abroad against Roman citizens, especially by foreign powers but even by Roman magistrates, was a serious offense. Citizens were entitled to Roman protections of law even if it meant returning them to Rome. This is why the declaration *"civis Romanus sum"* (I am a Roman citizen) kept St. Paul from being executed in Jerusalem and brought him to Rome. It was a cry that many Roman citizens had been able to rely on in the past.

Lend Me Your Ears

Cicero describes the far-reaching protections of Roman citizenship in the prosecution of the former governor of Sicily, Gaius Verres, in 70 B.C.E.:

"Verres, if you were captured by the Persians or in remotest India and brought to execution, what else would you cry out *except* that you were a Roman citizen? And if the noble and universally recognized name of your city would have protected you, an unknown among an unknown people, among barbarians, among people stuck in the most extreme and godforsaken corners of humanity—shouldn't that man, *whoever* he was, the one you were racing to crucify, even if he were unknown to you, when he began to say that he was a Roman citizen in your—the praetor's—presence, have been able to find, if not an escape from execution then certainly a stay, merely by his mention of Rome and claim to citizenship?"

When in Rome

The **Gracchi** refers to the brothers Tiberius (died 133) and Gaius (died 121) Gracchus, the tribunes who promoted land and voting reform in opposition to the senate. You can read more about them in Chapter 7.

Romans extended the rights of citizenship abroad in a couple of ways. Rome made some states allies (*socii*) through treaties with cities and kings, and citizens of allied states had whatever rights their treaty specified. In general, however, their status deteriorated as Rome became a world power and could pretty much do as it wanted no matter what any treaty said. Still, it mattered to be recognized as a member of a state having a formal relationship with Rome.

Secondly, beginning with period of the *Gracchi*, Rome began to settle displaced or disenfranchised citizens, veterans, and allies in colonies beyond Italy to help Romanize conquered lands. Colonists maintained their rights as citizens, and eventually, the native peoples who lived around the colonies integrated into them and became citizens as well. This process began to weave together the provinces with Rome in the same way that extending rights into Italy had.

Friends in High Places: Foreign Clients

As Rome conquered other lands, Roman officials went out as representatives, governors, and administrators. Generally, there were also already well established communities of Roman traders and businessmen integrated into the local economy who had political ties to Rome. Those without citizenship—the foreign nationals—needed friends who had it for access to power and protection. These foreign nationals established patron/client relationships with Romans—who became the representatives of foreign peoples and powers in Rome. Roman generals such as Pompey counted kings and entire peoples among their clients.

Follow the Money: Administration and the Perks of Conquest

After the conquest of Italy, Rome conquered huge areas of territory beyond. Some conquered cities and kingdoms became client states. Client states remained somewhat autonomous as long as their tribute was paid and they kept out of trouble. Other territory was under the control of no previous central authority. These conquests required Roman supervision both to maintain control and to organize ways to exploit the resources of the region. Other territories, such as those once controlled by Carthage and Macedonia, needed Roman administration to replace the authority that had been destroyed. These last two kinds of territories became *provincia* (provinces) and possessions of Rome.

Provinces were placed under the authority of a Roman governor with pro-consular or pro-praetorian *imperium* (the power of command). Minor officials were assigned within the regions and sub-regions of the larger provinces as well. General administration and taxes were drawn up in Rome as guidelines, but governors had full power to run their own affairs. Provincial governors and officials were in the position to win glory and become incredibly rich in clients and the spoils of conquest. Both became important components in the eventual rise of generals like Caesar, Pompey, Octavian, and Antony.

When in Rome

Provincia originally meant an area within which military *imperium* could be exercised; provincial governors were, in effect, military commanders in occupation of conquered territory.

Bringing Home the Bacon and the Bronze

After the initial conquest of a province and the extraction of tribute and booty, governors were in the position to exploit every aspect of conquest. There was no real bureaucracy connecting provinces to Rome; therefore, as long as the taxes were collected, order was kept, Roman interests were protected, and the governor was free to exercise his *imperium* as he saw fit. Governors administered their provinces as a way to increase their own wealth and power, and some virtually pillaged their provinces during their stay. Not just money, but art works, commercial goods, and more were shipped back for profit or the governor's private collection. Governors and lower officials were also in the position to demand kickbacks from the equites and *publicani* who were engaged in business or the collection of taxes.

Abuses of power became so infamous that Rome introduced laws for prosecuting governors and provincial officials. However, this didn't always have the desired effect. Verres, the governor of Sicily who was prosecuted by Cicero, told his friends that the enormous profit of his three-year term was divided three ways: The first year was to pay off his campaign debts, the second year was to pay off jurors when he got back, and the third year was for him. The problem of governors and commanders who exploited their positions to advance their own personal power helped bring down the Republic and plagued the empire over its history.

Got Plastic?

Rome didn't have the magic of magnetic strips on credit cards, but it came pretty close. Banking and finance operations were complex. Letters of credit, transfers of money or goods by ledger, and sophisticated lending practices enabled Rome to manage and exploit sources of wealth in its empire. The equites handled most of the financing, lending money to individuals, trading companies, cities, and even to kings

When in Rome

Mithridates VI (134–63 B.C.E.) was the powerful king of Pontus (on the Black Sea). Forty years of Roman oppression made the east ripe for rebellion against Rome and pro-Roman governments. When Mithridates invaded the province of Asia and then Greece in 88 B.C.E., these areas welcomed him as a liberator and attacked Roman citizens and interests. Sulla was appointed commander against Mithridates that same year.

Great Caesar's Ghost!

Cicero was a man of relatively modest means by Roman standards, but through his service as governor of Sicily, his representation of clients, and his connections with the elite, he became wealthy enough to buy eight country villas and a house costing 3.5 million sesterces (the Roman currency) on the Palatine hill (*the* district) in Rome, roughly equivalent to a penthouse suite in Manhattan.

who needed cash to pay their tribute or taxes. Rates were restricted to 12 percent officially, but with a little creative bookwork effective rates reached between 24 and 48 percent. This made Romans rich and kept client states in perpetual dependence.

Public-Private Partnerships

Public contracts for works and services were handled by groups of private contractors, called *publicani*. The *publicani* formed companies, which were incorporated, and sold public shares so that the companies could continue to operate as investors joined or departed.

Public contracts included the collection of taxes in the provinces. Rome set an amount that a province's taxation should be worth, and then private companies of *publicani* would bid on collecting them. The difference between the winning bid and the published amount was the tax cartel's to keep. This was big, big business, especially in the east, and the subject of tremendous exploitation. Each level of collection sought to maximize its profit, and each extorted the next level down, all the way to the taxpayers themselves. Roman governors and *publicani* were so harsh that the province of Asia erupted in revolt between 88–84 B.C.E.; up to 80,000 Italian *publicani* and merchants were reportedly killed in one day.

Senators were restricted from commercial business endeavors, but they found ways to reap profits in spite of such restriction. They became silent partners of the *publicani*, established shell corporations, and installed front men. They also went into money lending, especially to their foreign clients. Moreover, senators became patrons and partners of equites in many ways. Each needed the services of the other. Senators, for example, received loans for economic ventures, political campaigns, or private expenses at plumb rates. The equites in turn needed the favor of the aristocrats who became the magistrates, commanders, and provincial governors under whom they conducted business.

It's Who You Know: Lobbyists at Rome

Throughout the growing Roman Empire, political and economic business was still conducted on the basis of personal relationships, patron/client bonds, and personal authority. A senator who served abroad developed constituencies of Roman expatriates, businessmen, and important nationals who depended on him to protect and represent their interests in Rome. There was no state bureaucracy as such. Senators achieved both power and prestige by representing foreign interests; embassies, delegations, and private individuals streamed to Rome in order to affect business, bend the political process, or achieve redress against corruption. Such representation enriched an aristocrat's reputation, status, and purse.

Great Caesar's Ghost!

Today, with the advent of elevators, apartments on the top floor have a cachet for their views and their remoteness from the grime of street life. But in Roman times, the worst place to live in an *insula* (a multistory block apartment building) was the top floor. *Insulae* were notorious both for falling down and for burning up around the inhabitants.

Work, Work, Work

By the time of the later Republic, Rome had far outgrown the city of small farmers it had once been. Since the end of the Punic Wars (146 B.C.E.), Rome and Italy had moved toward urbanization where people lived and worked in urban centers instead of on small farms. Rome's conquests brought enormous changes in how Romans and Italians lived, worked, and fought. Huge urban markets were created that needed to be fed, housed, and entertained; new means of production were formed based on the enormous pool of slave labor; and a growing number of middle-class and fabulously wealthy upper-class citizens sought imported goods and services.

Roamin' the Romans

You can find the well-preserved remains of Roman *insulae*, working-class bars, and a port marketplace at Rome's port of Ostia—just a short hop from Rome.

Work in the City

The wealth of conquest brought great building projects—fabulous villas in and around the cities, public buildings, roads, and aqueducts. Middle class Italians and Romans ran small shops with small groups of slaves, imported and exported goods, and labored as tradesmen. But by and large the city was filled with unskilled workers. Rome grew to a population of nearly a million people, populations that London achieved only around 1800 and New York around 1850. Workers lived in the flimsy and squalid *insulae* (literally, islands), which were cheap multistory apartments that landlords threw up around the city. Crassus made a fortune buying burnt *insulae* on the cheap (some of which he had torched in order to buy them), renovating and re-selling them; others made money running private fire brigades (which went hand-in-hand with fire extortion rackets).

Over time, Rome attempted to settle the urban problem by establishing new colonies to which urban poor could relocate and homestead, settling veterans on public lands, and inaugurating public works projects. The numbers of urban poor, however, kept growing until they came to depend on the largesse of patrons, the import of subsidized grain, gifts provided to the public as a part of campaign elections, and the entertainment of public games. Bread and circuses.

Work in the Country

In the country, small landholders could manage to get by from their holdings and pick-up work from larger landholders. That is unless bad harvests, more powerful neighbors, extended military service, illness, invasions, civil disruption, or other such happenings got in the way. If you consider Roman history since the Second Punic War, there was scarcely a year in which several of these things weren't occurring simultaneously over much of Italy! (For more, see Chapters 6, "On Golden Pond: Rome Conquers Italy and the Mediterranean," and 7.) Many small farmers, overwhelmed by a variety of these factors, were displaced and left for the cities. Wealthy landholders and Roman aristocrats built huge country estates with the wealth of conquest, acquired failed land holdings, and reduced farmers to the status of tenants. Some small farmers who lived near enough to cities switched from growing grain to growing premium cash crops and vegetables for the urban market and were able to make it this way.

Veto!

You will sometimes read that the creation of *latifundia* (large corporate farms) and the import of slaves obliterated the Italian small farmer. *Latifundia* did have a decided impact, especially in Latium, Campania (southwest Italy), and Sicily; but in other parts of Italy small farms remained the norm.

Corporate Farms: Latifundia

From the time Rome began to conquer large portions of northern and southern Italy, it controlled huge tracts of public land (*ager publicus*). Even though there was a legal limit on the amount of public lands a private party could control, enormous parcels were leased long-term at rock-bottom rates to wealthy senators and equites hoping to make the switch to the noble life. They created huge corporate farms, *latifundia*, worked by gangs of slaves imported from Roman conquests and were able to produce grain and raise livestock at cheaper prices. Owners were able to weather price fluctuations by having *latifundia* in different districts to offset the uncertainties of local harvest conditions.

The *latifundia* compounded problems for the rural poor and contributed to urbanization. In addition, deplorable conditions on the farms in Campania and Sicily led to huge slave uprisings in the second and first centuries. Control of public lands by a relative few also led to conflict during the time of the Gracchae, when *populares* (see Chapter 7) attempted to portion out the *ager publicus* to the needy public. Citizens with vested interests, however, had come to consider the land as theirs.

Bringing Home the Prosciutto: Trade and Luxury Goods

Rome's wealth and the conquest of the provinces brought about a surge in trade and the development of luxury goods. Italy grew enough to feed itself and then some, but Rome was always in need of more than its direct environs could produce. Trade and shipping was big business with Italian merchants controlling much of the trade routes in the west. Italy exported wine and oil to France and Spain and imported raw materials. Wealthy Romans cultivated vineyards in Italy and other provinces. In the eastern Mediterranean, the Greeks continued to control most shipping. Italy imported grain, exotic materials, animals, fabrics, foods, and spices to meet the tastes and demands of Rome's economic and cultural elite.

So Go Join the Army: The Growth of the Professional Soldier

The gap, however, between haves and have-nots increased as the spoils of victory sifted into comparatively few hands while the burdens of conquest fell upon many who lost what little they had. By the second century, the loss of property was enough to threaten Rome's ability to field the forces it needed to continue and maintain the empire. Marius abandoned the conscription of citizens and made the army into a career (see Chapter 7).

Enlistment in the army was generally for 20 years (instead of the six years conscripts served), and bonuses were offered to veterans. For service, one received a steady paycheck (from which the cost of rations was deducted) and a job. It was a hard and grueling life, and some would rise through the enlisted ranks to the highest enlisted post of *centurion*. Soldiers fought for more than just the glory of Rome; their financial success depended upon their victories. They received a portion of the spoils taken as a part of conquest, a share of the commander's portion of booty, and other bonuses. These, when conquering the rich east, could be quite handsome.

Roamin' the Romans

Any soldier who saved the life of a citizen would be awarded the *corona civica*, the civic crown. An emblem of the civic crown, a woven crown of oak leaves, was proudly displayed by veterans. You can see one of them over the door of a house preserved in Pompeii.

When in Rome

Centurions were originally the leaders of the centuries (units of 100 men) furnished to the army by the property divisions of the ancient *comitia centuriata*. They became the Roman army's highest professional officer. After Marius's reforms, there were six centurions for each of the ten cohorts that made up a legion. Centurions were promoted in order within their cohort, and between cohorts and legions until they reached the highest post, the first centurion of the first cohort of a legion.

In the last century of the Republic, campaigns were long—six to ten years. Soldiers looked forward to returning to Italy, setting up a small farm with a land grant and retirement pension. What kind of honorable discharge (*missio honesta*) they got depended upon their commander winning confirmation of his arrangements (*acta*) by the senate. Thus, soldiers came to depend on, and to support, their commanders as a patron and protector more than they did the state.

The Least You Need to Know

➤ Roman citizenship evolved and broadened as Rome incorporated conquered peoples into its empire.

➤ Roman nobles and equites exploited provincial resources and sought personal power through wealth and the patronage of foreign clients.

➤ Roman conquests during the Republic brought enormous numbers of slaves and great wealth into Italy and created a powerful upper and middle class.

➤ Roman conquests took a toll on the small farmers and allies but improved the status of upper- and middle-class women.

➤ Roman culture became progressively urbanized in the Republic.

Chapter 11

Literature and Culture of the Republic

In This Chapter

➤ The growth of Latin literature

➤ Roman attitudes toward literature

➤ The Golden and Augustan Ages of Latin literature

➤ Principle authors of Latin literature

Most people are more aware of Roman conquest than they are of Roman (Latin) literature. That's a shame. Latin literature is rich and complex, influential and well worth the effort. But compared to Roman conquests, Latin literature had a late start: It didn't get going until the second century B.C.E. and came into its own in the first century B.C.E. In the time of Augustus (63 B.C.E.–C.E. 14), it flourished into a supernova, burned bright through the first centuries, and slowly faded until Boethius's *Consolation of Philosophy* but twinkled from his prison cell into the approaching dark ages.

In this chapter, we'll look at the rise and development of Latin literature and culture through the end of the Republic and the Augustan Age. I've chosen to tell you this story through short biographies of six writers from each period. You can pick up the literary story from where this trail leaves off in Chapter 21, *"Cogito Ergo Sum:* The Life of the Mind."

Importing Culture: Early "Roman" Literature and History

When thinking about Latin literature and culture in time, it's interesting to compare it to a rough timeline of Greek literature and culture.

Century	Romans	Greeks
800–700	Rome in mud huts.	Homer and Hesiod.
700–600	Rome in villages.	Sappho and Pindar.
600–500	Rome a small city.	Solon, Presocratic Philosophers.
500–400	Rome throws out kings. Plebs and Patricians struggle. Wars with Latins, Etruscans, and Samnites.	Golden Age of Athens. Persian and Peloponnesian Wars. Tragedy, comedy, history, philosophy, scientific medicine.
400–300	Rome conquers part of Italy against the Italians, Etruscans, and Samnites.	Decline of city-state. Plato, Aristotle, Menander, Demosthenes. Alexander the Great establishes his empire.
300–200	Rome conquers Magna Graecia, Sicily, Sardenia, Carthage, and becomes involved in Greece.	Hellenistic kingdoms. The beginning of the Hellenistic Age and Alexandrian literature. The Museum in Alexandria is established.

Greeks come to Rome as slaves and delegates. Greeks and Italians begin to write Roman history and adapt Greek literature to the Latin language.

200–100	Rome conquers Greece, Macedonia, and the Hellenistic East.	Greece and the Hellenistic East partially under Roman control.

Roman aristocrats begin to cultivate Greek language and thought; Latin writers continue to adapt Greek forms, develop Latin forms (such as satire), and refine the Latin literary language.

100–0	Roman literature comes into its own. The Golden Age (C.E. 14).	Greeks are educating young Roman nobles in Rome to and in Athens, which has become a college town. Egypt is conquered and becomes a province (31 B.C.E.), marking the end of the Hellenistic Age.

As you can see, Roman literature doesn't really begin until the second century B.C.E. There are several reasons for this late start. First, literary culture needs a certain amount of stability, time, and critical mass that the Romans just didn't have until they had established their presence broadly across Italy. Second, literary culture needs cultural place and value. High literature and culture weren't a part of the general Roman self-image nor were they among the values of the aristocracy (the class that typically cultivates literary pursuits). The *last* thing a Roman noble wanted to be known for was sitting around thinking and writing. Romans increased their political power, wealth, and *auctoritas* and *dignitas*. Romans, well, *did* things.

Consequently, during the conquest of Magna Graecia and Greece, Latin literature was mostly the work of ethnic Greeks from southern Italy. Writers began to compose the kinds of works that their conquerors wanted: translations of Greek works, comedies to entertain, and histories that took the Romans into account. Some of the important early writers were …

1. **Livius Andronicus** (284–204 B.C.E.), a Greek from the captured city of Tarentum. As a captive, Andronicus translated Homer's *Odyssey* into Latin according to a native Latin meter, and adapted Greek comedies and tragedies to Latin but kept Greek costume. Only about 100 lines of his work remains.

2. **Cornelius Naevius** (270–201 B.C.E.), a Roman plebeian who wrote comedies and plays on historical themes and used Roman costumes. Naevius got into trouble for his political attacks on the nobility and died in exile. He also wrote a patriotic Roman epic in Latin meter about the first Punic War. No work remains.

3. **Titus Maccus Plautus** (254–184 B.C.E.), a great Umbrian comic playwright and lyricist. Roman literature really begins with Plautus. About 20 of Plautus's comedies survive—all versions and adaptations of ancient Greek "New Comedy" (a combination of sitcom, musical theater, and vaudeville). Plautus's

Veto!

It's simplistic to say that the Romans copied or borrowed all their literature and culture from the Greeks. Romans decidedly had their own culture. Their literature developed from Greek models, but it, too, became uniquely "Latin" and "Roman." To say otherwise would be like claiming that contemporary Americans have no literature or art of their own because it has roots in European and African cultures.

When in Rome

Tragedy (a play about inescapable and inordinate suffering brought on by the human condition) and **comedy** (a play about the humorous interaction of people, events, and ideas) were invented by the ancient Greeks and came into full development in Athens during the fifth century B.C.E.

141

Great Caesar's Ghost!

Hint: Want to see something really close to a Plautine comedy? Rent yourself a copy of *A Funny Thing Happened on the Way to the Forum,* which comes complete with music, dance, stock characters, and the three-house set. Want something a bit more literary? Try Oscar Wilde's *The Importance of Being Earnest.*

wordplay, themes, and humor are decidedly Roman in sensibility and make for great reading.

4. **Quintus Ennius** (239–169). If you asked the Romans who was the father of Latin literature, Romans would point to Ennius. Ennius was from southern Italy in Calabria. He was trilingual, saying that he had three hearts: one Oscan (his native tongue), one Greek, and one Latin. Ennius was famous for his wit and learning, for adapting the Latin language to Greek epic and elegiac meters, and for making an epic of Roman history. He wrote tragedies, comedies, and other minor works, but his greatest achievement was the *Annales,* a patriotic epic reaching from mythological antiquity to the events of his own day. The *Annales* also featured portraits of famous Romans and their virtues; it was a foundation text of Latin school learning and influential on later Roman epic and history. Only fragments of Ennius's work survives.

Ennius was connected with prominent Romans of his time. He was brought to Rome by Cato the Elder to lecture and accompanied his patron, Marcus Fulvius Nobilior, on a campaign in Greece to write about his patron's achievements. Through these and other connections, Ennius was awarded Roman citizenship.

Great Caesar's Ghost!

Think the *Simpsons* are something new? *Au contraire.* Situation comedy began in Greece in the fourth century B.C.E. and came to its high point in the Greek comedies of Menander (342–292 B.C.E.) and the Latin comedies of Plautus. Menander's plays featured funny situations and stock family characters that everyone could recognize. There was the *senex* (old man), usually the crabby, stingy, lustful father of the family, or the *matrona* (woman), his nagging and worried wife. Plautus's comedies featured a stock set of three buildings and a long stage on which characters sing, dance, interact, escape, or overhear one another without exits.

Liberals at Large:
The *Scipionic Circle*

When Rome conquered Greece, some Roman no-bles became *philhellenes*. They began to cultivate Greek literature and learning, and to patronize Greek and Latin writers and intellectuals. In 155 B.C.E., Athens sent the heads of the philosophi-cal schools to Rome. Their lectures caused a stir among the young nobles of the day, and a fad for philosophy developed.

When in Rome

A **philhellene** is a lover of Greek culture and arts.

At the head of this movement was Scipio Aemilianus (ca 185–129 B.C.E.). Aemilianus was the son of the general who conquered Macedonia (Aemilius Paullus) and the adopted son of Scipio Africanus, the conqueror of Hannibal and Carthage (see Chapter 6, "On Golden Pond: Rome Conquers Italy and the Mediterranean"). Aemilianus became a famous general in his own right, successfully destroying both Carthage and Numantia.

Aemilianus and his associates were responsible for patronizing some writers and philosophers. These writers and Romans became known as the "Scipionic Circle." Cicero regarded Aemilianus as the finest example of a cultured, noble, and yet Roman, Roman. The Scipionic Circle included …

When in Rome

Satire is a Latin poetic form that addresses any subject of life. The Romans were very proud of satire, which was completely their genre, or, as the poet Horace put it, *satura tota nostra est* ("Satire is completely our own"). In modern terms, satire is the technique of ridiculing a subject by taking grains of truth and exaggerating them into biting caricature. We have this picture of satire mostly because of the works of Juvenal (C.E. 50–127), who lambastes urban crowding, immigrants, wives, and everybody else.

1. **Marcus Pacuvius** (220–130 B.C.E.). Pacuvius was from Brundisium and wrote celebrated tragedies. His works are lost.

2. **Polybius** (202–120 B.C.E.). Polybius was a noble Greek hostage who became a friend of Aemilianus and helped settle Greek and Roman affairs after 146. He wrote an impor-tant history of Rome, in Greek, to explain to the Greeks the Romans' rise in power.

3. **Panaetius** (180–110 B.C.E.). Panaetius was a Greek Stoic philosopher from the island of Rhodes. His philosophy and personality were highly influential upon philhellenic Romans. Aemilianus took him on embassies to Egypt and Asia. Panaetius then took over as head of the Stoic school in Athens.

143

4. **Gaius Lucilius** (180–102 B.C.E.). Lucilius was from Campania. He is famous for being the father of *satire,* which comes from the name of short hexameter poems on various contemporary foibles and subjects. He called this mixed bag of comment and complaint *satura* (grab bag), and the name stuck.

5. **Publius Terentius Afer,** or **Terence** (195–159 B.C.E.), was probably from Carthage. He is the other great early Latin comedic playwright; six of his works survive. Terence's work was more closely based on Greek originals. Terence's work was panned by some contemporary literary critics (the dark underbelly of the benefits of literary culture) and suffered a few setbacks in production. Once, a production had to be stopped because the crowd became more interested in a high-wire act going on in another part of the festival; another time, the audience stampeded out when it was announced that tickets for the gladiator fights had just gone on sale!

6. **Lucius Accius** (170–85 B.C.E.). Accius was from Umbria. He wrote celebrated dramas, some on Latin themes. He is the first known grammarian of Latin. This indicates how Latin was becoming codified as a literary language, complete with the annoying kind of people who know precisely when to use "which" and when to use "that." Only fragments of Accius's work survive.

Great Caesar's Ghost!

Terence's plays were picked up again in the Middle Ages. Hroswitha of Gandersheim, an important tenth-century nun, poetess, and playwright, found his secular popularity troubling. She composed a competing set of comedies, based on Terence as a model, which extol the joys of purity and martyrdom in comparison to unholy love. This is one reason why few people have heard of Hroswitha.

Made in Rome: Cato and Catonism

The Scipionic Circle was the avant-garde of the Roman nobility. Romans, in general, thought that they had little to learn from anybody. The fad of foreign ideas and literature created a backlash. Chief among early critics was Marcus Porcius Cato (234–149 B.C.E.), "the Elder," or "the Censor."

If Cato had a chariot, it probably had "Made in Rome" and "Rome, Love It or Leave It" bumper stickers. Cato promoted Roman ideals against what he found a decadent and frivolous cultural invasion. He was largely responsible for legislation that kept Greek philosophers from living and teaching at Rome. The Roman youth, he said, had better things to apply themselves to than verbal fluff. As *censor,* Cato applied himself to cleaning up the morals of the aristocrats (especially the Scipios) and to destroying Carthage.

> **When in Rome**
>
> The **censor** was an appointed magistrate who determined voting and property lists, the make-up of the senate, and acted as auditor for public works. For more, see Chapter 9, "The Romans Among Themselves."

In literature, Cato promoted Roman forms and language. He was famous for his *Origines (Origins),* one of the earliest histories of Rome in Latin, and for his *de Agri Cultura* or "On Agricultural Production," the oldest extant Latin prose work. Cato's cultural conservatism carried down to his great-grandson, Cato "the Younger" (95–46 B.C.E.), the poster child of moralists who mistake rigid adherence to their own ideals for integrity. Nevertheless, both Cato the Elder and the Younger became revered figures in their own day. They both became icons of old Roman values, and represented a broad current of distrust Romans never lost for un-Roman things and ways.

Latin Comes into Its Own: The First Century B.C.E.

But whether it was in Rome or out in the *provincia,* the impact of Greek culture was there to stay. Even Cato ended up studying Greek in his old age. Roman aristocrats found Greek education and rhetoric useful in their domestic and foreign public affairs and personally engaging. Moreover, Romans came to see that literature and learning gave Greek culture *dignitas* and *auctoritas* on the world stage. They wanted a part of it. In the last century of the Republic, Romans (this now includes Romans and Italians), always conscious of Greek predecessors, began to write in their own voice and to create what has come to be known as the Golden Age of Latin literature. Since the beginning of the Golden Age is also known as the "Ciceronian Period," let's start first with the defining author and voice of this time.

Marcus Tullius Cicero (Cicero)

Marcus Tullius Cicero (106–43 B.C.E.) deserves a whole chapter himself. Cicero was born at Arpinum to an upper-class equestrian family and became one of the preeminent Roman statesmen, orators, authors, theorists, first man of letters, and the bane of beginning Latin students everywhere.

Pater Patriae

Cicero came to prominence in his successful prosecution of the governor of Sicily, Verres, in 70 B.C.E. His oratory won him acclaim, and in 63 B.C.E., he was elected consul, the first *novus homo* since Marius. That year he foiled an attempted coup d'etat by a group of desperate nobles under the leadership of Lucius Catiline and executed the conspirators. The senate voted him the title *pater patriae*, although this acclaim was colored by the political maneuvering among the nobles of the day.

Cicero championed the idea of the *concordia ordinum* (concord of the orders), which (in his mind) was a cooperative partnership of *optimates, populares,* and equites for the good of the state. This didn't last, but Cicero remained an influential voice in Roman politics until he was proscribed and executed by Antony. His severed head and hands were nailed for display on the Rostra, from which he had delivered so many influential orations, as a lesson to others.

Lend Me Your Ears

"Quite rightly it was said by his contemporaries that Cicero reigned over the law courts, and those of subsequent ages give him such glory that Cicero is now not so much the name of a man as that of eloquence itself."

—Quintilian (ca C.E. 35–100), *Institutes of Oratory*, 10.110

When in Rome

Here's some Ciceronian vocabulary:

Pater Patriae means "the Father of his country," the title Cicero (and later Augustus) was given by the senate.

The **concordia ordinum** ("the harmony of the orders") was Cicero's phrase for the ideal cooperation between political and economic orders (nobles, equites, and so on) for the good of the state.

The **Rostra** was the speaker's platform in the forum from which orators such as Cicero delivered orations (public addresses). It was named for the Carthaginian ramming prows or "beaks" (*rostrae*) put on display there after the First Punic War (264–241 B.C.E.).

Besides his famous orations, Cicero published works of political science, practical philosophy, and literary criticism. He was also the first figure whose personal correspondence became a literary publication: Over 1,000 of his letters to and from friends and associates survive, collected and published by his publisher and friend, Atticus. These letters make Cicero and his period the best-documented figure and era in Roman history, sometimes giving us a day-by-day account of the final years of the Republic.

Cicero's Orations

Cicero's orations are among the world's finest oratory, and his flowing and balanced *"periodic"* style became a statement in and of itself of Ciceronian ideals. Many of the speeches were written but not delivered, and all were spruced up for publication. Some of Cicero's most famous orations include …

When in Rome

Periodic style refers to a style of composing complex sentences to contain clauses and subordinate constructions within the structure of the main sentence. These sentences have a form that goes somewhat like **A-b-c-c*-b*-A*** (if a letter indicates the beginning of a grammatical construction and the letter* indicates its completion). For example: "Periodic sentences are, for students who study Latin, the language of Cicero, or any language, very tedious to read."

➤ *In Verrem* [Against Verres], *Actio 1–2* (70 B.C.E.): These cases make up the prosecution of Verres that brought Cicero to acclaim. Only the first was actually delivered. Cicero surprised the defense and brought forth such a vigorous prosecution that Verres went into exile before the trial was concluded. Cicero then published the second case as a prosecution of Roman abuse of power in the provinces.

➤ *In Catalinam* [Against Catiline], *1–4* (63 B.C.E.): These are Cicero's best-known speeches, delivered at various stages of the debates surrounding the conspiracy of Catiline. In the first speech, he confronted Catiline in the senate, after which Catiline fled the city. Conspirators remained, however, and in the second and third speeches, Cicero lay out to the people the situation and how he came to discover and arrest the conspirators. The fourth speech was delivered in the senate on the question of executing the conspirators; Cicero and Cato prevailed against the moderating voice of Caesar. This action haunted Cicero: Caesar's political mob boss and tribune, Clodius, was able to exile Cicero for executing Roman citizens without trial.

➤ *Pro Archia* [For the Poet Archias] (62 B.C.E.): Cicero was called upon to defend the citizenship of the poet Aulus Lucinius Archias. The *Pro Archia* is an eloquent defense of the practical benefits of liberal education and the power of literature to an audience still deeply skeptical of both.

➤ *Pro Caelio* **[For Caelius]** (56 B.C.E.): After Cicero's return from exile, he became intensely involved in politics again, in particular against Clodius. Caelius was up on a charge of poisoning by Clodius's infamous sister, Clodia (the "Lesbia" to whom Catullus writes). Cicero's speech is half defense, half scathing attack on both Clodius and Clodia. Clodius was killed in a mob street battle in 52 B.C.E.

➤ *Philippica* **[The Philippics]** *1–14* (44/43 B.C.E.): Cicero became highly influential after the death of Caesar. He tried to undermine Antony's authority and support Octavian as a counterbalance, but in an effort to steer the state back toward his Republican ideas. In the chaos before the second triumvirate (see Chapter 7, "Let's Conquer … Ourselves! The Roman Revolution and the End of the Republic"), he delivered and published speeches and political tracts in which he explained his policy and attacked Antony.

These speeches range from careful outlines of policy to some of the best mudslinging you have ever read (*Philippic II*). Like what? Dear reader, why should I be forced to mention Antony's reported sexual perversions, heinous crimes, and other titillating tidbits? Who would want to read an extended catalogue detailing such unspeakable things? And so, let us leave them unmentioned. (In any case, once you read the speeches you'll better understand why Antony wanted Cicero's head.)

Golden Oldies

A single author, even a great one, doesn't make a Golden Age. Latin literature was finding many voices during Cicero's time. In prose and poetry, Roman writers were breaking new ground and laying down the foundation for Latin literature's florescence under Augustus. Like Cicero, many of these writers were as active in the politics of the day as they were in the literature of their time. Others were beginning to take the position that writing, in and of itself, was a "Roman" thing to do. The following are five influential writers of the Ciceronian Period.

Marcus Terentius Varro (Varro)

Marcus Terentius Varro (116–27 B.C.E.) was widely educated and a prolific writer. He is said to have written around 500 books on about 50 different subjects, including works on the Latin language, farm management, satires, and poetry.

Titus Lucretius Carus (Lucretius)

Titus Lucretius Carus (99–55 B.C.E.) was an Epicurean poet (Epicureanism was fairly popular in the turbulent last century B.C.E.). He wrote six books of florid verse called *de Rerum Natura* ("On the Nature of Things") in which he explains and argues for Epicurean philosophy. It's really interesting to read his approaches to the development of human civilization and language and to the place of religion in culture.

Gaius Julius Caesar (Caesar)

Gaius Julius Caesar (100–44 B.C.E.) was more than a great general: he was also a fine speaker and writer. He wrote six books of dispatches from his conquest of Gaul and three books about the civil war. The clear prose of these works, meant for public consumption, has often been used as Latin school texts.

Gaius Sallustius Crispus (Sallust)

Gaius Sallustius Crispus (86–34 B.C.E.) was from central Italy. He was an ally of Caesar who became a historian after a forced retirement from the senate. He is best known for two short historical monographs about pivotal events in Roman history. The *Bellum Jugurthinum* (Jurgurthine War) identifies Marius and Sulla's campaigns in Africa against the rebel Jugurtha as the time in which the ambitions of the nobility, corrupted by greed and power, turned against Rome. The *Bellum Catalinae* (Conspiracy of Catiline) shows the depths to which these ambitions had brought the state. Sallust's style and ideas were influenced by the Greek historian Thucydides; both sought to identify the human motivations and causes behind historical events. Sallust's writings were influential on the philosopher and writer Friedrich Nietzsche (1844–1900).

> **Great Caesar's Ghost!**
>
> Epicureans claimed that everything was composed of arrangements of tiny indestructible bits of matter, which they called atoms (un-cut-ables). Death was only the destruction of the arrangements and included the soul. Religion was an uneducated response to fear of the unknown, and institutional religion controlled people through fear with threats of eternal punishment. Epicurean ideas were influential on Karl Marx (1818–1883).

Gaius Valerius Catullus (Catullus)

Gaius Valerius Catullus (84–54 B.C.E.) was from Verona. Catullus was among a group of *poetae novi* (new poets, or neoteric) who came to prominence in the first century B.C.E. They adapted Greek lyric forms and wrote about the personal here and now: conversations, dinner, current events, and love. This direct approach to subjects and language was radical in that it exposed and elevated the personal over the philosophic, public, and civic. The neoteric writers also advanced the idea that being a writer *was* a worthwhile Roman thing to do. Catullus wrote poems of many kinds on many subjects, but he is most famous for his "Lesbia" poems, which describe the thrill and chill of love and betrayal with his mistress. "Lesbia" was a code name for Clodia, the powerful, educated, and infamous sister of Clodius, Cicero's potent enemy and Caesarian political mob boss.

The Augustan Period

Latin literature had been brewing and distilling under the pressure of civil war and strife for half a century, and creative energy strained against the effects of chaos and disruption. The settlement of Rome under Augustus created stability and took the lid off the cauldron. An explosion in Latin literature erupted, fueled in part by a healthy dose of patronage and especially of those poets who celebrated and advanced Augustan ideals. This second half of the Golden Age is called the "Augustan Period" or "Augustan Age." It begins with the death of Caesar in 44 B.C.E. and lasts to the death of the emperor Augustus in C.E. 14.

The primary patrons during this period were Gaius Maecenus, Augustus's chief advisor and friend; Augustus himself (usually with Maecenus as an intermediary); and Marcus Messala, an old Roman aristocrat who had fought with the Republicans but made his peace with the new regime. Augustan poets were urban writers, but some tended to romanticize and promote the easy and carefree country life of the hardy Roman peasant. Virgil and Horace had country villas given to them where they could play the role of the gentleman farmer.

Here are the primary writers of the Augustan Age.

Publius Virgilius Maro (Virgil)

Publius Virgilius Maro (70–19 B.C.E.), or Virgil, was born at Mantua (Mantova) and was the preeminent poet of this age. Patronized by Maecenas and Augustus, Virgil wrote pastoral poems (the *Eclogues*) that celebrated the Italian countryside, and poetry (the *Georgics*) that celebrated the rustic ideals and skills of Roman farmers. His greatest achievement, however, was the Roman epic *Aeneid,* which tells about the hero Aeneas's voyage from Troy to Italy. (In case you forgot the myth, it was Aeneas's descendants who founded Rome.) Virgil labored for nine years on this work, and willed that it be burned upon his death because it was not perfected. Thankfully, Augustus countermanded the order and preserved one of the West's greatest and most influential pieces of literature.

One of Virgil's pieces spoke of a golden age that would be ushered in by the coming of a divine son. Some early Christians, such as Augustine, took this to be a pagan prophesy of Christ. It was not (the poem concerned Augustus's heir apparent Marcellus), but it allowed Virgil's work a special place for Christian readers; Dante features the poet (and his work) as a guide through *Inferno* and *Purgatorio* in the *Divine Comedy.*

Roamin' the Romans

When in Rome, take a day trip outside of the city to the remains of Horace's Sabine Farm. It's only 50 km away, near the medieval town of Licenza. Horace loved this place, and it features in many of his poems. The American Academy in Rome and Italian Ministry of Culture have teamed up to preserve this, the only identifiable home of an Augustan writer.

Quintus Horatius Flaccus (Horace)

Quintus Horatius Flaccus (65–8 B.C.E.), or Horace, was born in Venusia in southeast Italy. He was well-educated and fought on Brutus's side at Philippi, but came home to make peace with the new regime, got a job as a clerk, and began writing poetry.

Virgil and a friend introduced Horace and his work to Maecenas. Things began to look up from there, and in about 33 B.C.E., Maecenas gave him the Sabine farm that was his joy. Horace composed some of the most finely crafted and beautiful Latin poetry, bar none. He was Augustus's poet laureate for his "Secular Games" in 17 B.C.E. and composed its famous hymn, the *Carmen Saeculare*. He published four books of lyric poetry (*Odes*), two books of Satires (*Saturae*) and Epistles (*Epistulae*), a work of poetic literary theory (the *Art of Poetry* or *Ars Poetica*), and other works.

Great Caesar's Ghost!

Ever read a story called something like "The City Mouse and the Country Mouse" about two mice who visit each other only to discover that their own haunts are really the best of all places? That's Horace's story and a parable about the romantic ideals that urban and rural dwellers have of each other.

Sextus Propertius (Propertius)

Sextus Propertius (ca 56–16 B.C.E.) was a poet from Umbria. He came to the attention of Maecenas, who asked him to write an epic about Augustus's deeds. Propertius declined to do so in a poem (2.1), but continued to be patronized by Maecenas and Augustus. Four books of intense elegiac poetry survive.

Albius Tibullus (Tibullus)

Albius Tibullus (48–19 B.C.E.) was a member of Valerius Massala's literary circle. He knew both Propertius and Horace, who addresses him in *Epistle 1.4*. Tibullus's poetry celebrates a romantic vision of the countryside (much like Virgil's) but also contains urbane renditions that put the lover in the position of being enslaved to his beloved. Tibullus (or his literary persona, at least) seems to have liked it that way. He published two books of poetry before his death; two more posthumous books were published, only a part of which may contain his work. Some of the later works may be by Sulpicia, the niece of Massala, who was a member of Tibullus's literary circle.

Titius Livius (Livy)

Titius Livius (59 B.C.E.–C.E. 17), or Livy, was from Patavium (Padua) in northern Italy. If you've ever had a class on Roman history, you've read his work. Livy romanticized the Republic and the heroes of Roman history who created it. Augustus, in fact, teasingly called him "My Little Pompeian" (after the party of Pompey the Great). Nevertheless, Livy's nostalgic and patriotic vision of heroes, old time values, stability, and discipline were in concert with Augustus's aims. Augustus patronized Livy's life and work, including setting him up as a tutor for the future emperor Claudius.

Livy's monumental task was compiling a complete and unabridged history of the Roman people. He called this work *ab Urbe Condita* (no, that's not a song by Iron Butterfly), "From the Founding of the City." Published in installments from about 27 to 8 B.C.E., it eventually reached *142* books. It brought Livy instant fame, but like all huge books (such as *War and Peace, Gone with the Wind, or* the *Iliad*) people didn't have the time, money, or inclination to actually *read* the whole thing. Within a few years, you could buy *epitomes* (condensed versions) of the volumes. (I wonder if there was a *Libellus ad ab Urbe Condita Intellegendum pro Stultissimis—The Complete Idiot's Guide to Understanding ab Urbe Condita?*) Most of these survive, and only the most popular sections (ancient Rome, the Wars with Carthage and Macedonia) survive in original form.

Publius Ovidius Naso (Ovid)

Publius Ovidius Naso (43 B.C.E.–C.E. 17), or Ovid, was from Sulmona (Sulmo) in central Italy. Ovid, like many of these writers, needed a book of his own. His father sent him to Rome to be a lawyer, but Ovid tells us that no matter what he tried to write, it just came out in verse. His witty, urbane, tongue-in-cheek, passionate, and irreverent work made him an instant success as an author.

The preeminent Roman poet of love and seduction, Ovid first published the *Amores,* vignettes from lovers' lives, in which he pokes as much fun at the literary tradition of love poetry as love itself. His *Ars Amatoria* (The Art of Love) brought him great fame, and eventually was published in three books. The first two might be entitled "How to Score with Women," and the third "How to Wring the Most out of the Guy Trying to Score with You." The *Remedium Amoris* (Remedies for Love) followed soon after; it could be titled something like "How to Get Over It."

Other works include the *Heroides* (imaginary letters from famous heroines to their lovers), *Fasti* (six books on Roman festivals and holidays), and the *Metamorphoses* (15 books of verse that tell the principle myths of Greece and Rome). If you have read and loved Greek and Roman mythology, chances are that you have read a version told by Ovid.

Roamin' the Romans

As you have read, few of the Golden or Augustan Age writers came from Rome itself. Especially if you have a car in Italy, you can have a wonderful time touring their home towns such as Mantova (Virgil), Padua (Livy), Sulmona (Ovid), and Verona (Catullus). If you happen to be in Romania and visit Constanta on the Black Sea (ancient Tomis), say hello or blow a kiss to Ovid's ghost.

Ovid was briefly patronized by Messala, but his popularity gave him independent standing and income. He ran afoul, however, of the Augustan program and perhaps even of Augustus himself. He was exiled in C.E. 8 by the Princeps to Tomis, on the Black Sea, for what Ovid says was a "poem" (the *Ars Amatoria?*) and "an error." Tradition has it that this error was connected with Augustus's problem daughter, Julia, but we will never know. Being exiled to Tomis was like a Parisian being exiled to a fishing village for life. No city, no Latin, no culture. He wrote some poignant works and letters from exile, and died without ever seeing his beloved city again.

The Least You Need to Know

➤ Rome literature didn't begin until the third century B.C.E. when Rome conquered the Mediterranean.

➤ Latin literature, with the exception of satire, evolved from Greek and Latin writers experimenting with and developing Greek forms.

➤ It was only in the first century B.C.E. that Latin literature really came into its own.

➤ Patronage, wealth, and stability in the Augustan Age helped Latin literature achieve its zenith under such authors as Virgil, Horace, Livy, and Ovid.

Chapter 12

If They Build It: Roman Engineering

In This Chapter

➤ How the Romans built to last

➤ Roman roads and aqueducts

➤ Urban planning and design

➤ Military engineering and building

The Romans were expert engineers and practical builders, and it's not hard to appreciate what they left behind. There are cities, buildings, roads, aqueducts, tunnels, and bridges all built to last and many still in use. These remains, however, followed conquests, and conquest depended on less permanent constructions for which the Romans were equally famous: military camps, siege engines, and the machines of war.

Besides being a professor, I've been a builder and a landscaper. From this experience, I've come to appreciate four consistent Roman approaches to enduring creations: do the math, prepare the earth, create a stable foundation, and build to last. I also admire two character traits that present themselves in their best work: practical problem solving and a tenacious determination to do things right. The Romans weren't necessarily fancy or experimental. You can attribute a great deal of Roman success to consistent and skillful application of fundamental techniques they had already learned by the sixth century B.C.E., such as digging ditches, working with stone, and building an arch. Once they found something that worked, they stuck with it.

In this chapter, we'll examine Roman building and engineering in civic and military areas.

The Empire Wore Cement Shoes

Roman building depended on concrete, which they began working with about 300 B.C.E. The Romans made two important contributions to concrete. First, they discovered that if they used hard volcanic sand from Mt. Vesuvius (*pulvis Puteolanus*) in the mix, the concrete became hard enough to withstand nearly any weathering, including immersion in flowing rivers. Concrete mixes today use super-hard particles (such as silica) to achieve similar durability. Second, the Romans refined their knowledge of mixing (using additives such as animal fat to manipulate cement properties), pouring, and curing concrete, and understood its properties even if they didn't understand its chemistry. With this knowledge, they could work concrete in dry and wet (including underwater) conditions.

Besides cranes, carts, shovels, and stone working tools, it doesn't take many tools to do good excavation and concrete work. Romans used a sighting instrument, called a *diptra,* to measure changes in elevation. To sight right angles, establish a parallel track with other lines, and calculate crossroads, they used an instrument called a *groma.* The *groma* looked like a crossroad sign with plumb lines attached to each end of the street signs. You sighted along either sign to find or establish new points. When establishing level or grade for aqueducts, the Romans used a long wooden table, called a *chorobates.* This table had a rounded, lengthwise groove in the top, which served as a water level.

Great Caesar's Ghost!

It may surprise you to learn that concrete is about as old as—well, about as old as concrete lasts. The ancient Mesopotamians and Egyptians used it. With apologies to "mud" contractors everywhere for the simplistic recipe, you make concrete by heating limestone until all the water molecules burn off. Pulverize the lime and mix in sand. This makes mortar. Mix mortar with small stone and gravel to get concrete mix. Add water to the dry ingredients, mix thoroughly, and let set. Chemistry takes over and produces (depending on mix and conditions) artificial rock (concrete).

How All Roads Led to (and from) Rome

The old proverb "all roads lead to Rome" is really backwards, of course. The Romans began constructing their extensive network of inter-provincial highways *from* the center of their city. Beginning with Gaius Gracchus (see Chapter 7, "Let's Conquer … Ourselves! The Roman Revolution and the End of the Republic"), distances were marked in mileposts measured from the *miliarium aureum* (golden milepost), a marker in the Forum. A Roman mile is 1,000 paces, and our word "mile" comes from Roman *mille* (thousand).

The Romans built roads to aid in the quick movement of defensive forces and to facilitate trade and commerce. Beginning with the famous *Via Appia*, successive roads were proposed and built by the censors to allow legions to protect Rome's interests. As Rome's reach grew, so did the length of its roads. The first great roads ran primarily north-south, but because troops were stationed in northern and southern Italy, east-west connecting roads were added, as well as roads in Gaul and Macedonia to facilitate troop movements to these new provinces.

Some of the major road projects of the Republic were …

➤ *Via Appia* (312 B.C.E.) from Rome to Terracina and to Capua.

➤ *Via Aemilia* (241 B.C.E.) from Rome to Piza along the coast.

➤ *Via Flaminia* (220 B.C.E.) from Rome to Rimini (Ariminum).

➤ *Via Valeria* (210 B.C.E.) in Sicily.

➤ *Via Aemelia* (187 B.C.E.) connecting (east-west) Rimini to Piacenza through Balogna.

➤ *Via Cassia* (177 B.C.E.) from Rome to Arezzo; reaching Florence and Pisa in 125 B.C.E.

➤ *Via Postumia* (148 B.C.E.) connecting Benoa, Piacenza, Cremona, Aquileia; *Via Aemilia* extends to Piacenza and Tortona.

Veto!

The *Via Appia* was not the first road from Rome; Rome was on the crossroads of several trade routes, and road maintenance is mentioned in the Twelve Tables (ca 450 B.C.E.). The *Via Salaria* (Salt Road) up to the mountains and the inland route to Capua, the *Via Latina*, were gravel roads built before the *Via Appia*.

Great Caesar's Ghost!

The primary reason for building Rome's major roads and its interstate highway system was military, not commercial.

➤ *Via Egnatia* (146 B.C.E.) from the Balkans to Greece; from Dyrrachium (Durazzo) to Thessolonica.

➤ *Via Domitia* (118 B.C.E.) in Gaul Narbonnensis from the Rhone River to the Pyrranees.

➤ *Via Emilia Scauri* (109 B.C.E.) extends *Via Aurelia*.

➤ A road from Turin to Vienne (in France) over the little St. Bernard Pass built by Pompey the Great (77 B.C.E.).

➤ Julius Caesar's improvement to the route over the Great St. Bernard Pass (57 B.C.E.).

Still miles to go: a Roman road.

How Roads Were Built

After a road was proposed, the censor figured the cost of the project, and bidding went out to the *publicani* (private companies). The road course was carefully laid out. Routes ran straight from one sighting point to the next (you didn't need banked or gentle curves for fast-moving traffic) or followed along natural topography.

Once the route was established, a roadbed (about 15 feet wide) was cut into the soil about 2 to 3 feet, and drainage ditches were added along the sides. A good bed was essential for the road to be strong enough to carry legions and huge transport carts (the ancient equivalent to the 16-wheeler) year around, day in and day out. In some wetter areas, this bed had to be built up to a firm platform, called an *agger* (we call this a "highway"). Drainage problems were then addressed (not only are wet roadbeds unstable and mucky, but they tend to buckle and shift when they freeze). Cisterns, for example, might be added to help shunt away road runoff.

A foundation of rock and gravel road ballast was laid down and compacted, and often a layer of sand or other impact-absorbing material was put on top of that. The final metalling surface had to remain stable and hard, and its composition depended upon its use, costs, and local materials available. Many roads were metalled with gravel or flint, and were paved only near the cities where traffic was heaviest. Near iron mines, the slag and mining tailings were used, which rusted together to create a hard surface. In Africa, the Romans discovered that a sloped dirt roadway became hard as rock and needed no *metalling*.

When in Rome

Metalling does not refer to "metal" (as in iron or bronze) in this context, but to the top surface of the road (such as the pavement), which bears the wear and tear of use and weather.

The most durable (and recognizable) metalling was multisided random stones, laid without mortar and cut individually to fit firmly against each other. (Appius Claudius the Blind was said to have examined the joint workmanship with his bare feet.) Fine sand and gravel was added around and over the top to sift into the cracks. It's not much different than what you do to build a patio of bricks or interlocking "pavers"—only the first Roman patio was 130 miles long!

The major Roman roads were called *viae publicae,* public highways, and funded by public funds. *Viae militares* were funded by the military. Local byways (*actus*) and private roads (*viae privatae*) were built to connect with public roads. Maintenance of public roads was highly organized and consistent; maintenance of local and private roads was the concern of those who needed and constructed them.

When the Mountain Was High

Roman roads generally followed the contours of the land, and large-scale excavation was impractical. Yet there were times when mountainous or rugged terrain necessitated excavation. When they needed to, the Romans cut into the hillsides to carve out a roadway, and it appears in places that they cut wheel grooves into the pavement to keep the wagons on the road at critical spots.

In certain places, it was better to go *through* the mountain rather than around it. The Romans were expert tunnelers (Rome conquered Veii by tunneling under its walls in 396 B.C.E.), a skill that they also applied to the construction of aqueducts. You can find Roman tunnels (they're not difficult to spot—you can drive through some of them) along the *Via Flaminia* at Furlo Pass and at the *Via Appia* at Cumae and at Pozzuoli. These two roads also feature impressive road cuts into the mountains and along the sea near Terracina.

When the Valley Was Low

At some points, the road had to cross valleys or rivers. The Romans used their skills with piers and arches to create bridges to span these obstacles. An arched bridge is an amazingly strong structure, and many Roman bridges remain in use today even with the weight and vibration of modern traffic!

The strength of the bridge depended upon a stable foundation. In valleys or in spots where an arch could span the water, the Romans dug down to bedrock and cemented in the foundations of the piers upon which the arches supporting the roadway were constructed. When these piers had to be in the middle of the river or in marshy soil, things were a little more complicated. Pilings were driven down around where the pier would go until a temporary dam could be built. The water was pumped out (the Romans had water pumps) and the earth dug down to bedrock where the Romans cemented massive foundations in place (fortunately, their cement hardened in wet conditions). Piers rose from the foundation to the beginning of the arches.

Roamin' the Romans

Hundreds of picturesque Roman bridges in various stages of repair from ruin to active use litter the Roman Empire. One of the most famous is at Alcantara (The Bridge) in Spain. The magnificent six arches rise 140 feet above the water, an enduring example of both Roman engineering and persistence. The remains of the old bridge, built by the engineer who created Trajan's famous column, were washed away by the wild Tagus river. The new bridge was built by Gaius Julius Lacer (whose spirit still looks on in admiration from his tomb nearby) in C.E. 105.

When the River Ran Wide

In places where there was a great deal of wetlands to cross, the Romans elevated their roadways. Timber piles were driven into the ground, and the frame for the road was built upon these. Limestone flagstones were laid on top of the wooden frame and the road was filled on top. In other places, causeways were constructed by pounding parallel lines of pilings and filling in between them to a height above flood stage.

In some places, a river was just too deep or too far across for the Romans to build a bridge, so ferries had to be used. One such place was at Forum Appii, where the last 20-mile stretch of the *Via Appia antiqua* had to be made by a ferry (pulled from the shore by donkeys) to Terracina. Other ferry crossings were broader. For example, ferries carried travelers over the Adriatic from the end of the *Via Appia* in Brudesium (from Rome) to the beginning of the *Via Egnatia* (to Greece) at Dyrrachium. After Caesar, Britain was put on the Roman road map, so to speak. It's a tribute to Roman road building that, in the Empire, a traveler could go from Hadrian's Wall to Rome and need only to take one ferry—and that was over the English channel.

Roamin' the Romans

Tavernae were pretty much the dive end of the accommodation line, but some were famous. The *Via Appia* had several well-known taverns; St. Paul stayed at one on his way to Rome, and the poet Horace spent an evening at another on his way to Brundesium with Maecenas.

The Open (and Clogged) Road

The major highways were thronged with travelers and transport, and became clogged at rush hour near steep inclines and cities, especially in Rome. Yes, just as now, Rome had terrible traffic problems. Julius Caesar decreed that heavy transport use the streets only at night, but the noise at night brought almost as much complaining as the traffic. Near and in cities, roads were lined with raised sidewalks for pedestrians and some roads featured stepping-stone crosswalks for dry pedestrian crossing. At the entrances to cities, major roads featured public baths, toilets, and places to stay.

Lend Me Your Ears

"Carriages in narrow streets and the bellowing of gridlocked drivers keeps even Rip Van Winkle awake! Mr. *Rich* (civic duty calls!) whisks by in his limo-litter over the yielding heads of the deferential crowd. *He* blithely reads, or sleeps all tucked-in with the windows shut for darkness. *He* sleeps and gets there before *me!* The surge blocks *me* no matter how hard I swim against it, a tidal wave of humanity pushes from behind. One idiot gouges me with his elbow, another with a stiff pole; one smacks me in the head with a beam and another with a barrel. My legs are sprayed with mud and soon I'm completely trampled under by huge feet and some soldier's boot crushes my toes."

—Juvenal, *Satire 3 (Against Rome)*, 234–248

On extended road trips, wealthy travelers often had their own (or friends') villas in which to stay. An official, who carried a *diploma* (travel permit), could also stop at various official stations (*villulae*) for a rest, and post-houses (*cursus publici*) for fresh horses. Other travelers had to depend upon travel inns (*mansiones*) and taverns (*tavernae*). The *mansiones* were built and maintained by local taxes and were required by law to provide food and shelter. Those who couldn't afford *mansiones* sought out the *tavernae* for their meals and overnight stays. Around all these accommodations stables, high-priced repair garages (what are you going to do—walk the 60 miles back to Rome for a wheel spoke?), fast-food outlets, and merchant shops sprang up.

Great Caesar's Ghost!

The poet Horace, in *Satire* 1.5, describes a journey that he made with friends Maecenas and the poet Virgil along the *Via Appia*, complete with road stops, friendships, travel disasters, and diseases. Maecenas and company were probably on the way to try to smooth out the relationship between Antony and Octavian during the rocky days of the second triumvirate (43–34 B.C.E.).

You Can't Lead a City to Water, But ...

The Romans learned early how to move water over and through the land, but it wasn't to get water—it was to get *rid* of it. Roman farmers used sophisticated drainage channels to manage soil conditions and reclaim land around the city. Later, the construction of the *Cloaca Maxima* by the Etruscans introduced the channel to the arch and created the great sewer.

It was only a matter of time until the Romans, in need of a drink and a bath, reversed the process—found water and brought it *to* the city. It was Appius Claudius the Blind who proposed the first aqueduct, the *Aqua Appia* in 312 B.C.E. It was a little over 10 miles long. The next, the *Anio Vetus*, in 272 B.C.E., was *50* miles long. Five hundred years brought 10 more aqueducts—one major water expansion every 50 years.

The principles and ideas behind an aqueduct aren't complex. You find water somewhere and collect it in a huge basin. From the basin, you let it run downhill in a big pipe to the city. There, you collect it again in a big basin, from which many little pipes distribute it around the neighborhood so that people can spend Saturday morning washing the chariot. Well, okay, it's a *little* more complicated than that (and washing vehicles wasn't a Roman obsession).

Roamin' the Romans

Earlier peoples used aqueducts, too, but it was the Romans who developed them into a signature architectural feature. The most famous aqueduct is probably the *Pont du Guard* in Provence (built by Trajan), but many other beautiful aqueducts grace the Roman Empire from east to west and north to south. Some, such as an aqueduct for the Vatican and one in Segovia, Spain, are still in use today!

Getting Water to the City

Once a source of water was found (such as a lake or springs), surveyors calculated the rise in elevation between it and the planned terminus of the aqueduct in the city. A route was then carefully planned and staked out to insure a continuous and gentle downward grade. Although people appreciate aqueducts for their graceful, arching elevations, most of the aqueducts were in fact underground. Burying the aqueduct not only kept water from evaporating, it kept it cool and protected it from potential tampering by enemies.

Beginning at the point of collection, a catch basin was built to collect the water. The delivery route was trenched if possible. Otherwise, shafts were then sunk every 20 yards or so along the route to the required depth, and tunnels dug from shaft to shaft using the *chorobates* to check for grade. These shafts could be reopened and used to enter the aqueduct at a later time for repairs, cleaning, and maintenance. Once the threat of enemies had been eliminated, the shafts were marked and numbered for ease of maintenance. A closed (usually arched) water conduit (*rivus* or *specus*) was created in the tunnels using stone and finished with concrete. The *specus* was made as tall as a man to accommodate adequate water supplies and to make it easier to clean and to inspect.

Pools (called fishponds or *piscinae*) along the route cleaned the water by allowing sediments and debris to filter out. Additional water was brought into the aqueduct from other sources through branch lines (*rami*), or water was drawn off into a distribution tank (*castellum*) for distribution through pipes (*fistulae*) to towns or individuals who had special water contracts. Tying into an aqueduct without permission would be akin to tying your farm into the electrical grid without permits. There were serious fines for such public theft.

When the topography didn't accommodate underground digging, the *specus* was elevated on earthworks, upon arches, or built into structures such as bridges or overpasses. These are the structures that inspire so much admiration. But they, and the underground structures and tunnels, are all the more impressive for their use of hydrostatic pressure and siphoning to get over rises and to distribute water in the cities once the aqueduct had reached its terminus.

The "Pont du Guard" near Nîmes in southern France, built under the emperor Trajan (98–117).

Water, Water, Everywhere

Roman cities used an incredible amount of running water. There were no faucets—water ran (at a measured amount) continuously. When the aqueduct entered the city, water was collected in an enormous distribution tank (*castellum*). From the *castellum* delivery pipes (*fistulae*) of lead, wood, or tile took water to different parts of the city.

The Roman engineer Vetruvius (ca 50–26 B.C.E.) lays out a hierarch of water distribution managed by three tanks in his treatise on architecture (*de Architectura*). The first tank supplied public fountains for drinking and personal use; the second supplied the public baths (which provided public hygiene and income to the state); and the third, which could run only when the other two had more than enough water, supplied private homes. Public water was available on most blocks, and many of these small running fountains are still a good source of a cool drink in Rome today.

Great Caesar's Ghost!

An abundance of running water and the technological know-how made for remarkably modern civic and domestic plumbing. Well-to-do Romans had water closet-type toilets, private fountains, and baths. Public sanitation (baths and toilets) was helped by using the outlet water from the baths to continuously flush public toilets. You can find an example of this sanitation plan along the main city street in Ephesus (Turkey).

Roamin' the Romans

When in Naples, be sure to visit the massive subterranean *castellum* that served as the fresh water tank for the Roman Navy and as a bomb shelter in World War II.

Great Caesar's Ghost!

The earliest public amphitheater was built for a colony of Sullan veterans at Pompeii around 80 B.C.E. Its builders called it the *spectacula.* (Nowadays, it would be called the "DictatorFelix.com Spectacula.")

The priority that public water distribution took in the aqueducts underscores that these public works were, in part, examples of Roman civic values and, in part, ways for political figures to win broad popular support. Agrippa, for example, won great acclaim for his repair of the aqueducts that were damaged by war and by "deferred maintenance" during the end of the Republic. Aqueducts also provide clues to population and economic growth in various parts of the city to archeologists.

I Like to Watch: Theaters and Amphitheaters

When you think of Rome, you probably think of the Colosseum, the great Roman amphitheater constructed by the emperors Vespasian (69–79) and Titus (79–81). Although you can find theaters and amphitheaters all over the Roman world, Roman buildings of these kinds were primarily built during the Empire. Rome didn't even *have* a permanent stone theater until Pompey the Great built one in 55 B.C.E. and no permanent amphitheater until 29 B.C.E.!

Nevertheless, it's important to distinguish between theaters and amphitheaters. Both of these buildings were developed for entertainment that, for the Romans, originated in temporary venues. Greek cities in Italy already had theaters, and when the Romans constructed their own permanent theaters, they used them as models. Theaters were composed of semicircular seating arrangements (the *theatron*—viewing place) around an orchestra (dancing circle), across from a raised platform for acting and a building *skene* (scene building) for backdrop and changing.

The amphitheater was another matter. The amphitheater evolved from the arena, a closed-off patch of ground surrounded by raised hills for viewing. The "amphitheater" literally means "two (*amphi*)theatrons," that is, two semicircular seating areas around an arena. The Romans used arenas for entertainment such as executions, hunts, and gladiatorial fights. The first amphitheaters were primarily seating enhancements (bleachers) added to the banks surrounding the arena. In time, however, the Romans created freestanding buildings and put their practical ingenuity into the creation of uniquely Roman entertainment centers.

The Roman Amphitheater in Nîmes, France.

Urban Planning

Urban planning preceded the Romans (remember Egypt?), and was (in the Mediterranean) systematized as early as 550 B.C.E. by the Greek architect Hippodamus. He proposed city planning on grid lines around a central marketplace; this became the model for the construction of Hellenistic cities founded after Alexander the Great.

The Romans based their urban planning, when they founded a colony, around the model of a Roman military camp, or *castra*. City walls were laid out in the shape of a square and fortified. Two principle streets (*viae principiae*) cut the square in half north-south (the *cardo*) and east-west (the *decamanus*) and met at a central forum. The streets met the walls at four city gates. Smaller streets were laid out parallel to the *cardo* and *decamanus,* forming blocks (*insulae*). At the corner of each *insula* a public fountain ran with water from the aqueduct. Each quadrant of the city had its purpose. In some cities, the lower rent districts were walled off from the wealthier citizens, a kind of early gated community.

In Rome, however, the Romans didn't have the advantage of beginning entirely from scratch. The Etruscan kings, who drained the marshes and created the civic, religious, and public spaces around which the later city grew, did the first central planning. Roman urban planning from then on consisted mostly of public works projects done on an *ad hoc* basis. The various forums were the public spaces in and around which most of this construction occurred. As Romans "romanized" foreign cities, they tended to focus rebuilding and development on forums and other urban projects that they identified with Roman civic identity. Urban planning, such as building codes and regulations (especially for fire), traffic regulation, and urban renewal projects, didn't begin until the very end of the Republic and Empire.

This sort of urban planning takes a kind of central authority that the Republic never had until Julius Caesar and Augustus made efforts to bring the teeming city into some kind of unified order. Of course, with such regulation came the dark minions of urban planning: boards of planning commissioners, inspectors, public works officials, and water meter readers.

Building for Victory

The Romans were famous for their engineering and building when it came to war. Roman legions had their own engineers, builders, stone masons, and surveyors. Their camps, earthworks, siege equipment, and catapults were legendary, as well as their ability to create and construct under horrendous conditions and in remarkable time.

Roman Camps

Roman military camps were set up, even while on the move, to protect troops and to serve as a defensive base. They had a standardized format so that everyone would know where things were, and troops were stationed within the walls according to military hierarchy. Camps were laid out in a square, surrounded by a ditch (*fossa*) and rampart walls of wood (*vallum*). Major encampments had towers added to the walls, and many permanent camps in the provinces became towns and then cities as settlements sprang up around them.

The camp was bisected by the *via principalis,* and troops were arranged by rank in lines perpendicular to it. There was a space of about 200 feet between the wall and the troops (*intervallum*). At the center stood the general's tent, the *praetorium,* flanked by centurions' tents and spaces for a forum and *quaestorium.* When camps were permanent, they included granaries to hold food, military hospitals, workshops, and VIP accommodations.

Roamin' the Romans

British place names with "Chester" or "Caster" come from Roman military *castra* (camps) that were located in Great Britain. These former camps are easy enough to recognize by their names, but there were many more camps than modern place-names preserve: At least 550 Roman military sites have been identified on the island. There are fine exhibits and museums all over Britain concerning its Roman heritage, including ones at major sites in Chester, York, and along Hadrian's Wall.

Siege Equipment

When attacking a city, the Romans first surrounded it with walls and ditches to keep the enemy trapped in the city and to prevent supplies and reinforcements from getting in. The ring might extend for many miles in circumference. The Romans then set to breaching the walls of the town in one way or the other. Approaches and workers were protected by wooden sheds, which were built out of enemy range and extended toward the wall until it was reached. Catapults and other troops covered the workers and tried to keep the enemy off the walls. To aid in this, Caesar built his own raised walls that were higher than those of the besieged town so that his men could fire more easily onto the wall and into the town.

Great Caesar's Ghost!

Catapults designed to shoot arrows and stones were first developed in Greece in the fifth century B.C.E. The Romans used two types of catapults: The *ballista* was a huge crossbow that shot arrows set afire; the *onager* shot stones. Each type of artillery came in various sizes. *Ballista* could fire arrows with deadly accuracy and in rapid succession depending on the size of projectiles that had to be loaded. Smaller *onegera* were mounted on wheels to be mobile. They shot either single stones or bags of stones, like huge shotguns, and had a range of about 1,400 feet. Large stationary *onagera* were the 16-inch guns of antiquity. They could hurl at the enemy up to 60-pound projectiles from half a mile away.

The main instrument for breaching the walls was an iron-tipped battering ram, called an *aries,* or a boring drill called a *terebra.* These were rolled up to the wall and were covered by a *testudo,* a structure with a fire-resistant roof. If they couldn't go through the wall, the Romans rolled a long work shed, called a *musculus* (mouse), up to the wall and dug a tunnel to the other side. Other times they constructed huge rolling assault towers and advanced them to the wall. From the top, soldiers would rain fire down on the defenders while a gangplank opened onto the wall and troops stationed inside the tower would rush across. With discipline in keeping supplies out and the inhabitants in, constant harassment of defenders, and aggressive try-and-try-again persistence, the Romans nearly always succeeded in finding a way to defeat a city.

The Least You Need to Know

➤ The Romans used their skills at tunneling, arches, and concrete to create enduring and practical structures.

➤ Roman roads were intended to serve in military defense. Major roads included sophisticated foundations, tunnels, road cuts, and elevated highways.

➤ Aqueducts were mostly constructed underground. Water distribution and plumbing were extremely sophisticated.

➤ Roman urban planning didn't begin until the end of the Republic. When Romans founded a small town they based its layout on the Roman *castra,* or military camp.

Part 3

Empire Without End: Roman Imperial History

Rome wasn't over with the Republic. Not by a long shot: You still couldn't hit the end of the Roman timeline with the best onager *(catapult). Augustus's Principate grew from the Republic's ashes into the Empire and at least another five hundred years of history. Or was it eight hundred years? Fourteen hundred? Fifteen? More?*

The next six chapters take you through the rise and fall of the Roman Empire as it was centered on Rome. We'll see emperors from the ridiculous to the sublime and watch the center of power shift away from "old" Rome to the provinces and finally to Nova Roma ("New Rome"), or Constantinople. Did Rome "fall" or "fall apart" in the West under the avalanche of barbarian invasions? Or had it simply packed up and moved corporate headquarters with Constantine?

Chapter 13

Easing into Empire

In This Chapter

➤ How Octavian transformed Rome

➤ The principate as transition between Republic and Dominate (Monarchy) during the Empire

➤ Octavian's policies as Augustus and as *princeps*

➤ Problems with Augustus's succession for the Julio-Claudians

By the time of Octavian's victory over Antony in 30 B.C.E., the Republic lay in ruins. The nobility and upper classes had been decimated by the wars. The senate, packed and repacked by Caesar and the triumvirs (Octavian, Antony, and Lepidus, discussed in Chapter 7, "Let's Conquer ... Ourselves! The Roman Revolution and the End of the Republic"), was too large to be effective and anyway lacked men of both character and experience to be effective. Besides, the "constitution" had now been changed, circumvented, or completely ignored for so long and in so many ways that it would be hard to know which Republic to return to. The economy was in ruins, the food supply was in jeopardy, and hundreds of thousands of people were homeless and dislocated. Moreover, the armies of the triumvirs, ostensibly Caesar's army, was now a restless and dangerous giant—homeless, unpaid, and without a settlement plan.

In short, the drive to be preeminent in prestige, power, and authority had destroyed the state that Romans like Caesar wanted to preside over. But it had also shown that the structure of the old Republic was incapable of governing both itself and its empire without strong centralized control. So long as politicians had the means to develop sufficient military power to threaten the state or could use violence at home to achieve political ends, there would be no order. And yet, the essence of the Republic was *against* centralized power and functioned, in the main, because it allowed for participation and competition; moreover, as the assassination of Caesar in 44 B.C.E. had shown, the Romans were unwilling to submit to anyone who appeared to be a king. Something new was needed, and in the aftermath of Octavian's victory over Antony at Actium, Rome needed it *now*.

In this chapter, we'll see how Octavian and the Romans transformed the Republic into an Empire, and transformed Octavian from Caesar's heir into the *princeps* and first Roman emperor, Augustus.

Okay, Now What?

The Mediterranean was exhausted and eager for some kind of stability and peace. Octavian was hailed as that peacemaker from the east to the west and returned to Rome in 29 B.C.E. to more than a hero's welcome. But what would he do? Clearly he was in the position to do *something*. Besides public adulation, he commanded the armies of Rome, had complete political authority, and possessed the vast wealth of Egypt as a personal fortune. Octavian would need all these, and the same guile and determination that he displayed in coming to power, to create stability. He did so remarkably well, walking a fine line between restoring the Republic and maintaining personal control over the military and political levers of power.

Great Caesar's Ghost!

Augustus's unofficial and official titles have later derivatives. Besides getting "principate" and "prince" from *princeps*, and "emperor" from imperator, his title of Caesar became an official name for the Byzantine emperors, and the source of both "kaiser" and "czar."

Officially, through powers given to him by the state, and unofficially, through his personal authority, Octavian presided over a Republic, which carried on (at least in name) as before but under the watchful and controlling grip of "Augustus," its *princeps*, Caesar, and imperator. Under Octavian's long tenure, Rome grew in stability, prosperity, literature and culture, while at the same time, the Republic evolved into a monarchy governing the Empire.

Octavian = Augustus

Before things get too confusing, you have to know that the triumvir "Octavian" and the princeps and emperor "Augustus" are names for the same person. The senate gave Octavian the name Augustus, which means Revered One, in 27 B.C.E. Giving Romans special names in recognition of their service was nothing new (remember Scipio Africanus or Sulla Felix or

Pompeius Magnus?), but here it's important to remember because classicists and historians refer to the upcoming period as the Augustan Age. If you miss it, all of a sudden Octavian disappears, and you read about this great Augustus and wonder "Where in the *infernis* did *this* guy come from?"

The Principate: It's the Same, Only Different

It's also easy to get confused with the term *Principate,* which was the transition between the Republic and rule of the Empire by a monarch. The Principate originates with Augustus (29 B.C.E.–C.E. 14), who ruled Rome as the *princeps,* or "first citizen," of Rome. It's an ambiguous title, but it reflects how much Augustus was able to deal with situations as they arose as much by means of his personal authority as simply by military or legal might.

Augustus's successors, however, continued to wear the title of *princeps*, and you'll read about the "principate" of various emperors until the time of Diocletian. At this point, the Principate ends and gives way to the "Dominate," because under Diocletian the emperor was officially recognized as *dominus* ("lord and master"). The practical transition to monarchy happened so much faster than the transition in official titles that, when people talk about the "Principate," they often mean "Principate (of Augustus)."

The Augustan Ages

The last century of the Republic had demonstrated that the Sullan conception of returning Rome to the "ancient constitution" (read: control by the senate and nobility) was inoperable. Caesar's career had shown the power of popular support and that centralized authority was needed, but he had been too obviously *autocratic* for the Roman nobility to tolerate. Antony's fall from power demonstrated that both the support of the nobility and a broad

When in Rome

The **Principate** (from *princeps,* "first citizen") covers the period from Augustus (27 B.C.E.) to the emperor **Diocletian** (C.E. 293).

The **Dominate** (from Latin *dominus,* "lord and master") covers the period from Diocletian (C.E. 293) forward.

The **Empire** generally refers to the period after the Principate of Augustus (C.E. 14) when it is clear (at least to us) that the Roman Empire was ruled by an emperor, whether he was officially recognized as a *princeps* or *dominus.*

Veto!

The term "Augustan Age" often applies to a literary period centered on Augustus's rule—it doesn't coincide precisely with Augustus's reign. Classicists usually think of this Augustan Age as dating from the death of Caesar (44 B.C.E.) to the death of the poet Ovid (C.E. 17).

When in Rome

Autocracy is rule by one person (the autocrat), whose power is unlimited and who rules subject to no higher power or authority. You don't need an official autocracy for someone to be an autocrat or to act in an autocratic fashion!

appeal to Roman patriotism and values were essential for maintaining control.

Octavian had to find a kind of hybrid solution that would be acceptable to all classes, and would balance Rome's need for central authority and stability with its tradition of freedom, participation, and individual ambition in the service of the state. You can roughly divide the evolution of his solution into three periods. These periods track a seesaw settling of Augustus's powers from extraordinary powers as triumvir to the established powers of an emperor, and the transition of the Roman state from Republic in emergency mode to monarchy with a republican veneer.

From Actium Until 27 B.C.E.

From 30 B.C.E. to 27 B.C.E., Octavian governed Rome as a sole ruler, but without any real formal definition to his duties and powers. He had allowed the law authorizing the powers of the triumvirs to lapse in 33 B.C.E. to deny legitimacy to Antony. The Romans had voted him a wide array of privileges and powers in the jubilation following Actium, and many cities and citizens had taken an oath of personal allegiance to him.

Even so, Octavian seems to have held off from trying to either solidify his authoritarian powers as Caesar had done, or to define his role vis-à-vis the senate, until things began to settle and he could see what was to be done for the long term. Officially, he was voted consul in 31 B.C.E. and every year after and remained imperator in command of the army. He, and a small group of intimates such as Maecenas and Agrippa, personally managed the affairs of the Empire and used his personal fortune to stabilize the entire system.

Caius Cilnius Maecenas became extremely powerful and influential as Augustus's friend, advisor, and patron of literature and the poets Virgil and Horace. Although he never held and office, he was Octavian's representative at many important occasions. Their friendship was said to have cooled somewhat in their later years, although Maecenas left a magnificent Roman estate to Augustus at his death around 8 B.C.E.

Marcus Vepsanius Agrippa was Octavian's right hand military commander and advisor. Agrippa was responsible for nearly all of Octavian's military successes on land and at sea, including Actium. Agrippa remained integral to Augustus's principate, and Augustus probably intended Agrippa to succeed him. He temporarily gave Agrippa his signet ring when it looked like he might die of illness in 23 B.C.E., gradually made Agrippa nearly his equal in power, and had him marry his daughter, Julia. But Agrippa died suddenly in 12 B.C.E. with children too young, and succession passed eventually to Augustus's stepson, Tiberius.

27–19 B.C.E.

In 27 B.C.E., Octavian convened the senate. He claimed that the burdens of sole leadership had become too great, and that the time had come for him to make good on his promises to return the state to the senate and people of Rome. He dramatically resigned his powers and declared that he had restored the Republic. The senate (at least those who had been unprepared) was stunned. It pleaded with Augustus to retain some part in the state, and he agreed to accept command and control of the provinces and legions of Gaul, Spain, Syria, and Egypt. The senate voted him the title "Augustus" in gratitude.

Although this meeting was probably carefully gauged and staged by Augustus, his supporters, and advisors, it marks the beginning of a seesaw settling in of official rights and powers between Augustus and the senate. Augustus remained one of the consuls until 23 B.C.E., when a near fatal illness seems to have changed his approach. From then, Augustus seems to have shifted his attention both to creating a successor and to establishing the position and powers of the *princeps.* He resigned the consulship. In its place, he retained command and control of the imperial provinces, but this command was declared to be *maius,* meaning greater than other authorities. In place of the consulship, he was given tribunician powers for life. This gave him the power of presenting and vetoing legislation, interceding where he saw fit for the good of the Roman people.

Roamin' the Romans

Augustus bragged that he had "found Rome in brick, and left it in marble." When you visit Rome, you can see one of these projects, the Pantheon, which was first constructed during this period. The building was destroyed by fire and rebuilt by the emperors Hadrian and Severus. The facade bears the title, *M Agrippa L f cos tertium fecit:* "Marcus Agrippa, son of Lucius, built this as consul for the third time."

19 B.C.E.–C.E. 14

In 19 B.C.E., Augustus received consular powers for life. Scholars debate the precise reasons why the shifts in powers and titles between 27, 23, and 19 B.C.E. came about. Nevertheless, it's clear that Augustus and the Romans were finding their way, within their own tolerances and with some semblance of rules, to something new that they didn't have, and for the most part didn't want, a name for.

From 19 B.C.E. onward, however, Augustus seems to have firmly established the power of his principate. His pervasive power and authority settled in to become a regular and (for the most part) accepted part of Rome. Elections continued, the senate met, debated, and managed a portion of the state, and trials were held, but all with a nod, a nudge, or with the conspicuous deference of the *princeps.* Romans not only looked to Augustus to guide matters, it practically demanded that he approve or sanction them. By the time that he was made *pontifex maximus* in 5 B.C.E., Augustus had come to both embody and symbolize Rome.

Besides administering the Empire, Augustus was primarily concerned about firming up the Roman borders and establishing a successor. He was never in good health, and a nearly fatal illness in 23 B.C.E. put the question of succession on the front burner. Although that was technically up to the Roman senate and people, it was up to Augustus to assure a smooth transition and to avoid another civil war after his death. He had difficulty with this. Although Augustus tried to arrange for a successor from the Julian side of his family to follow him, he eventually was forced to settle on Livia's son, Tiberius, who peacefully succeeded Augustus after his death in C.E. 14.

Augustus's Powers

Augustus's gradual, though decisive, approach to the principate can be summed up in one of his favorite expressions: *festina lente*, "Make haste, slowly." This, coupled with Augustus's willingness to intervene and oversee practically everything, and his 41-year position at Rome's helm, allowed for the changes he brought about to become, for the most part, permanent.

Lend Me Your Ears

"He abandoned being a triumvir and fashioned himself a consul or, as tribune, content to protect the people. When he had seduced the military with gifts, the people with food, and all with sweet tranquility, he gradually usurped the powers of the senate, magistrates, and courts. No real opposition remained—the bravest men were casualties of battle and proscriptions. He elevated the remaining nobility financially and politically according to their willingness to serve him and they, enriched by his regime, preferred the safety of their new arrangement to the dangers of the old. Nor did the provinces object: competition and greed of the wealthy and the governors had undermined the Republic's legitimacy; power, favoritism, and primarily money had rendered the laws no help whatsoever."

—Tacitus, *The Annals of Rome*, 1.2

If you look back at his career, you see that Augustus's official powers stemmed from his control of the imperial provinces and their armies, his continuous power as consul or proconsul or tribune. These, however, are only an expression of the personal power and authority that Augustus had over Rome. The Romans not only recognized him as the *princeps,* but (and with good reason) as the *pater patriae,* "father of his country." Augustus's prestige went hand in hand with his political and military powers, and he could use his immense personal wealth, which was sufficient to bail the entire state and military out of several financial crises, to bring about results. In addition, Augustus formed and sometimes served on municipal boards, served on juries, heard cases, and advanced a whole cultural, not just political, agenda for the reforming Roman state. He was, in effect, everywhere.

Rome Under Augustus

Augustus transformed Rome—that is, both the city of Rome and the larger Roman provincial system—from a patchwork of provincial administrations loosely (or in name only) supervised by Rome to a truly imperial system centered on an imperial capital and administered by a budding imperial bureaucracy. While he revolutionized Roman politics, Augustus fashioned himself a social conservative, and in propaganda, as well as in his personal life, expounded a Rome still founded on old-fashioned and traditional Roman values and mores. The economic boom, relative stability, and cultural resurgence brought forth a literary and artistic boom that became Rome's Golden Age of literature.

Getting Back to Roman Values

Augustus promoted a broad "back to traditional values" program in Rome that went hand in hand with creating the impression of continuity and stability. These included campaigns in religion, social values, and civic pride. He restored temples and resurrected ancient religious offices such as the *flamen dialis* (see Chapter 9, "The Romans Among Themselves," for more about the flamen). He instituted morality laws and laws penalizing unmarried individuals as well as rewards for marriage and children. Laws against extravagant expenditures were passed in keeping with traditional Roman frugality. Ancient noble families were brought into the civic limelight once more, and the civic unity of Italy was encouraged and celebrated.

Augustus himself modeled his conservative approach in public; the biographer Suetonius marveled at his modest (by that time's standards) accommodations on the Palatine. Augustus and his advisor Maecenas encouraged literature (such as the *Aeneid* of Virgil and Horace's *Odes*) that promoted these values, and Augustan monuments, such as the Ara Pacis Augustae, portrayed him and his family as pious and traditional role models.

Augustus's daughter, Julia, was Augustus's Achilles' heel on the role model front. He married her to Marcellus, Agrippa, and Tiberius in order to procure a direct heir. Notorious for her affairs and sexual appetites, and a loose cannon as the potential mother of Julian heirs from who-knows where, Julia was finally banished by Augustus to the little island of Pandateria in 2 B.C.E. He allowed her to return in C.E. 3, but only so far as the very tip of Italy at Rhegium, where she remained until her death.

In the City

Augustus and his colleagues such as Agrippa worked to transform Rome with monumental public works projects and buildings that projected the image of a great world capital and played upon the principate as the fulfillment of a long progression of traditional Roman history. These projects included …

➤ The first imperial forum (the Forum of Augustus).

➤ Great temples such as that of Mars the Avenger, the Pantheon, and the temple of Apollo (the first to be made entirely of the white Carrara marble with which Rome is associated).

➤ Public libraries and baths.

➤ The Theater of Marcellus.

➤ The great Mausoleum of Augustus, which served as the imperial tomb for over 100 years.

➤ Aqueducts and roads.

➤ The *Ara Pacis Augustae* (Altar of Augustan Peace).

On the Borders

Augustus worked to fully conquer and solidify the borders of the Roman Empire, and discouraged expansionist policies. He worked through his prefect, Gallius, to solidify the southern border of Egypt against African invasions, and came to an eventual settlement with the Parthians through Tiberius over the eastern border and Armenia. With this settlement, he regained the standards lost with Crassus's defeat, and gained an enormous propaganda victory without a great war. His forces subdued, fortified, and reinforced the borders along the Alps, the Danube, and the Rhine, and established military colonies in Spain and Gaul. He attempted to push the frontier in Germany to the more easily defendable Elbe, but the disaster at the Teutoburg Forest made him change his mind and resolve to keep the border along the Danube and Rhine.

Remains of the Forum Augustum and the Temple of Mars Ultor (Mars the Avenger), where Julius

Caesar's sword was kept.

In conjunction with the building and expansion at

Rome, the provinces also saw a period of economic stability, growth, and prosperity. This was encouraged by Augustan building programs, colonization, urban development, and road building, especially in the west.

Great Caesar's Ghost!

P. Quinctilius Varus, Augustus's governor of Germany, was attempting to put down a rebellion in C.E. 9 led by the chieftain Arminius. Arminius's army surprised three legions in the Teutoburg Forest (between Osnabruck and Padoborn) and massacred them. Varus committed suicide. The disaster stunned the aging Augustus. He wandered the halls calling on the dead Varus to return his legions, and withdrew from attempts to conquer Germany to the Elbe. Later, Tiberius's adopted nephew Germanicus defeated Arminius's forces, but without establishing Roman control in Germany. Arminius was eventually murdered by his own feuding family.

The Era of Big Government

In order to communicate with and manage both the provinces directly under the *princeps* and his involvement in the affairs of state, Augustus and his advisors developed a fledgling bureaucracy, which was to become the vast imperial administrative system of the later Empire. This system was especially important for the class of equites, who served as financial administrators and imperial representatives in the provinces, and the class of freedmen (freed slaves), who took over the keeping of imperial correspondence, records, and accounting.

Freedmen were to become extremely important and powerful in the Empire, and some became more powerful than any senator or equites. They were part of the administration, and had the ability to bring matters to the attention of the emperor (or not), to make sure that things ran smoothly (or not), and to grease the wheels of imperial bureaucracy and finance (or not).

Not Too Successful with Succession

The area in which Augustus's efforts were the least successful was in his attempts to secure a successor from his own Julian line. Here he showed that, beneath the public image and rhetoric, the principate became, especially in the mind of its architect, essentially a hereditary kingship. His convoluted attempts at establishing a hereditary dynasty were to plague the entire history of succession in the Empire.

Augustus had few direct descendants. He had one child, Julia, by Scribonia, whom he had divorced (on the day of Julia's birth) to marry Livia. Other than Julia, his closest heirs were the children of his sister, Octavia. There was a son, Marcellus, who was the product of Octavia's first marriage to Gaius Claudius Marcellus. He was about the same age as Livia's son, Tiberius. Then there were two daughters, Antonia Maior (the elder) and Antonia Minor (the younger), who were the children of Octavia and Mark Antony.

Technically, of course, Augustus could not name a successor, but he could, as he did with other magistrates, make it known whom *he* would choose. Augustus's first choice was his nephew Marcellus, whom he married to his daughter Julia in order to solidify the family tree in 24 B.C.E. Unfortunately, Marcellus died unexpectedly in 23 B.C.E.

Trying to Get Agrippa on It

The death of Marcellus and the near fatal illness of Augustus himself brought his friend, colleague, and general, Agrippa, to the fore. When it looked like he might die, Augustus indicated Agrippa as a successor by giving him his personal signet ring. Over the next 10 years, he groomed Agrippa as the heir apparent. He married Julia to him in 21 B.C.E. She bore Agrippa three sons (Gaius Caesar, Lucius Caesar, and Agrippa Postumus) and two daughters (Julia and Agrippina). Augustus adopted his sons in 17 B.C.E. Agrippa's powers and responsibilities were gradually increased until they were nearly equal with Augustus's. Then, Agrippa became ill and died suddenly and unexpectedly in 12 B.C.E.

Turning to Tiberius

Agrippa's sons were too young to rule, so Augustus turned to Tiberius. It was clear, however, that Tiberius was only a stopgap. Augustus forced him to divorce his wife and marry Julia. Tiberius, apparently put out by the whole thing, retired to the island of Rhodes. But Lucius and Gaius both died young, and Augustus had to turn to Tiberius, who was 50, and again adopted him in C.E. 4. He was, like Agrippa, given powers commensurate with Augustus. Augustus continued, however, to try to ensure some Julian would follow him by having Tiberius adopt Germanicus, the 18-year-old son of Antonia Minor. Germanicus was married to Agrippina, the daughter of Agrippa and Julia, so Augustus hoped that finally a nice, clean Julian line would be assured.

When in Rome

Adoption (*adoptio*) was a legal action whereby a Roman citizen entered another family under the *potestas* of its head. In the Republic, both men and women could adopt. Some Romans used adoption to move between classes for political advantage; others, such as the emperors, indicated successors by adopting the man (at times as old or older than himself) whom he wished to succeed him as his son.

Roamin' the Romans

In Ankara, Turkey, you can find an inscription of the *Res Gestae* (Accomplishments), Augustus's autobiographical account of his achievements. Augustus had this text put on bronze tablets for display on his mausoleum in Rome. The original is lost; fragments remain from the copies that were put on public monuments in the provinces, of which the copy in Ankara is the best preserved.

Intriguing or Intrigue?

It didn't turn out that way. As we'll see, Augustus's torturous attempts to forge a hereditary dynasty created a complex intermingling of families, rivalries, jealousies, and competing ambitions. The combination of unforeseen and early deaths, larger-than-life personalities, and complex infighting led authors (such as Tacitus) to suspect foul play at every turn both before and after Augustus's death. But at least when Augustus died in C.E. 14, the transition to Tiberius seemed as well-prepared as it could be. Octavian had stepped into a republic in civil, military, financial, and social crisis. As Augustus, he left it a stable, prosperous empire fumbling a bit through its first succession.

The Least You Need to Know

➤ Octavian and Augustus refer to the same person in different stages of career.

➤ The principate refers to the era of Roman government that originated in Augustus's evolving balance of military, civil, and personal powers.

➤ Augustus stabilized Rome internally and externally and was, for the most part, both successful and popular.

➤ Augustus carried out reform efforts in civic, religious, and moral practices that he promoted as a return to traditional ways and values.

➤ Augustus's efforts at securing a direct heir were unsuccessful.

Chapter 14

All in the Family: The Julio-Claudian Emperors

In This Chapter

➤ The Julio-Claudian dynasty and the development of the principate

➤ Tiberius, stepson of Augustus

➤ Gaius (Caligula), the megalomaniac "Little Boots"

➤ Claudius—half-wit or clever emperor?

➤ Nero, the flamboyant showman burned by his own self-aggrandizement

After the death of Augustus in C.E. 14, the first Roman emperors of the emerging Empire belonged to two hereditary dynasties. The first was Augustus's own family; the second came to power in the chaos that followed the death of Nero.

In this chapter, we'll follow the careers of the Julio-Claudians, who are the most famous (and infamous) emperors of the time. Besides their larger-than-life personalities, we'll see how the imperial family, staff, and personal bodyguard of the emperor (the Praetorian Guard) became more powerful and influential than the senate.

As you can see from the accompanying chart of the Julio-Claudian dynasty (the thing that looks roughly like a schematic for a circuit board), Augustus's tenacious attempts to ensure that a Julian would inherit his position created a tangled web of marriages, divorces, adoptions, and sour grapes that would make any soap opera producer proud. You have to admit that it was successful in that, of the first four emperors (Tiberius, Gaius, Claudius, and Nero), only Tiberius had no Julio in his Claudian. But if Augustus could have seen what kind of rivalries, not to mention what kinds of emperors, came of his efforts (in Gaius and Nero), he may have rethought his strategy.

The tortuous Julio-Claudian dynasty.

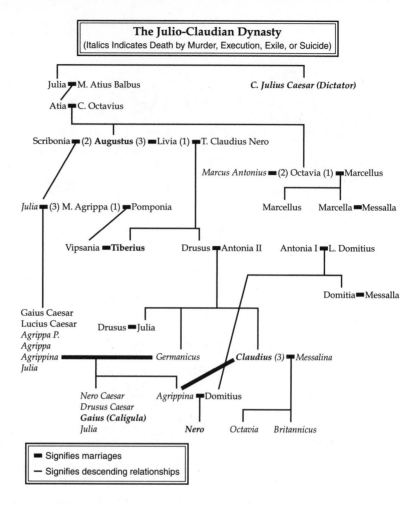

The Julio-Claudian Dynasty
(Italics Indicates Death by Murder, Execution, Exile, or Suicide)

Tiberius (c.e. 14–37)

Tiberius was proud, dour, and embittered by Augustus's treatment of him and by his marriage to Julia in 12 B.C.E. He did what was asked of him well, but probably would rather have pursued other things. Passed over most of his life for younger Julians and forced to divorce his wife and marry Julia as a caretaker, he had retired to Rhodes and was later yanked back to Rome when young Julians kept dropping like flies. By Augustus's death, he was 56, a well-trained general and administrator, and obviously the heir apparent. He already shared Augustus's *imperium* and tribunician powers. The transition went smoothly.

In many respects, Tiberius was a success as an emperor. He was an experienced and efficient administrator, and judicious with foreign policy. He consolidated Augustus's borders, firmed up the frontier with Germany, and stabilized the eastern Empire mostly through diplomacy with the Parthians. In all the provinces, he worked at financial and tax reform, instituted the building of roads and other public works, and appointed (mostly) qualified governors. He also encouraged provincials to communicate directly with the emperor when they felt that the governors were not handling things properly. Economically, the Empire went through a boom, and Tiberius was able to reduce taxes and still leave Rome 20 times better off than he had found it.

But to turn a campaign phrase, "it's not just the economy, stupid." Tiberius's principate was marred by personality conflicts with the senate, suspicions of imperial intrigue, and struggles within his administration to become the next *princeps*.

Veto!

Our sources for the early Roman emperors are biased against them. The historians Dio, Suetonius, and Tacitus all belonged to a class of senators who had good reason to resent the growth of imperial power. These writers tended to favor (or even foster) dark, scandalous, and scurrilous explanations and reports over others.

Germanicus and Agrippina

Tiberius's primary conflicts within the family came from his popular and volatile nephew, Germanicus, and his popular, volatile, and ambitious wife, Agrippina the Elder.

Germanicus was a good commander but a loose cannon, prone to overstepping his bounds at the prospect of a great war for the glory of Rome (and the glory of Germanicus). Tiberius sent him to fight Arminius (who defeated Varus) in Germany. Although he was largely successful, he was also reckless. Tiberius recalled him from Germany and sent him to the east, where he again overstepped himself against the Parthians and in Egypt (the *princeps*'s personal province). Tiberius suspected that Germanicus and Agrippina were attempting to build popular support against him and moved against Germanicus in the senate.

Germanicus also came into conflict with Piso, Tiberius's governor of Syria. Piso refused to recognize Germanicus's authority, and Germanicus ordered the uncooperative Piso to go home. Then Germanicus took mysteriously ill. As he died, he accused Piso of using sorcery and poison against him and called for vengeance. Piso later committed suicide. This set up a simmering public and private confrontation between the *princeps* and his mother, Livia, and Agrippina and her supporters in the senate, who suspected (or encouraged the suspicion) that Piso and Tiberius had been behind Germanicus's death.

Despot or Dilbert?

Tiberius's relations with the senate were uncomfortable and frustrating. It was, in the words of today's human resources personnel, a bad fit. He disliked pretense and lacked Augustus's diplomacy. He tried to make the senate a partner in managing the state and

187

When in Rome

Maiestas, or prosecutable treason, came to include, by Julius Caesar's time, affronts to the dignity of the state. This law could become a capricious and dangerous political weapon in the hands of emperors (who were the state) and in the hands of unscrupulous accusers called delatores.

Roamin' the Romans

When in Italy, you can visit the hauntingly beautiful remains of Tiberius's Villa Jovis, the best preserved of his 12 villas on the island of Capri. This remote and secluded site says a lot about Tiberius's need for privacy, study, and his desire to remain apart from the pretentious and contentious role into which he had been thrust as Augustus's eventual heir.

encouraged senators to speak their minds. Nevertheless, his proud nature and surly mannerisms were ill suited to inspiring confidence in how open he really was.

The more Tiberius pushed, the more senators balked. All knew that the *princeps* possessed the ultimate power and, eventually, that accusations of *maiestas* (real or contrived) could come against them. A senator once asked, "Would you please tell me when you're going to vote? If you go first I'll have an example to follow; if you go last I'm afraid that I might accidentally disagree with you." This reality led to Tiberius's increasing distaste for the senate (whom he once called "men too ready to serve") and the politics of Rome. He eventually withdrew from Rome to Capri, where he governed from afar and, for a time, through his prefect, Sejanus.

Sejanus

Lucius Aelius Sejanus rose to power as Prefect (commander) of the Praetorian Guard, a position that became powerful and influential. Sejanus "protected" the *princeps*'s interests, and convinced Tiberius to remove himself from the increasingly dangerous capital to Capri.

Sejanus was, however, scheming for himself. Gradually Sejanus's powers were increased, and he virtually ruled Rome through power and prosecution while keeping Tiberius largely in the dark. He battled Agrippina's faction and married into the imperial family. Only Caligula, whom Tiberius had named as an heir, stood between him and the principate. There was a plot, and here something went very wrong for Sejanus. Antonia the Younger, Gaius's grandmother, sent a secret envoy on a mission to Tiberius and was able to reach him. Gaius was whisked to safety with Tiberius at Capri.

Tiberius turned on Sejanus in a way that was fitting for a student of Greek tragedy and rhetoric. He sent a carefully guarded letter to the senate. The letter first praised Sejanus, then expressed reservations, moved to accusations, and ended in a scathing condemnation and call for execution. The senate complied, and by nightfall, a mob had brutally and gleefully dispatched Sejanus, his family, and their supporters.

Stay Away ... and Stay Dead

After Sejanus, Tiberius was determined to root out the conspiracy that he thought might have extended even beyond Sejanus. He continued to rule from the seclusion of Capri until 37, when the dying *princeps* attempted to return to Rome, probably, as a last act, to arrange for a successor other than Caligula. He fell into a coma on the way. He is said to have revived temporarily, but Sejanus's successor Macro (who had had already nominated Caligula at Rome as the succeeding *princeps*) came and smothered Tiberius with his own bedding.

Gaius (Caligula) (c.e. 37–41)

Although Tiberius saved Gaius from Sejanus, Tiberius never really groomed Gaius for the responsibilities of becoming *princeps* and probably would have preferred his own grandson, Tiberius Gemellus, whom he made a co-heir. Tiberius probably saw in Caligula what others later wished they had seen. But Tiberius died before Gemellus could come of sufficient age, and without dissent the senate accepted Caligula, the son of the popular Germanicus and Agrippina, as *princeps*.

Caligula had spent a good deal of his life with his grandmother Antonia in the company of eastern potentates and with Tiberius in the confines of Capri. His models for a ruler were more autocratic than Augustan. Nevertheless, he had a very popular start. His courteous and generous manner pleased people and senate; he cut back the *delatores* and acted to consolidate and unify the imperial family. He also announced a return to the glory of expansion with big plans to attack both Parthia and Britain. Things were very upbeat. Then he became ill and almost died.

Veto!

Tiberius's seclusion at Capri led to reports of his cruelty, debauchery, sexual perversions, and sorcery. These reports made for great fodder for writers like Suetonius. In reality, Tiberius surrounded himself with the scholars and tutors that he really enjoyed and was probably busier with these and with running the empire than with sexual escapades.

Great Caesar's Ghost!

Caligula got his name from spending time with his father, Germanicus, and his mother, Agrippina, on campaigns along the Rhine. The soldiers affectionately dressed their commander's son as a mini legionnaire, complete with the little boots (*caligulae*) that became Gaius's moniker.

When in Rome

Delatores were informers who accused others of treason or other offenses against the state. By law, delatores received one quarter of the property of the accused upon conviction (kind of like turning someone in for tax evasion today). Tiberius, contrary to some accounts, did not institute a reign of terror with this law, but his precedent-setting uses of it and the delatores became infamous.

When in Rome

A **megalomaniac** (Greek for "huge madness") has delusions of grandeur and conceives of himself as a person or divinity of enormous power and prestige.

Something Lost in the Recovery

Whether it was an effect of the illness, the psychological stress of a brush with death, the absolute corruption of absolute power, or some combination of all three, Caligula emerged from his illness a whacked *megalomaniac.*

Determined to prove that he was immortal, Caligula exalted himself as a god in the manner of an Egyptian pharaoh. He sat in temples, dressed as one of the gods, and engaged the gods in conversation. He perpetrated outlandish acts such as appointing his favorite horse, Incitatus, to the senate. He humiliated senators by forcing them to swear to lay down their lives for him and his sisters and to serve them like slaves at table. He squandered the surplus that Tiberius had accumulated on incredibly stupid and garish expenditures until he had to raise taxes and go after personal property with prosecutions and *maiestas* trials.

Schizophrenic Adventures

Caligula was erratic with foreign polity. His insistence on being recognized as a god in the temples of other gods nearly caused a revolt among the Jews (avoided by his death). Longing to be another Alexander the Great, he careened from decision to decision, from big plan to big plan, but never really followed through with any of them. He built a bridge from boats over the Bay of Baiae and rode his horse across wearing Alexander's breastplate (part of the bridge sunk in the drunken celebration that followed). He marched an army to the channel for his grand invasion of Britain, erected lighthouses at Boulongne and Dover, and then suddenly abandoned the expedition. He did, however, order his soldiers to gather seashells in their helmets to take back as "spoils from the sea." (Imagine the T-shirts: "My legion went to Britain, and all I got ….")

Enough Is Enough

Caligula was just as unbalanced with the imperial household. He had Gemellus killed, as well as Macro, who had replaced Sejanus as praetorian prefect and had proposed

Caligula as *princeps*. (Ironically, he seems to have spared his uncle Claudius because he was thought to be an idiot and not a threat.) Finally, four years of him was enough. Senators, members of the imperial household, and military agreed to kick a little booty (pun intended). A disgruntled praetorian killed Caligula in a secret passage, and the praetorians ran amok in the palace.

Rome was rid of a tyrant, but nobody had a plan for what to do next. For a brief moment, a group of senators had a chance to effect some kind of change. They debated whether to return to the Republic or to adopt an elected principate. Deliberations were cut short, however, by the announcement that the Praetorian Guard had proclaimed Caligula's uncle, Tiberius Claudius Nero Germanicus, *princeps*. The senate protested, but this was a done deal. Opportunity knocked, and then was gone. The senate approved the new *princeps*.

Roamin' the Romans

When in England, head to Dover. Upon the white cliffs, the lighthouse at the castle of Dover is the oldest in England, built by Caligula for the grand, but abandoned, conquest of all Britain.

Claudius (C.E. 41–54)

Suetonius tells a great story about how the praetorians, ransacking the palace, spotted feet jutting out from behind a curtain. Ripping it aside, they found the cowering Claudius, the 50-year-old stuttering imperial family buffoon. Instead of killing him (as they did Caligula's sisters and daughter), they carried him off like a mascot to the barracks where they proclaimed him emperor.

Like most of Suetonius's stories, however, things were more complicated than that. When Claudius was discovered, he was smart enough to work the situation and become emperor. He recognized that the power lay in the Praetorian Guard's hands, offered them large bonuses to support him (a disastrous precedent), and seized the day. Pretty smart moves for an idiot.

Lend Me Your Ears

"Because Caligula was bald, he made it a crime for anyone to look down on him from above as he passed along, or to utter the word 'goat' for any reason whatsoever. He even made a great effort to render his naturally horrible face hideous as well by practicing each and every look of terror and dread in front of the mirror."

—Suetonius, *Caligula*, 50

Will the Real Claudius Please Stand Up?

There are two conflicting views of Claudius. Some see him as someone mistaken for an idiot who became an educated and effective emperor at the center of an efficient imperial administration. Others see him as a marginally functional man managed by the imperial household (or, as Dio says, "by slaves and his wives") and an effective administration of freedmen who really ran the empire.

The evidence can go both ways, because the essential character at the center of the Empire is a mystery. If you look at what his administration did, you would tend to favor the former view; if you look at the ancient sources (which are biased to be sure), his personal life, and a few candid moments, you begin to suspect that the emperor was without his genius at least part of the time.

Most contemporaries, however, thought Claudius a freak. A birth defect or early childhood seizure had given him a deformed physique, a head he couldn't hold still, strange expressions on his face, and stammering speech. These physical traits may have gone hand in hand with mental or developmental impairments, or simply been taken to indicate them. Claudius was also (understandably) very socially awkward and timid. Caligula made him into the imperial court jester.

Augustus had, however, recognized there was more to Claudius than met the eye. His letters and actions show that, although he never meant for Claudius to have a public presence and distrusted his ability to be influenced, the *princeps* thought that Claudius had a brain. He gave him scholars (such as the historian Livy) and scientists as tutors, and Claudius eventually became a published expert on Roman law, history, and languages (Etruscan and Carthaginian). He never had, however, direct experience with imperial administration or military command before becoming emperor.

Freedmen and Administration

As emperor, Claudius followed Augustan tradition and participated in senate meetings, encouraged senators to take up their duties seriously, and (with his interest in law) was very active in the courts. These attempts were mostly met with suspicion and the same kind of awkward posturing that Tiberius had experienced.

Great Caesar's Ghost!

Claudius not only suffered indignities during his lifetime, but was ridiculed after his death by Nero in his accession speech, and by the famous author and philosopher Seneca (Nero's tutor), who wrote a satirical work about a botched deification of Claudius, called the *Apolcolocyntosis*. This roughly translates, instead of "Claudius becomes a god," as (pun intended) "Claudius becomes a gourd."

Great Caesar's Ghost!

Roman intervention in Britain under Claudius was in part instigated by British chieftains who feared the growing power of the kingdom of Comulodunum (Colchester). Its great king, Cunobelinus, was the source of Shakespeare's *Cymbeline*. His son, Caratacus, championed both British independence (under *his* rule, of course) and Druidism until defeated by Claudius's troops in C.E. 43.

In addition, Claudius streamlined and centralized many administrative functions for the empire in a working cabinet of talented and ambitious freedmen. Chief among them was Narcissus, his cabinet secretary, and Pallas, the minister of finance. The senators hated and envied the freedmen's power, wealth, influence, and access. Nevertheless, under Claudius, Britain, Thrace, and Mauretania (North Africa) were added to the Empire, provincial citizenship and urbanization was increased, and the Empire thrived generally. Great building projects, such as the artificial harbor of Ostia, were also part of Claudius's principate.

Watch Out for the Wives

Claudius's reign was haunted by personal problems with and weaknesses for gambling, drinking, and wives. These are probably understandable, given the way he was treated. While drinking and gambling didn't turn out to be a terrible problem, his troubles with women did. He divorced his first two wives for adultery, and then was married by Caligula to Messalina Valeria, another Julian, and only 15 years old.

Claudius doted on her and she bore him a son, Britannicus (named in honor of the conquest of Britain), whom Claudius favored as his heir. Messalina, however, spent most of her energy messin' around. She not only slept around, but allied herself with Claudius's freedmen to manipulate Claudius. Among other things, she used her influence with him to prosecute and execute her enemies and former lovers. Finally, she contrived with a lover, the consul Gaius Silius, to take over the principate. While Claudius was away, she openly married Silius. Claudius was alerted by his freedmen, however, and was able to execute Messalina and Silius before the conspiracy could spread.

Claudius then married his niece (the law had to be changed to allow this), Caligula's ambitious younger sister, Agrippina. Claudius's freedman Pallas (Agrippina's lover) was the matchmaker. This marriage brought Agrippina to the power she had craved and (in her mind) deserved as the daughter of Germanicus. Claudius's son Britannicus was only five, so he adopted Agrippina's son Lucius Domitius Ahenobarbus. The boy took the family name of Nero. Claudius put the philosopher and rhetorician Seneca the Younger in charge of Nero's education. Agrippina's ally, Burrus, became praetorian prefect, and everything was in place for her.

Four years later, when Nero was just old enough to take power, Claudius conveniently died, perhaps (as the story goes) poisoned by Agrippina with mushrooms. If Agrippina didn't arrange it, she certainly was well prepared for it. She, Pallas, Seneca, and Burrus pulled off a well-orchestrated and smooth transition to power, and a joyful inaugural celebration ensued for the beginning of Nero's reign.

Lend Me Your Ears

"And yet there were those who for a long time adorned his tomb with flowers each spring and summer; they kept putting dressed statues of him on the Rostra, or his edicts, as if he were alive and would return shortly to the great harm of his enemies ... and finally when in my own youth (about twenty years after Nero's death) a certain man of unknown origin came forward and claimed to be Nero, the Parthians still so regarded his name that they supported him strongly and scarcely gave him up."

—Suetonius, *Nero*

Nero (C.E. 54–68)

This is where an author of a book like this comes to a grinding and terror-stricken halt. How *does* one cover Nero in a few paragraphs? What, by Jove, does one leave out? With Nero, it's impossible either to exaggerate or to qualify enough. But let's try.

First, remember that Nero came to the principate at the age of 16. *Sixteen.* Think back to when *you* were 16, and consider the possibilities. Second, consider that, as a 16-year-old, he had three important influences: his powerful teacher, Seneca; his powerful praetorian prefect, Burrus; and ... his mother. Like most adolescents, he rebelled against all of them eventually. Third, realize that Nero's ego was rather like that of Mr. Toad—he craved recognition and importance. He was given to effusive and melodramatic self-indulgence, self-adulation, self-reproach, and self-aggrandizement. Take all these things, mix in a dangerously volatile temperament, add in all the power in the world, and you get what you get.

Nero, for all his faults, had talent. He was a creative and imaginative person, an artist (though not to his own estimation), a person with star power. Hated by senators, he continued to be venerated by a loyal following of people. Suetonius comments that flowers mysteriously appeared on his grave for years, his edicts still circulated, and rumors abounded around the Empire that, like Elvis, Nero was still alive and would soon return to the stage.

Good Beginnings and Mommy Dearest

Nero's first eight years went well for Nero and generally for Rome. He and Agrippina poisoned Britannicus at dinner in 55. Under the guidance of Seneca and Burrus, Nero and Claudius's bureaucracy managed the state and provinces well, provided for the people, and gained victories (through his generals) in the east and in Britain. But a power struggle developed with Agrippina, who considered herself the real font of power. She *was* powerful, popular, and connected. Nero feared her, and eventually killed her after plots that would rival any Batman movie. Burrus, in 62, died and was replaced by Tigellinus (a cruel and ruthless prefect who encouraged Nero's worst capacities and insecurities); Seneca retired in dismay, and Nero was free to be Nero.

Great Caesar's Ghost!

Nero's efforts to blamelessly rid himself of his arch-nemesis mother sound like a comic book. He constructed a ship in which the cabin would cave in, kill Agrippina, and sink the ship. After a mock reconciliation, he sent her off in the boat. When the ceiling crashed down, the high sides of a couch saved Agrippina and a maid. When the maid tried to save herself by calling out that she was Agrippina, the sailors clubbed her to death and started to sink the boat. Agrippina secretly swam to safety at her nearby villa. When Nero's men arrived to finish her off, her last words (melodramatic like her son to the end) were "Strike here!" as she pointed to her womb.

I Gotta Be Me

From there, things went pretty much up in flames. Nero began appearing increasingly in public as a competitor in musical competitions, acting, and chariot racing. This was encouraged by staged public adulation and culminated in a grand concert tour of Greece in 66 and 67. Some of the famous games of Greece were moved to allow him to appear in them. Nero received carefully prepared adulation, awards (many awarded to him before he got there), and left having granted his hosts freedom from Macedonia. He was a success.

In Rome, however, things had not been going well. Nero ruthlessly persecuted political enemies and anyone he felt rivaled his popularity. This led to intense hatred from senators and the upper class, who considered his artistic pursuits, especially in public, to be appalling and demeaning. He confiscated large estates and lands, mishandled the provinces, and ignored the legions. Fear, loathing, and discontent bred plots against him, including a famous one in which Suetonius, the writer Lucian, and the satirist Petronius all lost their lives in 65.

Veto!

The saying that "Nero fiddled while Rome burned" comes from the story that, while observing the flames, Nero donned a dramatic costume and sang "Disco Inferno." Okay, really it was "The Fall of Troy," and his own composition. But if he accompanied himself, it would have been on the lyre, not the fiddle (which hadn't been invented yet).

Over time, Nero also became increasingly despotic and depraved in his personal life. He was rumored to roam the streets in disguise for fun, mugging, stealing, and sexually assaulting people. (He was once badly beaten up by a senator whose wife he assaulted, and from then on, Nero kept guards close by on these escapades in case things went badly for him.)

He divorced and exiled his first wife, Octavia, in 62 in order to marry his beautiful mistress, Poppaea Sabina. He had Octavia's head brought to Poppaea to gloat over, but later kicked Poppaea to death in a rage while she was pregnant in 65. He married Messalina in 66, but turned his attention to a boy, Sporus, who resembled Poppaea. Nero had Sporus castrated and "married" him. Nero was also "married" to another lover, Pythagoras, although the saying was that whereas he was Sporus's husband, he was Pythagoras's wife. And this is only *some* of the naughty bits.

Roamin' the Romans

When in Rome, you can visit the remains of Nero's unfinished *Domus Aurea*, or Golden House—or at least the grounds. The house, on the Mons Oppius, had an entrance high enough to house Nero's 125-foot-tall statue, a mile-long colonnade, rooms with panels that sprayed guests with flowers and perfume, and a dining hall rotated like the heavens by water power (a precursor to Seattle's Space Needle restaurant). The Coliseum, which is named for the same statue of Nero that stood there, is roughly situated on the site of the artificial lake built for the extensive grounds.

Burn, Baby, Burn

A great turning point in Nero's career came in 64, when the city of Rome caught fire and burned for three days. Most of the city, including the imperial quarters and the city center, was obliterated. Nero was not in Rome, but he rushed back and tried to organize the fighting of the fire. When that proved impossible, he opened public buildings and his own gardens as shelters, brought in subsidized food, and worked tirelessly (and often in the face of personal danger) to help the victims of the blaze.

The rumor, however, that he had started the fire to make way for his own grandiose plans for the city, soon took hold. It is probably not true, but his dramatic changes to Rome (including many good building and urban planning developments) and his construction of a stupendous imperial residence named the "Golden House" encouraged suspicion. Nero tried to deflect suspicion and criticism by making a small and secretive sect of Jews, the Christians, into scapegoats. It didn't work, and rebuilding the city and Nero's palace brought on a currency devaluation that fueled Nero's now smoldering reputation.

Trouble began to brew among the legions, in the provinces, and in Rome itself. Increasingly harsh taxes, Nero's excesses, his confiscations, his un-Roman ways, and growing despotism were alienating everyone who mattered.

Great Caesar's Ghost!

Nero's was the first persecution of Christians and the first time that Christianity was officially recognized as a sect distinct from Judaism. Several factors may have contributed to singling them out. St. Paul had been executed previously, and may have brought Christians name recognition and public suspicion. Some speculate that singling out Christians both served its purpose and shielded the larger Jewish community, who lived primarily in one of the quarters that hadn't burned. In any case, Christians were executed with all the exquisite horror of Roman spectacle. Some were put in animal skins and torn apart by dogs in the amphitheater; others were crucified and then burned as lamps after dark.

Nero on the Tracks

By 67, when Nero returned from his concert tour of Greece, things were beginning to close in. In 68, the legions of Gaul and Spain began to revolt under their governors and commanders. Vindex, one of the governors of Gaul, revolted and raised troops. He had the support of Servius Sulpicius Galba, the governor of Hispania Terraconensis (Spain). The loyal commander of Germany, Rufus, defeated Vindex. But then *his* troops revolted and proclaimed *him* emperor. Rufus declined, but Galba had been building support for himself at Rome. He offered the praetorians large sums to support him, and they deserted Nero as he contemplated flight. Other legions began to declare for Galba or for their own commanders.

Nero tried to flee to the east by ship, but couldn't persuade the guards to help him and he returned to Rome. He apparently contemplated making a dramatic and pathetic appeal to the people in the Forum, wearing black, and composed part of such a speech. Later that night, he awoke to find the palace deserted. He ran about calling and searching for someone, and finally ran out into the street. There he found one of his freedmen, Phaon, who convinced him to go in disguise to a nearby villa outside of town (probably not to save but to betray him). Nero was recognized along the way, terrified by what he heard people saying about him, and periodically engaged in more self-pitying displays and comments. Phaon brought a letter to the villa from the senate declaring Nero a public enemy.

Nero tried to muster the courage to kill himself (he encouraged others to go first as an example), but hesitated, berated himself, and delayed. As the guards arrived at the villa to take him back, Nero stabbed his throat with the help of his secretary. Melodramatic to the last, his final words were reported to be either, "Such an artist dies in me" or, to a centurion who tried to stop the blood flow, "Too late, but ah, what loyalty!" Whichever it was, it was a fitting tag to the end of the Julio-Claudian line.

Augustus, on his deathbed, had asked his friends if they had enjoyed watching all the parts he had played so well. He asked them to applaud as he departed the comedy of life, and then had his jaw set and hair combed for his exit. Nero died a grandiloquent death, a tragic actor upon the stage that Augustus had built and that the Julio-Claudians had transformed into high opera.

The Least You Need to Know

➤ The outrageous personal details of the Julio-Claudians come from mostly hostile sources.

➤ During the reign of the Julio-Claudians, the Roman Empire became more economically, politically, and culturally cohesive.

➤ As it became clear that the *princeps* held the power, the senate became less involved, and the *princeps* became an emperor.

➤ Those close to the emperor (family, lovers, freedmen, and guards) became extremely powerful and influential.

Chapter 15

The (Mostly) Good Emperors: The Flavians to Marcus Aurelius

In This Chapter

➤ The Roman Empire after the Julio-Claudians

➤ The chaos after Nero

➤ The Flavian dynasty and stability

➤ The so-called good emperors

The rebellions that led to the death of Nero were an ominous blast from the past. Provincial legions proclaimed their own commanders emperor, and factions of the Praetorian Guard complicated the dangerous situation in Rome. For a year, the Roman Empire wobbled like a top as commanders from both west and east moved on Italy to claim power. In the end, however, the chaos of a year led back to a stable and a hereditary dynasty: the "Flavians," from the family name (Flavius) of its founder, Vespasian. Vespasian was rightly recognized as a second Augustus. This dynasty, however, marked the end of the old Roman nobility's hold over the principate, the increasing importance of provincial armies and citizens in Roman affairs, and the growing cohesion of Rome as a world state.

The Year of Living Dangerously

After Verginius Rufus crushed the rebellion of Vindex, one of the governors of Gaul, in 68 (see Chapter 14, "All in the Family: The Julio-Claudian Emperors"), and refused to be named *princeps* by his own forces, there was a revolving door into the office of the *princeps*. This year is sometimes known as "the year of four emperors."

Galba (68–69)

Servius Sulpicius Galba, the aging (he was in his 70s) governor of Spain, next maneuvered to power. Galba belonged to an ancient and distinguished Republican family, but his hold on the principate was brief because he failed to make good his financial promises to the praetorians and to the military. There was a good reason for this—Rome was broke—but it wasn't a good enough reason for Galba to stay emperor.

Galba alienated the legions by replacing the commander Verginius Rufus, and he alienated his most important supporter, the governor of Lusitania, Marcus Otho, by appointing Otho's rival, Piso, as colleague. Otho took matters into his own hands and secretly bribed the Praetorian Guards to proclaim him emperor. His supporters murdered Piso and Galba and paraded their heads around the palace.

Otho (69)

Otho was one of Nero's intimates (perhaps quite intimate), and the former husband of Nero's mistress and then wife, Poppaea. He had a reputation for decadence and dissolution. This reputation, his ties and falling out with Nero, and his violent coup against Galba made nearly every faction deeply suspicious of him. He surprised most, however, by being moderate and trying to work with both Nero's supporters and enemies.

This didn't keep trouble from brewing. The legions of the Rhine and Gaul had declared their commander, Aulus Vitellius, to be the Empire's rightful emperor. Full-scale civil war appeared imminent, but when Vitellius's forces defeated Otho's in battle, Otho advised his supporters to look after themselves as best they could, and committed suicide. This may seem like a coward's way out, but contemporary Romans saw his suicide as a heroic act to spare Rome civil war. He had come a long way in just three months.

Vitellius (69)

If our sources are to be believed, you can't say enough bad about Vitellius. He was a flatterer of Caligula and Claudius, a crony of Nero and Galba. His German legions declared for him in an attempt to secure their commander the place of power (and payment) at the head of Rome. The legions of Gaul and Britain soon followed.

Despite his position, Vitellius had no real military experience—he didn't even command the troops that invaded Italy and defeated Otho. He did, however, come to observe the battlefield and made the chilling remark that the smell of dead enemy was sweet and the smell of dead citizen sweeter. He entered Rome a short time later and set up his own troops as the Praetorian Guards and urban cohorts.

Vitellius is known mostly for his ability to eat Rome out of house and home. He spent 900 million *sesterces* on dining alone! (At one banquet, 2,000 fish and 7,000 birds were reportedly consumed.) But Vitellius's principate was running afoul (so to speak) in another way: The legions of the east had declared for Titius Flavius Vespasianus, a general with definite military credentials. Vespasian had been sent by Nero to quell a revolt in Judaea. Now he was holding Egypt while his commander, Mucianus, moved on Italy. Soon the legions of Illyrium and Pannonia joined in and these forces met and butchered Vitellius's forces at Cremona, in almost the same spot that Vitellius had defeated Otho's.

Vitellius tried to abdicate and save his skin, but his supporters declined to accept his resignation. When word of this attempt got out, Vespasian's brother, Sabinus, and friends tried to seize power. Vitellius got the upper hand and had them killed. Two days later, Vespasian's forces fought their way into Rome. Vitellius tried to escape disguised as a commoner (a commoner with a big money belt hidden under his clothes), but he was discovered, tortured to death, and thrown into the Tibur river.

Working Stiffs to Lord and God: The Flavian Dynasty

Flavian forces were now in control of Rome. The commander of Syria, Mucianus, administered things until Vespasian arrived. Vespasian's younger son, Domitian, was also in Rome. He came out of hiding and began to act out a version of "I just can't wait to be king."

When in Rome

The **sesterce** was a primary coin of the realm. It was worth 2½ of the main small coins, **asses** (no relation to the animal), and four sesterces made up a **denarius**, the principal large coin. A Roman soldier made about 900 sesterces a year, so Vitellius's banquets could have funded the legions for about a millennium!

Great Caesar's Ghost!

Domitian's premature affectations of power should have been a warning bell. Vespasian, who had a dry sense of humor, got wind of his son's pretensions and wrote him as he traveled to Rome. He thanked his young son for allowing his father to hold office and for not yet dethroning him.

201

Vespasian not only provided the Empire with a capable emperor, but established the second hereditary imperial dynasty, the Flavians. He was succeeded by his son Titus, and then by his younger son Domitian.

The Flavians brought about a renaissance of Roman stability and prosperity that was compared to Augustus's creation of peace out of the anarchy of the end of the Republic. The Flavian dynasty began with an emperor whose roots, perspective, and work ethic grew out of the equestrian middle class, and concluded at an ultimate end of the ambition for independence and power: the demand to be recognized as lord and god.

The Flavian dynasty.

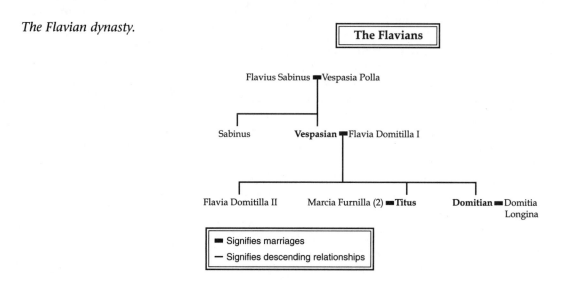

Vespasian (69–79)

Vespasian's parents were middle class Italians (his father was an auctioneer). He had served all over the Empire and gained both experience and accolades under emperors from Tiberius to Claudius. His brother, Sabinus, and he were the first of his family to enter the senate. Vespasian was promoted under Nero to a "companion" and traveled with Nero to Greece, but fell out of favor when he drifted to sleep during one of the emperor's performances. Nevertheless, he was put in charge of quelling a Jewish revolt in Palestine, and was in the process of putting it down and besieging Jerusalem when Nero committed suicide and Rome began to spin into anarchy.

Vespasian stayed in Alexandria holding on to the imperial province of Egypt; he hoped to both conclude putting down the rebellion in Palestine and fulfill his legions' proclamation of him as emperor. He had to leave for Rome before the first was completed, however, and left his son, Titus, in charge. Once in Rome, Vespasian proved to be an able, determined, practical, and down-to-earth emperor. His background, practical approach, and what one might call "common" humor put off some of the high society, but overall, Vespasian was both respected and successful.

Vespasian and his colleagues such as Mucianus had a reputation for a love of money, and Vespasian maintained a decidedly business-like attitude toward finances as an emperor. Accused by Titus of stinky financial associations, he picked up a coin and remarked, "This, my boy, does not stink." Despite some rather questionable practices, Vespasian managed the Empire out of destitution into sound fiscal shape. He spent a great deal on public works projects aimed at restoring Rome after Nero's fire and the pillage of the last year. His most famous project was the Colosseum, which he built on the site of the artificial lake of Nero's Golden House.

Great Caesar's Ghost!

Vespasian enjoyed witty observations and snappy comebacks, and according to Suetonius, the more lowbrow the better. Nevertheless, he is best known for another of the famous imperial exit lines, and one that displays his practical and sometimes tongue-in-cheek approach to the principate. "Dear me," he commented on his deathbed, "Methinks I'm becoming a god."

Roamin' the Romans

The Colosseum could seat around 50,000. It featured easy and well-designed exits, a retractable roof (an awning on ropes and pulleys that took a crew of 1,000 to raise), and something that beats even monster truck rallies—the ability to be flooded for mock naval battles. Today, you can peer down into the labyrinth of underground passages and cages under the floor and gaze up the 160 feet to the nosebleed section, where women and lower classes were allowed to sit.

Vespasian faced turmoil and resistance in the provinces, but handled them well. He put down the remains of the rebellions, reformed and spaced out legions along the borders, and moved to separate recruits from their own territory. In doing so, he increased Rome's border defenses and contributed to a process of homogenization of the Empire. He went far beyond his predecessors in also strengthening provincial participation by extending citizen rights, promoting urbanization, and adding provincials to the senate. He removed some older members and added many more new. While the senate's power continued to decline, the cohesion between Rome, Italy, and the provinces increased.

Vespasian held and was active in numerous consulships and offices such as censor, and fully promoted his sons as his heirs. For this he earned both blame as a shameless dynasty promoter and a measure of relief for providing a clear path for succession. But although he had critics and enemies in the senate and among the upper class, he took most of this in stride and with a degree of indulgence. He showed less favor toward the criticisms of intellectuals. He expelled Stoic and Cynic philosophers, whose criticisms he considered irritating and superfluous, from Rome.

When Vespasian died, he left the principate prepared for a smooth transition of power. Titus not only had his father's powers and *imperium,* but was praetorian prefect. This gave him an unobstructed path to the principate.

Titus (79–81)

Titus succeeded to the principate without issue, but there were some misgivings. He was reputed to be a wild character, immoderate, and, as praetorian prefect, had a nasty reputation for doing Vespasian's dirty work no matter what it took. He also had a thing going with Bernice, a Judaean royal whom he met while finishing up for dad in Palestine. Another eastern seductress? Shades of Cleopatra! Titus brought her to Rome in 75, and they were momentarily a public item, but she was such a political and public relations nightmare that Vespasian made Titus break things off and send her back to Judaea. Rome virtually groaned when Titus came to power, however inevitable it was.

Roamin' the Romans

Not much remains from Titus's short reign, but in the Roman Forum, you can view his spectacular triumphal arch still standing and complete with reliefs depicting his triumph and the spoils of Jerusalem.

But to everyone's surprise, Titus was a much different emperor than heir. He was kind, compassionate, fair, intelligent, and deferential to the traditions of his office. Vesuvius blew up and destroyed Pompeii and Herculaneum; Titus heaped disaster relief on and personally visited the area. Another huge fire swept through Rome; Titus rebuilt it bigger and better and put on public celebrations. A plague swept into Italy; Titus again organized and provided public relief and aid. His generosity and moderation stunned his critics, and his response to this series of disasters earned him public adulation. Then, only slightly two years after taking office, he suddenly died. His enigmatic dying remark, "I have made only one mistake," led to centuries of speculation.

Domitian (81–96)

Rome was unprepared for Titus's death. He had no children and no designated heir. But his brother, Domitian, filled the gap and had himself proclaimed emperor by the praetorians before Titus had turned cold. This was the second time Domitian had moved to grab the opportunity for power. He had come out of hiding after Vitellius's death to take on a role in ruling Rome before his father arrived. He took this role a bit *too* seriously and too much to heart, however, and for this it looks like Vespasian and Titus kept him somewhat under wraps. But with dad and big brother gone, Domitian was *princeps* at last.

Roamin' the Romans

In wandering the ruins of the great imperial residences of the Palatine hill, such as Domitian's, you'll realize why we get the word "palace" from the name on the hill on which they were constructed.

Domitian has a terrible reputation, worse than he probably deserves. He appears to have administered the Empire remarkably well. He completed his father's and brother's projects, put on extravagant games, suppressed rebellions in Germany, expanded and solidified Roman holdings along the Rhine, and raised the pay of the legions. Through shrewd, though not popular diplomacy, he made the kingdom of Dacia (modern Rumania) a client kingdom and buffer instead of trying to conquer it. Imperial palaces, roads, and frontier settlements were also constructed throughout the Empire. All this and no harsh taxes, no debasing the currency, and still an Empire in the black.

Domitian was hated for openly acting as an autocrat. Of course, this was basically *true,* but part of the deal with the *princeps* was that you weren't supposed to *act* like it. Domitian never understood that part. He paraded around in royal garb. He built an enormous imperial palace on the palatine and conducted there what amounted to a royal court. He encouraged others to recognize him as *dominus et deus,* lord and god. He treated the senate as inconsequential and subservient.

Roamin' the Romans

We owe one of the most beloved Roman squares, Piazza Navona, to Domitian. I recommend that you go there at night. Wander among the street artists, have your fortune read, and see Bernini's famous fountain statue recoiling in horror at Boromini's (Bernini's rival) church. As you promenade, you'll recognize that the piazza preserves the outline of Domitian's stadium and the buildings still line the racecourse like spectators.

Domitian recognized that a strong central religion could bring cohesion to a broadening Roman civilization. He championed himself as a defender and center of Roman religion and *Romanitas* (Roman-ness). Impiety, including failing to worship the emperor and imperial gods, became treason. Tradition has it that he persecuted religions, including

Judaism and Christianity, that refused to recognize the emperor as *dominus et deus*. The actual evidence for this is slim, however, and rests mostly on interpretations of the New Testament book of *Revelation* (which has never been an easy text for anyone to interpret).

As time went on, Domitian became increasingly paranoid, saw conspiracies everywhere, and attacked those he suspected. Finally, realizing that they would all be suspected sooner or later, his wife, the praetorians, imperial servants, and high ranking senators conspired against him and murdered him in his bedroom. Rome celebrated and pulled down the autocrat's statues.

Adopting a Better Succession Policy: The Five Good Emperors

No chaos or uprising followed the assassination of Domitian. The Flavians had left the Empire stable and centered on Rome. There was no question of returning to the Republic, no revolting legions, no rampaging praetorians. There was, however, also no dynasty. Instead, a kind of compromise between traditions came about, whereby an emperor designated a successor by adoption, passing on the office both by heredity and by merit but *not by blood.* This worked remarkably well, and ushered in a period known as the "Five Good Emperors."

The "good" emperors.

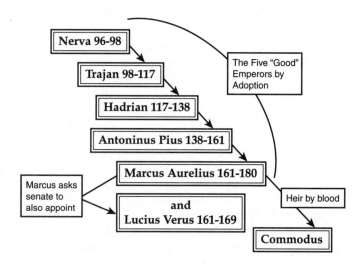

Nerva (96–98)

Nerva was an aging senator without an heir who was appointed emperor by the senate following the assassination of Domitian. But Nerva was unable to maintain order. Those who had been repressed by Domitian began to push the envelope while the military, which admired their soldiering (and well-paying) warlord, began to grow discontented.

Finally, revolt broke out. Soldiers forced their way past Nerva and executed Domitian's assassins, whom Nerva was harboring. The end was near, but Nerva made the astute move of adopting the popular and respected governor of Upper Germany, Marcus Ulpius Trajanus (Trajan), as an heir in 97. This quelled problems and earned Nerva the title *Pater Patriae* (father of his country) as well as the right to live out the rest of his life in peace and security. It wasn't very long—Nerva died just a few months later.

Trajan (98–117)

Trajan has been one of Rome's most influential and popular emperors. His 20-year rule was marked by military conquest, good government, good relations with the senate, and an overall sense of grandeur, competence, and maturity.

Trajan, a distinguished and imposing figure, looked the part of the *princeps,* and he played it, too. In time, the highest wish of the senate for a new emperor was "more fortunate than Augustus and even better than Trajan." This reputation remained into the Middle Ages, when Dante allowed him, of all the emperors, into paradise in *The Divine Comedy.*

Trajan was the first emperor born in the provinces. He was of Spanish origin (born near Seville), and through good family connections and personal merit, he rose under Vespasian and Domitian to become the governor of Lower Germany. He was so secure in his position that he did not go directly to Rome after Nerva's death but spent two years making sure Rome's northern defenses were secure before proceeding to the capitol.

When in Rome

By Trajan's time, Italy was struggling economically and population was on the decline. To help, Trajan instituted **alimenta,** public funds that were used to subsidize education and food for needy families and children. Funds were acquired from a system in which large landowners pledged small portions of land as collateral for government loans. The small interest payments that they paid for these loans funded the alimenta.

His arrival in Rome was impressive: Tall, handsome, and rugged, Trajan looked the part of a world commander. He treated the senate with deference and respect and pursued popular and progressive public politics. Of these, most point to his *alimenta,* subsidized public assistance for poor children. Trajan was also a prolific builder in both Rome and the provinces. In Rome, he is chiefly known for his magnificent Forum, market, and his spectacular Trajan's Column, a remarkable complex of public buildings that demonstrates the intertwining of Roman conquest, culture, and economy. Trajan celebrated his Dacian conquests by building an enormous forum, basilica, and two public libraries from which visitors could view his famous carved column (still standing). He also built, overlooking the civic buildings, a magnificent market that featured imports from the Roman world. There, Romans could not only see the grandeur that the spoils of war could bring, but they could also purchase

207

food, spices, and luxury goods coming from these far-flung conquests. Besides Rome, you can find other projects such as his harbor at Ostia, his remarkable villa (near Civitavecchia), roads, and bridges throughout the Empire.

The remains of Trajan's magnificent market and forum.

Roamin' the Romans

Trajan's Column is one of the most famous monuments of Rome. Presented by the senate as a part of Trajan's Forum (see Chapter 1, "Dead Culture, Dead Language, Dead Emperors: Why Bother?"), it served both as a burial chamber and a monumental record of his achievements. The 100-foot column was cut with a spiraling relief and was intended to be viewed from the library balconies that graced either side of the column as a part of the Forum. The relief shows scenes from Trajan's Dacian campaigns and is a source of both artistic wonder and historical information. A spiral staircase inside the column leads up to the top, where a statue of Trajan originally stood. The statue of St. Peter replaced Trajan's in the late 1500s.

Trajan is chiefly known, however, for his military exploits. He fought wars in Dacia (modern Rumania), Armenia, and Mesopotamia. While his settlement of Dacia stood, his conquests in the east were less secure. He realized at least some of Caesar's and

Antony's Alexander-esque ambitions and pressed the Roman border all the way to the Persian Gulf. There he reportedly sighed, "Had I been younger I would have liked to have gone to India too." But Trajan's eastern conquests were crumbling behind him. Revolts in Judaea and Mesopotamia, Parthian troubles in Armenia, and other eastern turmoil forced him to return. While trying to deal with these problems, he fell ill. He put Publius Aelius Hadrianus (Hadrian) in charge of the east and left for Rome but suffered a stroke and died without boarding the ship.

Hadrian (117–138)

Hadrian rose through his connections with Trajan's family, and eventually his friendship with Trajan and Trajan's wife, Plotina. When Trajan died, it appears that things were not quite settled. Plotina sent the senate documents confirming Hadrian's adoption as successor, but these had her signature. To this day no one knows exactly how, or by whom, Hadrian became emperor.

Hadrian suffered by having to follow in Trajan's immensely popular footsteps and having to clean up messes that Trajan's policies and exploits left behind. While Trajan's exploits were legendary, they left Rome virtually depleted while defenses cracked at the edges. Hadrian decided to return to an Augustan approach—to a Rome that was non-expansionist in temperament, stable, and with firm and delineated borders. He gave up some of Trajan's conquests in the east, which upset both military and senatorial expansionists. He worked to firm up Roman borders with projects such as the famous *Hadrian's Wall* built between England and Scotland.

Hadrian was an admirer of all things Greek. He started a trend for the next several emperors by sporting a beard, studying Greek literature, and patronizing the city of Athens. Unpopular at Rome, Hadrian traveled the Empire extensively, visiting every corner of the realm. He founded cities, including an attempt at restoring Jerusalem as Aelia

Veto!

Not *all* reports of Trajan were glowing. While he and his wife, Pompeia Plotina, had sterling reputations, there were reports of dark eddies under the still waters of the imperial family. Trajan, for example, reportedly was a bit too fond of wine and young boys; Plotina is said to have encouraged Hadrian to marry into Trajan's family behind Trajan's back, and to have forged documents confirming him as Trajan's heir.

When in Rome

Hadrian's Wall was an 80-mile wall roughly separating England from Scotland. Built first of dirt and timber, and then stone, the wall featured forts, supply roads, and settlements at regular intervals along its way. It is not only a major tourist attraction and important archeological site but features beautiful walks along its ruins.

Roamin' the Romans

The Mausoleum of Hadrian in Rome is known today as Castel San Angelo. This imposing structure was incorporated into Rome's and the Vatican's defenses in the Middle Ages and has served as a fortress, a prison, and a museum. The present name comes from a vision of an angel over the mausoleum, which signaled the end of a plague to Pope Gregory the Great in 590.

Capitolina with a temple of Jupiter on the site of Solomon's temple. This attempt resulted in a major Jewish revolt under Simon Bar-Kochba, which was suppressed at an enormous cost and loss of life. He also founded a city in Egypt in honor of his young companion, Antinous, who died under mysterious circumstances while traveling with Hadrian in Egypt.

Hadrian's many buildings and projects, such as Castel San Angelo and his villa in Tivoli, remain as spectacular monuments today. You would think that these projects, coupled with discipline in the army, extension of the *alimenta* and citizen rights, reforms of military and provincial administration, and Hadrian's exhaustive attention to legal, civil, and administrative reforms and organization would make him a popular emperor. Not so. Hadrian was cranky, a strict disciplinarian who was difficult to be around. He was reportedly also a voracious sexual switch-hitter and seducer of married women. Only the soldiers adored their commander, who marched alongside of them and seemed to demand as much of himself as he did of them.

Hadrian lived out his final years in his magnificent villa at Tivoli, lonely and in growing pain from a medical ailment. This pain grew so bad that he sought suicide in attempts that ended in darkly comic frustration. Attendants kept sharp implements out of reach. He commanded his doctor to give him poison, but the panicked doctor took it himself. He commanded a servant to kill him and even marked out the spot to stab ("right here at the blue line"), but the servant bailed at the last minute and ran. Hadrian transferred power to his successor, Antoninus, and finally died at Baiae. Even in death, the traveling emperor traveled. With his mausoleum unfinished, Hadrian's body was first buried at Puteoli, exhumed to temporary digs in Rome, and then brought to his completed tomb.

Antoninus Pius (138–161)

Antoninus was from a prominent family and had limited military and administrative experience. He was 51 and probably chosen by Hadrian to hold things down until Hadrian's nephew, Marcus Aurelius, could become emperor. Antoninus adopted Marcus, who also married Antoninus's daughter. He was given the name "Pius" (Pious) for successfully opposing Hadrian's enemies in the senate who wanted to nullify his acts and desecrate his memory. Antoninus pointed out that his accession depended upon the authority and legitimacy of the man and the acts that they were condemning, and he quelled their opposition.

An artificial island in Hadrian's villa at Tivoli, where the emperor sought solitude from imperial pressures.

History seems to have taken a mostly "If you can't say anything bad, don't say anything at all" approach to Antoninus Pius. He was, by all accounts, fair, judicious, good-looking, well-spoken, even tempered, and a relatively unpretentious man who preferred administering the Empire from his country estates. Antoninus ruled for 23 years and never left Italy. Some of his most significant reforms were judicial, including the precedent of presumption of innocence and tie verdicts going in favor of the accused. Although there were no major wars during his reign, there was plenty of trouble on the borders to attend to. Antoninus did not put much effort into the military, however, and by the time of his death in 161, Rome's defenses and military were worn very thin.

Marcus Aurelius (161–180)

Marcus Aurelius is one of the best-known emperors. People admire him for his nobility of character, which comes from the contrast between the emperor who relentlessly campaigned to hold the Empire together against enormous odds and the man who

211

wrote his simple and unpretentious Stoic reflections in the journal that has become known as the *Meditations*.

Raised by his beloved adopted father and educated for duty, Marcus spent most of his years on the borders fighting the Parthians, Germanic invasions along the Danube (where he wrote the *Meditations*), a revolt in Syria, and the effects of a plague that ravaged the Empire.

Lend Me Your Ears

"Tell yourself each morning, 'Today I'm going to meet nosey, ungrateful, arrogant, untrustworthy, envious, and antisocial people. Bear in mind that they act this way because they don't realize what good and evil really are. I, however, realize that the nature of the good is beautiful and that the nature of evil is ugly, and that the nature of the person who does me wrong has a share of the same intelligence and divinity as I do. I can't really be hurt by any of them (since no one can pin ugliness on me) nor be angry at and hate my fellow human being. For we've been made for cooperation, like feet, hands, eyelids, and rows of teeth.'"

—Marcus Aurelius, *Thoughts to Himself* (in *Meditations*), *Book II;* after a translation by George Long

When Marcus was recognized as emperor, he insisted that his colleague, Lucius Varus, be given equal and commensurate power. Varus, according to imperial biographies, was a less dutiful leader than Marcus, and more interested in enjoying the power and luxury his position gave him. Nevertheless, he appears to have been a loyal colleague, and died while campaigning with Marcus in 169. The model of co-emperors was picked up later by Diocletian in an attempt to distribute the burdens of administering and defending the vast Empire. Marcus later faced down a strange uprising in 175 when his trusted governor of Syria, Cassius, was proclaimed emperor by his troops based on the rumor that Marcus was dead.

While Marcus was a pious philosopher, he wasn't necessarily a tolerant man. The Empire was under terrible strains, and Marcus viewed Roman traditions and religion as a part of the fabric that (barely) held it together. He therefore persecuted Christians as members of a secretive and subversive cult. Overall, however, he worked tirelessly and fairly at hearing law cases, issuing imperial decisions and edicts, and defending the borders—all of this apparently in the face of painful and deteriorating medical conditions for which he took the opiate theriac.

Marcus became very ill in Vindobona (Vienna), in 180. Advising his friends not to grieve for his death, for death was common to all, his last words were "Go to the rising sun; mine is setting." So died the last of the "good" emperors, a man who, according to Dio, "both survived himself and preserved the Empire amid the most unusual and extraordinary troubles." Unfortunately for Rome, however, these troubles survived Marcus, and passed on to his son and heir, Commodus.

Roamin' the Romans

When in Rome, be sure to see the statue of Marcus astride a horse on the Capitoline, a stunning combination of serenity, grace, power, and movement. You should also visit his column at Piazza Colonna, which was modeled on Trajan's and shows scenes of Marcus's campaigns. Like Trajan's column, a statue of Marcus once stood at the top where St. Paul now surveys the prime minister's office.

The Least You Need to Know

➤ Nero's death put Rome into a brief time of anarchy.

➤ The Flavian emperors put Rome on a firm military and financial footing.

➤ The "good" emperors are known for adopting successors instead of passing power on to blood relations. Of course, it helped that only Marcus Aurelius had a son!

➤ The expansion of Rome under Trajan and Hadrian began to strain under Antoninus Pius, and to crumble under Marcus Aurelius.

Chapter 16

The (Mostly) Not-So-Good Emperors: Commodus to Aurelian

In This Chapter

➤ Pressures on the Empire after the "good" emperors

➤ The Severan dynasty

➤ Roman disintegration following the Severans

After Marcus Aurelius's death in 180, the Empire slipped into a period of decline and fragmentation with continual warfare on the borders. Rome became more of a symbolic capital; power concentrated in the provinces responsible for Rome's defense. This trend helped to transform regional warlords into emperors, and citizens under them eventually became more like serfs. But, if not for the restoration of the Empire under Diocletian in 285, we might have had the Dark Ages (ca 476–1000) a few centuries earlier.

People usually skim through this period. Understandably so—it's one of the most complicated and obscure periods in Roman history. Nevertheless, it contains some of the most interesting history of Rome and the early Christian church, which grew through persecutions both against and within itself in establishing doctrinal orthodoxy and institutional hierarchy. But by piecing together early Christian writers (such as Tertullian and Eusebius), fragments from Dio and other minor writers, and archeological evidence from the provinces, we're getting a better understanding of what went on. (For really detailed information you'll have to wait for *The Complete Idiot's Guide to the Barracks Emperors, 235–285*.)

In this chapter, we'll break up the period of the not-so-good emperors into three sections. The first goes from Commodus to the accession of Septemius Severus in 193. The second section covers the Severan dynasty, which ended with the murder of Severus Alexander in 235. The third is a black hole of assassinations, emperor-for-the-day military coups, invasions, and breakaway provinces that threatened to suck the Empire under until Diocletian reestablished order and stitched things back together in 285.

A "Good" Hangover: Commodus to the Severi

The Flavians and the "good" Emperors presided over 150 years of relative stability and development, but it had come with some weak links and at a price. Trajan's conquest of Dacia brought in the rich gold reserves of that country, but it masked the fact that Rome's economic systems were unequal to its size and needs. As these resources played out, the cost of maintaining social programs, not to mention the military and its loyalty, was a burden that could not be sustained. Marcus Aurelius, for example, had to sell off the imperial dinnerware to fund his campaigns! Rome was never very good at long-term budgeting, but then the record for economic long-range planning isn't very good for most states.

This period also witnessed the emperor's increasing power over and involvement with military, civil, judicial, and religious aspects of imperial Roman life. As the *princeps* drew power to himself, and the senate either lost or relinquished it, the emperor and his staff became the micro-managers of a macro-system. This led to a situation wherein one person could not attend to the whole, but the whole depended on the one to function. This system often experienced large-scale paralysis, disenfranchisement, and apathy while awaiting the emperor's direction.

Defense of the borders increasingly occupied most of the emperor's time and resources. Trajan had taken the Empire beyond the limit of what its populations, resources, and technology could maintain. Hadrian scaled back these borders, but Rome still barely managed, and only through great effort, to maintain territorial integrity. As pressures increased, especially along the Danube, in Dacia, and in the east, Rome needed more resources. Without new sources of revenue, it could raise money only by increasing taxes and diverting resources from the center of power toward the provincial armies.

Succession in the Commodus, Again

Despite these preexisting conditions, you will often read that things went bad when Marcus Aurelius abandoned the "good" emperors' practice of adopting a successor by merit and went back to the practice of hereditary succession. Trust me: There were enough problems with the Empire already going bad. To single out Commodus's succession is a kind of *post hoc propter hoc* argument. Besides, no one was waiting in the wings who could have stopped the downslide. Marcus Aurelius himself couldn't do it, and odds are his successor, whoever that was, wouldn't have either.

Besides, what if the best man for the job (which includes keeping the peace among rival armies and such) *is* your son? Marcus tried to buffer his son Commodus's inexperience by surrounding him with trusted advisors. It is unfortunate, however, that Commodus turned out to be a disaster of Herculean proportions.

When in Rome

Post hoc propter hoc is one of many informal logic fallacies that still bear Latin names. In English, it translates as "after this (then) because of this" and describes the fallacy of claiming a cause and effect between two events based on their succession in time. For example, it may *seem* that your purchase of a particular stock causes its value to drop because that's what happens after you buy it, but there isn't really any correlation between *your* purchase and the stock's performance.

Commodus (180–192)

Marcus Aurelius, Commodus's father, had groomed Commodus from youth to be emperor, and Commodus had accompanied him on his military campaigns. Commodus was on campaign with him when Marcus died in 180. He settled affairs in Germany by negotiation (which some thought cowardly but which really made sense) and returned to Rome. There he let a series of personal advisors run the Empire while he pursued what every red-blooded 18-year-old Roman male with all the power in the world wants: sports and sex. These advisors became notorious and were either assassinated by the senate or by Commodus as he fell out with them. A few to mention are …

➤ **Saoterus,** who first appeared in a chariot with Commodus in the new emperor's first triumph. Commodus shocked the crowd by making a display of periodically kissing him. Saoterus was murdered by opposing senators in 182.

Veto!

Many blame Marcus for making his son his heir, but it wasn't as if the emperors before him had abandoned the practice. They preserved the concept of dynastic succession by adopting their successors. Furthermore, by marrying successors into their own families, the good emperors showed that they retained dynastic aspirations of their own. Besides, of the "good" emperors, only Marcus had a natural son!

➤ **Perennis,** commander of the Praetorian Guard. Commodus put him in control of the government after Saoterus. Perennis indulged the emperor's interests, but Commodus had him and his sons executed when disgruntled soldiers accused Perennis of plotting Commodus's death.

➤ **Cleander,** a Phrygian slave who rose to power in the imperial household. He became notorious for indulging Commodus while running the government for his own profit. Commodus had him killed to save his own skin during riots against Cleander.

Great Caesar's Ghost!

Commodus's gladiatorial fervor and madness recently came back out of the mire to serve as the historical backdrop and story line for the film *Gladiator*.

Commodus is most famous for his sex-capades (he is said to have kept a supply of 300 concubines and 300 young boys) and his enthusiasm for gladiatorial games. He became very skilled at archery and javelin throwing—he could cut the head off of an ostrich at 50 paces. He participated in games of the hunt and reportedly even finished off a few cripples in the arena. The senatorial class was disgusted. It would be as if a president or governor became a participant in professional wrestling. The crowds, however, loved it and flocked in from beyond the city to see Commodus, who demanded a high fee for his appearances.

Commodus slipped into megalomania during his reign. He insisted on being called "Hercules" and demanded that the senate deify him while alive and worship him. He wore a Hercules outfit in public and appeared as the hero in the games. When a fire ravaged the city, he decided that he would be the second founder of Rome and officially renamed Rome "Colonia Commodiana" ("Colony of Commodus," or "Commodeville").

After surviving several assassination attempts, Commodus began to threaten both the senate and those around him. In one particularly vivid display, he walked around the arena shaking a severed ostrich head and bloody sword at senators. Finally a group of senators and Commodus's favorite concubine, Marcia, pulled their collective head out of the sand. They poisoned him the night before a big event in which the emperor planned to appear as "Hercules, Founder of Rome." When he threw up the poison, they called in his personal trainer to finish him off.

Pertinax (193)

That same night the assassins smuggled Commodus's body out of the palace. They brought it as proof of the tyrant's death to the house of a respected senator, the 66-year-old Publius Helvius Pertinax, and offered him the emperorship. With large bribes to the Praetorian Guard, Pertinax was "reluctantly" proclaimed emperor in a midnight meeting of the senate worthy of any Fellini movie. Calling Commodus "more savage than Domitian and more foul than Nero," senators called for the desecration of Commodus's body, but Pertinax and cooler heads prevailed. They wiped Commodus's name from all monuments but eventually buried him in Hadrian's Mausoleum.

Pertinax sold off Commodus's gladiator outfits and other personal paraphernalia, and tried to bring finances back in line. But he didn't last long—he didn't pay off the praetorians while trying to rein them in. They tried to assassinate him several times. Finally, about 300 of them broke into the palace, and Pertinax bravely tried to talk them down. "Hey," a soldier shouted as he stepped forward with his sword, "The soldiers have sent you this sword!" and struck. The rest then hacked Pertinax to death. He had been emperor for 87 days.

Didius Julianus (March 28–June 1, 193), Come on Down!

Pertinax was dead. As the soldiers stuck his head on a pole and paraded it around a bit, they realized that they had no exit strategy. They beat a quick retreat to their barracks and waited. As news spread, a candidate for emperor, a senator and Pertinax's father-in-law, Sulpicianus, showed up. He promised them a big bonus to support him. Then *another* senator, the wealthy Didius Julianus, showed up and offered them a bigger bonus. A bidding war for emperor went on until Julianus won. (Just think if they had had eBay at that time.) His wife, who always wanted him to amount to something, was very pleased.

But neither the people nor the provincial armies were pleased. In Rome, people jeered and threw stones, and then voted to ask Niger, the governor of Syria, to take the throne. Meanwhile the legions of Britain proclaimed their commander, Albinus, and the legions of the Danube proclaimed their commander, Septimius Severus, emperor. All three commanders made a rush for Rome, and Severus's forces got their first. Julianus tried to organize resistance and then to negotiate, but the senate proclaimed Septimius emperor and Julianus a criminal. Guards found Julianus deserted in the palace, wailing something akin to "Why *me?* What have *I* done?" and killed him. He had been emperor for 66 days.

Roamin' the Romans

The magnificent ruins of Leptis Magna in Libya show Septimius's success at furnishing his home provincial city with all the grandeur of a capital. The artificial harbor, temples, public buildings (such as the basilica), four-sided triumphal arch, and other urban developments made Leptis Magna into a shining star along the Empire's African coast.

The Severi

Septimius Severus was born in Leptis Magna (a spectacular site in Libya) and spoke Latin with a recognizable African accent to his death. Emperors of the provinces to the last, the Severans governed Rome from the periphery, as Rome itself and the senate slid into increasing irrelevance. The provinces and provincials became more important than Italy and the Italians, and the army of the borders was held together, not from the center, but from around the edges. These developments proved nearly fatal to the integrity of the Empire once the Severans passed from the stage.

The Severan dynasty.

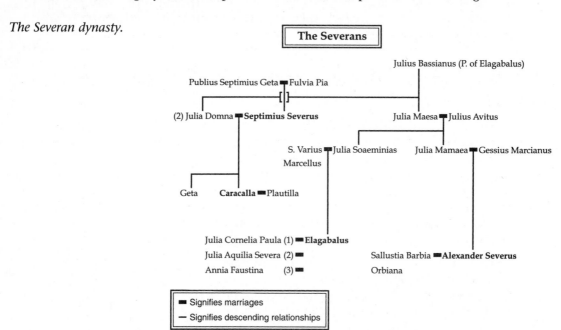

Septimius Severus (193–211)

Septimius had come up under Marcus Aurelius and profited from the patronage of other influential Africans in Marcus's circle. He married Julia Domna, the daughter of a powerful Syrian family in Emesa. Highly educated, he was nevertheless extremely superstitious. Septimus reportedly married Domna because an astrologer told him that she would wed a king. The wedding ceremony took place in Britain—how much more multicultural can you get!

When Septimius got to Rome, he dispatched the disloyal praetorian guards in the name of avenging Pertinax and replaced them with troops loyal to himself. He then defeated Niger, the rival governor of Syria, in 194 and quelled an uprising supporting Albinus, governor of Britain, by 197. Both of these men had supporters in the senate, and Septimius purged them all by execution.

Great Caesar's Ghost!

Julia Domna and her sister Julia Maesa were the daughters of a powerful Syrian high priest of Elagabalus in Emesa, Julius Bassianus. This family played an influential and sometimes controlling role in the Severan dynasty. The women became infamous for their ambitions, their plots, and their adulteries. Domna, in the last stages of breast cancer, starved herself to death instead of surrendering to Macrinus (you'll find out more about Macrinus later in this chapter). Maesa ruled the Empire after the death of her grandson Elagabalus until she died in 226 and her daughter, Julia Mamaea, ruled the Empire as the mother of the young Alexander Severus until both Julia and Alexander were killed together in 235.

Septimius was a brutal man, and he earned the name "Punic Sulla" both for executing his enemies and for confiscating their estates. However, unlike Sulla, Severus was not about building up senatorial power. He made extensive use of equestrians, ended the distinction between senatorial and imperial provinces, and added many provincials from the east to the senate. He was about increased military pay and privileges and promoted the idea of imperial divinity, portraying both himself and members of his family in connection with gods.

Gout and other illnesses plagued Septimius, but he was a restless commander and expanded Roman territory in the east by conquering parts of Parthia and Mesopotamia. He returned to Rome, but soon headed back to the frontiers with his sons Caracalla and Geta. The brothers were bitter rivals, as were their respective supporters. Septimius had elevated Caracalla to co-emperor and Geta to Caesar in 198. He left Geta in Gaul in charge of the Empire while he took Caracalla with him to Britain. Septimius hoped to bring about a conquest of all Britain, but died in York (Eburnacum).

Septimius's death reportedly came none too soon for Caracalla, who was tired both of fighting Scots and of waiting for his old man to die while his brother gained power. Septimius's parting advice

Veto!

Caracalla is a nickname. The emperor's full name was Imperator Caesar Marcus Aurelius Severus Antoninus Pius Augustus. Caracalla got his name from the hooded Gallic overcoat (*caracalla*) that he wore, which became a fashion during his reign.

221

to his sons was, "Get along, enrich the soldiers, and to hell with everyone else." Caracalla apparently missed the first part of that advice.

Caracalla (211–217) and Geta (211)

The brothers were supposed to rule jointly, but their bitter rivalry led to their splitting the imperial palace into two separate houses (kind of like the movie *War of the Roses*). They contemplated splitting the Empire, but their mother put the nix on that by asking them how they intended to split *her*. According to the historian Dio (who is not always the most trustworthy source), Caracalla eventually lured Geta into their mother's apartment and killed him. That solved *that*. He then engaged on a ruthless purge of upward of 20,000 of Geta's supporters. Whatever the case and the actual numbers were, Geta's murder seems to have become a dark cloud that hung over Caracalla's reign and his conscience.

Things were shot with the senate, and following his father's advice, Caracalla concentrated on the military and the provinces. He left for Germany, where he was generally successful in defending and securing the borders, and became very popular with the soldiers as "one of the guys." He issued a declaration of universal citizen rights to all free people of the empire, the *Constitutio Antoniniana*. But as he worked his way down toward the east, Caracalla became entranced with fashioning himself as another Alexander the Great. He began emulating Achilles (Alexander's role model) with a visit to Troy, and made a great show of visiting Alexander's grave in Alexandria. In Alexandria, criticism (probably concerning his murder of Geta) seems to have led him to emulate his role models' worst traits by having his men murder scores of civilians.

Caracalla also tried to revive a version of the Macedonian phalanx for the army before attempting to conquer the Parthians. It was during these campaigns that Macrinus, the praetorian prefect, hatched a plot against him. Caracalla was 29, nearly the same age Alexander the Great was when he died at 32, but Caracalla didn't go very heroically. While the army had discreetly turned its back, a paid assassin stabbed the emperor as he was relieving himself. (I wonder if that's where the phrase "caught with your pants down" comes from?)

Macrinus (217–218)

Macrinus was a Moor and the first to attain the emperorship without even having been elected or appointed to the senate. He was campaigning with Caracalla in the east and took control of the army there. At first, he left mommy dearest, Julia Domna, alone in her palace at Antioch, but she started conspiring to regain control for her family before she died from advanced breast cancer. Macrinus finally ordered her to leave, but she starved herself to death instead.

Macrinus became unpopular with the soldiers, both for negotiating with the Parthians and for failing to heed Severus's deathbed advice as much as he should have. Rumors started that the grandson of Julia Domna's sister Julia Maesa was really Caracalla's. Maesa's lover and supporters smuggled the boy, named Varius Avitus but known as Elagabalus, into a legion who proclaimed him emperor. Things started to fall apart from there for Macrinus, who shaved his hair and tried to flee to the Parthians in disguise. He was betrayed, caught, and executed in 218.

Elagabalus (Hierogabalus) (218–222)

Elagabalus was 14, and the hereditary high priest of the Syrian sun god, Elagabal. The five years of his rule were bizarre, to say the least. Before coming to Rome, his mother (Julia Soaemias) and grandmother (Julia Maesa) made sure that they were in control of things. Rome was shocked by the arrival in the capital of what was, for all purposes, the entourage of its eastern monarchy and priesthood.

Elagabalus tried to compel the Romans to make Elagabal their supreme deity. He built a magnificent new temple, treated Roman gods as subordinate to Elagabal, and carried out daily rituals and sacrifices that the Romans found strange and creepy. More that that, he was notorious for his sexual practices. Leaving aside the number of his marriages (five in three years), he was a cross-dresser who reportedly frequented smarmy clubs where he prostituted himself in drag. He fell in love with and "married" a slave who was allowed to beat his "wife" (the emperor). He sought out the possibilities of a sex-change operation from doctors. He was also charged with promoting lowlifes to high places, such as the Praetorian Guard commander Comazon, whose family were cabaret dancers. Who would put up with this? No one, eventually.

Elagabalus's grandmother persuaded him to adopt her other grandson, Gessius Bassianus Alexianus, as heir. This led to a power struggle between the mother of Elagabalus, Soaemias, and the mother of Alexianus, Maesa. Public and military opinion shifted rapidly toward Alexianus. The praetorians mutinied against Elagabalus, discovered him and Soaemias hiding in a latrine, and killed them. Their bodies were dragged around the city, loaded with weights, and thrown into the Tibur river.

Great Caesar's Ghost!

Maximius was the first enlisted man to become emperor. His chief credentials were his size and strength. Reputed to be a gigantic 8-feet-plus tall, he could pull around fully loaded carts by himself! (Always a good thing to look for in an emperor.) His shoes were so big that they spawned the expression "Maximius's boot" to refer to a tall person.

Alexander Severus (221–235)

Alexianus was only 13 when he became the emperor Alexander Severus. He ruled for 13 years, or rather, his mother, Julia Mamaea, did. Cleopatra's ambitions were realized at last.

Mamaea ruled both Rome and her son—she even banished his wife out of jealousy while Alexander could only wring his hands. There were continual disruptions in Rome with the praetorians and abroad with the legions, and many, such as Mamaea's close advisor, the famous Roman jurist and writer Domitius Ulpianus (Ulpian), lost their lives in the literal cut and thrust of politics.

Alexander made a well-advised attack upon the growing power of Persia, but the attack was poorly carried out and ended in a stalemate that was bad for morale. Later, Alexander went to quell Germanic invasions along the Rhine, but instead of attacking the Germans, he bought them off. This angered his legions. Under their commander, Maximius, they rebelled. They found Alexander in his mother's tent, clinging to her while he berated her handling of things. His inner child never got that chance to grow up; the soldiers killed both him and Maesa, and made Maximius Thrax ("the Thracian") emperor. Maximius was the first of a long line to rise through the ranks to (ostensibly) rule Rome.

Another Day, Another Emperor (235–284)

For the next 50 years, things, quite literally, went to pieces. Plagues swept across the Empire, earthquakes leveled whole regions, and legions promoted their own emperors (the so-called "Barracks" emperors) and assassinated them in turn. There were at least 25 emperors, 16 from 244 to 260, and few died naturally. Under such stress, the provinces began to break away from the powerless core, and it began to look like the Roman Empire would split into several kingdoms just as Alexander's empire had done. But a series of Illyrian emperors helped to bring things back together just in time for Diocletian to stitch it together, temporarily, again.

The Roman Empire was besieged during this period from every side but along the Sahara. Franks, Jutes, and Germanic Alemanni invaded across the Rhine river, and

Vandals and Goths across the Danube river. The Emperor Decius (249–251) was killed fighting against them at Abrittus, the first emperor to die in battle against a foreign enemy. Decius was also the first emperor to institute systematic persecutions of the Christians (for more see Chapter 20, "(Un)Protected Sects: Religions, Tolerance, and Persecutions"), so his early demise was welcome in some quarters.

In the east, the Persian empire began to encroach. The emperor Valerian (253–260) tried to recapture the eastern Empire from the Persians, but he was captured by the Persian king, Shapur, while trying to negotiate terms. A gruesome tradition has it that Valerian ended his days as a movable footstool (he had to bend down so that Shapur could step on him to mount his horse), and that when he died, Shapur dyed his skin green and hung it in a temple as a warning to future visitors. This may only be inspired from a Persian relief (sculpture carved into stone) that shows Valerian kneeling before a mounted Shapur. Nevertheless, news of the emperor's capture was hushed up, but it leaked out. This precipitated the provinces of Gaul breaking away, and the rise of the Palmyrene empire in the east.

I'll mention two major developments you should know about and a couple of the emperors who might interest you.

Great Caesar's Ghost!

Rome's invaders at this time left a lasting imprint upon our modern world. The Franks settled into France (which bears their name), and there, great Frankish dynasties developed. The greatest of these was headed by Charles the Great (Charlemagne), who became the first Holy Roman Emperor. The Alemanni echo in the Franks' name for Germany (Alamands). The Vandals became a synonym for a destroyer, and the Goths live in all things Gothic.

The Gallic Empire

With all the turmoil and without an emperor, provincial areas began to split off to fend for themselves. The largest and longest lasting of these splits was the Gallic empire established by Postumus, the governor of Lower Germany. When Valerian's capture was made known, Postumus, supported by legions of Britain and Spain, formed a breakaway empire against Valerian's son, Gallienus. This empire, whose capital was Trier, survived until 274 when Aurelian defeated the Gallic emperor Tetricus's forces at Châlon-sur-Marne and reabsorbed France, Spain, and Britain back into the Empire.

The Palmyrene Empire

Palmyra was an ancient trading city between Syria and Mesopotamia. After Valerius's capture, the Palmyrene king, Odaenathus, stopped Persian encroachment into the

Lend Me Your Ears

Gallienus was a literary figure as well as emperor. Several speeches and poems survive. Here's a translation of a poem he wrote for a family wedding:

"Okay, kids, go on and together work every part of you into sweat, and don't let the doves outdo your murmurs, the ivy your arms, or the sea-shells your kisses. Go on and play! But don't put out the lamps that keep watch through the night. At night lamps see everything, but at tomorrow's light remember nothing."

Roamin' the Romans

The ruins of Palmyra in Syria show the grand, but ephemeral, power of this city that rose to prominence after Valerian and then fell into obscurity after Aurelian's forces sacked it in 272. Some of the grandest parts of the city remained unfinished after Zenobia's capture in 274.

region. Odaenathus was proclaimed the guardian of the east by the Roman emperor Gallienus, who had the breakaway Gallic provinces to deal with. Odaenathus went on to conquer much of the region. His wife, Zenobia, who in turn became a powerful and famous queen, succeeded him. She ruled the area and broke with Rome in an attempt to control Egypt. She proclaimed her son emperor, but was eventually captured by Aurelian in 274. Aurelian reportedly exhibited her in his triumph at Rome and put her in house arrest at Tivoli until her death.

The Illyrian Emperors

It was a series of valiant Illyrian emperors that gradually conquered the Goths, stabilized the center of the Empire, and reunited the eastern and western portions that had broken away. The most famous of these were Claudius III "Gothicus" (268–270) and Aurelian (270–275). Claudius's short reign was marked by important victories over the Goths (who were able to penetrate into Greece and sack Athens) in 268 and 269, but he fell victim to the plague and died. Aurelian, after abandoning Dacia and calming what remained of the northern borders, was able to capture Zenobia and bring the Palymrene empire back under control and, in the same year (274), defeat the Gallic empire in the west. He is also remembered for constructing a massive defensive wall around Rome that bears his name to this day.

Aurelian also recognized the need for a cohesive element to the Empire. He tried religion by instituting a new religious cult of the Unconquered Sun, Lord of the Roman Empire, and by presenting himself, the emperor, as the divinely appointed representative. Thus, the emperor finally passed from a human office to one achieved through divine will and sanction. This concept reappeared with Diocletian and continued to influence the office once the Empire was Christianized. Aurelian did not live long enough to consolidate and stabilize his achievements, however. He was murdered by a conspiracy of his own men.

Roamin' the Romans

The invasions of the Alemanni and Juthungi into Italy in 271 compelled Aurelian to recognize the vulnerability of Rome. He constructed a massive defensive wall around the city. The Aurelian Wall is about 12 miles in length and originally contained 18 gates. You can find its remains all around Rome, often as a part of later refortification and buildings. The wall marks the decline of Rome from an imperial capital with a wall of legions to a medieval city vulnerable to invasion and pillage.

Following the assassination of Aurelian, the Empire remained united, but the imperial palace on the Palatine resembled a combination of residence and mortuary with a revolving door: From 275 to 285, Rome was ruled by six emperors, all thrust into place by the armies, and all meeting unnatural deaths, mostly at the hands of those who put them in power in the first place. The last of these were the emperors Carinus (283–285), in the west, and Numerian (283–284), in the east. Numerian was assassinated and succeeded by Diocletian, who defeated Carinus in 285 to bring this period to an end.

The Least You Need to Know

➤ The period from Commodus to Aurelian is one of the most complicated in Roman history.

➤ The Severan dynasty resulted in an eastern monarchy ruling the Roman Empire.

➤ The chaos following the Severans, northern invasions, and plagues nearly shattered the Empire.

➤ During the period of the "barracks" emperors, a Gallic empire in the west and a Palmyrene empire in the east temporarily broke away from Rome.

➤ The Illyrian emperors (such as Aurelian) were able to defeat the Goths and regain both the eastern and western Empire.

Chapter 17

Divide and (Re)Conquer: Diocletian to Constantine

In This Chapter

➤ The dominate of Diocletian

➤ The tetrarchy and its breakdown

➤ The rise of Constantine the Great

➤ The Christian emperor and empire

By the time of Diocletian, the Empire was completely mobilized for chaotic war and defense. Provincial armies fought invaders, fought themselves, or fought both while provincials suffered under the boot of repeated conquests and requests. Something new had to happen. The emperor needed to be more than a warlord, central authority and control had to be reestablished, and some binding imperial culture had to be developed. Most of all, stability of some kind had to settle in, or be imposed upon, the seething mass.

In this chapter, we'll follow how Diocletian set about imposing a new kind of structure, cohesion, and stability upon the Empire, and how this structure fell apart and came back together under Constantine the Great, who transformed the Roman Empire into a Christian enterprise.

Diocletian (284–305)

Diocletian was an Illyrian soldier who rose through the ranks to become head bodyguard of the eastern emperor, Numerian. Numerian died mysteriously and the army proclaimed Diocletian emperor. The western emperor, Carinus, refused to recognize him, and the two armies fought. Carinus's army was on the point of winning when it discovered that it had no leader—a jealous tribune had knifed Carinus (who liked to sleep around with his officer's wives) during the battle. Both armies then accepted Diocletian as sole emperor.

Diocletian and Constantine.

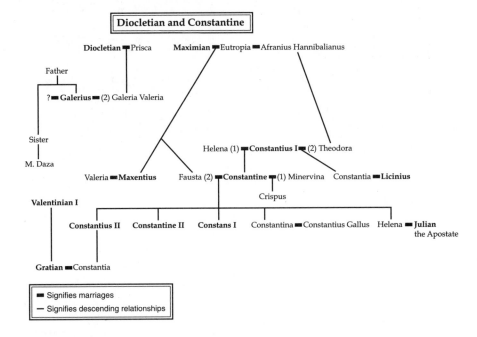

Diocletian faced huge problems in trying to complete the reunification and restoration of the Empire that Illyrian emperors such as Gallienus and Aurelian had started. Central authority had to be permanently reestablished around the emperor, who needed to become a unifying element to the whole in order to exert control. Imperial succession needed to be predictable to get the focus away from competing for succession and on to advancing the Empire. The huge provincial armies had to be redeployed to protect the Empire, not the provinces. The economy of the Empire needed stabilization and systemization to make state finances predictable.

The Dominate

Diocletian needed support from both east and west. He incorporated Carinus's supporters into his administration, building support and using their expertise. He himself, however, dispensed with any pretense of a principate and adopted the official title of "dominus," or "lord and master." Thus began the dominate (as opposed to the principate). He made the emperor more than a military and political autocrat by fashioning himself as "Jovius," Jupiter's chosen one.

The emperor became the representative of the divine order of things, the Empire's right hand, heart, *and* soul. Public images showed his divine aspect by depicting him surrounded by an *aura,* or halo. Diocletian reinforced the image by becoming a figure of mystery and awe. He rarely appeared in public and then only in wondrous regal and ceremonial garb. People were required to treat the emperor as divine, prostrate themselves before him, and kiss his robe. Prayers and sacrifices were offered to him.

Did he believe his press? Probably not, at least not in the way that Caligula and Commodus believed in their own divinity. Diocletian's actions speak of a man who had a method rather than a madness, and who was acting in line with a progression that stretched from Caesar through Aurelian.

Great Caesar's Ghost!

Early Christians had problems with Diocletian's attempts to unify the Empire around a divine emperor. They already had a reputation as subversive because they refused to participate in state sacrifices and prayers. After problems at imperial ceremonies, Diocletian first purged Christians from civil service and the military in 298. He went after churches and clergy in 303, and decreed in 304 that all Christians were to offer sacrifice to the emperor and the Roman gods on pain of death. Large-scale persecutions ensued, urged on by Diocletian's Caesar and heir, Galienus.

Maximian

Diocletian recognized that the unified Empire was still too big for one man to govern effectively. He put a trusted colleague and general, Maximian, in charge of the west with the title of "Caesar" (Diocletian was "Augustus").

Maximian was a Disneyland rags-to-riches story, the son of shopkeepers who rose through the military to become first a hero, then a co-emperor and a god. Raised to the title of "Augustus" in 286, Diocletian, in line with his program, made Maximian divine with the title "Hereculius." The parallels between Jove (Diocletian) and Hercules (Maximian) were not lost on Maximian, who remained a loyal colleague of Diocletian.

Empire in Four-Wheel Drive: The Tetrarchy

Diocletian still needed to ensure a stable transition of his two-ruler system. He created a solution by having himself and Maximian (together called the Augusti) appoint heirs that would take over if either man died or retired. Each heir, or Caesar, would

Roamin' the Romans

Maximian lost control of the north briefly when his naval commander, Carausius, revolted, took control of Britain, and declared himself emperor of the north alongside Maximian and Diocletian. Maximian was unable to bring Carausius under control, but Constantius succeeded in defeating Carausius and reconquering Britain. You can still find some of the fortifications from this period along the British coast, such as the Saxon shore fort at Burgh Castle, Suffolk.

assist his Augustus in ruling his respective hemispheres. Each Caesar also married into his Augustus's family to preserve the dynastic element.

Maximian appointed and adopted his praetorian commander, Constantius Chlorus. Constantius married Maximian's daughter, Theodora. Diocletian similarly adopted Galerius Maximianus as his Caesar, and Galerius married Diocletian's daughter, Valeria. This arrangement of four rulers is known as the *tetrarchy* (from Greek *tetra*, or four). Diocletian clearly had the dominant role, but imperial edicts and proclamations were made in all four tetrarchs' names. Each tetrarch had his own court and defended his territory from regional capitals. Maximian was based in Milan to protect the frontiers along the Rhine and Danube, while Constantius protected Gaul and the Rhine, and went on the reconquer Britain from his capital at Trier. Diocletian saw to the east from his base at Nicomedia (on the Sea of Marmara in modern Turkey), and Galerius saw to the lower Danube and northeast empire from Sirmium (on the Sauve in modern Yugoslavia).

Notice something here? Not one of the tetrarchs resided at Rome. Diocletian himself visited the city only once.

The tetrarchy worked remarkably well. Each tetrarch saw to their own areas and worked to pull the Empire together. The most notable achievements were probably those of Constantius. He put down Carausius, Gallic and Germanic rebellions, and then invaded Britain in 296. He reestablished Roman order from Hadrian's Wall south, cleared the area of pirates, and beautified Trier (Augusta Treverorum) as a thriving capital. Over their tenure, the tetrarchs worked together to defend the Empire efficiently, settle barbarian invaders, and stabilize Rome in a way that allowed the Empire to remain intact for another 200 years. But, the unifying element of the equation remained the personality, character, and drive of Diocletian; as soon as he was gone, the arrangement fell apart in typically Roman-esque fashion.

Emperor, Reformer, and CEO

Diocletian did much more than reform the way that Rome was governed from the top. He applied innovations and complete overhauls to practically everything. He reorganized the provinces under the tetrarchs, grouping them into 12 dioceses under the administration of vicars. These terms, ironically (since Diocletian is known for persecuting Christians), remain active in the administrative language of the church.

Neither the provincial governors nor the vicars had military capabilities and were appointed by the tetrarchs. This arrangement kept provincial power fragmented and under control. In this reorganization, the Italians lost their tax-free status and became just another diocese.

The legions were broken into smaller units so they could be spread out along the borders more efficiently. Diocletian divided them into two classes: border guards (*limitanei*) and imperial troops (*comitatenses*). The latter were more highly trained and paid troops. They were held back from the border for rapid deployment to where they were needed once the *limitanei* were attacked.

Diocletian was a prodigious builder of roads, bridges, and palaces throughout the Empire. This activity and his sweeping administrative reforms took money and brought him face-to-face with a financial crisis of imperial proportions. Rome was mired in a manpower shortage, runaway inflation, currency problems, and layer upon layer of hodgepodge tax and tribute legislation.

Diocletian met these challenges head on—he reformed the currency and established a regular tax collection system in the dioceses and provinces. Taxes on production were paid *in kind* (that is, if you made olive oil you paid in olive oil), and taxes on other assets or labor were assessed by a complicated system of tax units. Workers were organized into guilds (*collegia*) and required to remain where they were. Sons were required to take over their father's occupations. In this way, Diocletian made long-range planning possible and imperial revenues predictable.

Lend Me Your Ears

"And so we encourage the diligent observance of all, so that the matter established out of public convenience might be safeguarded by willing compliance and religious obligation. Mostly, let it appear to have been established by a statue of this manner not just for particular cities, peoples and provinces, but for the whole world, to whose detriment a few people are known to have raged to the utmost extent, and whose greed neither an enormous span of time nor riches (for which they clearly have been eager), have been able to lessen or to satiate."

—Diocletian, from the Preface to his *Edict of Maximum Prices and Wages*

But while the systemization and stabilization of the tax system was good for the Empire, it essentially reduced the common people to the position of serfs bound to the land or to their hereditary occupation. Rome had essentially become a totalitarian state. What's more, although Diocletian set the death penalty for law-breakers, his legislation broke economic laws that could not be repealed, even by a god. Prices continued to climb to the point where no one could afford to produce. Neither Diocletian's monetary reforms nor his famous *Edict of Maximum Prices and Wages* (published with a scathing attack on speculators) in 302 could stop this process.

When in Rome

Diocletian's **Edict of Maximum Prices and Wages** of 302 set price ceilings on over 1,000 goods and services. But prices continued to rise to the point were official production became unprofitable. In the face of declining production and a growing black market, the law was relaxed and finally canceled by Constantine, who nevertheless increased the burden of some of Diocletian's economic reforms.

Too Many Augusti and Not Enough Caesars

After a prolonged illness in 303, Diocletian did something remarkable in 305. He retired. He spent the remaining eight years of his life at his fortified palace at Split. Begrudgingly, Maximian retired as well and left Milan, heading to Lucania to brood and wait for events to change. Constantius became the senior Augustus and was to rule the northwest quadrant; he named Flavius Valerius Severus his Caesar to rule Italy and Africa. Galerius succeeded as the second Augustus to rule the northeast and nominated his nephew, Maximinus Daza, as Caesar to rule the eastern provinces and Egypt.

Okay, let's recap. In the east, we have the tag team of Galerius and Daza; in the west, we have Constantius and Severus. What happens next is predictable. Everybody (including the retired Maximian) wants to be Augustus, nobody wants to be Caesar, and two sons of the tetrarchs, Maximian's son Maxentius and Constantius's son Constantine, force their way into the picture. The system that Diocletian set up to avoid competition and confrontation, well, ensured competition and confrontation in the end. But Diocletian had a retirement.

Roamin' the Romans

Two of Diocletian's most famous building projects, ironically, were partially transformed into centers of Christian worship. The imposing fortress-palace to which he retired remains at Split (Spoleto). The palace is constructed like a fort, with massive defensive gates and towers. The octagonal cathedral there now was originally Diocletian's mausoleum. (Talk about dancing on someone's grave!) The other site is the remains of Diocletian's enormous public baths in Rome. Remains are preserved in the Church of Santa Maria degli Angeli (built by Michelangelo), the National Museum, the church of San Bernardo, and other structures.

Maxentius and Constantine

Constantine was the illegitimate child of Constantius's concubine, Helena. Brought up in Diocletian's court, Constantine was kept by Galerius as insurance against aggression by Constantius (it's always handy to have a rival's son around). But finally, Galerius signed for Constantine to travel to join his father Constantius in 305.

Constantine took no chances that Galerius might change his mind and decide to keep holding onto him. He fled as soon as possible in secret and as he took a new horse on route, he destroyed the old to keep from being pursued and stopped. He was just in time. When he accompanied his father to Britain the next year (306), Constantius died and the army proclaimed Constantine "Augustus" in his father's place. Constantine, however, accepted the title of "Caesar" from Galerius, who promoted Severus to Augustus.

Maximian's son, Maxentius, was enraged; *he* was the son of an Augustus and got nothing! Maxentius seized Rome from Severus in 306 and was soon joined by his father. Maxentius proclaimed himself Augustus, recognized Constantine as Augustus, and nearly undermined Galerius, who had come to Italy to settle things. Maximian got out of hand and tried to retake the mantle (literally) from his son in front of the soldiers and had to be hustled off. Nobody could persuade Diocletian to come out of retirement. Things were getting out of hand.

Great Caesar's Ghost!

Constantine's mother, Helena (St. Helena), made a pilgrimage to the Holy Land in 326. There she identified the stable in which Jesus was born, the place where he was crucified, and the tomb from which he rose. Inspiration led to excavation and the discovery of three crosses at the sight of the crucifixion. A miracle reportedly revealed which was the "true" cross of Christ. Fragments of the True Cross became important relics. Constantine built the original Church of the Holy Sepulcher over the site of the tomb in Jerusalem.

Shakedown

Galerius tried to resettle things in 308 by appointing a colleague, Licinius, as Augustus of the west, keeping Constantine and Daza as Caesars, sending Maximian back to pasture and outlawing his son Maxentius—all of which achieved nothing. Constantine and Daza were angered by the appearance of Licinius. Maximian went to Constantine and, when he got no respect there, started a rebellion, was cornered in

Marseilles, and killed in 310. Constantine then claimed to be a descendant of the Illyrian emperor Claudius Gothicus, thus giving him the hereditary right not to rule as tetrarch (like Maxentius) but as emperor.

By 310, there were five emperors: Galerius and Licinius Augusti, Constantine and Daza Augusti, and Maxentius Augustus. Diocletian refused to come out of retirement (really, what's the use?). Galerius grew ill and needing all the divine help he could get, issued the famous *Edict of Toleration* for Christians in 311—but died anyway. This left Constantine and Licinius to maneuver against M&M (Maxentius and Maximinus Daza).

When in Rome

According to Lactantius's *On the Deaths of the Persecutors,* Christ appeared in a vision to Constantine before the battle of the Mulvian Bridge and commanded him to put the sign of the Chi-Rho on his soldier's shields. The **Chi-Rho** is a symbol made up of a combination of Chi (Greek "ch" [χ] in the shape of a cross) and the head of a Rho (Greek "r" [ρ]), the first two letters in "Christ."

The Mulvian Bridge and Maximinus Daza

Constantine invaded Italy in 312 with a small army and won swift victories on his way to Rome. Maxentius was holed up behind the mighty Aurelian Walls with plenty of food and men, but came out to fight Constantine's smaller army. The night before the battle, something occurred to Constantine. As the result of a vision, he made his battle insignia and soldiers' shields carry the Christian symbol *Chi-Rho.* According to Eusebius, Constantine claimed that he had seen the Chi-Rho blazing across the sun with the words "You will conquer by this sign." The two forces met at the Mulvian Bridge, a pontoon bridge over the Tibur, and Constantine's forces won the day. Maxentius was drowned in the battle. Constantine was proclaimed senior Augustus of the west.

Constantine ordered Daza to stop persecuting the Christians. Later that year, Constantine and Licinius met in Milan where the two men solidified their relationship with Licinius marrying Constantine's half-sister, Constantia. They also reaffirmed the complete freedom of religion in their realms and granted churches corporate status as legal persons with the right to own property. Daza, completely shut out by the two Augusti, made an attempt on Licinius from the east while Constantine was occupied with trouble along the Rhine. Daza was defeated, fled into Asia dressed as a slave, and died of illness. Licinius now ruled the complete east, and Constantine the complete west.

I'll bet you can't guess what happens next.

When in Rome

The **Edict of Toleration** allowed Christians to practice their faith and for their churches to operate legally. Galerious had vigorously pursued and encouraged Christian persecutions while under Diocletian, but this policy was unsuccessful and costly. Whether Galerius decided that religious persecution was practically impossible or was simply hedging his bets on his deathbed is hard to tell. A terrible cancer-like disease may have suggested to him, as it did to Christian historians like Eusebius, that a god was not pleased. He asked for Christians to pray for both him and the state, but remained less than charitable, executing doctors who were unable to stand the sight of his decaying flesh or who failed to arrest the progress of the disease. He died, from all accounts, a horrible death.

Showdown

From 313 to 316, the Empire remained in an uneasy balance. Constantine eventually provoked a dispute over whether his or Licinius's sons would succeed him and invaded eastward. Although things went well for Constantine at first, he bogged down in the Balkans (doesn't everyone?), and the two came to a truce.

Over the next six years, Constantine began to cooperate with and elevate the status of the Church. He gave it greater power and privileges until Licinius began to suspect a holy conspiracy against him. Licinius eventually turned against some of the Christian bishops in his realm, executed them, and razed their churches. This gave Constantine the pretext he needed to invade again and defeat Licinius at Chrysopolis in 324. Constantia made a plea for her husband's life and Constantine granted it—for about a year. Then he had Licinius and his nine-year-old son hanged.

Veto!

Constantine was the first Christian emperor, but his conversion to Christianity was gradual and complicated. He continued to officially patronize traditional gods, to hold pagan state religious offices, and to represent himself with both Christian and pagan religious symbols on his coins. He was not baptized until just before his death in 337 (a practice that was common to assure purity on death), and then—ironically—deified by the Roman senate.

Constantine the Great (324–337)

Constantine changed the course of European history by converting the official Empire to Christianity and by moving the capital to Constantinople (ancient Byzantium, modern Istanbul). He set the stage for over a thousand more years of Roman imperial survival.

Christian historians have portrayed Constantine as the opposite of the Dark Lord Diocletian, but in fact, Constantine continued many policies of his predecessor. Although he was sole ruler, Constantine passed on divided rule to his sons (it didn't work any better with them). During his rule, he adopted some aspects of the tetrarchy by appointing four prefects over the most important prefectures (Italy, Gaul, Illyrium, the east) and giving them executive control over all facets except military command. He continued military reorganization along Diocletian's model.

Constantine also continued Diocletian's economic and social programs. His laws bound people even tighter to their occupations, social positions, and location. One of his new taxes was so onerous that it was said that every collection year wailing went up throughout the cities in anticipation of the beatings people would get for failing to pay in full. Parents reportedly had to sell children into slavery and prostitution, and the provinces complained bitterly about being forced into destitution. On the other hand, Constantine *was* able to stabilize the currency and imperial finances for the future. So, at least in business ethics, you could see his practices as a good thing.

Great Caesar's Ghost!

Istanbul, the modern name for Constantinople, has been in use since about the eleventh century. It comes from a corruption of the Greek *eis tēn polin* (to the city), the reply travelers gave when asked where they were going. Sacked by the Crusaders in 1204 and eventually conquered by the Ottoman Turks in 1453, modern Istanbul remains a luscious and cacophonous mix of ages, cultures, sights, sounds, and tastes.

Finally, by aligning himself with the church, Constantine turned himself into the figure that Diocletian had sought to become. He rewelded politics and religion and expanded upon Diocletian's practices of imbuing the imperial court with pomp and an aura of sacred importance. But instead of the earthly representative of Jupiter, Constantine became the earthly representative of God. You can see this idea in his self-proclaimed title of *Isoapostelis* (Equal of the Apostles) and especially in his planned burial in the Church of the Holy Apostles. Surrounded by 12 sarcophagi for each apostle, Constantine's sarcophagus was placed in the center, the symbolic place of Christ. He remains venerated as a Saint by the Greek, Armenian, and Russian Orthodox Churches.

Moving the Center of the Empire

The tetrarchs transformed their regional capitals into imperial cities. Constantine looked for a new center of power from which to rule without the baggage and isolation of Rome. He chose the site of the ancient

Greek city of Byzantium, which lay along the Bosporus strait. The site offered rich trade routes, commanded the entrance to the Black Sea, and sat on the fault line between Asia and Europe.

Constantine's rebuilding program began in 325 and laid the foundations of the great walls in 328. It was an enormous building program, and Constantine was determined to make the city a worthy capital. An imperial palace and senate house, libraries and universities, hippodrome and forum looked back to one history; magnificent new churches (Holy Peace, Holy Wisdom, The Twelve Apostles) looked back to another. He had to pillage a lot of material from pagan shrines such as Delphi to do it, but on May 11, 330, the new city, *Nova Roma,* had its opening ceremony and received privileges formerly granted to Rome. Nova Roma soon was called Constantinople, but in all respects was intended to be the "new" Rome, the center of a new Empire summed up a new sound bite: one ruler, one world, one creed.

Roamin' the Romans

Constantine continued to patronize the former capital with buildings and churches. He completed the Basilica of Maxentius and the last of the great imperial public baths. Constantine's religious building construction in Rome included the original churches of St. John Lateran and St. Peter's. Helena, Constantine's mother, was buried in Rome at Tor Pignattara and Constantina, his daughter, in a mausoleum that is now the Church of Santa Constanza. You will find the remains of his famous colossal statue in the Palazzo dei Conservatori on the Capitoline.

The Christian Empire

Well, the "one creed" part was tough. Constantine's first taste of discord was the Donatist Schism in Africa while he was still an Augustus. Donatists were radical followers of the bishop Donatus. They felt that the pope was too forgiving of backsliders during the Diocletian persecutions. They elected Donatus, who had endured nine rackings (a rack is an instrument of torture) during the persecutions, as a rouge bishop of Carthage. Widespread riots broke out when Constantine summoned two councils in 313 and 314 and backed their decisions against the Donatists. Constantine ordered the Donatists suppressed in 314, but gave up the persecution in 321 in frustration. He was just feeding the fire: These martyrs weren't amateur, they were *professional.*

Later, another major doctrinal controversy arose between the church hierarchy and followers of the bishop Arian concerning the nature of Christ's divinity. Under Licinius, the controversy raged between Christian communities and among the clergy until Licinius, angry at the disturbances and suspecting Constantine's complicity, began to persecute both sides again.

Great Caesar's Ghost!

At Nicea, the difference between the Arians and the others came down to one letter. The Arians asserted that Christ was *homioousios* (of a like, but not identical, substance) while the others asserted that Christ was *homoousios* (of the exact same substance). Arian lost because the majority refused to budge an iota—the name for the Greek letter "i" that the Arians wanted in the language of the Nicene Creed. Arianism became a heresy, and the other became orthodox (correct belief) doctrine.

When in Rome

The **Nicene Creed** ("Nicene" from the Council of Nicea, "Creed" from the Latin *credo*, "I believe") is a fundamental declaration and definition of what (orthodox) Christians believe. It lays out the basic tenants of faith regarding the nature of God, the trinity (God the Father, God the Son [Jesus], God the Holy Spirit), and the Church.

As sole emperor, Constantine wanted the same organizational unity in the church that he wanted for the Empire. He didn't care so much for the fine points of the Arian dispute, and said so in a letter to the respective leaders in which he asked for reconciliation. When that didn't work, he brought bishops, at state expense, from all over Europe to a council at Nicea in 325. There, he gave the council's keynote address (in Greek) and oversaw the debate.

The Nicene Council developed the famous *Nicene Creed*, established the date for Easter and other matters of orthodox belief, organized the Catholic Church, and rejected Arian and commanded his writings to be burnt. This did not end things, however, because Arians remained a prominent unorthodox sect of heretics. Some later emperors saw things their way, and Arian missionaries made great strides among the Germanic and Gothic peoples who overran the Nicene west. Later popes found orthodox champions in the Frankish kings, but the Arian controversy packed a lot of punch into one small iota.

Love and Loss

Faith and hope may have abided in the imperial household, but love was a problem. Constantine's son Crispus by his first wife, was a successful and talented heir. But Constantine's second wife, the Empress Fausta, wanted her sons to succeed in Crispus's place. She accused Crispus of trying to rape her. Constantine's edicts on sexual crimes saw to his execution. Later, Fausta found herself in hot water for this accusation. Helena convinced her son Constantine that Fausta had concocted the story, and Constantine had his wife scalded to death in a steam bath.

Great Caesar's Ghost!

Constantine's harsh laws concerning sexual crimes are indicative of a deep distrust of women. Rapists were burned alive, but girls who were raped away from home were also harshly punished (a version of "If you were there you must have done something to deserve it or wanted it to happen"). Girls who eloped with lovers were burned along with their lovers. If a female attendant helped in the elopement, she was executed by pouring molten lead down her throat. If parents concealed the fact that their daughter was pregnant out of wedlock, they were deported.

Constantine's last plans were to conquer the Persian Empire and Christianize it. He grew ill along the way, died in Ankyrona in 337, and was buried in the Church of the Holy Apostles at Constantinople (much to the Romans' dismay). He left to his three sons an empire completely transfigured and transformed into a theocratic state. Constantine was fittingly both the first Christian emperor and the last deified by pagan Rome. The trinity of the sons, however, was unable to maintain the unity of the father until one became the *dominus* if no longer a *deus*.

When in Rome

In a **theocracy** the state is ruled by a god, or by an authority thought to be divinely guided and ruling in the god's name.

The Least You Need to Know

➤ Diocletian promoted the divinity of the emperor in a program to unify the Empire.

➤ Diocletian established a tetrarchy that ruled effectively as long as he remained active.

➤ After Diocletian's retirement, the tetrarchy fell apart until Constantine the Great unified the Empire again.

➤ Constantine maintained many of Diocletian's reforms but transformed the Empire into a Christian, not pagan, theocratic state.

Chapter 18

Barbarians at the Gates: The Fall of the Western Empire

> ## In This Chapter
>
> ➤ Dissolution after the death of Constantine
>
> ➤ Upheavals in the Empire and culture from Julian to Theodosius II
>
> ➤ The barbarian hordes
>
> ➤ The "fall" of the western half of the Empire

Constantine's motto of "one ruler, one Empire, one creed" didn't outlive him. The Empire split into east and west, and no one creed held either together. Things were, at least for the western half, on the downhill side as a landslide of barbarians surged across the borders. As you now understand, barbarian invasions had been going on for a millennium. Nevertheless, something "Roman" had previously been able to rise up through the new layer, break it down through conquest and assimilation, and re-grow. But after Constantine, the waves were too great, too frequent, and too deep.

Rome, the city, was buried under the barbarian avalanche with little more than the trappings of an illustrious history and a few churches protruding. A wild western forest of Frankish, German, Vandal, and Ostrogoth stock grew up, away from, and often in opposition to "Roman" Constantinople. Eventually, the barbarian kingdoms matured and nourished, based on the old Rome, the hopes of empires to come, which were only marginally "Holy" or "Roman."

"My Three Sons"

Constantine left the Empire with many possible heirs but without a succession plan. After initial bloodletting in which most of Constantine's half-brothers and their families were killed, rule of the Empire passed to his three sons by Empress Fausta.

Constantine II (337–340) took the prefecture of Gaul, Constans I (337–350) took the prefecture of Italy and Illyria, and Constantius II (337–361) took the prefecture of the east. Constantine II (the eldest) was supposed to have greatest authority, but you know how it goes with brothers in one room. Constans I kept putting his toe (so to speak) into Constantine II's side, and in 340, big brother came into Italy to teach Constans a lesson. Constantine, however, was killed, and Constans got the prefecture of Gaul instead of a lesson.

The Roman Empire after Constantine.

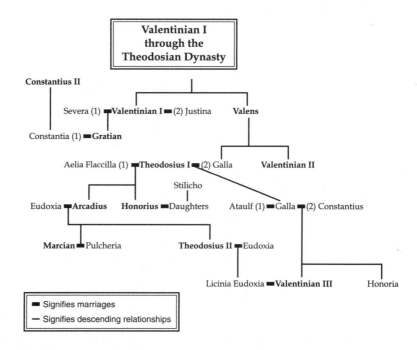

This arrangement lasted until Constans was assassinated in 350 and replaced by his general, Magnentius. Constantius II was having problems fighting the Persians in the east, but he was not about to let Magnentius usurp two-thirds of the Empire. He defeated Magnentius in 351, and by 353, the whole Empire was back under the rule of one emperor.

Constantius was a moderate Arian (see Chapter 17, "Divide and [Re]Conquer: Diocletian to Constantine," for a discussion of Arianism) and encouraged the church to incorporate doctrinal differences. Beyond Christianity, he was less open-minded. He further Christianized the state against paganism and kept his father's ban on pagan temples and sacrifices.

Constantius was indecisive and suspicious, which led him to be manipulated by people in the imperial household, bureaucracy, and church. His temperament played out when he appointed Gallus, one of two remaining sons of Constantine's half-brother Julius, as Caesar in the east. Constantius surrounded him with his own people, and when Gallus turned out to be mildly successful and a potential rival, had him beheaded.

Can't Rewind: Julian the Apostate (361–363)

Trouble in both Gaul and Illyria meant Constantius was needed in two places at one time. He recalled Julian, Gallus's 23-year-old brother, from his studies in Athens, named him Caesar, and sent him to Gaul.

Julian turned out to be an intelligent, likeable, and successful commander. He restored the borders, won some spectacular victories, and became endeared to the people and army for limiting the abuses of Roman officials. This didn't sit well either with the officials, who denounced him to Constantius, or with Constantius, who feared Julian's growing popularity. He commanded Julian's troops to fight in the east, but Julian refused to send them. This made him even more popular with the local legions and their families. They proclaimed Julian "Augustus" in 360.

Julian protested the proclamation (so he said), tried to negotiate with Constantius (who was having none of this), and then marched out to meet Constantius, who was already headed his way, in battle. But Constantius died along the way without leaving an heir. Julian became the sole emperor.

When in Rome

Remember that the Christian **Church** of this period saw itself as a whole: It was organized under bishops and guided through the decisions of councils, such as the council of Nicea. Organized sects and denominations were, for the most part, a later phenomenon: Eastern and Western Orthodox churches, for example, didn't formally split until 1054.

Great Caesar's Ghost!

Julian remains a controversial figure today. He still remains, to some, the apostate—to others, the vilified, if outdated, pagan and intellectual who attempted to roll back Christianity's hold on Rome.

Julian was raised a Christian, but his studies and the fact that his entire family had been murdered by Christians combined to bring him back to traditional pagan values. He declared himself to be a pagan and rescinded laws against non-Christian practices. Julian was a prolific writer, and many of his works survive. Although he claimed freedom for religion and tolerance for Christianity, he attempted to advance a kind of official Neoplatonic paganism as a state religion in its place.

When in Rome

Neoplatonism was the most influential pagan philosophy of late antiquity, and was a complicated synthesis of philosophic and spiritual teachings. It not only influenced early Christian theologians (like Augustine), but also Medieval and Renaissance thinkers and writers.

When in Rome

Pagan comes from the Latin *paganus*, meaning "country peasant," and stems from Christianity being mostly an urban phenomenon in which the country dwellers (the *pagani*) were the last to convert. The same is true of the term "heathen," which refers to the primitive dwellers who lived in the wild "heaths" of Europe and England.

Julian authored significant administrative and tax reforms, and gave the Jews permission to rebuild the temple in Jerusalem, but his promotion of pagan ways met with outrage and resistance among the Christian communities that had thought the church triumphant. They termed him "the apostate," or "backslider." This was particularly true in Antioch, from which Julian mounted an attack upon Persia. Antioch was heavily Christianized in politics and religion, and Julian's efforts there met with rejection.

A spear, reportedly thrown by one of his own Christian soldiers, wounded Julian during the campaign against Persia, and he died shortly thereafter. He remains a controversial figure today—still the apostate to some, the vilified pagan intellectual to others.

Julian's demoralized army, hounded by the Persians as they retreated, elected another commander, Jovian, as emperor. Jovian was a moderate Christian. He rescinded Julian's edicts and negotiated a settlement (a very bad one) with the Persians before he died just eight months later.

Roman Gothic: Theodosius to Alaric and the Sack of Rome

Julian was the last of Constantine's line, and Jovian had left no heir. The officers and officials in Constantinople chose Valentinian, and Valentinian chose his brother, Valens; they ruled over west and east respectively in 364. The mishandling of invasions plagued this dynasty. Valentinian, in an audience with barbarian envoys along the Rhine, died from a stoke brought on in a fit of rage; he left his 16-year-old son, Gratian, in charge.

In the east, Valens settled many of the migrating Goths on Roman soil, but his administrators abused them so badly that they revolted and, together with the Ostrogoths, defeated and killed Valens in battle in

378. Gratian appointed a Spanish commander, Flavius Theodosius, as emperor of the east. Gratian completely offended the remaining old Romans by ordering the removal of the statue of Victory from Rome at the urging of Ambrose, the bishop of Milan. Even the old gods, who had served the city well, had now abandoned Rome. The end could not be far behind.

More pious than effective, Gratian was killed in 383 by rebellious troops. His brother, Valentinian II, briefly recovered the throne, but he, too, was assassinated by his commander Arbogast. Arbogast appointed a puppet emperor, Eugenius, to the throne, but they were defeated by Theodosius in 394.

Theodosius the Great (379–395)

Theodosius settled the Goths and negotiated a treaty with them in 382, which was to have grave consequences for the Empire. He allowed the Goths to settle as a kingdom under the jurisdiction of their own kings. While this allowed them to handle many of their own affairs and brought them into the Empire as a fighting force with their own organization and training, it also established a precedent for barbarian kingdoms to be set up within the borders of the Empire. When these kings eventually became the western emperors themselves, the "fall" of Rome was (at least in the historian Edward Gibbon's mind) complete.

Lend Me Your Ears

"Those following our law shall be known as 'Catholic' Christians and the rest, since we judge them fools and madmen, shall endure the infamy of heretics nor call their gatherings 'churches.' They are to be punished by divine retribution and by whatever vengeance we, in accordance with heavenly judgement, decide to inflict."

—Theodosius I, from the *Theodosian Code* 6.1.2

"It's a reasonable assumption that we all worship essentially the same thing. We gaze up at the same stars, the same sky is above us all, the same universe surrounds us. What difference does it make which system we each use to arrive at the truth? We cannot arrive at so great a mystery by one way alone."

—Symmachus, *Dispatches to the Emperor*, 3.9–10, adapted from Shelton

Veto!

Paganism didn't die out with Theodosius. Although its vitality declined and waned, pagan religion was still practiced into the sixth and seventh centuries. Pagan philosophy and ritual were profoundly influential upon Christianity, and some of it was incorporated, in different guises, over the centuries into Christian practice, thought, and doctrine. Neoplatonism, for example, profoundly influenced Christian conceptions of angels and demons, while December 25th was the birthday of *Sol Invictus*, the monotheistic "Unconquered Sun" god patronized by emperors such as Aurelian and Julian. It became the date for Christmas in the fourth century.

Theodosius, an ardent Nicene Christian, also influenced other important developments. With the council and urging of Ambrose, he first pursued making Nicene Christianity the only Roman Christianity, and then Christianity the only Roman religion. He completed Constantine's work by officially banning both public and private pagan religious observations in 391 (Jews were not included in this proclamation). But Theodosius found that religious sanction can bite even an emperor. He allowed his forces to massacre civilians in Thessolonika in 390 and found himself excommunicated by Ambrose. With the gates of paradise shut off from him, Thedosius was compelled to do penance. This set the stage for similar confrontations between state and ecclesiastical power in the west.

The Boy Emperors

When Theodosius the Great died in 395, the traditional interpretation has been that he left an Empire stumbling under enormous taxes, corrupt officials, and depopulated cities. More recent archeological evidence, however, provides a different picture at least in places: Britain, for example, was extremely prosperous even as the Romans left the province! In any case, Theodosius divided the Empire that he had unified among his sons. He left the eastern half to his 18-year-old son, Arcadius, and to his 10-year-old son, Honorius, he left the wild, wild west. It was an uneven division. Rebellions and invasions kept Honorius's hold over the west very weak and very insecure. He spent most of his time hiding out in his capital at Ravenna, which was impregnable because of marshes on all sides and offered a sea escape and supply route.

Arcadius died in 408 and left the east to his 7-year-old son, Theodosius II. Theodosius II ruled for 40 years, mostly under the eye of his sister, Pulcheria, and his wife, Eudocia. His most famous achievement came when he formed a board of scholars to compile a codification of Roman laws since the time of Constantine. This compilation, known as the Theodosian Code and published in 438, was intended to bring a unified legal system to the whole Empire. One of Theodosius's other projects suggests the dangerous times in which he lived. He completed a massive defensive wall around Constantinople, which, like Rome, had become vulnerable to attack by Goths and Huns, whom he paid massive yearly tributes to keep away.

Theodosius fell from his horse in 450 and died. His death without an eastern heir firmly entrenched the split between east and west. Factions of the eastern empire were left to contend for political and doctrinal dominance under the emperors Marcian (450–457), Leo I (457–474), and Zeno (474–491), who was the eastern emperor when the west "fell."

The succession of boy emperors in both east and west helped to bring on the permanent division of the Empire. In short, these youngsters required adults (who were not emperors) to do their jobs. Sometimes these adults were powerful imperial women. Sometimes they were high-ranking court officials. Both attempted to maneuver the emperors according to their own rivalries and ambitions. All eventually became powerless to control the barbarian warlords and commanders who ostensibly served them.

None of these barbarians (and often Arians) had hope of becoming emperor in the face of Rome and Constantinople. Instead they sought their own kingdoms within Rome in some cases, and in others sought to become supreme commander, *Magister Militum* (Master of the Soldiers) and achieve the status of patrician. From these positions, they could control the Empire and the emperors, and through marriage into the imperial families attempt to establish dynasties of their own.

Women of Influence

A number of imperial women played important roles in the Theodosian dynasty. Some of the most important of these include …

➤ **Gallia Placidia,** the half-sister of Honorius and Arcadius, and mother of Valentinian III. She was captured when the Goths sacked Rome and carried off. Later, she became the practical ruler of the west and rival of the general Aetius. Some of her correspondences survive as well as the churches she built at Ravenna.

Great Caesar's Ghost!

Besides the legal code that bears his name, Theodosius, under the influence of Eudocia, established and endowed a great university in Constantinople to rival earlier centers of learning such as Athens and Alexandria. This university was responsible for preserving much of the Greek classical culture that passed eventually to the west and fueled the Italian Renaissance.

When in Rome

Patrician was an honorary title bestowed by the emperor, not an official office.

➤ **Pulcheria**, the older sister of Theodosius II. She was a powerful figure, committing herself to orthodoxy and to chastity, which she maintained through her dynastic marriage to the emperor Marcian in 450. She was influential and active: She ruled as regent over Theodosius II, issued edicts against pagans and Jews (the famous Greek female philosopher *Hypatia* was killed in Alexandria during this time), and convened the Council of Ephesus in 431 to debate ongoing doctrinal differences among the bishops. Pulcheria vied for influence over religion, politics, and Theodosius II with Eudocia, and eventually won.

Great Caesar's Ghost!

Hypatia (ca 370–415) was the leader of the Neoplatonic school in Alexandria (Egypt). She was a famous philosopher, mathematician, astronomer, speaker, and popular teacher. Supporters of Pulcheria's bishop, Cyril, feared her influence with city authorities. A mob of them attacked and killed Hypatia in her own home.

When in Rome

The **Magister Militum**, or "Master of the Soldiers," was the military title for a supreme commander (under the emperor) of both infantry and cavalry.

➤ **Eudocia**, the wife of Theodosius II. She was the well-educated daughter of a philosopher, and a poet of some distinction. She converted to Christianity for the marriage and fought a long battle with Pulcheria for influence. Eudocia was eventually disgraced by rumors of adultery (started by Pulcheria) and left for Jerusalem to devote herself to better things.

Stilicho and Alaric

Two important figures illustrate the power of the times struggles between east and west and between barbarian and Roman forces. The first is Stilicho, a Vandal who became *Magister Militum* under Theodosius the Great. The second is Alaric, the great king of the Visigoths.

Stilicho married Theodosius's niece, Serena, and was entrusted by Theodosius with the fortunes of the young heirs Arcadius and Honorius. Stilicho became Honorius's regent in the west, but fostered imperial ambitions of his own, including plans for his son to marry Gallia Placidia, a patron of churches, and his daughter to marry Honorius.

His ambitions conflicted with those of Rufinus, one of the high officials in the court of the boy emperor Arcadius in the east. Rufinus and Stilicho began to seek advantage over each other's half of the empire and to gain possession of Illyria, ostensibly in the name of their respective emperors. But before the two sides could deal directly with each other, they had to deal with the Visigoths, who were rebelling under Alaric.

Alaric was a king of the Visigoths who had been allowed to settle on Roman lands by Theodosius. Since then, the Visigoths had helped to defend the Empire against other barbarian invaders and felt poorly paid in return. Alaric rebelled and plundered almost to Constantinople itself, but was captured by Stilicho in 395. He was ordered released, however, by Arcadius (on Rufinus's advice) and allowed to regain his strength. Alaric then left Constantinople alone and led this army south on a swath of destruction down through the central empire into Greece. Stilicho finally arranged Rufinus's assassination in 395, but by then, the eastern empire feared his power. When Stilicho intervened and attacked Alaric's forces in 397, Constantinople declared Stilicho a public enemy for interfering outside of his jurisdiction.

After Rufinus's death in 395, the eunuch Eutropius, Arcadius's chamberlain, ran the eastern government in Arcadius's name and continued to deploy Alaric against Stilicho and Honorius. He gave Alaric a high command, and in 401, the Visigoths invaded Italy. They had Honorius cornered in Milan, away from the safety of Ravenna, but Stilicho brought his forces down from the north and captured Alaric's family. Alaric's forces withdrew but invaded again in 403. Again Stilicho defeated him, but the enormous invasions along the northern borders meant Stilicho could not stay. Alaric invaded Italy again in 407, demanding a huge tribute and employment for his army. This time Stilicho persuaded the Roman senate to accept the terms. Anger in Rome over the terms fueled the suspicion that this time Stilicho and Alaric might be working together and led to Stilicho's arrest and execution by Honorius in 408.

Roamin' the Romans

Gallia Placidia, half-sister of Honorius and Arcadius and mother of Valentinian III, was a patron of churches such as the basilica of St. Paul Outside-the-Walls in Rome and the Church of the Holy Cross in Jerusalem. During a voyage, a storm threatened to sink the ship with her and her children (Valentinian III and Honoria) on board. Placidia made an "Oh Lord, if you save me I will …" vow. You can read about it on the dedicatory inscription of the Church of the Holy Cross in Ravenna.

Barbarians in the Gates: Alaric and the Sack of Rome

With Stilicho dead, Honorius reneged on his bargain with Alaric. Alaric was not amused and laid siege to Rome. The Romans agreed to pay him a huge ransom to stop, but when he did, Honorius backed out before payment was made, and Alaric resumed the siege in 409. Finally, the Romans, mostly the pagans who had opposed the outlawing of their traditions and practices, elected another emperor and established a new administration with Alaric as commander.

As Honorius waffled as to what to do about his Roman rebellion, Alaric tried to play both sides against the middle. He agreed to dump the Romans and side with Honorius, but a rival barbarian leader came over to Honorius first. This left Alaric out of favor with both sides again. Alaric then turned his forces on Rome and sacked the city in 310. For three days, the Visigoths pillaged and burned, and when they left, they took a bundle of loot and Honorius's sister, Gallia Placidia, with them and marched south. Alaric, however, was not long for this world. He died on the way but received a fitting burial: His people diverted a river, buried Alaric under the bed, and turned the river back into its channel to hide and protect his grave. True or not, it's a great story!

Great Caesar's Ghost!

Alaric's conquest of Rome brought about a great "We told you so" outcry from the pagans of Rome. The statue of Victory had been removed, pagan rites were forbidden, and then, for the first time in 800 years, Rome was sacked. It appeared clear that the gods had abandoned Rome because Rome had abandoned the gods. The power of this sentiment compelled Augustine's 14-year effort to reconsider and recast history in his late, great work, *The City of God.* Augustine became the bishop of the North African city of Hippo, where he died in 430 just as it was about to fall to the Vandals.

In Alaric's place, the Visigoths elected Athaulf, who married the kidnapped Placidia (with her consent). It's actions like these that show that the Gothic tribes' bottom-line aim in engaging Rome was not plunder, but incorporation into the empire. Honorius and the in-laws responded by sending Stilicho's replacement, Constantius, with an army instead of wedding gifts. They cornered the Visigoths in Spain and got Placidia back. Honorius settled the Visigoths under Athaulf's successor, Vallia, as an independent nation within the province of Aquitania (west-central France, modern Gascony). Vallia's successor, Theodoric I, eventually became king of the entire province.

The End Is Near

In the late fourth and fifth centuries, the northern Roman borders from the Black Sea to the North Sea were awash in barbarian migrations, invasions, and dislocations. Barbarian tribes took advantage of Roman disorganization and weakness in the west, but they also were being pushed from behind by the rapid encroachment of the Huns. As tribes poured across the borders, they tended to settle down (after a suitable amount of pillage) and become federated allies of Rome. These former invaders allied with Rome to defeat Attila and save Europe from the Huns, but by then the western empire had become a patchwork of barbarian kingdoms. The western imperial family (and later the popes) tried to manipulate these kings against each other for their own purposes, and the kings did the same in return.

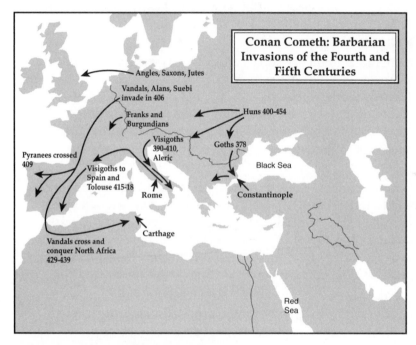

Conan cometh: the barbarian invasions.

Know Your Barbarians

Okay. We've already talked in various chapters about "barbarians," such as tribes of Gauls, Germans, Visogoths (Eastern Goths) and Ostrogoths (Western Goths). So were these new invaders more of the same? Well, yes and no. Some of the barbarian invasions of this period were Gallic and Germanic tribes though different tribes from previous centuries. Others came from as far away as central Asia. Here are the most important tribes to be familiar with for understanding the fourth and fifth century invasions:

➤ **Angles, Saxons, and Jutes.** These Germanic tribes lived along the North Sea in what is now Denmark and northwest Germany. Their raids on Britain in the fifth century led to invasions in 408 and settlements that drove the Romans out of Britain for good in 442.

➤ **Franks and Burgundians.** These peoples invaded across the Rhine in 406 to 407. At first fought by the Romans, they eventually settled parts of Gaul and became autonomous but federated allies that helped the Romans defeat Attila and the Huns in 451.

➤ **Vandals, Alans, and Suevi.** These people came from a swath of territory extending from about Mainz, Germany, east through Hungary. They invaded across the Rhine at Mainz in 406 and made their way down through central France and across the Pyranees into Spain by 409. There they were partially contained by a combined force of Romans and Visigoths, who had gotten to the area first under Alaric and Athaulf.

A particularly ambitious group of Vandals under king Gaeseric invaded across the Straits of Gibraltar in 428 and conquered all of North Africa, Sicily, Sardinia, and Corsica. Gaeseric sacked Rome again in 455 and carried off Valentinian III's widow, Eudocia, and two daughters. The eldest, Eudocia, married Gaesaric's eldest son, Huneric, but the Vandals remained an outlaw nation until the eastern emperor Zeno recognized their legitimacy in 476. By then, however, the west was over.

➤ **The Huns.** These were a fierce nomadic people and tremendous cavalrymen, who originated in central Asia. They pressured the Ostrogoth and Alan kingdoms, and under their king, Rua, became powerful enough to exact a yearly payoff of 350 pounds in gold from Theodosius II to keep them away. Rua and the Huns were particularly helpful to Aetius in his attempts to maintain power over the west and over the imperial family.

Rua's nephew, Attila, succeeded him in 434 and turned the Huns into an empire. He was encouraged by the Vandal king Gaiseric to attack the Visigoths, and by Valentinian III's sister, Honoria, to attack Europe and establish himself, and her, with an empire of their own. Attila's forces got as far as Orleans, but had to turn back in 451. On the Mauriac Plain, a combined force of federated barbarians and the Roman army under Aetius fought Attila's army to a draw. Attila then attacked Italy to demand Honoria, but was turned back by the plague, the arrival of an army from the east, and the intervention of Pope Leo. He died in 454 while settling for marriage to Burgundian royalty.

Aetius and the End of the Theodosians

After Stilicho and Alaric, the heirs of Theodosius struggled for position and control of the west. Constantius married Gallia Placidia. Their child, Valentinian III, became a threat to Honorius' position, so mother and child saw to their protection and took refuge with Theodosius II until Honorius's death in 423. By the time Theodosius decided to install the six-year-old Valentinian III as emperor, a certain "John" had been proclaimed emperor at Ravenna with the support of the general Aetius. In sorting it all out, Gallia Placidia became Regent, the six-year-old Valentinian III became Emperor, and Aetius became *Magister Militum* (Supreme Commander).

For the next 20 years, Aetius managed to control the imperial family and play off the various barbarian warlords against each other. His masterful management of the western empire has led some to call him "the last of the Romans." Aetius's close ties with the Huns, among whom he had lived as a young man as a hostage, helped him greatly. His defeat of Attila in 451 brought him still greater power, to the resentment of Gallia Placidia and Valentinian III. Even though Aetius's son had married Valentinian's daughter, mother and son conspired with a powerful Roman senator, Potronius Maximus, to lure Aetius to a meeting in 454. There Valentinian himself killed Aetius, who was the last "Roman" with the power and skill to keep the west together.

Looking down on the ruins of the ancient forum and the remains of the Basilica of Maxentius where Constantine's colossal statue once stood.

When Valentinian didn't give Maximus the position he expected (namely Aetius's), Maximus conspired with Aetius's officers and assassinated Valentinian in 455. Maximus attempted to establish himself as emperor by marrying Valentinian's widow, Eudoxia, and her daughter, Eudocia, to his son. However, Gaeseric (king of the north African Vandals) had arranged for *his* son to marry Eudocia. This explains what brought the Vandals to Rome that year and why, besides their plunder, they carried both Eudoxia and Eudocia back to Africa with them.

And Maximus? He was killed by a stone thrown at him while he fled the attack. The house of Theodosius was over in the west; it was up to the barbarians now.

The Western "Fall"

"Stop! Stop!" I hear you saying, "I can't keep it all straight! *I* want to destroy the west!" Well, hang in there—it's almost over. We're perilously close to 476, the year of Rome's fall (according to Gibbon, remember). The western Empire is spinning out of control and spiraling into the beginnings of the Middle Ages. Before we proceed, however, think back to the different theories we looked at in Chapter 2, "Rome FAQ: Hot Topics in Brief," regarding why Rome fell. Well, does the impending fall sound like a problem of lead pipes to you? Global warming? Simple economics? No, many things came together to destabilize, demoralize, and decentralize the Empire, and led to the loss of the West.

Roamin' the Romans

The Visigoths under Athaulf established Tolosa, modern Tolouse, as a great capital. It was there that the Visigoths elevated Avitus to emperor in 455, the first emperor elected outside of Rome.

Rimicer (455–472)

After the death of Maximus in 455, it was all barbarians in the west. The Visigoths, under Theodoric II, elected one of their own, Avitus, as emperor in the West. Avitus appointed Rimicer, half Visigoth and Sueve, to the powerful position of *Master of the Foot Soldiers*. Rimicer turned on Avitus, deposed him, and manipulated a series of western emperors for the next 16 years. During this time, the western Roman emperor's (whoever he was) sphere of influence shrunk to include only Italy (caught between eastern emperor to the east), the Visigoth kingdoms to the north, and Gaiseric (the Vandal king of north Africa) to the south.

When Rimicer died in 472, two factions, one backed by the barbarians under a certain Orestes, one backed originally by the eastern emperor Leo II (who died in 474), fought for control. The barbarians got the upper hand and forced Nepos, Leo's choice, into exile in Diocletian's palace. While the eastern emperor Zeno struggled to maintain his hold on the eastern throne, the barbarians crowned the 16-year-old Romulus Augustulus, Orestes' son, western Emperor at Ravenna.

Okay, This Is Almost It

Orestes had procured the Germanic mercenaries' support for his control of the west by promising them land to settle on, just as other barbarians had been allowed to do elsewhere in the Empire. Orestes, however, tried to keep Italy intact. When the barbarians who had supported Orestes didn't get what they thought they had coming to them, their chieftain, Odoacer, gave Orestes what they thought he had coming to him: a chop with a sword.

With Orestes dead, Romulus Augustulus was deposed and sent off to Naples with an allowance. Odoacer settled his people on a portion of Roman lands and was recognized as patrician of the west by the eastern emperor Zeno. This is where historian Edward Gibbon drew the line and proclaimed the Empire fallen, since the (albeit fuzzy) line of emperors from Augustus to Romulus was permanently severed. The last western Roman emperor was a 16-year-old usurper who had made it to emperor and early retirement. Even the dot.com generation would find that hard to match.

I Said, "Almost"

Zeno was worried about Odoacer's plans and plagued by a major uprising of Ostrogoths who were pillaging the lower Danube regions clear to the gates of the city. Their king was Theodoric the Amal, who had been a hostage as a young man in Constantinople while his father was king. Zeno hit upon a way to both get rid of Odoacer *and* give Theodoric something more productive to do. He sent Theodoric into Italy as his representative to conquer Odoacer. Theodoric invaded Italy in 489 and had mopped up Italy, including Odoacer, by 493. He became the eastern emperor's representative and the virtual king of Italy.

Rome, in the west, was no more. A patchwork of independent kingdoms emerged, built upon the ruins of Rome's imperial legacy, and moved into the darkness of the early Middle Ages. The Roman past continued to echo in some institutions (especially the church), laws, and learning. Rome's imperial idea, however, continued to haunt the dreams of the west into the modern age.

When in Rome

Constantine the Great replaced the Praetorian Prefect (the commander of the Praeteorian Guard) with two posts, the **Master of the Foot Soldiers** (*Magister Peditum*) and the **Master of the Cavalry** (*Magister Equitum*). Only the supreme commander, the **Master of the Soldiers** (*Magister Militum*), had a higher command.

Veto!

As you can see, it's simplistic to talk about the "fall" of either Rome or the Roman Empire. Just what fell, when, and to whom, gets pretty complicated. The western empire "fell apart" more than "fell," making it hard to mark a definitive end.

The Least You Need to Know

➤ Constantine's sons split the Empire and fought for control of it.

➤ Disputes in Christian doctrine (such as Arianism) and the suppression of paganism became important forces in imperial history and politics.

➤ The Theodosians ruled over an empire mostly divided between boy emperors in which powerful regents and military commanders held sway.

➤ Huge barbarian invasions and migrations overwhelmed the western Empire in the fourth and fifth centuries.

➤ The settlement of independent barbarian kingdoms within the Empire and the reliance on barbarians for imperial defense and civil conflict, contributed significantly to the destabilization and loss of the west.

➤ The western Empire did not "fall"; it was transformed even as it "fell apart."

Part 4
Roman Imperial Life and Culture

Imperial Rome affected cultures from India to Ireland and Sudan to Sweden. These effects go a lot deeper than the scattered ruins that litter the landscape of Asia Minor, Europe, and North Africa. The broad scope of Rome's influence not only impacted cultures individually, but drew from, mixed, and united them in ways that still profoundly influence the world.

In the next chapters, we'll take a look at three aspects of McRoman culture with enduring legacies: its approach to religions, its literary legacy, and its public entertainment. In all three of these areas, the transformation of the Empire from pagan to predominantly Christian was a process of synthesis, as much as it was of conversion.

Chapter 19

Roman Mass Culture of the Imperial Period

In This Chapter

➤ Roman imperial culture

➤ Joe (and Josephine) Roman

➤ A tour of the Latin provinces

From the time of Augustus's victory over Antony in 30 B.C.E., the Roman world underwent remarkable transformation. Augustus had, in his words, found "Rome brick and left it in marble," and over the next 200 years the city became the central hub of a world state and the enforcer of what Pliny called *immensa Romanae pacis maiestas*, "the immense majesty of Roman peace." Some may have pointed out that this peace was at times enforced by creating a desert, but for a considerable period of time, a person might travel from Hadrian's Wall to the Sudan or from Lisbon to the border of Parthia. Not only could he travel there, but he also would find it relatively stable and bound by common legislation, education, and urban and civic culture.

In this chapter, we'll take a look at Roman culture and society as it developed in the first and second centuries of the Empire. We'll see how fortunes waxed and waned in the final centuries of the western Empire, and take a look at the western provinces' role in the Empire. (We'll save a closer look at the eastern half of the Empire and Byzantium for Part 5, "Where Did the Romans Go?")

Great Caesar's Ghost!

There isn't enough sidebar space in this chapter to call full attention to it, but notice the number of imperial towns, cities, and garrisons that have grown into modern cities, and you'll begin to get a picture of the impact of *romanitas* (Roman-ness) upon the formation of Europe.

When in Rome

Remember, **Hellenistic** refers to the Greek kingdoms and culture that continued to control the eastern Mediterranean basin after the death of Alexander the Great until their conquest by Rome.

The Fabric of Empire

Rome began this period as a city that controlled conquests through military occupation, colonization, and treaty. Its Empire was a quilt of languages, peoples, and cultures ranging from wild tribes to already ancient civilizations. The Roman military held it together under the strain of exploitation and taxation. Over time, however, Roman law, citizenship and military service, Greco-Roman education, travel, trade, and the development of a uniform urban culture combined to give the whole a sense of unity that went beyond conquered and conqueror.

By the end of the third century, provincials came to feel that an attack upon the province was also an attack upon Rome, not just upon their own particular locality. The barbarian invasions of the fourth and fifth centuries tore apart the social, cultural, and economic fabric of the Empire in the west, but the fabric of religious belief and church structure, and the idea of a united Empire, remained.

East Is East and West Is West

It's convenient to divide the Roman Empire into the east and west, and to a degree, this broad division holds. In the east, Rome conquered great cities and civilizations in Greece, Ptolemaic Egypt, and the Seleucid Empire; these already had highly sophisticated cultures, histories, and systems of governance. Rome may have brought order, but none of these conquered territories would have recognized Rome as a "higher" civilization. They each had their own underlying culture and were bound together by a broad overlay of *Hellenistic* culture that everyone there recognized. Few in the east, for example, aspired to learning Latin except to use for conducting imperial business, but both east and west recognized the cultural and practical value of Greek.

The Romans of the Imperial Period administered and taxed, but left areas largely to govern themselves, as long as the locals did not get out of hand and the taxes got paid. Some areas in the east such as Philippi and New Corinth were highly Roman in population (veterans and freedmen), but elsewhere, older cultures largely retained their pre-Roman ways and identity even as they came to view themselves as "Roman" in the sense of an imperial system. Constantine's establishment of a new capital in Constantinople gave the eastern provinces a cultural, not just imperial, center on which they could continue to identify themselves.

The west was much different. Here Rome not only provided the urban centers that brought *romanitas* to the western provinces, but the infrastructure, civic structure, and high culture adopted by the Celtic and Germanic peoples. Latin language and Roman culture *was* high culture, and the western provincials added new strength and vitality to it as they came to identify themselves as Romans of the Empire with the city of Rome. The western provinces came to supply Rome with more than raw materials and manpower. They supplied it with poets, generals, and emperors.

Major Cities and Capitals

The primary engines of Roman mass culture during the Imperial Period were the cities in which imperial bureaucracy, military headquarters, and major religious and economic centers were located. Here, Roman urbanism encouraged cultural, civic, and economic relationships that had parallels throughout the Empire. The same laws, currency, civic institutions, range of religious practices, and imperial language(s) bound these centers together and extended from there into the smaller cities and the hinterland.

Migrations between urban centers, especially from the provinces to Rome, were frequent and fervent. Juvenal the satirist would have us believe that second century Rome was awash in foreigners—and from grave inscriptions it appears that he may have been right! Notwithstanding Juvenal, however, the multicultural mix in the cities also encouraged a level of common culture throughout the Empire.

Veto!

When reading Juvenal, you have to keep in mind that you're reading satire. Remember that satire comes from real conditions and experiences (so what you read is, in some ways, true), but is exaggerated so that the problems or vices the satirist is attacking take on the proportions of caricature (so, in other ways, it isn't).

Cities began to decline with the economic and provincial troubles of the third century (see Chapter 18, "Barbarians at the Gates: The Fall of the Western Empire"). Nevertheless, the Augusti and their Caesars built their regional capitals (Rome, Constantinople, Trier [*Augusta Treverorum*], Milan [*Mediolanum*], and Antioch) into imperial "Roman" cities. Rome, which essentially remained a parasitic resource drain on the rest of the Empire (it got huge subsidies and produced primarily lawyers and administrators), survived better than most.

Lend Me Your Ears

"Romans, I can't stand a Greek Rome, although what percentage of our city scum really comes from Greece? The Syrian river Orontes has long since tainted the Tibur with its weird language, weird customs, weird music and the weirdoes who prostitute themselves at the Circus. Come on down, all you who have a thing for foreign chicks in tie-dyed hats! That good country boy of yours, citizen, now wears *Berkinstocks* to dinner and triathlon ribbons around a neck smeared with sunscreen. Foreigners come from all over Hell-(and gone)-ism and make a beeline for Rome's bowels to become our future masters."

—Juvenal *Satire* 3.60–72

The imperial capitals and Alexandria remained centers of imperial culture until the massive invasions of barbarians and Persian Wars in the fourth and fifth centuries. Rome survived Alaric and the Vandals (see Chapter 18) primarily because the barbarians had little interest in adopting urban culture. They left after they got what they wanted. Elsewhere in the west, however, where the barbarians settled, cities never really regained their central role.

In the east, only Alexandria and Constantinople remained vital after the wars with Persia had destroyed Antioch. It took a Roman, however, to complete the destruction of the two great classical cities: Rome and Athens. Justinian's reconquest of the west wiped out Rome in the sixth century, and he pulled the plug on Athens in an effort to stamp out the last vestiges of pagan legitimacy.

Civis Romanus Sum: The Roman Citizen of the World

A Roman citizen was, at the beginning of the Empire, either a Roman or an individual of a community with a special relationship to the city of Rome. In the Republic, this relationship was exclusive—that is, the citizens of different communities didn't necessarily have the same relationship with each other that they had with Rome. After the Social War (see Chapter 6, "On Golden Pond: Rome Conquers Italy and the Mediterranean"), however, all Italians had similar rights, and Italy began to develop a sense of "Roman" cultural identity. Emperors in the early Empire broadened this trend by granting the status of *colonae* to more and more provincial cities and municipalities.

As Roman culture broadened and deepened in Italy and the provinces, the meaning of Roman citizenship did as well. By the end of the second century C.E., the Roman citizen was subject to an emperor who rarely was in Rome and to legislation that extended from border to imperial border. Citizens and delegations traveled to provinces, rather than to Rome, to meet with the emperor or awaited his arrival in their capitals. The emperor had become the emperor of a world state, and his subject citizens came to see themselves as members of that larger order as well. They may have belonged to very different social classes, had different rights and privileges, and spoken different languages, but as the *Constitutio Antoniniana* in C.E. 212 had affirmed (see Chapter 16, "The [Mostly] Not-So-Good Emperors: Commodus to Aurelian"), there was a basic "Joe Roman" with whom all had something in common.

Have a Little Class

The Romans were a very class-conscious culture, and during the period of the Empire social classes became both marks of prestige and important demarcations of civic protection. This became clear when Septimius Severus (see Chapter 16) divided Roman citizens into ranks: *honestiores* and *humiliors*. *Honestiores* were senators, equites, the municipal magistrates, and all military personnel. *Humiliores* were all the "lower" people. *Honestiores* retained the right of appeal to the Emperor and the right to a swift and clean execution or exile as punishments; *Humiliores* did not have the right of appeal and could be thrown to the beasts or shipped off to the mines.

Great Caesar's Ghost!

Not only did the two-tiered punishment system begun by Severus survive into the Middle Ages, but some of the Roman nobility titles such as "duke" (*dux*) and "count" (*comes*) did as well.

As imperial structure became more regal and formalized, titles and class hierarchies were created to distinguish among the rich and powerful. The highest noble ranks were the *clarissimi* (most glorious) and the highest equestrian the *ementissimi* (most eminent). *Duces* (dukes), vicars, and governors were *perfectissimi* (most accomplished). Individuals who met with the Emperor's favor from any of these orders might be given the title of *comes* (count), which meant "companion." There were first, second, and third class (*ordo primus, secundus, tertius*) companions to distinguish these special people.

The Rich Get Richer

The economic good times of the first two centuries of the Empire brought a degree of prosperity to all levels of Roman society. Wealth and urbanization created Italian and provincial upper classes who had more in common with each other than they did with their own, less wealthy, people. Although they came from different ethnic backgrounds, they had similar education, similar means of access to imperial power, and similar benefits.

As the emperors brought upper-class Italians and then provincials into imperial service and into the senate, new kinds of Roman aristocracies arose based throughout the Empire and not just in Rome. As provincials themselves became emperors, this homogenization increased even as the split between the wealthy and everyone else continued to widen. As the fortunes of the Empire waned and urbanism declined, the aristocracy were able to retreat to their fortified country villas and continue their lives more in the manner of feudal lords than civic leaders. The wealth of the upper echelons of imperial and provincial classes continued to increase, a kind of "suck up" as opposed to a "trickle down" economic syndrome that continued to concentrate wealth and power into the hands of a few even as the general civilization and culture disintegrated beneath them.

In parts of the west, the settlement of barbarian peoples and tribal warlords only quickened that cultural shift. Romans in Gaul and Italy were required to give at least one third of all possessions (including land and slaves) to the newcomers. Romans retained some separate legal rights and provisions. The Vandals in north Africa simply confiscated everything and sent the Roman nobility packing or reduced them to *coloni* (tenement farmers). Over time, the upper classes of the western Empire either made the shift to the new world order or joined the church hierarchy where they could retain power. This led to further conflicts between old and new Romans as the old converted to orthodoxy while the barbarians remained Arian (see Chapter 17, "Divide and [Re]Conquer: Diocletian to Constantine," for a discussion of Arianism).

The Poor Get Poorer

In the first two centuries, sufficient public income allowed cities and municipalities to provide subsidized or free food and education services for the poor, and games and festivals kept the city masses entertained, if not satisfied. As inflation soared, however, and imperial revenues had to be diverted to defense, funds for these services disappeared until the poor in Rome and Constantinople only could hope for some kind of relief. Even with imports of subsidized food, the capitals had deplorable urban conditions in the later Empire.

Urban flight from cities and from wretched rural conditions brought imperial edicts against translocation. These edicts primarily succeeded in creating a class of workers and serfs for the remaining aristocracy.

The Middle Gets Squeezed

The middle class grew and did well for the first two centuries. The stability of the *pax Romana*, the influx of wealth, the development of the provinces, and the ability to travel made for entrepreneurial times. A blossoming system of imperial roads within and between the provinces made business and pleasure travel possible as never before. Mid-sized landholders and producers and businessmen, especially in the provinces, exploited local markets for local and export trade. Traders, especially those who dealt in luxury imports, could do very well. These middle-class people came to make up the *curiales,* the people who made up the town councils (*curiae*) of their towns and cities, who funded civic improvements and functions, and who collected taxes for the Empire.

When in Rome

Pax Romana means "the Roman Peace" and is the term that refers to the peace and stability that Rome maintained (within its borders) during the early Empire.

Great Caesar's Ghost!

For travelers, the homogenization of urban culture in the high Empire allowed one to enter a city nearly anywhere in the Empire, get a bath, find a place to stay, take in a gladiator fight, get some dinner, wake up, and think, "Geez, now *where* am I again?" Plus, more vacation spots and amenities became available to the middle–class traveler. A tourist of the Empire could, for example, visit ancient Greek antiquities and take a guided climb of the Mt. Etna volcano. At the top, he could camp with his guide overnight on the mountain to watch the sunrise and then soak away sore muscles in one of the many hotel/hot springs that dotted the mountain the next day.

But as inflation and civil disruption hit in the third and fourth centuries, the middle class suffered and declined. Caracalla's *Constitutio Antoniniana* in C.E. 212 had broadened the tax base by making all freedmen tax-paying citizens, but then as now, who was *eligible* to pay taxes was much different than who actually *paid* taxes. The increasing burden of taxation and the enforcement of tax revenues fell hard on the middle

class and *curiales*. Many were driven into ruin when they couldn't enforce taxation upon the wealthy and couldn't squeeze it out of the poor. Urban flight ensued, which Constantine put a stop to by legally tying the middle-class citizens to their professions and locations. Those that did escape became *coloni* and hired workers for the wealthy or joined the military.

Women

Augustus's laws on morality attempted to roll back and restrict the gains that women, at least upper-class women, had begun to enjoy in the late Republic. These laws were unsuccessful in putting the genie back in the bottle. In fact, the law making women who bore three children (or produced a document so stating) free from their guardians actually did the opposite! After Augustus's death, women continued to make slow gains, and the role of a woman's "guardian" became more like a lawyer: Wealthy women could hire and fire their guardians based on petitions to the court.

It's important to realize that legislation, especially Roman legislation, is a very conservative thing, and it often reflects realities and attitudes that have already been present for some time. Women of the politically powerful class were assertive and active; besides the biographies of the women of the imperial household, inscriptions and dedications from around the Empire make it clear that women were civic patrons and an established presence in civic and imperial circles.

Their legal status improved officially little by little. In C.E. 126, Hadrian increased women's power over their personal property by loosening restrictions on their ability to make wills, and Diocletian (284–305) abolished the guardianship of women altogether. This gradual emancipation of women coincided with a decrease in the official power of the *pater familias* (the head of the family), which, judging from inscriptions and from practice, had become largely moribund long before.

However, women's personal power and autonomy rose or fell, depending on what class they belonged to. Women of the upper class exercised considerable power and independence; women of the *humiliores* mostly exercised by getting their chores done. The remains of Pompeii and the portrayal of women in the

New Testament (*Acts*) show that a great many middle-class business women were an influential sector of society. As gender roles in Christianity became entrenched, church doctrine about women provided an additional force for restricting women of all classes.

Roman women work out (note the medicine ball and "executive" dumbells) among the mosaics of the Roman villa at Piazza Armerina (Sicily), third century C.E.

Slaves and Freedmen

Slaves continued to remain a part of the fabric of everyday life throughout the Empire and throughout the Imperial Period. But manpower, including slave labor, became in short supply during the Empire. The slave populations were replaced in large part by poor laborers and *coloni*. Just as women achieved gradual improvement in their status, slaves received marginal, and relative, improvements under the emperors. These improvements only amounted to the right not to be castrated for profit and not to be arbitrarily killed.

As the numbers of slaves dropped, the population of freedmen did as well. As former slaves, freedmen made up a large segment of the poor, middle-class businessmen, and bureaucrats. Some, however, who were connected with the wealthy or the imperial household became fabulously wealthy and powerful during the early Empire. Under Claudius, freedmen, such as the notorious Pallas and Narcissus (see Chapter 14, "All in the Family: The Julio-Claudian Emperors"), were feared and loathed by the nobility for their personal influence, wealth, and power. But as power and wealth concentrated into fewer hands, there was also less opportunity for anyone, much less freedmen, to achieve economic and social mobility.

The Army Life

The army was an important factor in providing unity and cohesion to the Empire, even though it was also armies that supported generals as emperors against each other, attacked each other's provinces, and serially murdered emperors during dark periods of instability. Nevertheless soldiers, especially in the upper ranks, served commanders in campaigns all over the Empire and conceived of "Rome" as the sum of its provincial parts. Army life and culture, no matter in which province soldiers were stationed, venerated the idea of there being a *Roman* Empire and that they were *Roman* soldiers. These Joes looked forward to the rewards of an honorable discharge: a pension and *Roman* citizenship for himself, one wife, and their descendants.

Ring Around the Latin Empire

Let's make like Hadrian and take an imperial survey of the Latin provinces. As we tour, we'll take a look at each area during the broad span of imperial history.

The Imperial Roman provinces and regions. After a map from the "Rome Project" of the Dalton School (http://www.dalton.org/groups/rome/).

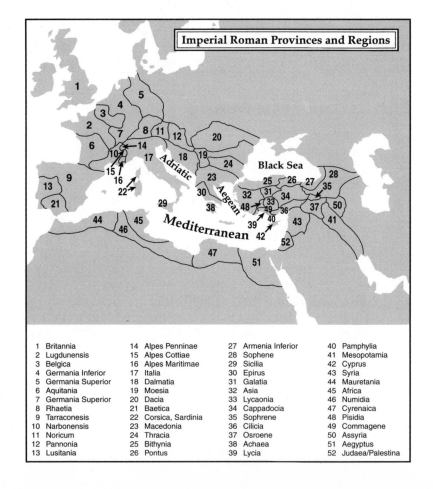

Imperial Roman Provinces and Regions

1 Britannia	14 Alpes Penninae	27 Armenia Inferior	40 Pamphylia
2 Lugdunensis	15 Alpes Cottiae	28 Sophene	41 Mesopotamia
3 Belgica	16 Alpes Maritimae	29 Sicilia	42 Cyprus
4 Germania Inferior	17 Italia	30 Epirus	43 Syria
5 Germania Superior	18 Dalmatia	31 Galatia	44 Mauretania
6 Aquitania	19 Moesia	32 Asia	45 Africa
7 Germania Superior	20 Dacia	33 Lycaonia	46 Numidia
8 Rhaetia	21 Baetica	34 Cappadocia	47 Cyrenaica
9 Tarraconesis	22 Corsica, Sardinia	35 Sophrene	48 Pisidia
10 Narbonensis	23 Macedonia	36 Cilicia	49 Commagene
11 Noricum	24 Thracia	37 Osroene	50 Assyria
12 Pannonia	25 Bithynia	38 Achaea	51 Aegyptus
13 Lusitania	26 Pontus	39 Lycia	52 Judaea/Palestina

Northern Africa

North Africa had been lightly held together by Carthage, the major city in the region, but *Punic* influence never went very deep. Punic continued to be spoken in the large cities, and both Septimius Severus's and Augustine's African accent showed in their Latin. Rome, however, made the northern continent "Roman" within about 200 miles south of the coast—estimates range in the number of 200,000 settlers. The Romans were able to put their practical knowledge to good work. Aqueducts and a string of fine roads served well-founded cities and agricultural farmlands. These provinces were lost first to the Vandals, then to the Arabs, and then (depending on your politics) to the French or Islam.

Roamin' the Romans

If I could get into Algeria again some day, I'd like to visit ancient Lambessa (modern Tamzult-Lambese). This city became the headquarters for the Third Legion around C.E. 129. Marcus Aurelius gave the settlement the status of a city, and Septimius Severus made it the capital of Numidia. Lambessa declined after the Romans withdrew from the area in the late fourth century, but its settlers left impressive ruins and reportedly the best preserved Roman military camp in the world.

The North African provinces were great exporters of grain, figs, and olives as well as exotic materials and animals. The emperors from Nero onward came to "inherit" huge estates there, from which they earned enormous revenues. The ruins of Leptis Magna (in Libya from which the Severan dynasty came) and those at Dougga (in Tunisia) are probably the most impressive, but many wonderful ruins await travelers throughout North Africa, if one can but get to them. Besides the Severans, many of the great early Christian writers (St. Augustine, for example) and early Christian controversies had their beginnings in North Africa.

When in Rome

Punic refers to Carthaginian culture. It comes from the Latin term for Carthaginians, *Punici*, which derived from their origin as Phonecians.

Spain

Spain was one of the earliest provinces, and certainly one of the most important, for the Roman economy, Roman literature, and Roman politics. Spanish gold, silver, copper, and other mineral mines were leased out to private concerns and provided rich returns for the state. Spanish wines, olive oil, fish products, and other natural resources were exported throughout the western Empire. The Spanish tribes, especially along the Mediterranean coast, became thoroughly Romanized and provided not only military manpower, but a host of important imperial authors (Seneca, Lucan, Quintilian, and Martial) and even emperors (Trajan and Hadrian).

When in Rome

Romanitas is the Latin term for "Roman-ness" and refers to the Roman way or manner of doing things.

Spain is riddled with Roman ruins, roads, and bridges, and many of its cities have Roman roots. The extent to which Spain and Portugal achieved *romanitas* remains in its languages, which, with the exception of Basque (the Romans were only marginally better at conquering the entire Pyranees than the modern Spanish), are all Latin derivatives.

Gaul

The provinces of Gaul were hard to conquer but well worth the effort for the Empire. In the north, Augusta Treverorum (Trèves) grew from a garrison colony of Claudius into the imperial capital of the western Augustus. In the northwest, Gaul remained a wild mix of Celtic and Roman elements, never really suited to the kind of urban and agricultural development upon which *romanitas* was based. Aquitania, however, with its capital Burdigala (Bordeaux) quickly became a wine producing and exporting region of estate villas. Claret has been flowing from here to the British isles for a long, long time. Inland, Lugdunium (Lyons) was a thriving imperial city and capital of Gallia Lugdunensis. And if you have ever been to Provence, you already know that you can't visit a city without seeing evidence of the thriving "more Roman than Rome" province of Gallia Narbonnensis. This province featured its own spa, Aquae Sextiae (Aix en Provence), and summer resort, Genava (Geneva).

Roamin' the Romans

France is known for its modern chateaux, but there were many ancient Celtic/Roman examples throughout France as well. You can find one of the best preserved near Toulouse at Martres-Toulousaine. This villa, furnished with sculpture and building materials from around the time of the Empire, was unearthed only in 1826!

Gaul was (and is still) served by a fine network of Roman roads and rivers for transportation, and you can see how these provinces could become their own mini-empire during the third century.

Besides wine, Gaul exported fine foods, pottery, and glass (somehow, that doesn't surprise you, does it?). At its height, about C.E. 150, greater Gaul was heavily populated, prosperous, and well-educated in Latin. Celtic was also spoken and taught, although from present-day languages one can see that only in Brittany (where a dialect of Gaelic is still spoken) and along the Rhine (where Germanic languages prevailed) did anything but Latin dialects survive.

The barbarian invasions of the next centuries brought upheaval, but in time the Frankish and Gothic invaders became the sword of the Popes, the Medieval crusaders, and emperors of the Holy Roman Empire. They were also responsible for bringing Latin back to the continent as a book language from Ireland and England, where their barbarian ancestors had helped to push it in the fifth and sixth centuries.

Britain

The Romans threw a lot of resources into Britain, but one has to wonder why. It returned little to the Empire and took a whole lot of men and money to keep. The island exported some raw materials, including famous oysters, but primarily was just able to meet its own and legionary needs. The latter was substantial. Forces required to settle and protect the lowlands, plus those required to maintain defenses at Hadrian's (and for a short time, the Antonine) Wall, made up a fair percentage of the Empire's manpower. The periodic revolts, such as those of Boudiccea (61) and Carausius (287–293), took enormous effort to suppress.

Great Caesar's Ghost!

In C.E. 410, the Emperor Honorius issued a letter to Britain explaining that Alaric had sacked Rome and that the Brits were on their own. He withdrew Roman troops and commanded Britain to fend for itself against the invading Saxons. Unfortunately, the Romans had never helped the lowlands learn to organize or defend themselves, and the only people who were able to resist the Saxon invaders were the same people who had given the Romans their own trouble—the tribes of Wales, Cornwall, and the Scottish Highlands. Everywhere else became Anglo-Saxon before the Normans arrived and altered that.

Moreover, Romanization, which to a large degree was built upon replicating Mediterranean agricultural and urban culture, simply wasn't very adaptable to British people or climate. Urban centers were moderate—Londinium (London) reached 25,000—although throughout the island there were many impressive buildings and villas. The impressive spa resort of Aquae Sulis (Bath) is but one of these remains. Nevertheless, the Romans were unable to hold off the northern Picts of Scotland and the Saxons from across the channel while lands closer to Italy were being ravaged. When the Romans withdrew in 410, although the province was in a prosperous stage, they left little remaining imprint behind but for place names, ruined fortifications, and a Celtic Christianity that clung to the places that even Saxons wouldn't go.

The Germanys

Germany had been the bane of the early Empire, and Domitian finally brought it under some control. This area remained a wild land of border fortifications, small settlements, and great forests. Garrisons allowed the Rhine to become somewhat Romanized and grew into the cities of Cologne, Mainz, and Strasbourg. But migrations, tribal rebellions, and harsh weather kept *romanitas* isolated, just as happened in Britain.

Along the Danube

It's easy to think of the provinces along the upper Rhine and Danube (Raetia, Noricum, Pannonia, Illyricum, Moesia, Dacia) as wild and hostile outposts of Roman fortifications against the barbarians. Control of these areas protected Italy and secured imperial mobility by allowing for a northern land route linking northern Gaul with the eastern provinces. But Roman traders and businessmen had been plying the regions along these rivers before the Roman legions arrived and set up their standards and camps. By the time the legions and Roman patrol fleet had secured the lands between modern Switzerland and the Black Sea, there was already a thriving border-zone culture of Romans—"Roman" and non-Roman Celts and Goths. You might think of these areas as analogous to the mixture of cultures along the United States's border with Mexico. Borders make for sharp demarcations on a map, but when families, cultures, tribes, and businesses settle in large numbers on both sides, the line is anything but sharp.

The garrison towns of these northern reaches grew into important cities. Rhaeta's capital, Augusta Vindelicorum, grew into Augsburg. In Pannonia, the legionary quarters at Vindobona and Aquincum grew to Vienna and Budapest. This province became heavily Romanized with bustling cities, such as Singidunum, now known as Belgrade. To the south of Pannonia was the large province of Illyricum, from which the Illyrian legions and emperors such as Diocletian brought the Empire back together from chaos.

East from Pannonia toward Constantinople was Moesia. This province was full of Latin colonists and settlers from the time of Claudius, and it was from here that Trajan pushed northward into Dacia (see Chapter 15, "The [Mostly] Good Emperors:

274

The Flavians to Marcus Aurelius"). This was also the area into which the eastern emperors tried to settle the troublesome Visigoths (see Chapter 18) and from where they revolted. South from Moesia were the provinces of Thrace, Macedonia, and Greece. These areas remained in relative obscurity and produced soldiers, wine, and livestock from large estates and ranches while the cities declined. Athens, of course, was an exception. It continued to enjoy the patronage of students studying at its schools, travelers, and even emperors until the sixth century.

North from Moesia was Dacia, which was conquered by Trajan between 101 and 106. Dacia's mineral and economic wealth was such that enough cash could be sucked out of the province and into the Empire to fund Trajan's conquests, to cut taxes, *and* to carry out his building program. On the other hand, enough colonists and Latin speakers were sucked into Dacia to establish the Latin roots of Rumanian language. Not only Romans wanted into Dacia, however: This province was the subject of Gothic invasions and attacks by the Huns. By the time of the fall of the western Empire, the east was able to hold onto Dacia, Moesia, and Thrace south through Greece, but it lost the lands west of their eastern borders to the kingdom of the Ostrogoths.

The Least You Need to Know

➤ The Romanization of the Latin provinces had a profound effect upon the geography and urban landscape of Europe.

➤ A broad urban imperial culture developed throughout the Empire. This worked best where Romans could also reproduce their agricultural and cultural ways.

➤ The huge gap in wealth and privilege between the rich and everyone else became progressively worse through the Empire.

➤ The status of Roman citizens, women, and slaves made progress in the Empire, but these gains were offset in the later Empire by economic hard times, the reduction of lower classes to serfs and laborers, the disruptions of invasions, and the Church.

(Un)Protected Sects: Religions, Tolerance, and Persecutions

In This Chapter

➤ Roman attitudes toward other religions

➤ Mystery religions

➤ Roman "persecution" of Druids, Jews, and Christians

In this chapter, we'll take a look at Roman religious attitudes and practices, official and unofficial, during the course of the Empire. The picture is rather complicated. Romans of the Empire made up a religiously pluralistic society and incorporated beliefs that ranged from the ancient cults of Egypt and Asia to the Teutonic and Celtic tribal gods. This was not particularly a problem as far as Rome was concerned. Romans had, since the time of the kings, begun to incorporate other gods and religious practices into, or on top of, their own native beliefs. As they conquered the peoples of Italy and then the Mediterranean, they brought their gods with them and often came to equate their gods as versions of those worshipped by other people. They never, however, suppressed or tried to convert inhabitants away from their own religions. They did try to eradicate elements that they considered seditious and politically disruptive.

Through conquest, Rome encountered other religions abroad and brought them home. Huge numbers of foreigners came to Italy and Rome (often as slaves), and Romans found themselves confronted with a broad and exotic mix of religions on their own turf. And while the city itself tried, from time to time, to put a lid on religious practices, such as those of Bacchants (followers of Dionysus, or Bacchus, a god of vitality,

Veto!

Cult in the language of classicists and historians of religion does *not* indicate a radical group of true believers who follow a quasi-divine authoritarian leader and live an unconventional lifestyle. Cult here refers to the organized system of traditions and ritual practiced by followers of any god or deity.

When in Rome

Charismatic (from the Greek *charis*, "grace, "charm," or "gift") here refers to religious practices whose key element is participants' experience of spiritual or physical abilities (speaking in tongues, for example) that are understood to be manifestations of the god.

Ecstatic (Greek for "being stood outside of one's self") refers to the experience of emotions or sensations so strong that they overwhelm and drive out one's normal faculties and self-possession.

wine, and revelry) or the followers of Isis and Cybele (both "great goddess" figures), it never persecuted the followers of other religions for what they believed per se.

Why, then, are the Romans popularly known for religious persecutions? Well, it would be better to say that they are known for *a* religious persecution—the persecution of the Christians. Only two other religious groups—Druids and Jews—received some of the similar treatment. Still, it's important to have an idea of how these persecutions took place and the attitudes behind them. It helps explain why, despite persecution, Christianity conquered the Empire, Druids are no more, and why the temple in Jerusalem still isn't rebuilt.

Family, Public, and Personal Religious Practice

Roman attitudes toward religion aren't easy to describe, particularly over such a long period of time. The Romans were an extremely religious and superstitious people, but this worked itself out in different ways depending upon whether you talk about the private family or the public sphere.

As members of a family, the Romans had family gods (Lares and Penates, for example). Practices of family religion survived in the home and were handed down from generation to generation. Especially in the countryside, where family traditions and its ties to an agrarian life remained strong, these cults persisted into the Middle Ages, where they became synthesized with Christian practice. They remain a part of European peasant culture even today.

One Nation Under God(s)

The official Roman state gods represented Rome as a whole, and their patronage and protection of the state was taken very seriously. Over the course of the Republic, the nobility's manipulation of religious ritual and tradition helped to fuel a growing cynicism among Romans about state practice. Nevertheless, the Romans were *as Romans* religiously conservative and suspicious of foreign cults—especially *charismatic* and *ecstatic* cults. The Roman senate allowed only the *Magna Mater* ("Great Mother") Cybele (begrudgingly) and Julius Caesar into the official pantheon during the Republic.

The Romans also took seriously the recognition of their state gods by other people as a sign of acknowledgement and respect for Roman power and authority. These kinds of gestures toward political and religious symbols pack a lot of punch. Remember the anger and outrage kindled in the United States when images of foreigners burning the U.S. flag in other countries first flashed across the TV screen? Mutual recognition of Roman and "barbarian" gods was made easier by the tendency to see each other's gods in terms of one's own and to allow a tolerant *syncretism* of rituals and beliefs.

When in Rome

Syncretism (Greek for "blended together") is the blending of different beliefs and customs into a synthesis that accommodates elements of each.

In the course of the Empire, the figure of the emperor became a symbol of Rome itself and an object of veneration. Many Romans throughout the Empire kept an image of the emperor in their house and venerated it as a part of their household devotions. (A similar image of FDR graced the dining room of many of our ancestors who experienced the Dust Bowl and the Hoovervilles of the Great Depression.) The Illyrian emperors Aurelian and Diocletian made themselves into figures who combined Rome and the divine. Nevertheless, even these emperors never claimed that participation in state rites had to preclude other beliefs or practices. What was mandatory was a recognition and acknowledgement of the state's primary authority and legitimacy as represented in the state cult.

This is where Jews (who were exempted) and Christians (who were not) were unable to comply. Christians' personal religious practices contradicted state practice in a manner that could not be solved without one party giving way. Neither was very good at that.

Following One's Bliss

As individuals, however, Romans who had the time and ability were relatively free to pursue their own religious thought and practice as long as it didn't conflict with either their family or state obligations. Many of them were attracted to *mystery religions* and religious philosophies that gave the individual a personal relationship with divinity and some personal assurance (usually through direct charismatic experience) of a place in the cosmos and in the afterlife.

When in Rome

Mystery religions contain secret forms of religious practice
and doctrine, which are revealed
only to initiated members and
usually involve beliefs about the
afterlife. Initiates generally must
undergo trials and oaths of secrecy before being allowed the
revelations that admit them into
the circle of believers.

Great Caesar's Ghost!

In Ephesus, St. Paul ran into
trouble with the *collegia* of
artisans for the great Ephesian
temple of Diana (Acts 19). They
incited a riot against him that
was fueled as much by economic
as religious fervor. A local official
calmed the crowd, and Paul and
his companions headed for
Greece.

The Empire was a large, multicultural, and in many
ways identity-less place. In an age in which the individual seemed powerless, small, and subject to arbitrary circumstance, people looked for a personal
experience upon which to pin their hopes or into
which to escape. Great numbers of people turned to
astrology, divination, and other magical practices to
establish (if only by foreknowing) personal control
over their lives. People who promised such control
were also popular: Miracle workers, preachers, and
soothsayers developed enormous followings of devotees, and some were worshipped after their death. The
early Empire was an age of gurus and star power.

In the course of the Empire, popular religions tended
to succeed where they gave the individual a personal
sense of place with the divine *and* a community of believers to which he or she could belong and find care.
Local clubs and associations, or *collegia,* were popular
throughout the Empire. Sometimes, these collegia
were religiously based; others were defined by trade or
ethnicity (but still under a patron deity). Funeral
clubs, which were organized to help pay the costs of
burial, were popular as social groups with the lower
classes. *Collegia* sometimes became powerful elements
in fostering local tensions, rebellions, and local
persecutions.

Protected Sects: Religious Philosophy and Mystery Religions

The first two centuries of the Empire was a time of intense and broad philosophical and religious searching
for meaning and place. Teachers, preachers, revivalists,
gurus, and true believers intermingled in a cacophony
of religious beliefs, rituals, and devotion. Over time,
fads and charlatans ebbed and faded from the scene,
but several philosophical schools and religious cults
became influential on each other and upon the eventual victor in the struggle for the soul of the Empire:
Christianity.

Think It Through (Our Way)

Some philosophical sects took on religious overtones and roles. Philosophers made up a kind of intellectual clergy and dispensed advice and reprimand to all levels of society. Schools of thought vied amongst themselves for converts. Words such as dogma, heresy, and conversion originally applied to philosophers, not Christians!

Cynic philosophers preached a practical morality for the streets, a kind of religious and moral reality therapy. Stoic philosophy held that God was ascertained through reason, and that all things were held together by divine reason and providence. Knowledge of this and a realization of what one was really in control over (namely, one's own reactions to things) gave one the strength and moral fiber to do one's duty and face any hardship. Stoics, moreover, believed in the brotherhood of humanity, where all men were essentially equal.

When in Rome

Both **Stoic** and **Cynic** philosophies came to Rome from Greece. Stoics emphasized self-control, detachment, and independence from the world, which they nevertheless believed was regulated by a divine reason for the common good. Cynics emphasized a frank practical morality, which confronted pretentious shallow morality and custom. The most famous Cynic, Diogenes (ca 340 B.C.E.), lived in a dog house to repudiate the "civilized" customs for which he had contempt. (*Cyn* is the root for "dog" in Greek, and Diogenes' famous home may be what gave the Cynics their name.)

The stoic philosophy became especially influential under the teachings of Epictetus, an ex-slave and teacher who was expelled from Rome by Diocletian. Epictetus's teachings were influential on the emperor Marcus Aurelius and his *Meditations*. The teachings of Neoplatonism also became influential, if never very popular. This philosophy developed from the more mystical elements of Plato's teaching. Adherents, such as Plotinus, sought a mystic communion with God, whom they conceived as pure Mind. Neoplatonism had a rich hierarchy of angles and demons, rejected the flesh as contaminating the spiritual, and emphasized spiritual communion to achieve a unification with God.

All these philosophies were influential on other religious movements of the Empire.

Stop Making Sense and Just Sense: Mystery Religions

For a much broader cross-section of the Empire, mystery religions were particularly popular. They all featured common elements—a kind and benevolent divine figure with whom believers could have direct personal contact, secret rites, and celebrations (mysteries) that initiated believers into special knowledge and understanding. Manifestations of ecstasy, inspired behavior, visions, and glossolalia (speaking in tongues) confirmed the initiates' experiences and the religion's claims. These experiences mystically connected believers to the god and to each other in a community of believers and spiritual family.

Roamin' the Romans

We have very little evidence of mystery rites. A few pictures of initiation ceremonies have been found painted on the walls of a house in Pompeii, which is (aptly) called "The House of the Mysteries."

We know little about the actual religious practices of these cults because they were, of course, *secret*. Later, hostile Christian writers did little to illuminate what they knew of them.

Republican Rome had an uncomfortable and tense relationship with ecstatic cults, but in the early Empire, the emperors reversed course and allowed—even encouraged—them. Cults of Cybele, Isis, and Dionysus had all come to Rome in the Republic and been periodically booted out or bolted down. By the time of the Empire, however, these were an imperial phenomenon and found patrons in Caligula and Claudius.

Besides these cults, those of Mithras competed for initiates among the urban centers and in the military. In addition, the ancient Greek mysteries of Demeter at Eleusis (a short way from Athens) inspired and drew devotees from all over the Mediterranean world, including the emperor Hadrian.

The Cult of Isis

Isis was originally an Egyptian nature deity, but in Hellenistic times, she became the subject of a massive mystery cult. Isis, who found and resurrected Osirus, became the benevolent mother of all who could rebirth the believer into a happier life on earth and a life of eternal bliss after death. The mysteries and ceremonies of Isis were full of grand ceremony, wild music, and emotional charge. Our only hint of what these mysteries contained, as well as the devotion they inspired, comes from passages in Lucretius and a long episode in Apuleius's *The Golden Ass*.

Lend Me Your Ears

Lucius, who is transformed back into a man by the grace of Isis during a procession, alludes to his ecstatic experience after his conversion, baptism, and initiation:

"Listen then and believe, for it is true: I passed over the threshold of death's door, through the elements of the cosmos and returned. I saw the sun ablaze at midnight, and came into the very presence of gods above and gods below and did them reverence."

—Apuleius, *The Golden Ass*, 11.22

The Cult of Mithras

Mithras had Persian (Zoroastrian) origins, but during the Empire, he had become a more popular savior-god than even Isis. He was the god/hero of light, truth, and the intermediary between humanity and the supreme Sun God. His miraculous birth was witnessed by shepherds (a story influenced by Christianity) who brought him gifts. When he grew to manhood, he accomplished many heroic feats fighting evil, including the sacrifice of a great bull from which good things and the promise of salvation came to mankind. He then ascended to heaven to join his father and care for the souls of those who followed him.

The worship of Mithras was especially popular among the soldiers, many of whom came from the east. They admired his heroic deeds even as they were comforted and strengthened by his care and presence. His worship also fit in with the ambitions and program of the Illyrian emperors Aurelian and Diocletian. They styled themselves, in part, after the invincible Sun god and led their armies of little Mithras to victory.

Great Caesar's Ghost!

The fifth of March was the day of the *navigium Isidis* (ship of Isis). A representation of Isis' sacred ship (upon which she sailed to find and bring Osirus back to life) was launched amid a crowd of masked revelers and a great parade. Some scholars have thought that this is the real origin of *Carnevale* celebrations in the Mediterranean.

Roamin' the Romans

Some *Mithraea* (places of the worship of Mithras) became places of later Christian worship. You can find one beautifully preserved under the Church of St. Clement in Rome.

Veto!

Most of what we know about Druids comes from Roman sources and some mythic elements preserved in the late middle ages by Welsh and Irish monks. Modern Druidism, whose conception of druids and druid practice comes mainly from a romantic revival begun in the eighteenth century, bears little historical resemblance to its ancient namesake.

Mithraic rituals were held in underground caves or in temple basilicas. Groups were kept small, and worship caves or temples were owned by their congregations. Mithraic ritual had sacraments of baptism, confirmation, and communion. There were several grades of initiates for which there were elaborate ceremonies of advancement. "Ordained priests" instructed initiates and conducted the ceremonies. Mithraism included strict moral guidelines and promised eternal life. This way, however, was only open to men. No women were allowed, and this was a fundamental problem for Mithraism against Christianity.

Unprotected Sects: Druids, Jews, and Christians

There were, however, some religions or religious orders that Rome did not tolerate—namely those that did not recognize the Roman state's authority or legitimacy and who (in the Romans' view) undermined stability and fostered discord. These cults were called *religiones non lictae* (unsanctioned religious cults). Over the period of the Empire, three major groups were persecuted at various times: Druids, Jews, and Christians.

Druidism

The Druids were a combination of Celtic judge, sage, doctor, historian, and scholar. They made up the intelligentsia of Celtic tribes, learning their craft and history through an arduous and lengthy oral education (it was forbidden to write down Druidic lore). Greeks and Romans admired their intellectual and scientific knowledge, but abhorred their practice of human sacrifice.

Both Julius Caesar and Augustus had trouble with the Druids in trying to suppress the Gauls. Caesar, one of our sources about them, portrays them as a noble, powerful, and yet savage caste that fostered Celtic resistance and unity. Caesar's conquests in Britain were short lived, but Claudius returned to the island in C.E. 43, aided by the invitation of British chieftains afraid of the power of Caratacus, the king of Camulodunum (Colchester), who championed the Druids as a force against Roman occupation of Celtic territories.

Claudius's armies defeated Caratacus, but problems with Druids persisted. The emperor declared Druidism illegal in 54, and in 61, the Romans drove most of them to their sacred island of Anglesey in Wales, and exterminated them.

Judaism

The Jews in Hellenistic times had established large settlements all over the east, especially in Alexandria. The Romans' relationship with them, and with Judaism, went far back. The senate had offered the Hasmoneans support against the Seleucids in 161 B.C.E. (renewed in 141 B.C.E.). At Rome, however, the senate banned Jews and Jewish preachers in 139 B.C.E. and refused to recognize synagogues as places of worship.

Pompey the Great, however, who had helped to settle affairs in Palestine in 68 B.C.E., allowed Jewish refugees to come to Rome. Julius Caesar, as compensation for the Alexandrian Jews' assistance to him in Egypt and for the support in Judaea of Antipater, King Herod's father, allowed Jews to worship freely and established Judae as a client-state. Augustus proclaimed synagogues to be sacred places and exempted Jews from appearing in court on the Sabbath (Saturday). The Jewish presence in Rome over this time grew in numbers and in stature, and many Romans were attracted to Hellenistic Judaism's thought and elegant monotheism.

Great Caesar's Ghost!

The Celts and Romans believed that mistletoe was a sacred plant that fostered peace and love. Combatants who found themselves under the sacred plant were to lay down arms and maintain the peace for the day. The plant was also a part of cultural rituals intended to foster peace and friendship. We, of course, use the plant at Christmas to foster a similar kind of good cheer.

Veto!

Jewish "persecution" is kind of a misleading term. The roots of anti-Semitism are more in Christian than pagan Rome. Pagan Rome did not persecute Judaism or Jews (in fact, Rome exempted Jews from emperor worship, military service, and certain court obligations in order to allow their beliefs). The Jews ran into problems with Caligula—but didn't everybody—and Jewish *nationalism* became problematic in Palestine in the early Empire. Hostility to Jews started to become official Roman policy under Constantine.

But troubles between Jews and other ethnic groups abroad, and between Jews and Romans in Rome, caused problems in the early Empire. Judaea was put under direct Roman control as a province in 6 until the rule of Herod Agrippa I in 41. Tensions with the urban population caused Tiberius to ship 4,000 of them to Sardinia in 19. More trouble came under Caligula, who attempted to set up an image of himself in the Temple of Jerusalem despite pleas to the contrary from Jewish delegations from around the world. He also allowed those hostile to the Jews in Alexandria to ransack and desecrate their holy places. A rebellion in Palestine was barely avoided by his assassination. Claudius, who was in the process of stamping out Druidism, made Judaea into a province again on the death of Herod Agrippa in 44, which set the stage for the Jewish rebellion under Nero (see Chapter 15, "The [Mostly] Good Emperors: The Flavians to Marcus Aurelius").

The Flavians conquered Jerusalem and the rebels and attempted to stamp out Jewish nationalism once and for all. They abolished the Jewish high council (Sanhedrin) and high priest, forbade Jewish proselytizing, and destroyed the Temple. Jews were still allowed to practice their faith and were exempt from Emperor worship in the Empire, but they paid a yearly head tax to compensate for the former revenues generated by the Temple for Rome. Later, the emperor Antonius Pius (138–161) allowed them the right of circumcision as a part of his tolerant approach to religious sects of all kinds.

When in Rome

Diaspora means "dispersal." At times it refers to groups of people living outside of the homeland; at others it refers to the forced displacement of people from their lands. Here I am referring to the period after 135 when Rome banned the Jews from living in Jerusalem or Judaea.

Christianity

Christians, who had begun as a Jewish sect, held an ambiguous relationship with Jews and Judaism in the early Empire. Christianity was broken off from Judaism both by Roman policy (such as the prosecutions under Nero), by Jewish and Christian antagonism, and by the Jewish *Diaspora* following the Bar-Kochba revolt (132–134).

After the second century, Christian writers and theologians took an increasingly harsh stance against the Jews, and when the Roman Empire became Christian, the Empire took an increasingly hostile stance to them. There was a brief reprieve when Julian the Apostate, in his attempt to revive paganism and strengthen Christianity, made provisions for the Temple of Jerusalem to be rebuilt, but this was abandoned after his death. The emperor Justinian, in particular, persecuted both Jews and Monophysite Christians; both these groups were happy to see the Muslims take control of the Holy Land from Constantinople.

Christian Persecutions

We first hear of Christians as a troublesome sect of a troublesome Jewish people during the rule of Claudius. Jesus' opposition to the Jewish hierarchy favored by Rome and the community chaos that followed preachers like Paul probably contributed to this impression. Whether this trouble had something to do with Nero's blaming Christians for the fire in 64 isn't clear. Distinguished from Judaism, especially after the destruction of Jerusalem, Christians were viewed as suspicious because of their secretive and strange practices. Their refusal to acknowledge the Roman gods of state or the Emperor resulted in their being branded "atheists" in the larger Roman world, a charge that fueled many of the persecutions by state and local authorities.

And yet Christianity, especially that which Paul brought to cities around the Roman world between about 30 and 60, spread to all levels of Roman urban society. It offered a benevolent savior, personal salvation and the promise of eternal blessings, a strong moral and social code, and an organized community of believers. This organization was developed at the congregation level, at the city level under the bishops, and between the bishops and a growing number of Christian thinkers and writers. This organization gave Christianity a foothold from which neither persecutions nor doctrinal controversy could shake it.

Early Christian communities were popular refuges for the poor, but relatively well-off converts provided their leadership and patronage. Early Christian writers also came from this class of people. The whole was held together by a theoretical breaking down of barriers, or in Paul's words, a lack of distinction between "Jew and Gentile, slave and free man, Greek and barbarian, male and female." This last pair was particularly important, because the development and maintenance of early Christian communities depended in large part upon the leadership and money of women. It also gave Christianity an important social and cultural inroad that Mithraism lacked. This mixing of classes and sexes, however, offended the sensibilities of many prudish pagans, who refused to associate or even speak with people who conducted themselves in such inappropriate ways.

In parts of the Empire, people brought charges against Christians for a variety of motives. Roman magistrates and emperors of the early Empire were not, for the most part, overly concerned with pursuing or protecting them. Domitian went so far as to send representatives to interrogate Jesus' family,

Lend Me Your Ears

"In the meantime, I have followed the following procedure for defendants who were brought before me as Christians. First, I asked them if they were Christian. If they admitted it I asked them a second time and then, having warned them of the punishment, a third time. I ordered those who still persisted to be hauled off: I had no doubt that—whatever it was that they were admitting—such pigheadedness and rigid obstinacy should be punished."

—Pliny the Younger (*Letters*, 10.96)

but when all they found was a few poor farmers who included a great-nephew, he apparently decided that Christ represented no real threat. The emperor Trajan made it a policy that Christians, even though they were participating in an unsanctioned secret society, were not to be hunted down or prosecuted on anonymous evidence. This comes to us in correspondence between Pliny the Younger, the governor of Bithynia in C.E. 113, and the emperor. Pliny, who had no previous experience with Christians, decided to make it illegal to charge Christians anonymously, and gave those brought before him every opportunity to get off the hook. Those who persisted, he figured, deserved what they got—whatever it was that they believed—simply for being so obstinate. Trajan, in a reply, confirmed Pliny's approach.

Tensions between Christian communities, which spread all over the Empire by the second century, and local governors and populations increased. Christians openly refused to recognize and participate in state rituals and sacrifices. To the others, they were unpatriotic and irreligious in an age when the Empire was stressed, under siege, and in need of cohesion. Their exclusivity and detachment threatened local order and was a direct rejection of what it meant to be Roman.

The Emperor Antonius Pius attempted to quell religious intolerance, but during the reign of Marcus Aurelius major attacks against Christians by angry mobs erupted around the Empire. Christians, charged with impiety and atheism, were tortured and killed in Lugdunum (Lyons), Smyrna (Izmir), Vindobona (Vienna), Rome, and other cities. The heroic manner in which many Christians faced their deaths won more converts in some cases. Still, Christianity had many friends in high places in the Empire. Traditionally it was Marcia, the Christian concubine of Commodus (she also helped plot his assassination), who secured the release of Christians condemned to the mines during the reign of Commodus's father Marcus Aurelius.

In the chaos after Commodus, there weren't systematic persecutions again until the Illyrian emperors advanced imperial religion, with the emperor at the center, as a unifying element to the Empire. Aurelian promoted himself as the divine representative of the Invincible Sun God and Diocletian expanded upon this by making the figure of the emperor one of veneration and worship. He intended to establish a strong religious cult and figure at the center of the Empire and at the head of the military. When Christians in the civil service and the military refused to go along with the program, Diocletian issued edicts in 299 against them, and in 303 against their churches.

Civil unrest, arson, and riots broke out, first at the imperial residence in Nicomedia, then around the Empire. Diocletian and the tetrarchs then issued edicts that all who would not perform state sacrifices should be put to death or sent to the mines. These persecutions lasted between 303 and 311 and were carried out to various degrees by the different tetrarchs in their respective areas—mainly in the cities. By 311, it was clear that the persecutions were a failure, and even Galienus, the most ardent persecutor, became convinced that it was better to have everyone—anyone—praying for his soul (see Chapter 17, "Divide and [Re]Conquer: Diocletian to Constantine"). His *Edict of Toleration* put an official end to the Roman State's persecution of Christians.

Roamin' the Romans

Sites commemorating lives and deaths of Christian writers, saints, and martyrs cover the lands of the Roman Empire. In Rome, you can visit St. Peter's and St. Paul's resting places in Rome: the Basilica of St. Peter and the Basilica of St. Paul's Without the Walls (meaning outside the walls of Rome). In Greece, you can visit the Island of Patmos, where St. John, in exile, wrote *Revelation*. Even though the Byzantines didn't accept *Revelation* as gospel, they took John seriously and founded a monastery there.

Christian Versus Christian

By the time Constantine the Great fought under the banner of the Invincible Christ instead of the Invincible Sun God, Christians were already beginning to engage in persecuting each other in the mob riots caused by the Donatist controversy (see Chapter 17). As Emperor, Constantine attempted to bring unity to the Empire through unity of religion. Despite the council at Nicea in 325, differences in Christian doctrine (especially Arianism and Monphysitism) and concerning scripture continued to keep Christians occupied with the faithful for centuries to come. Except for the pagan hiccup of Julian the Apostate, however, no later emperor (Orthodox or otherwise) conceived of Rome as anything but a Christian empire. Rome had found the match of state and religion that could claim both absolute sovereignty and exclusive truth without getting in each other's way. If Diocletian had listened to his Christian wife, he might have unified the Empire 30 years before Constantine.

From this point on, persecutions were by Christians against other Christians, pagans, or Jews. With the removal of the altar of victory from Rome in 381 and the edicts of Theodosius, paganism's historical and practical legitimacy was rejected and outlawed. When Justinian closed the philosophical schools in Athens in 529, its independent intellectual history was subjugated as well. From now on, Greek philosophy would live as the clever slave of a Christian master.

Great Caesar's Ghost!

There's never been agreement among Christians as to what constitutes "scripture." Additional gospels, such as the *Gospel of Thomas*, epistles (letters) of Peter, Paul's *Epistle to the Laodicians*, the *Acts of Peter*, and the popular *Shepherd of Hermas* were elements of an elastic scriptural tradition. Early Christians viewed *Revelation* and *Hebrews* (eventually accepted into the canon) with great suspicion. In the west, the works of the New Testament remained open until the Council of Trent in 1546, when they were closed by a less than a ringing endorsement (24 votes for, 14 against, with 16 abstentions). Protestants further restricted the canon to match their own approach to scripture. In the east, Greek, Russian, and Ethiopian orthodox churches developed a different approach to scripture and have different scriptural canons.

The Least You Need to Know

➤ Pagan Rome was generally tolerant of other religions and beliefs.

➤ Rome persecuted Druids, Jews, and Christians for opposition to the state.

➤ Christian persecutions were periodic and localized.

➤ The Christian Roman Empire persecuted Jews, pagans, and heretical sects.

Chapter 21

Cogito Ergo Sum: The Life of the Mind

> **In This Chapter**
>
> ➤ The Silver Age of Latin literature
>
> ➤ Christian and pagan writers of the Empire
>
> ➤ The end of Latin literature in the western Empire

With the close of the Augustan Age, Latin literature and culture was at its high point and poised for the wild roller-coaster ride to the end of the western Empire. In this chapter, we'll follow that ride through the twists and turns to the time of Marcus Aurelius, including the beginnings of Christian scripture and literature. Then we'll climb the giant loop in which pagan thought infuses Latin Christendom before plunging into the dark tunnel of the Middle Ages. In each section, we'll pick out a couple of writers that exemplify a kind of literature or a trend in the Empire's life of the mind.

The Silver Age of Latin Literature

The first two centuries of the Empire are called the Silver Age of Latin literature. Latin forms and style developed and perfected what the Augustans had established; although it produced a great *quantity* of literature, it doesn't match the vitality and *quality* of the end of the Augustan Age. But that's rather like saying silver serving pieces aren't quite up to gold. It's true that gold is more valuable, but it's all sterling (so to speak), and depending on the use—some people prefer silver.

Poetry and Epic

Virgil's *Aeneid* was the high point of Latin epic, but his work inspired others to write in this style. Two particular poets who found worthy subjects and wrote epics worth knowing about are Lucan and Statius.

Marcus Annaeus Lucanus (39–65) was born at Cordoba in Spain. Lucan was the nephew of Seneca (Nero's tutor). He wrote, among other works, an epic called *Pharsalia* about the war between Pompey and Caesar. His popularity brought on Nero's jealousy. Lucan was implicated in the same conspiracy in which both Seneca and Petronius lost their lives and was forced to commit suicide. Lucan's work was highly admired in the Middle Ages and Renaissance.

Publius Papinius Statius (ca 45–96) was from Naples. He wrote two epics, the *Thebaid* (about Oedipus's sons' fight for the throne of Thebes) and *Achilleid* (about the Greek hero Achilles). Only parts of these works survive.

History and Biography

Livy's history of Rome ended with Augustus and featured the heroes of the Republic he idealized. In the principate, the emperors became the central heroes and villains of the new Rome. Two particular writers known for chronicling the early history of the principate and the transition from Republic to principate to dominate are Tacitus and Suetonius.

Veto!

Seneca ridiculed Claudius to glorify Nero; the senatorial Tacitus looked darkly on the authoritarian underbelly of the principate. Suetonius loved juicy scandal and naughty bits. I'm just saying, don't take everything—especially reported rumors or suggested interpretations of motives—in these histories as unbiased reporting.

Cornelius Tacitus (ca 55–115) served under the emperors from Vespasian to Trajan. He married the daughter of Cornelius Junius Agricola, the governor of Britain. Tacitus wrote several important works. He wrote a dialogue concerning orators (or how bad Roman education had become), the *Dialogus de Oratoribus;* the earliest ethnography of the Germans, the *Germania;* and a famous biography of his father-in-law, the *Agricola,* which also contains important information on early Britain and the Celts.

Tacitus's major works, however, were his histories. The *Annales,* which covers the reigns of Tiberius through Nero, survives in portions; the *Histories* covers the years 69 to 96. Parts of these works survive. Tacitus's dark and suggestive histories are primarily responsible for the suspicious and grim image we have of the workings of the early principate.

Gaius Suetonius Tranquillus (70–140) was a friend of Pliny the Younger in Rome. Pliny secured favor with Trajan, and Suetonius became an imperial secretary.

This gave Suetonius access to the imperial archives. He published numerous works (parts of which are lost), but he is most famous for his *De Vita Caesarum* (Lives of the Caesars), which covers the period from Julius Caesar to Domitian. There isn't much depth, but you'll find a host of personal anecdotes, rumormongering, and juicy tidbits about the emperors.

Novel and Satire

Tacitus's history had a sharp note of bitterness and cynicism, and this edge is also felt in writers of fictions and satire who commented upon the foibles of their times. Even though times were pretty good for all classes, optimists are always disappointed, moralists are constantly chagrined, and life seems to have lost its grounding in the international swirl of Roman affairs.

Gaius Petronius Arbiter (ca 20–65) was a member of Nero's circle and was looked to by Nero as his judge of good taste. Petronius's novel, the *Satiricon,* concerns the adventures of two young rogues on the loose in the southern Italy of Nero's day. Only fragments of this work remain, the episode of the *Cena Trimalchionis* (Trimalchio's Dinner) the most famous. Petronius lost his life with Lucan and Seneca in the conspiracy of Piso against Nero in 65.

Marcus Velerius Martialis (40–104) was born in Spain. Martial is best known as a master of epigram: short pithy poems on personal topics done in a biting, ironic, and satirical manner. Many famous English epigrams are really translations of Martial.

Decius Junius Juvenalis (ca 50–127) was probably born in the Italian city of Aquinum. When you think of satire, you're thinking of the form of the invective perfected by Juvenal. Sixteen satires rake Romans, foreigners, writers, wives, and Rome itself over the coals. Juvenal was indiscriminate in his attacks: He hated *everybody.*

Lucius Apuleius (ca 123–180) is famous for the *Metamorphoses,* or alternatively, *The Golden Ass.* This tale concerns a young Greek who accidentally becomes transformed into an ass, and passes through the hands of a series of owners (each with his or her own virtues and vices) before being transformed back into himself by the benevolence of Isis. The mysteries and worship of Isis are lovingly portrayed at the end, but the most famous part of the story are the Greek fairy tale of *Cupid and Psyche.*

Great Caesar's Ghost!

Apuleius's tale of *Cupid and Psyche* is one of the best-known Western fables, and has been translated, painted, and adapted by writers and artists throughout history, including C. S. Lewis in *Till We Have Faces.*

How To, and Bet You Didn't Know

As we've seen in the previous chapters, the early Empire was an age of seekers and of a growing body of specialists and professionals. It was accordingly an age that produced works of information, advice, and knowledge for both laymen and professionals of all kinds. And like today, where there is so much—too much—to know, people needed advice on what one *should* know to be educated in general or in a particular subject. This climate in turn created a need for the know-it-all, writers who churn out encyclopedic works on various topics or who prescribed how or in what to be educated. The following are some various areas and major writers in each.

Philosophy, Rhetoric, and Letters

Marcus Fabius Quintilianus (35–95) was from Caligurris in Spain. He was a rhetorician and educator. His work, *Institutio Oratoria,* is a comprehensive treatment of rhetorical education (including the skills of reading, writing, listening, and speaking) and includes valuable annotated lists of Greek and Latin authors that Quintilian thought worth studying and why.

Roamin' the Romans

As you read about the authors in this chapter, you'll notice just how culturally important the province of Spain was to the early Empire. The next time you go to Spain, take note, especially in the city of Cordoba from which Seneca the Elder, Younger, and the poet Lucan came.

Plinius Caecilius Secundus (61–114), or Pliny the Younger, was Pliny the Elder's nephew and was adopted by him. Pliny the Younger was a friend of Trajan's and wrote a long, long speech praising the emperor (a eulogy) called the *Panegyricus.* Ten books of letters survive, including his famous letters to and from Trajan concerning the Christians in Bithynia and his recollection of Mt. Vesuvius's eruption and death of his uncle.

Lucius Annaeus Seneca (ca 4 B.C.E.–C.E. 65) was born in Cordoba, Spain and was the son of the famous rhetorician Seneca the Elder (ca 65 B.C.E.–C.E. 37). Seneca became Nero's tutor, but later "retired" and was forced to commit suicide when he was implicated in the conspiracy of Piso. Seneca wrote works and letters on Stoic philosophy, natural science, tragedies, and a satire on the deification of the emperor Claudius. His tragedies were translated into English in 1581 and became influential on the Elizabethan court and upon writers such as Ben Johnson and Shakespeare.

Technical Subjects

Vitruvius Pollio (fl. under Augustus) wrote an important treatise, *De Architectura,* which is our major source of information on Roman city planning, architectural design, aqueducts, and the machines of war.

Sextius Julius Frontinus (ca 30–104) was *praetor urbanus* of Rome in 70 and *consul suffectus* in 73; he then was governor of Britain. In 97, the emperor Nerva appointed him *curator aquarum* (water commissioner). Frontinus wrote a major work on the history, workings, management, distribution, and construction of Rome's aqueducts and water works, called *De Aquis Urbis Romae* (Rome's Water Supplies).

Medicine and Science

Aulus Cornelius Celsus (*fl.* 20?) wrote encyclopedic works of which only the medical portions survive. He wasn't a doctor, but he wrote a clear and comprehensive work for laymen describing medicine from Hippocratic works to current practice.

Galen (ca 129–199) of Pergamum was a Greek doctor, scientist, rhetorician, and philosopher who rose from the position of doctor to a gladiatorial school to imperial physician for Marcus Aurelius in Rome. Galen's voluminous works on Hippocratic medicine, anatomy, physiology, neurology, case studies, and other subjects, as well as his philosophical and religious approach to medical knowledge, became standard through the Middle Ages and Renaissance.

Antiquarians and Encyclopedists

Gaius Plinius Secundus (24–79), or Pliny the Elder, was a prolific writer and self-styled investigator. He was killed while checking out Mt. Vesuvius during the same eruption that buried Pompeii and Herculaneum. His *Historia Naturalis* (Natural History) is 37 books of information on everything from physics and geography to magic charms. While interesting, it contains a great deal of misinformation and has been called "a compendium of all the errors in the ancient world."

When in Rome

The abbreviation **fl.** stands for *florit*, Latin for "flourished," and is used when we know when a particular author was active, but don't have a good idea when he or she was born or died.

Marcus Cornelius Fronto (ca 100–170) was Marcus Aurelius's tutor. He was a traditionalist, and wanted to get back to using "real Latin." To get the vocabulary that this would take (imagine trying to describe our global world using only English words) he researched obscure words and phrases and tried to create a Latin that was more precise in terminology and expression. His letters to the young Marcus Aurelius survive.

Aulus Gellius (ca 125–175) started writing little discourses for his children. These included a host of obscure facts, odd bits of cultural information gleaned from a wide range of authors, and probably a whole garage of information. The collection of these writings is known as the *Attic Nights* in honor of his time in Athens.

It's Greek to Everyone

While Latin literature was going silver, Greek literature was beginning to enjoy the beginnings of a Renaissance. Greek was still the lingua franca of the ancient world and still the primary language of education and culture. With the prosperity and stability of the Empire, Greek writers and educators enjoyed a wide audience and a broadening interest by both Greek speakers and Romans in what was emerging as Greco-Roman culture. Two representative writers are Plutarch and Pausanias.

Plutarch (ca 45–120) wrote moralistic biography and philosophical essays that became highly influential in the fifteenth and sixteenth centuries. His *Bioi Paralleloi* (Parallel Lives) pairs biographies of influential Greeks and Romans and concentrates on actions, words, or circumstances that might pass unnoticed but reveal the character of each subject. His other work was a collection of 83 essays on topics that bear on moral character and guidance. This work is known as the Moralia.

Think travel guides began with Michelin? Pausanias (fl. 150) wrote a practical guidebook to Greece for tourists interested in Greek antiquities. Pausanias based his work mostly on his own experience and included first-hand commentary on ruins, statues, and local attractions (such as marvels that local tourist attractions advertised but didn't materialize while he was there). His works have been crucial to identifying and reconstructing buildings at archeological sites.

Rise of the Romance Novel

Does the reading public want highbrow literature? Not now, and not then. Many readers went for romance novels, which started to become popular during this time (probably to read instead of Pausanias while on vacation in Greece). If the Empire had had supermarkets, you would have found beautiful women swooning, handsome heroes with intense stares, menacing pirates, and exotic settings depicted on the covers of *Chaereas and Callirhoe, An Ethiopian Tale,* and *Daphnis and Chloe*—probably right next to *Kosmopolitana* magazine and the display of *Tik-tak*s.

The Second Sophistic

I should tell you about the "Second Sophistic," a period of intense interest in Greek rhetoric in performance (rhetoric as performance art) and public lectures given by Greek orators on various subjects of public concern.

The original "sophists" were professional rhetoricians, teachers, and public lecturers who became active during the fifth century B.C.E. in Greece, especially in Athens. This period would be the "First Sophistic," although it's never called by this name. "Sophist" comes from the Greek *sophistēs*, or "learned man." Some sophists claimed not just to teach skills but virtue. Those in Athens were confronted by Socrates (who was nevertheless accused of being a Sophist himself) and attacked by Plato in his various dialogues for teaching young men how to win arguments with clever rhetoric (hence our term "sophistry" to indicate dishonest verbal sleights of hand). The "sophists" of the "Second Sophistic" were also rhetoricians, teachers, and public speakers who achieved great popularity in the revival of Greek culture that occurred during the early Empire's period of prosperity and stability. Two famous speakers of the period are Dio Chrysostom and Aristides.

Dio Chrysostom (ca 40–115) had a pleasant style that earned him the title "Golden Mouth" (Chrysostom). Dio was born in Bithynia and was a popular lecturer who spoke on culture, politics, morals, and virtues.

Aelius Aristides (ca 120–189) was a widely popular inspirational orator and speaker. He delivered showpiece orations on a variety of topics and grand public eulogies of Rome and Athens when in those cities. Over 50 speeches remain.

Early Christian Writers

The Apostle Paul's letters comprise the earliest Christian texts. Despite all the literature and writers you're reading about in this chapter, the ancient world relied heavily on oral tradition, and the early Christian church relied on preaching and the idea that Christ would come back *soon*.

However, as the Apostles and first-hand witnesses of Christ began to die out and the Kingdom of God began to look like it might be a while in coming, Christ's sayings and teachings were written down. These sayings began to be woven together with narratives of his ministry in the later first and early second centuries. Some versions apparently relied on a common source of sayings (known as "Q" for *quelle,* meaning "source"). Luke put what he knew into the form of Hellenistic history and included the story of Jesus' birth. As the Apostles' own generation passed, their acts also were written down for reference and edification.

Besides scripture itself, however, Christians began to write *about* scripture and about the beliefs that made them who they were. Christian scholarship therefore developed to support or oppose differing views and approaches, although politics and doctrine fettered these discussions as often as it informed them. Some influential writers of the early Christian church included Irenaeus, Tertullian, and Origen.

Irenaeus (ca 130–202) of Lyons was one of the Christian church's first systematic theologians and proponents of the authority of apostolic succession in church doctrine and teaching.

Great Caesar's Ghost!

Most Christians have seen study Bibles in which translations are lined up for comparison. This goes back to Origen, whose *Hexapla* compared six versions of the Old Testament. There were columns for Hebrew, Hebrew transliterated into Greek, and three Greek versions, including the *Septuagint.*

Tertullian (ca 160–230) of Carthage was influential in helping to determine the early Christian canon and in arguing against *Gnostic* beliefs. He himself was a proponent of the apocalyptic writings of *Montanism*, which was condemned. Tertullian's language and style were famous and helped establish Latin firmly as the language of the Western church. It was he who coined the term "New Testament."

Origen (ca 185–254) was an Alexandrian and became one of the most learned of early Christian scholars. His works on Biblical criticism, systematic theology, exegesis, and doctrine were influential, but his unorthodox teachings and ordination got him booted from Alexandria by his bishop. He continued his work in Palestine, was tortured in the persecutions under Decius, and died a short time later.

When in Rome

Montanism developed from the apocalyptic prophesies of Monatanus (ca 172), a charismatic Phrygian priest and preacher. His followers (Tertullian was the most prominent) treated his writings as scripture in their fervor for the end times. The sect was suppressed quickly but continued in remote parts of Phrygia into the seventh century.

Gnostic is a term that applies to sects that believe in a kind of secret knowledge (Greek *gnosis*) that depends on revelation. There were gnostic aspects to many Hellenistic religions and philosophies, and gnostic sects were an influential element of early Christianity. The gospel of John appears to have been written, in part, to contradict some of their claims.

From Marcus Aurelius Until the Fall of Rome

After Marcus Aurelius, who wrote his own *Meditations* in Greek, Roman Latin literature was largely lost in the chaos of the times, and Roman literature in Greek took on the glow of an aging pagan aristocrat. Christian writers, however, were on the move and gaining strength; pagan writers and thinkers engaged them in a battle of words and culture.

After the triumph of Christianity under Constantine, noble pagans attempted to carve out for themselves a place in a Christian Rome based on their knowledge, history, culture, and contributions to Rome and humanity. This was a losing battle. Nevertheless, by the time of the end of the western Empire, Christian writers (such as

Augustine, Boetheus, and Cassiodorus) had assimilated enough of pagan Latin literature to both triumph over it and yet preserve a place for it in the west if only as a means to preserve Latin education. In the east, Constantinople remained a repository of classical Greek until the Renaissance.

Some Roman Greek Authors

Cassius Dio Cocceianus (ca 150–235) was one of several historians during the time of Alexander Severus. He was consul at Rome and the governor of Africa and Dalmatia. He spent over 20 years researching and writing a history of Rome, in Greek, from Rome's beginnings to C.E. 229. His work, only part of which survives, contains information that is missing otherwise, such as a description of Claudius's invasion of Britain.

Athenaeus (fl. 200) was a Greek writer of *Deipnosophistai* (Wise Guys at Dinner), conversations of imaginary dinner parties featuring both fictional and historical guests ranging over a variety of topics, personalities, and anecdotal stories.

Diogenes Laertius (ca 200–250) was a Greek from Cilicia who wrote a work of 10 books concerning the lives, opinions, and principle doctrines of 82 philosophers from the early pre-Socratics to Epicurus.

Authors of Pagan Pride

Porphyry (233–305) was the student of the famous Neoplatonic philosopher Philostratus and a scholar of comparative religion. His treatise *Kata Christianon* (Against the Christians) was a powerful pagan salvo against some Christian doctrinal and historical claims (such as the early composition of the book of Daniel). The work was decreed banned and copies were burned in 448.

Quintus Aurelius Symmachus (ca 340–402) was the powerful pagan Roman senator and the center of opposition to the complete Christianization of the Empire. He vigorously opposed the removal of the Altar of Victory from Rome but lost the battle to his cousin, St. Ambrose, the bishop of Milan. Nevertheless, Symmachus was influential in preserving the pagan heritage of Rome, such as making sure editions of Livy survived. His letters to

Great Caesar's Ghost!

Historia Augusta (fourth century) was an anonymous tract detailing the reigns of the emperors from Hadrian to Diocletian. It pretends to be the work of six biographers from Diocletian and Constantine's time, but it was written by one person, probably during the time of Symmachus.

prominent people of the day and bits of his speeches survive. A conversation between Symmachus and his friends about pagan scholarship and culture is portrayed in another contemporary's work, the *Saturnalia* of Aurelianus Macrobius, who was possibly the emperor Honorius's chamberlain.

Ammianus Marcellinus (ca 330–?) was born a pagan in Antioch. Although his native tongue was Greek, he wrote a Latin history of Rome from 96 (where Tacitus's work left off) until the battle of Adrianople in 378. Much of this work, unfortunately, is lost.

Zosimus (early fifth century) wrote a history covering the period from Augustus to Alaric's sack of Rome. He identifies Christians and Rome's neglect of its gods for its decline and fall. You can see here and in Symmachus the kind of thing that Augustine was trying to contradict in his *City of God* (discussed in the next section).

When in Rome

Monasticism is the practice of living as a monk (from the Greek *monachos*, "hermit"), usually according to practices prescribed by tradition and rules passed on by other monks of a certain order.

Roamin' the Romans

The famous *Codex Sinaiticus*, housed at the British Museum since 1933, has been thought to be one of the copies that Eusebius made for Constantine the Great in 331.

Christian Literature of the Later Empire

In the era of crumbling cities and doctrinal strife, becoming an ascetic monk and living a monastic life became popular as a way to live a pure and uncompromising Christian life. One monk in particular, St. Anthony of Egypt, became a popular icon of the monastic life in the fourth century and inspired the beginnings of western monasticism. Monastic communities began to spring up. Eventually, rules of conduct and organization were composed, such as the rules of St. Basil (329–379) in the east and St. Benedict (480–547) in the west. Meanwhile, in the cities, writers were trying to make sense of the chaos and decline that they found around them. Some of the important institutional writers in this time were Eusebius, St. Jerome, and St. Augustine.

Eusebius (ca 260–340) lived through the great persecutions and the Edict of Toleration and became the associate of Constantine the Great, whom he represented at the Council of Nicea. Eusebius wrote histories of the early church, a life of Constantine, a discussion of historical chronology, and an explanation of how pagan history and culture also led to the triumph of Christianity. Eusebius was also commissioned to provide 50 copies of scripture for the emperor. These early renditions of scripture may have helped in the formation of the early canon.

St. Jerome (ca 348–420) was a student of Donatus, the great pagan grammarian, and was so enriched by classical pagan culture that he once dreamt Christ accused him of being a Ciceronian instead of a Christian! He became, after a period of study and monastic asceticism, the advisor and secretary to Pope Damasus. Damasus commissioned a translation of the Gospels and the Psalms from Jerome, who had mastered both Hebrew and Greek. The rendition of these works into popular Latin, *Latina vulgata,* became the Vulgate Bible.

St. Augustine (ca 354–430) was a classically trained educator and rhetorician who became (after a long period of spiritual struggle) a Christian, the bishop of Hippo, and one of Western Christianity's most influential writers and theologians. Augustine's most famous work is probably his *Confessions* in which he details the long road of his spiritual odyssey. His monumental work, *City of God,* is a Christian theory and exegesis of history. Using his philosophical and rhetorical training, he expounds a history in which the Christian is not a citizen of any earthly city (such as the recently sacked Rome) or empire, but one who enjoys the rights, privileges, and comforts of God's eternal city and the citizenry of believers.

Augustine's letters and sermons also survive. He died in Hippo as the Vandals were laying siege to his city, but his synthesis of classical and Christian learning, reasoning, and writing lived beyond them.

Writers at the Passing of the Greco-Roman Tradition in the Latin West

Anicius Manlius Severinus Boethius (ca 480–524) was a Christian who both respected and used pagan literature and philosophy. He was patronized by the Ostrogoth king Theodoric and consul in 510. Boetheus was a prolific orthodox writer and scholar. He started complete translations of both Plato and Aristotle into Latin, but he was charged with treason by a friend and was condemned to execution. While he waited, he wrote *De Consolatione Philosophiae* (The Consolation of Philosophy) an imaginary conversation with *Philosophia* the (mostly pagan) personification of Philosophy, who comes to visit him in his cell. With the death of Boetheus, the Greco-Roman literary tradition's last hope in the west was snuffed out until the Renaissance.

Flavius Cassiodorus Magnus Aurelius Senator (487–583) was from a very noble Roman family and one of the last Roman consuls. After a period of service, Cassiodorus retired and founded a monastery in which he built a library and established a collection of books. He wrote numerous works, but his chief importance lies in his model for other Christians and monastic orders of a writer who was Christian but yet knew, used, and respected pagan Latin literature for learning and education.

The Least You Need to Know

➤ The Silver Age of Latin Literature ranges from the death of Augustus to Marcus Aurelius.

➤ Both Latin and Greek writers were important in the sacred and secular literature of the Empire.

➤ Latin and Greek literature of the Empire ranges from technical and literary works to popular fiction and travel guides.

➤ Early Christian writers formulated theology and debated conflicting doctrines within the context of a flexible canon of scripture.

➤ Pagan and Christian writers waged a culture war in the late Empire in which pagan literature, traditions, and thought were infused into Christianity.

Chapter 22

That's Entertainment! Public Spectacles

> **In This Chapter**
>
> ➤ Roman games and spectacles
>
> ➤ Chariots and gladiators
>
> ➤ Where was the V-chip?

Roman public games (*ludi*) developed in the Republic, but they came to their full measure of intensity, grandeur, and bloody drama in the Empire. In this chapter, we'll review a bit of the history of Roman games and see how the different kinds of public entertainment—including gladiators and chariot racing—kept the urban public thrilled and chilled.

They Liked to Watch

It's good to keep in mind that the spectator culture of Rome was just that—Romans watched but for the most part did not participate. There weren't permanent sites for entertainment, with the exception of the Circus Maximus, until the late Republic and early Empire. Festivals and the entertainment that went with them were transitory affairs, and Romans looked upon the performers, whether they were actors, dancers, and musicians, as carnies.

Being a charioteer or gladiator was the work of slaves. No good Roman would stoop to appear on stage or compete, like the Greeks, in competitions such as the Olympics. Such exhibition was not only silly, but it had no practical application to work, politics, and conquest that Romans engaged in. This is why Nero's appearances on the stage, Commodus's ambition to be Rome's main attraction, and the occasional appearances of noble Romans (including women) in the arena shocked the upper classes and titillated the common folk. Those nobles and emperors might as well have played a saxophone on late night television, publicly enjoyed pork rinds at a Texas BBQ, or been a part of WWF wrestling matches.

History of the Games

The ancient world had a history of public entertainment and competition connected with holidays and festivals. The competitive performance of Greek tragedy and comedy in Athens is a famous example, the Olympic games are another. Sacred holidays or occasions also involved parades, dances, and both solemn and carnival-like public activities. Two of the most famous examples are the portrayal of the *Panathenaic* procession on the frieze of the Parthenon in Athens (the Elgin Marbles of the British Museum) and the reliefs of the *ara pacis* of Augustus in Rome.

The major festivals of Rome were based in religious celebrations of the early Republic,

but came (like in our own day) to be more "holidays" than "holy-days." Not all holidays included *ludi*. By the time of Sulla, there were six major Roman religious festivals (57 days) that included *ludi;* other towns and cities would have had approximately the same schedule. Festivals that did have *ludi* usually had several days of performances culminating in a day of big-ticket games (races, hunts, or gladiatorial combat). Here are the major Roman state games:

When in Rome

The **Panathenaic** festival was a yearly civic and religious festival held in Athens in honor of the city's patron goddess, Athena.

➤ *Ludi Megalenses* (April 4–10) celebrated the arrival in Rome of the cult and sacred stone of Cybele in 204 B.C.E.

➤ *Ludi Cereales* (April 12–19) were celebrations of Ceres, the goddess of grain.

➤ *Ludi Florales* (April 28–May 3) were festive celebrations of Flora, an ancient Roman goddess of flowers and fertility.

➤ *Ludi Apollinares* (July 6–13) were dedicated to Apollo from the time of the Second Punic War in thanks for his help.

➤ *Ludi Romani* (September 5–9) was an ancient celebration that occurred in thanks to Juno, Jupiter, and Minerva (Athena) at the end of the military campaigning season. This was one of the first festivals to which dramatic performances were added.

➤ *Ludi Plebii* (November 4–17) were apparently an early plebeian version of the patrician *Ludi Romani*.

In the first century B.C.E., generals such as Sulla, Pompey, Caesar, and Octavian began to celebrate their own victories with holidays (like our modern V-E Day) and games funded by their conquests. Special games, such as the *Ludi Saeculares* which gave thanks for the end of a long period (*saecula*), could also occur. Under the Empire, games were also instituted to commemorate emperors' birthdays (like our Presidents' Day). By the fourth century C.E., Romans could enjoy *ludi* 177 days of the year.

During the Roman Republic, the aediles (officials in charge of urban affairs) oversaw public funding and production of *ludi*. Ambitious politicians, such as Julius Caesar, used their own revenues or borrowed heavily to win public favor by adding to the public funds to create spectacular games. Gladiators weren't a part of the publicly funded entertainment until late in the Republic (more on that later). Instead, public events included dramatic performances (such as comedies, tragedies, pantomimes, and rustic farces), staged hunts, animal exhibitions, and the biggest event: chariot races.

During the Empire, gladiatorial fights were added and shows of all kinds got bigger, bloodier, and more elaborate. These shows became a staple all over the Empire for urban populations that, in Juvenal's words, demanded their *panem et circenses* (bread and circuses).

The interior of the Colosseum, with the vestal virgins' box seats (center).

The Circus

Chariot racing was the big event of ancient spectator sports and went way back before the Romans: The Olympic and other Greek games featured wealthy aristocrats from all over the Hellenic world competing at the "sport of kings."

By the time of the Romans, chariot racing was a for-profit operation. Four teams, the Reds, Blues, Whites, and Greens, competed all over the Empire, a bit like Team Porsche and Team Ford do in professional car racing. These teams were run by wealthy owners just as professional teams are today. It took a lot of money to breed, maintain, and train champion horses, and have a supply of chariots and drivers.

How the Races Were Done

Before the *ludi,* the aedile or public official in charge of setting up the race entered into negotiations with the four teams to rent horses, drivers, and support teams for the period of the games. Officials tried to get top-notch teams of drivers and horses for their events. Teams received a negotiated fee for participating and then any purse money they won. Purses ranged in amounts, but big ones ranged between 40,000 and 60,000 sesterces.

On the day of the race, crowds crammed into bleacher-style seats. You know how some guy or family will hog bleacher space by spreading out their stuff on either side of them? No such thing allowed in Rome. The rule was that you had to be touching your neighbor; this allowed as many as possible to get in. The poet Ovid points out that this made for a great way to meet girls. Here is a quote from his *Art Amatoria* (1.134–162) in which he describes seduction strategy in the Circus:

> Don't let the contest of the noble chariots escape your notice; a racetrack full of people offers many opportunities. You don't need to communicate secrets with finger-talk or make do with a nod and a glance, just sit right next to your heart-throb, no problem, touching and joined at the hip by the narrowness and regulation of the seats!

> Start conversation in the usual friendly way, and let what's being said around you get you started. Ask the girl eagerly whose horses are running that day and don't hesitate, whoever it is, to be for the same as she is! Then, when the statues of the gods are brought in, be sure to clap loudest for Venus, the Goddess of Love.

> Now, if by chance a little bit of dust falls into the girl's lap—Oh! It simply *must* be bushed off with your fingers. And if there's no dust … brush it off anyway. Any excuse to get involved warrants your attention. … The Circus presents these openings to new love.

Races featured two-, four-, or sometimes even six-horse chariots, depending upon the event. Numbers of chariots in the race depended on the size of the venue; the Circus Maximus could run up to twelve four-horse chariots. In the Circus Maximus, races lasted for seven laps (about two and a half miles). A long low wall down the center kept chariots from cutting corners, and terminated in a turning post at each end. Chariots and horses lined up against a starting gate with grooms to help hold them in position. At the signal (a blast from a horn), the chariots flew down the stretch with the drivers leaning forward over the front of the chariots, whipping the horses, and bracing for turns.

Racing chariots were like skateboards hitched to horses: small, light frameworks with wheels about the size of a wheelchair and a platform just big enough for the driver to stand on. Racing was an all-out contact sport. Drivers jockeyed for position and rammed each other out of the way. Knowing how to navigate the turns was crucial to staying in the race—and staying alive. Crashes were frequent, and frequently fatal.

The Drivers

Chariot drivers began as slaves or the children of drivers. Even though the owners won the purse money, some of it must have gone to the drivers because winning drivers were able to purchase their freedom (if they lived that long). Still, winning one race paid as much as a schoolmaster earned in a year, and winning drivers became celebrities. A big-name driver could scarcely go out in public without being mobbed by women and men. One of the most famous, a late first-century charioteer by the name of Scorpus, appears in several of the poet Martial's poems. Scorpus won an amazing 2,048 victories and died in a crash at the age of 26. Martial (in two other poems) and Scorpus's fans mourned him after his death just as modern fans mourned the loss of NASCAR racing legend Dale Earnhardt.

The Crowds

Supporters from all levels of society cheered the colors of their favorite teams. When the race began, crowds leapt to their feet and began cheering and waving banners and togas. If there was a false start, people shouted and waved their togas for the race to begin again. Can you imagine this with up to 250,000 fans at the Circus Maximus? It must have been wild. Groups of supporters were called *factiones* (gangs). Besides cheering on their team, chariot hooligans traded insults and fought before, during, and after the races. In Constantinople, the factions became so powerful and dangerous that they nearly toppled the emperor Justinian.

Gladiators

The other major attraction of the games were exhibitions that featured life and death struggles.

It's important to distinguish what kinds of people killed each other in the Roman games: They were either criminals or professional gladiators. Convicted criminals were fed to the beasts or were forced to kill each other by pitting an unarmed man against an armed one. After each death, the victor was disarmed and faced the next armed opponent. This kind of carnage was lunchtime fare (*meridianum spectaculum*) before the battles of the professionally trained fighters in the afternoon—the gladiators.

The spectacle of gladiatorial combat originated in Etruria as a part of aristocratic funeral games and sacrifices. For this reason the matches were known as *munera* (obligations to the dead) rather than *ludi*. They were introduced into the Roman aristocracy in the mid third century B.C.E. They were privately funded events and became a way for aristocrats to develop popularity and prestige. By the first century B.C.E., Caesar's lavish use of gladiators and the revolt of Spartacus show that gladiatorial combat had become a popular and lucrative spectator event. Augustus and the emperors exploited the mass popularity of the games and gladiators by offering games in

307

Great Caesar's Ghost!

Athletic games and contests were a part of the aristocratic funeral celebrations in the ancient Mediterranean. If you've read the *Iliad* or the *Aeneid,* you know about this. The Olympic Games, in fact, were by tradition the funeral games of the hero Pelops. Julius Caesar put on games to honor the death of his daughter, Julia.

their own names. These games were an important part of the emperors' public relations.

Arena spectacles and executions followed wherever Romans established themselves, and although they were protested by some, executions and gladiatorial fights became a successful popular export of Roman mass culture.

Gladiatorial contests were originally held, like the *ludi,* in temporary venues in the markets or forums with fights between only a few pairs of gladiators. In spectacles, however, bigger is better. Caesar featured many pairs of gladiators sparing off against each other at one time; in Augustus's games, 5,000 pairs of gladiators fought over the course of the games, and 5,000 fought in Trajan's games over the course of a month. Venues also became professional: the most famous, of course, is the Colosseum.

The entrance to the Roman arena in Nîmes, France.

The cost for these kinds of games was enormous and could be afforded only by the emperor. Smaller games outside of Rome might be put on by local magistrates or officials, but for anything of size, permission (and perhaps funding) had to come from Rome.

Who Were the Gladiators?

Gladiators came from slaves, war captives, and criminals. Men were sold to a gladiatorial school under the supervision of a trainer (*lanista*) and the owner. Yes, sometimes free men in desperate circumstances entered the schools on their own. If so, they had to swear an oath of complete submission to be enrolled in the *familia* of the school. Once they agreed "to be burned, to be bound, to be beaten and to be killed by the sword," they were trained and hired out to games three or four times a year. Most gladiators died in the arena fighting beasts or members of their own *familia*. The talented, however, could hope to win their freedom and the honorific wooden training sword that gladiators were presented with at their retirement. Retired gladiators sometimes returned to the schools as trainers/ coaches or hired out as private bodyguards.

Roamin' the Romans

You'll find the remains of a gladiatorial school and barracks in Pompeii, where the first permanent amphitheater was built.

Top gladiators were, like top chariot drivers, objects of public adoration. Inscriptions in Pompeii record how certain fighters made girls swoon, and Juvenal (in *Satire 6: Against Women*) tells us about Eppia, the wife of a senator who ran off with a gladiator to Alexandria and joined his school (I'll bet you wouldn't want to get between those two in a spat!). Fighters in the Thracian style (see the following section, "Specialists"), who wore the least clothing, were apparently especially popular with women. From funerary monuments, it appears that many gladiators took a grim pride in their profession, combining a measure of fatalism with a sense of duty that often accompanies public figures who—in one way or another—sacrifice themselves to the desires of "their" public.

Specialists

Originally, gladiators were captive warriors and fought each other with the equipment they had. Since they came from different backgrounds, they fought with an exotic array of arms. As the sport became more professional, a variety of fighting styles and equipment emerged and gladiators specialized to match their bodies and abilities. Matches pitted different types of fighters against each other to make them more interesting by balancing strengths and weaknesses.

At the bottom of the food chain, so to speak, were the *bestiarii,* who fought for their lives against wild animals. These men were rarely armed with more than a whip or a spear and some leather protective clothing. *Venatores* were specialists in the hunts (*venationes*) that obliterated so many animals from around the Empire. It's not clear if trained gladiators or simply condemned captives fought in the staged naval battles (*naumachiae*) that occurred in the Colosseum or artificial lakes flooded for the games.

Great Caesar's Ghost!

Gladiators lived in a highly regimented and disciplined hierarchy. Owners (or imperial managers) of gladiatorial schools took great pride in providing the best in facilities and specialist trainers. Besides living quarters, facilities featured places for fans to watch gladiators train (like spring training facilities). Owners also took good medical care of their valuable investments, retaining on staff both physicians and dieticians who were often first-rate professionals. The famous physician Galen (Marcus Aurelius's doctor) began in a gladiatorial school and was proud of his reduction of its mortality rate.

At the top of the ranks were the highly trained and specialized fighters. There were many kinds and tended to be named either for the country of their fighting style's origin or for the distinctive weapon they used. Generally, however, they can be broken down into two groups: fighters who relied on strength and armor, and those who relied on speed and mobility.

Heavily armed fighters included …

➤ **Secutores** (pursuers in the Samnite Style). Secutores were armed with a large shield, a sword, a heavy simple helmet with eyeholes, one protective arm sleeve, and a protective greave for their forward leg. They were originally called Samnites, but after the Samnites became allies and Romans, this name was dropped (an early example of PC language change?) and the name "pursuers" was adopted, probably because they had to pursue the more lightly armed fighters who relied on mobility.

➤ **Thraeces** (Thracian-style). Thraeces had a helmet with a wide brim, crest, and protective visor. They were armed with a scimitar (curved sword) and small shield and wore greaves on both legs.

➤ **Myrmillones** (Gallic-Style). Myrmillones were heavily armed fighters who were named for an emblem of a fish on their helmets.

Lightly armed fighters relied on speed, mobility, and trickery to defeat their opponents. They included …

➤ **Retiarii.** The Retiarii were armed with only a net and a tether to ensnare their opponents and a trident to strike from a distance. Their only defensive armor was a shoulder piece to protect their net arm.

➤ **Laquearii.** These fighters used a lasso.

➤ **Sagittarii.** The Sagittarii were armed with bow and arrows.

➤ **Essedarii.** Essedarii fought from Celtic war chariots (probably introduced by Caesar's conquest of Britain).

➤ **Dimachaeri.** These gladiators fought with two swords.

Some gladiators apparently fought with highly specialized weapons or armor. We don't know too much about them, but their names make you think as much of the movies featuring Mad Max or Luke Skywalker as they do of Romans. Three of them were …

➤ **Scissores.** Scissores were gladiators whose name means "carvers" or perhaps "slicers and dicers."

➤ **Provocatores.** Provocatores means "challengers" and refers to the calling of an enemy out to fight. No one knows what this means, but since gladiatorial pairs were drawn by lots, I've wondered if this might indicate some kind of challenge bouts where gladiators could challenge specific opponents (sort of like challenging the heavyweight for the title).

➤ **Andabatae.** These were gladiators whose helmets blocked their vision so that they had to fight opponents blindly. Can't you hear the *lanista* (trainer): "*Utere illa vi, Luce*" (Use the force, Lucus)?

Dwarfs, Amazones, and Amateurs

As gladiatorial combat became more a spectator spectacle than a solemn funeral rite, the Roman spectators' desire to see the bizarre and strange, as well as the fans' fantasy of participation, affected the games. Both dwarf and female gladiators (Amazones) are mentioned as a part of the games of Nero, Domitian, and Commodus. Female gladiators were especially popular, and although there couldn't have been many, they appear to have been a fairly regular part of the top entertainment bills. The emperor Diocletian spoiled the fun in 200 and banned women from the arena. Dwarfs, however, apparently still continued to be a part of the games.

Even though some had huge followings, gladiators as a group (along with actors and prostitutes) were *infames:* "slime balls" or "(social) trash." As it is

Roamin' the Romans

The funeral remains of what is believed to be a female gladiator were unearthed in London in the summer of 2000. The London amphitheater where she would have fought and died lies under London's guildhall and held about 7,000 spectators.

Veto!

Don't get the idea that Romans were the only people to employ cruelty and a macabre use of realism in their productions. When Crassus was defeated and killed by the Parthians, his head was cut off and sent to the Great King. The king, who was viewing a production of Euripides' *Bacchae,* had Crassus's head used as the main prop.

with all disreputable sports, the arena nevertheless appealed to some wealthy Roman enthusiasts, including women, who trained and participated in the events. These bigwigs brought both enthusiastic crowds and condemnation from their peers. The most blatant class-jumpers were Nero and Commodus. Since these emperors were also the ones under whom aristocrats, dwarfs, and women entered the games, it seems that these emperors set the tone for these other performances.

The Greatest Show on Earth

Another stupefying kind of Roman spectacle sounds like Olympic Games Opening Ceremonies run amok: reenactments of mythological or historical events, complete with real suffering and death. Roman spectators loved big shows with realistic effects, and the games gave the opportunity to put the "real" into history and myths. Does the story have a burning house? Then burn a real house down! Nero's games featured just such a prop (the actors were allowed to keep the furniture they saved out of it for themselves). Does the story require a murder?

An immolation? Someone to burn their hand off? One of those things that it's really hard to get the screams and smells just right? No problem! The games provided a ready supply of actors and extras perfect for those kinds of "one night only" parts.

Sea battles (*naumachia*) were among the grandest of the spectacles. Caesar was the first to organize a battle of 3,000, and Augustus followed by creating a drainable (for sanitation and smell) venue by the Tibur in which to stage his sea battles. Claudius celebrated his tunnel at Lake Fucini with a massive battle on the lake involving 19,000. The participants fought so well that the emperor let the survivors go free. Titus, Domitian, Trajan, Diocletian, and Philip the Arab also put on *naumachiae*.

A Day at the Games

Games were announced beforehand by heralds, and the venues for the different events and performances were posted. Programs were distributed to increase interest and people studied their programs to determine where to go and who to bet on. A feast (or last supper) for the gladiators was put on the night before their show. On the day of the games, the participants paraded to music and great fanfare past the sponsor of the games (*editor*) and then retired to their stations for the games to begin.

The morning program was a warm-up for the big events. Morning games included mock duels and martial arts displays with wooden weapons and displays of wild or trained animals. Morning was also when the *venationes* and other hunts took place, pitting beast against beast (the more exotic the better) or man against beast.

Great Caesar's Ghost!

Productions of *Peter Pan* or even Wagner's *Ring* feature flying characters hauled about in the air to simulate flight. That's nothing new. A production of *Daedalus and Icarus* during Nero's games featured characters flying about on wires. Unfortunately this production was a little *too* true to form: The actor who played Icarus crashed and burned (or, in Icarus's case, burned and crashed) when his gear broke; he landed by Nero's seat and splattered on the emperor.

Lunch featured a half-time show of executions. In the more mundane games, this is when criminals were thrown to the jungle cats (which were usually bound to stakes) or forced to kill each other. The afternoon featured the gladiatorial pairs. The pairs were drawn by lot, and each fight was refereed by a *lanista.* If the gladiators weren't giving it their all, it was the *lanista*'s job to (literally) whip them into fighting shape. When a gladiator was wounded or defeated (and yet alive), he could appeal for mercy and concede defeat by holding up his index finger (a kind of "Excuse me, I believe I'm dying here" gesture). Whether he lived or died was up to the *editor* (sponsor) of the games, but the crowd got into the picture by waving, cheering, and making hand gestures to either spare or kill the fallen participant.

Gladiators given a reprieve (*missio*) might have to fight again the same day; others were expected to be true to their oath and take the final blow without fear or flinching. After someone dressed as Charon (the spirit who ferried souls to Hades) or as Mercury (the god who escorted them there) tested to make sure that he really was dead, the fallen gladiator's body was dragged off with a meat hook by a slave through the *Porta Libitinensis,* or Death's Gate (*Libitina* was a goddess of death) and disposed of.

Veto!

Gladiators are popularly known to have said, "Emperor, we who are about to die salute you," before each match. Not really. Suetonius (in *Claudius* 21.6) reports that that captives who fought a sea battle said this to Claudius. There isn't any evidence that gladiators ever said this in the arena, much less that the phrase was a regular part of the games.

The End of the Games

You'd think that the coming of Christianity would have ended the brutality of the Roman arena, but not completely. It is true that Constantine the Great issued an order in 326 against gladiatorial games, but neither edict nor the Christianization of the Empire stopped either the spectacles of execution or the gladiators. Constantine himself, in fact, had German captives thrown to the animals and was praised by Eubebius for destroying the Empire's enemies.

Honorius closed the gladiatorial schools in Rome in 399. However the games continued; we find Symmachus still putting them on. St. Augustine (ca 400) writes of a friend who was reluctantly dragged to the arena by friends, only to become an ardent fan. Such fans were so ardent that when a monk tried to interpose himself between two fighters in the arena in 404, the crowd killed the monk. This, at least, allowed Honorius the excuse to close the gladiatorial games themselves. In the east, gladiatorial combats ended about the same time. Entertaining executions by wild animals continued, however, to be officially sanctioned until 681.

Why?

I'm guessing that as you've been reading through these descriptions, you've asked yourself, "Why?" How could people have done these kinds of things and found them *entertaining?* Why were the Romans so warped? Some Roman writers defended the games as exhibitions that taught courage and spirit; others gave that defense all the contempt it deserved.

Before you attempt an answer, however, keep a few things in mind. Consider the public exhibitions of Medieval punishments and torture. Take a look at the crowds of families picnicking at public hangings in the American West in the 1800s. Take a look at footage of the parties and celebrations outside of prisons on the eve of executions enjoyed by people who are in no way connected with the victims of the condemned. Take a look at popular horror films, books, and magazines. Consider why people slow down at traffic accidents. Before you write the Romans off, ask yourself if their entertainment was warped or manifestations of desires that lurk in all humanity.

The Least You Need to Know

➤ The Roman games involved more than gladiators and gore.

➤ Chariot racing was the most popular spectator sport throughout the Empire.

➤ Roman fascination with spectacle, death, and pain permeated the most popular events.

Part 5

Where Did the Romans Go?

Rome didn't fold. Like a big family with a common business, different branches of the Roman cultural clan went their separate ways while maintaining ties (in imagination if not in lineage) with their ancestors. In the east, the Byzantine Empire kept the business open in one form or the other until the fifteenth century; in the west, the popes kept the coals of the old headquarters alive until a merger with the Franks brought the western Empire back on line in C.E. 800. Reincorporation of the two regional bodies was a shared goal, but by then their corporate culture was neither compatible nor particularly willing to combine. Hostile takeovers of the east by the Crusaders and by the Turks brought about the dispersal of the east's hard and soft assets to the benefit of the Renaissance, Imperial Russia, and the Ottoman Empire.

In the following chapters, we'll follow the history of Rome in both east and west, and see how some different periods continued to capitalize on Rome's legacy. I hope that you'll come to understand how big of a market share Rome has on our contemporary world, and speculate how future profits might come from an understanding of its case study. After all, we're all in the business.

Chapter 23

And the East Goes On

In This Chapter

➤ The end of the eastern Roman Empire

➤ The beginning of Byzantine civilization

➤ Byzantine history in four Byzantine steps

➤ The fall of Byzantium and contributions to the West

The "fall" of the western Empire was not something that either the western or eastern Empires marked at the time. The making of Italy into a Germanic kingdom was not the decisive affair that it appeared in retrospect to Edward Gibbon (the famous writer of *The Decline and Fall of the Roman Empire*) in later days. In fact, the eastern Empire, the Orthodox Church (which included the bishop of Rome—the pope—until 1054), and even nonorthodox sects continued on the idea that "Rome" was still functioning. Latin continued (for a time) to be the language of administration and of the army, and both emperors and patriarchs conceived of the Empire as still comprising the peoples, lands, and economies living within the bounds of Constantine the Great's day.

The east made one more heroic effort to reclaim this legacy under the emperor Justinian but was unable to maintain its gains. From that point, the divergent paths of east and west began to go their own ways. The east, compacted by pressure on all fronts, remained predominantly Greek in language and culture. The west spun out of the east's orbit toward Europe. The popes, unable to be protected by Constantinople, sought power and protection amid the tumultuous tribes and against the pressures of Islam in southern Sicily and Spain by allying themselves with the Frankish kings. This alliance spawned the birth of a new "Holy" Roman Empire, whose drive to reconquer the Empire for Christendom brought the crusades (see the next chapter) both to Constantinople and to Jerusalem.

A struggle for dominance in the orthodox church came to a head at this time as well, and the pope in Rome and the patriarch in Constantinople excommunicated each other in 1054. After this divorce, the western orthodox church became known as the "Roman Catholic" (Latin) Church, while the national eastern orthodox churches (Serbian, Greek, Armenian, Syrian, Russian, and so on) are usually clumped under the name "Eastern Orthodox." Constantinople, as the center of what remained of the eastern Roman empire and the Eastern Orthodox Church, developed into the civilization we know as "Byzantium." In this chapter we'll see how that civilization developed, flourished, and fell, giving back to the west a legacy that it had lost and largely forgotten.

Roamin' the Romans

Istanbul is a wonderful, stewing city, piled with layers of history and culture and constantly mixing east and west at the crossroads of Europe and Asia. Spending time there means experiencing Byzantium, *Nova Roma,* Constantinople, and modern Istanbul all at once.

Nova Roma (Constantinople)

The opening of Constantine's new capital, Constantinople or *Nova Roma,* on the site of the ancient city of Byzantium turned out to be a stroke of genius. The city held a position that offered many advantages for the present and well into the future. It was easily defensible. It commanded access to the Black Sea and all of the rich trade routes to and from that area. It lay on the fault line between Asia and Europe facing the Greek, Oriental, Egyptian, and Barbarian quarters of the Empire like the hub at spokes of a wheel. It was an optimum place for a power base in the east.

Byzantine Beginnings

The turbulent fifth century put the east through a tumultuous time of upheaval and both internal and external pressures. The Persians continued to press the Empire from the east, the Huns from the northeast, and the Goths from the northwest. The emperors kept these tribes at bay by a combination of military strength, defensive building, diplomacy, and a whole lot of tribute payments. These payments were bitterly resented by the wealthy from whom the money was extracted. Following the breakup of Atilla's empire after his death in 454, a people known as the Bulgars (hence Bulgaria) arose from its remnants and became a constant threat to Constantinople and its lands to the northwest.

Internally, the fifth through seventh centuries were dominated by struggles for central control of both political and religious matters by the capital, Constantinople. Doctrinal differences continued to plague the Christian ideal of unity, and regional conflicts often made these differences worse. Constantinople was not the definitive center of ecumenical power. Alexandria, Jerusalem, Antioch, and Rome all had powerful bishops who competed with each other for power, in establishing doctrine, and for imperial favor. When the west was lost to the Germans and Islam conquered the other areas in the seventh century, Christianity in these cities became both politically and doctrinally isolated from the capital.

The primary doctrinal dispute of the early period continued to be the question of Christ's nature. Did Christ have two natures (human and divine) that existed independently in the same person or only one prevailing nature (the divine assimilating the human)? Bishops of Alexandria, such as Cyril, held one view, the bishops of Constantinople, such as Nestorius, the other. When it looked like Alexandria would become more powerful than Constantinople in determining doctrine, the emperor Marcian called the Council of Chalcedon in 451 to resolve the issue.

The early Christian Church wrestled with understanding the precise nature of Jesus, who gazes out from a mosaic in Justinian's church of Hagia Sophia in Constantinople (Istanbul).

What came of the Council of Chalcedon was the decision to adopt the opinion of the bishop of Rome (Pope Leo I), namely that Christ's human and divine natures were united within one person, but that they remained (in that one person) distinct and separate. This view (*hypostasis*) is still the dominant view in the west and Greek Orthodox Churches. However, the prevailing opinion of most of the eastern bishops and—interestingly enough—most of the emperors of this period was that Christ's divine nature had absorbed the human and was one nature in one person, or *Monophysite*. Despite Chalcedon, this view remained predominant in Egypt and Syria.

When in Rome

Hypostasis is the condition wherein Christ's two natures (human and divine) remained separate and distinct in one person.

Monophysitism holds that Christ's two natures (human and divine) had become one (divine absorbing human) in one person.

Trouble continued between rival factions, including riots, lynchings, and forced resignations throughout the Empire. In 482, the emperor Zeno tried to bring some space for order by issuing a declaration of unity, called the *Henotikon*. While the *Henotikon* ratified the decisions of the councils that established, it also left some room for interpretation and debate for the Monophysites. What it called for, however, was a recognition of one catholic church whose decisions were orthodox and binding.

We've followed the emperors in the east up through Marcian (450–457), but here are two more influential emperors leading up to the reign of Justinian:

➤ **Zeno** (474–491) came up with the idea of co-opting the troublesome Theodoric the Amal and using him against Odoacer in order to retake the west (see Chapter 18, "Barbarians at the Gates: The Fall of the Western Empire"). This deflected the Ostrogoths from Constantinople and relieved the Balkans of their pressure but led to the end of Italy as an independent province. Zeno tried to reestablish central control and authority over the doctrinal warring among Christians in the east by issuing the *Henotikon*.

➤ **Anastasius** (491–518) was a Monophysite but was crowned only with a pledge to uphold orthodoxy and the *Henotikon*. He put down much of the political violence and intrigue of his day and worked to balance Monophysite and Chalcedonian interests in the appointment of bishops. Although his reign was marked by attacks from the Bulgars and Persians, he was nevertheless able to reform the Empire's finances and tax laws so that when he died he left an enormous surplus of gold in the treasury. Like most surpluses, however, it didn't last long.

Great Caesar's Ghost!

Justinian's reign is one of the best documented in Roman history. The historian Procopius witnessed much of Justinian's reign and published several works on its events. But Procopius was not a fan. After Justinian's death, Procopius published the *Secret History,* a libelous attack upon Justinian and his wife, Theodora. In Greek, this work is the *Anekdota,* the term from which we get *our* word "anecdotal" describing published but unconfirmed reportage.

Justinian (518–565)

Justinian was the nephew of Justin I, the Illyrian head of the imperial guard who succeeded Anastasius. He is the last *Roman* emperor and the first Byzantine. After him, the west was lost, the east became Byzantine, and the armies of Islam swept through the southern hemisphere of the old Rome. Justinian was intelligent, very well-educated, orthodox, and ambitious. His western roots probably only fueled his drive to reestablish the Roman Empire over both east and west.

Besides Justinian, the most powerful person in the Empire was the empress, Theodora, who was Justinian's wife, partner, and close councilor. Empress Theodora was the daughter of a bear keeper and may have been a courtesan (a prostitute with a rich clientele) with a daughter before she met Justinian. Her background earned her the contempt of the upper class (Procopius reports all kinds of libel) and the tough mind-set of someone who came up from the streets. It was Theodora who told Justinian to have some backbone and convinced him to stay in the capital during the bleakest moments of the *Nika Rebellion*. The empress (perhaps because of her background) championed rights and protections for women, including buying impoverished women out of prostitution with her own money and setting up a foundation and home for them. Her influence with Justinian was profound even though she stayed independently powerful and sometimes (such as in her promotion of Monphysitism) opposed him. Justinian deeply mourned her death, by cancer, in 548.

When in Rome

The Blue, Green, White, and Red *factiones* of the Constantinople chariot races became highly organized, powerful, and violent. These factions could threaten emperors and patriarchs with riots and demonstrations. When Justinian tried to clamp down on them both, Blues and Greens joined under the slogan of *Nika* (Conquer!) and attempted to drive him from power in 532. Their massive riots, called the **Nika Rebellion**, were nearly successful, but Theodora's determination, Justinian's strategy, and Belisarius's loyalty turned the tide at the last minute. The subsequent destruction of the factions' power firmly established (and perhaps motivated) Justinian's autocratic rule.

Justinian's greatest achievements were the outgrowth of his zeal for order, splendor, and control. His most enduring achievement was to cause Rome's historical law codes and judicial opinions to be ordered and codified. To these works, he added a manual for legal studies and a work of laws passed under his own administration. This monumental compilation of scholarship, the *Corpus Juris Civilis* (completed in 534), became the foundation for all canon law and most European civil law. His reforms of tax codes and administrative procedure and his attempts to reduce corruption also deserve commendation although they weren't always successful. His monumental building projects, best represented in the wonder of Hagia Sophia (dedicated in 537) in Constantinople and the churches of Ravenna, are breathtaking. Their wondrous mosaics, which utilized artistic trends developed from Persia, helped to develop the ethereal and otherworldly style associated with Byzantine art.

On the flip side, Justinian's autocratic nature led to the centralization of power and decisions in the person of the emperor. He attempted to systemize everything throughout the Empire *his* way with *him* at the controls. In addition, he insisted upon arcane ritual and pomp that made him a figure of mystery and awe. The centralization of power under him, including the elaborate court ceremony and etiquette, and the arcane knowledge needed to get anything done were in large part responsible for giving the term "Byzantine" its meaning today of something that is overly and purposefully complicated to the point of being incomprehensible to an outsider.

His hands-on approach and desire to systemize everything extended into both secular and religious practices. He attempted to enforce his version of orthodoxy throughout the Empire, and vigorously persecuted all (especially Jews and Monophysites) who wouldn't fall into line. He was, in today's colloquialism, a control freak (albeit a capable one!) along the lines of emperors such as Diocletian.

How the West Was Won—And Lost for Good

Justinian's greatest failure was his determined attempt to reconquer and hold the full extent of the Roman Empire. Starting with a deceptively easy campaign against the Vandals in 532, his great general Belisarius quickly reconquered all of North Africa. The campaign bogged down in the quagmire of Gothic and Germanic Italy. Roman commanders were divided in their aims, Gothic armies could not be constrained from transferring alliances and raising trouble under new chieftains, and Justinian considerably underfunded the war effort. Persians, Huns, and Bulgars all took advantage of the Empire's stretched resources to attack in the east.

Roamin' the Romans

You can find portraits of Justinian and Theodora in the famous mosaics of San Vitale, in Ravenna, Italy. Justinian attempted to make Ravenna, which had served as an imperial residence and stronghold since Honorius, into the new capital of the west.

Nevertheless, Justinian was momentarily able to retake Spain and the Balkans, and to impose an imperial settlement on Italy. This attempt, however, bankrupted the Empire and left it so strained that it began to fragment immediately upon his death. It was as if the Empire suddenly sat up from its deathbed and grabbed the world once more by the throat, only to collapse and die.

The eastern emperors continued to assert that they rightfully ruled over the whole, but this was an assertion without teeth and without basis. The time of universal empire was past. If Justinian had concentrated his energy and resources on building up what he had, he could have made an enormous difference over the course of his long reign. He didn't, but perhaps we shouldn't fault him too deeply given his proximity to a unified Roman state. He wasn't the last leader to let the siren's song of reestablishing the Empire put his ship of state upon the rocks. There's been a lot more wrecks on those shoals since Justinian.

Byzantine History: It's Called "Byzantine" for a Reason

Justinian left no clear successor, which put the eastern Empire into a period of crisis after his death in 565. A new dynasty under Heraclitus (610–641) established itself just in time, but by then, the eastern Empire was surrounded on all sides by hostile or dangerously unstable states. The emperors and patriarchs of Constantinople clung to their identity as the continuation of Rome and citizens knew themselves as *Romanoi*. We know them, however, as "Byzantine" for the distinct civilization that grew up and inward from Justinian's time.

There are three intertwining facets that made up the distinct character of the Byzantine Empire: First, it was a Christian empire; second, its law and administration were Roman in form and heritage; and third, it was based on Greek (not Latin) language, literature, and culture. The last of these facets was largely responsible for the dogged preservation of Greek learning by scholars and copyists in Constantinople and the various Greek communities in southern Italy, Sicily, and Greece. They preserved this heritage until the Turks sacked Constantinople in 1453 and drove the accumulated remains of Greek and Roman civilization into the waiting arms of the Italian Renaissance in Venice, Florence, and Rome.

Between Justinian and the fall of Constantinople in 1453, however, Byzantine history can be thought of as falling into roughly four periods (610–711; 717–867; 867–1200; 1200–1453). During these centuries, Islamic armies, religion, and culture spread from Arabia; conquered the richest parts of the eastern Empire; and spread along Africa up through Spain. Ties with the western Latin church, which were always strained, continued to fray as the bishop of Rome looked to alliances with the Franks for protection in the west.

The popes came to assert primacy over the western church and eventually over all of Christendom. But by then, an iron curtain of differing orthodoxies had settled over Eurasia. Rome had Christianized in Latin as far as Scandinavia and Britain and Constantinople in Greek up through Russia. East was east and west was west. The pope of Rome and the patriarch of Constantinople excommunicated each other in 1054 and set the stage for the west's reconquest of the east, including the Byzantines, in the name of Christ and the crusades.

C.E. 610–711: Fighting to Keep Place

The first centuries of Byzantium were occupied by fighting to keep from being overrun by the Bulgars from the north and by Muslims from the south and east. With the death of Muhammad in 632, Muslim armies set out to conquer the world for Islam. By 680, Muslim armies were raiding all the way up to the city of Constantinople cutting it off from the rest of eastern Christianity. A series of energetic emperors were kept busy fending off the Slavs, Bulgars, and Muslims. With developments in military tactics and equipment (including the use of *Greek Fire*), along with the best navy of the time, Constantinople was able to maintain its hold over its heartland and the trade that kept it vital.

323

When in Rome

Liquid Fire, more commonly known as **Greek Fire,** was the secret weapon of the Byzantine Empire that turned the tide of battle for Byzantium against the Muslim fleets in 678 and 718. A Syrian refugee to Constantinople, Calinicus, created a chemical mixture that could be shot from a tube on a boat at an enemy warship. The gelatinous mixture would burst into flames like napalm, stick to boat and enemy, and burn fiercely even in water. The recipe was a state secret—so secret that the formula was eventually lost and never recovered. We still don't know what it was made of or how it was ignited when deployed.

This period of Byzantine history ends in the tumultuous reign of Justinian II, the son of the emperor Constantius IV. Justinian was emperor from 685–695, but his loss of Asia Minor to the Arabs and his despotism triggered a revolt. The rebels cut off his nose and sent him into exile. Justinian "Rhinotmetus" (Greek for "guy with the cut-off nose") came back 10 years later with Bulgar forces, retook the throne from 705–711, and wreaked revenge upon his enemies. In the words of the proverb, however, this was "cutting off your nose to spite your face": Justinian was again deposed in 711 and this time his enemies made sure that he lost his whole head.

Breaks Me Up: Icons and Iconoclasts (717–867)

Emperor Leo II repulsed the last serious attack of the Muslims on Constantinople in 717. For several centuries thereafter, Byzantium remained strong enough externally to keep it safe from foreign attacks. Doctrinal disputes, however, continued to damage its internal stability. In addition to the Monophysite controversies between the various national orthodox churches (Greek, Armenian, Syrian, Egyptian), a particularly violent controversy erupted over the use of sacred images (icons) in worship.

One side, which was particularly influenced by beliefs in the far eastern portion of the old Empire, contended that venerating images was idolatry and that these images should be destroyed. That's how they got the name "iconoclasts" (icon smashers). This approach was especially prevalent among the well-educated and upper crust of the clergy. The other, which was more identified with the west and with the practices of Christians in Greece and Italy, fought to maintain a cherished tradition of worship that still exists today. And, as it was more connected with a contemporary practice, those that defended the use of icons tended to be the monks and clergy associated with these practices and the people who admired them.

This controversy, then, was fueled by regional and class, as well as by theological, antagonisms. Violent clashes between the iconoclasts and their opponents occurred as bishops, emperors, and empresses (such as Constantius Copronymous and the famous Empress Irene) on both sides took power and persecuted each other.

During this period, relations between east and west hardened. The east, under the bishop Photius, worked to head off the pope's influence with the Illyrians and the recently Christianized Bulgars. Byzantine emperors and patriarchs still claimed authority over the whole west of the ancient Empire, but with the Muslims taking Byzantine, Sicily to the south, and Spain and the Lombards pressing hard from the north, the popes needed real protection. They also needed secular muscle to back up their ecclesiastical wrestling match with the patriarchs. They found it in the Frankish kings, and in 800, the popes established the west on equal footing with the east by getting an emperor of their own in Charlemagne. Two nationalistic Church/State systems, one Latin, one Greek, both claiming to be the legitimate heir to the restoration of Christian "Rome," were now fully in place.

Veto!

Orthodox Christians do not worship icons although they do *venerate* them. Icons are holy objects that serve as a focus for meditation, contemplation, and prayer and provide a means through which to respond respectfully to that which the icon represents.

Power and Splendor (867–1200)

In this period, Constantinople acquired a Macedonian dynasty and a series of military emperors who reestablished Byzantine control over a vast territory eastward into Palestine and into the Balkans and Caucuses. Constantinople now controlled most of the east of the old Roman Empire, but its harsh treatment of these "liberated" lands was so cruel that the inhabitants were eventually inclined either (like the Bulgarians) to break away or (like in Armenia) to have the Turks back.

Although it lost Sicily to the Muslims in 902 and later to the Normans, Constantinople recaptured southern Italy all the way to Naples, where the emperors opened relationships with the west. The first crusades drove out the Arabs; the disarray of European crusading aristocracy, Germanic emperors, and papacy gave Byzantium an opportunity to reassert control. For a while, the emperor Michael IV the Paphlagonian (1034–1041) attempted to recapture Justinian's dream, but it slipped away. The rift that had been growing between Greek and Latin churches was unable to be crossed; when the western representatives came to Constantinople, there was no common ground. Both sides excommunicated each other in what is known as the Great Schism in 1054.

Meanwhile, Greek antipathy against the Latin crusaders and against the Italian city-states (Venice, Florence, Genoa), which began to prey on the Empire, was also starting to grow. The loss of Bulgaria and Greece had weakened Constantinople. The Byzantines, who had hoped that the Latins would help them regain these territories, were incensed when the crusaders intervened in an internal dispute and set up their own emperor. A rebellion against the Latins brought massacre and counter massacre, with rival factions competing to establish an emperor in the capital. And so, weakened internally and externally, the Byzantine Empire was poised for its decline.

Great Caesar's Ghost!

One of the most interesting writers of this period is Anna Comnena (1083–ca 1150), the daughter of the emperor Alexius Comnenus (ruled from 1081–1118). After her husband failed to win the throne, Anna retired to her mother's monastery and wrote the *Alexiad*, 15 books of history concerning her father's reign. This work is a daughter's work, to be sure, but also the work of a historian who used a wide variety of source material in addition to her own personal knowledge of the Byzantine court and the events of the day. Her work is also interesting for a Byzantine perspective on the Latins and the Crusaders, who (according to Anna) entered Byzantium with all the grace of a motorcycle gang and proceeded to occupy her father's time.

Nevertheless, at the height of Byzantine power, Constantinople and its lands developed in regal splendor. Great landed families and barons grew in the regions, and in the capital, the emperor ruled amid a maze of ceremony and wonder complete with mechanical lions that roared and birds that sang. The splendor, however, masked the Empire's growing dependence of the land power of foreign mercenaries and upon the sea power and commerce of the growing navies of the city-states of Italy. By the end of this period, the Turks had taken Armenia, and the Normans had taken southern Italy and Sicily. This left Byzantium caught in a pincer movement between the forces of Islam and western Christendom.

With Friends Like You … the Crusades and Conquest (1200–1453)

Constantinople was sacked by the soldiers of the Fourth Crusade in 1204. The Latins set up their own emperor and patriarch confirmed by Pope Innocent II, and although the Byzantines were able to retake their city, they had to play off of three powers who continued to seek the capital as its prize. The first was, of course, the Turks themselves. The second were the powers in the Bulgarians and the Serbs, who would have taken Byzantium for the Slavs if they hadn't lost to the Turks in the famous battle of the Field of Blackbirds (1389). The third were the Normans, who continued to try to take the Holy Land and to govern Byzantium. Normans such as Charles of Anjou tried to become a Norman Justinian, but Byzantine emperors such as Michael Paleologus (1259–1282) kept him at bay by negotiating with the papacy for a reconciliation with Rome.

As this process dragged on, the Byzantine Emperor became more and more reliant on western military and monetary help to fend off the ever-encroaching power of the Ottoman Turks. The Council of Florence (1438–1439) declared a reunification of eastern and western churches but too late for Byzantium: the Turks captured Constantinople in 1453. From that time on, Roman dreams of empire without end would move among the kaisars and czars of Rome's former barbarian enemies.

Falling Star: The Influence of Byzantium

The fallen Byzantine Empire left behind a strong regional structure of orthodox churches throughout the east. This was a legacy of Constantine's establishment of the close link between Christian state and church authority. Over the course of Byzantine history, some national churches became autocephalous, or under their own authority and empowered to elect their own head. These churches retained, just as the Byzantine empire did, their fiercely independent and nationalist character. They also maintained the use of many rituals and vestments (clothes) that the ancient Byzantine emperors and patriarchs used. Several orthodox churches refused to recognize the unification between Constantinople and Rome decreed in the council of Florence. When Constantinople fell, they continued under their own authority.

Lend Me Your Ears

"[The Emperor Alexius] feared the [Frankish crusaders'] arrival, for he already knew of their raging and unstoppable attacks, their thoroughly unstable and violently capricious character, their insatiable hunger for money, and their readiness to betray a truce for their own momentary advantage."

—Anna Comnena, *Alexiad* 10.5

Roamin' the Romans

If you want to see some of the treasures of Constantinople, visit Venice, Italy. The Venetians were one of the major naval powers in the Aegean in the 1200s and ferried many crusader armies to the Holy Land. Venice's magnificent Basilica of San Marco is home to some of the spoils from the Crusader's sack of the Byzantine capital.

Veto!

If you ever doubt the way tradition colors history, compare historical accounts from both Greek (eastern) and Latin (western) perspective. Whether you're reading the contemporary accounts of Anna Comnena or Geoffrey de Villehardouin's *Conquest of Constantinople* (a crusader's account of the Fourth Crusade) or whether you're reading online resources such as *OrthodoxInfo* or the *New Catholic Encyclopedia,* you'll be struck by the similarity of facts and the dissimilarity of interpretation.

Veto!

Medieval European scholars also received a great deal through Muslim and Jewish scholars living in Spain and in the Holy Lands, who were far advanced beyond their European counterparts in many areas. Some works of Aristotle, for example, survived only in Arabic translations; St. Thomas Aquinas (fl. 1260s) needed Aristotle translated from Arabic into Latin in order to complete his monumental and still influential works.

In the waning centuries of the Byzantine Empire, and especially after the fall of the capital, Greek refugees fled to the West bringing the Greek language, learning, and texts that had been preserved as a part of the eastern Empire's heritage. This included works of classical Greek literature and history that were virtually unknown until that time. It's no accident that Italian cities who had large Greek refugee populations, such as Venice and Florence, became the centers for the infusion of Greek learning into the west. Without this influx, we would have had Virgil but no Homer, nor the works of the famous Greek historians and tragedians. In this way, the fall of Byzantium helped to ignite the growing Italian Renaissance and led to the combined study of both Latin and Greek traditions that still is the hallmark of a Western liberal education.

Ironically, the classical heritage preserved by the Roman east has served as a kind of cultural Trojan horse within the idea of "Roman" civilization in the West. The legacy of classical Greece became a revolutionary idea for those who found hierarchic authorities to equate with Rome's legacy. German and English Romanticism, Protestants who equated Rome with the Pope, and strains of American politics have tended to equate Rome with a stultifying tyranny of authority and tradition.

The interior of Hagia Sophia, which was converted into a Mosque and is now a world heritage site.

American culture, focused on individualism, youth, and vitality, finds something more alluring in Calvin Klein–like athletic Greek statues than the furrowed brows of middle-aged Roman ancestors. And I've got to admit, however, that there's something sexier in individual excellence (Greek *arete*) than duty (Latin *officium*) to others. Nevertheless, to read some Western Civ. outlines, you would think civilization submerged after Pericles (the famous fifth century B.C.E. Athenian leader) caught a quick breath in the Renaissance and Reformation and finally reemerged in Thomas Jefferson! This is, as you now know, an oversimplification of a very complicated history.

The Least You Need to Know

➤ The Byzantine Empire is the continuation of the eastern half of the Roman Empire figured roughly after the reign of Justinian.

➤ Three things distinguish the Byzantine Empire: It was Christian, it had Roman law and administration, and it was based on Greek (not Latin) language, literature, and culture.

➤ The Byzantine emperors maintained that they had authority over the west, but this was never realized.

➤ Byzantine civilization flourished between the ninth and eleventh centuries C.E.

➤ Pressure from the Slavs, Bulgarians, Franks, Crusaders, and Turks contributed to the decline of Byzantine civilization.

➤ The Turks conquered Constantinople (modern Istanbul) in 1453.

➤ Byzantine refugees brought Greek literature and culture to the West. This had a profound impact upon western history and culture.

Chapter 24

Nothing Quiet on the Western Front

In This Chapter

➤ The history of the west after the "fall"

➤ The papacy and the Holy Roman Empire

➤ Crusades and crusaders

➤ The ambiguous legacy of Rome in the west

And so, at last, we come back home to "old" Rome in the west for our concluding chapter. It's fitting—after all, this half of the Empire is the reason most readers are interested in Rome.

What a long, strange trip it's been! But we can't leave off just yet. We've traveled together over the fortunes of Rome—the city, Republic, and Empire—and followed the continuation of that Empire in the east after the west fell. Now it's time to pick up the ashes of Rome itself and show how the Western orthodox church, under the leadership of the popes, breathed life back into the coals of the old Empire and ignited the dreams, culture, conquests, and learning of Europe.

Instead of a super-condensed "history of the West" chapter, we'll take a look at some of the legacies that Rome has left the West over the course of the centuries.

Rome After the Fall

The city of Rome was not as damaged by the sacks of Alaric and the Vandals as you might imagine, but after Odoacer and Theodoric (see Chapter 18, "Barbarians at the Gates: The Fall of the Western Empire"), it became progressively a backwater. There was still a class of powerful and incredibly wealthy pagan nobles who owned huge estates throughout Italy. Pagan hostility to the Christianization of the Empire helped lead to Rome's isolation from Constantinople. These people could afford to continue with their ways and traditions even though the world was changing around them. Nevertheless, the aristocratic traditions of patronage and civic involvement became an important facet of the western church as the aristocracy gradually became Christianized.

Meanwhile, the western emperors had been building Ravenna and Milan into leading cities. Justinian, in his attempted reconquest of the west (see Chapter 19, "Roman Mass Culture of the Imperial Period"), ignored Rome altogether and made Ravenna into the new capital. It was here that Rome had to look for assistance from the east. When the *Lombards* (sixth century) invaded from the north, they virtually cut Rome off from Ravenna. By then, many residents had fled the city and pagan Rome fell into ruins, a moldering pile of abandoned monuments around the ancient forum.

When in Rome

The **Lombards** were a Germanic people from west–central Germany who invaded over the Alps in the sixth century, settled, and established a kingdom along the northern part of modern Italy (still called Lombardy).

The Papal Tiger

Around the geographical periphery of the city, however, the bishops of Rome were taking up the role that the pagan aristocracy had played. Popes were instrumental in providing for the material needs of both Rome and the needy of the less wealthy bishops. Endowed by Constantine with the Basilica of St. Peter and the Lateran palace, the popes created a network between these and the other major churches to care for both the spiritual and physical needs of their central Italian flock.

Constantine had allowed the church to own, sell, and manage property. As the nobility came into the Christian fold, they brought with them the riches of their estates and their experience at administration. It's no accident that the vestments of the Roman Catholic Church are those of the old Romans! The popes used revenues from these possessions to stabilize and oversee an area that the Empire had largely abandoned. In a time of extreme crisis and dislocation, the Church of Rome grew largely on its ability to meet people's pressing needs. Catholic social services have a long and well-documented tradition.

From their relative position of isolation, the popes had to fend for themselves and fill a number of important roles left in the power vacuum. Without the rod of military might, they established direct relations with the western barbarian kings, and negotiated among them for the protection of Rome, church possessions, and Christian communities. They sent out missionaries to Christianize them to orthodoxy and established bishops with lines of authority back to Rome. Efforts that began as attempts at self-preservation and practical administration grew into autonomy and then dominance in the west. By 800, the bishop of Rome was in the position to challenge the authority of Constantinople by crowning Charlemagne his own western emperor.

Roamin' the Romans

When you visit the Vatican City, you're not in Italy—you're in the capital of an independent state. Papal estates and territories in parts of northern Italy held out against the Lombards and became the so-called Papal States in the early Middle Ages. The Papal States grew throughout the Middle Ages and large sections of Italy remained state lands of the Roman Catholic Church until 1870 when Rome fell to republican forces. Italy as a modern country was born, but the question of just who owns just what remains unresolved. The Vatican and two other properties (the Lateran in Rome and the pope's summer quarters at Castel Gondolfo outside of Rome) remain "extraterrestrial" to Italy and Italian jurisdiction to this day.

The popes' independent authority over the west continued to grow until they established themselves as the preeminent authority in spiritual—and often temporal—matters in the twelfth and thirteenth centuries. Besides the church, they controlled vast territories and, at times, armies. So powerful and pervasive was their reach that from the late Middle Ages until the present day, "Rome" has more often meant "the Holy See" (Vatican, the pope) than either the city or the ancient Romans.

Like a Rock: Pope Gregory the Great

Pope Gregory the Great (pope from 590–604) was from an ancient, aristocratic, and wealthy Roman family. Trained for a career of Roman civil service, Gregory changed tracks and became a determined Benedictine monk. He sought a life of secluded spirituality, but his talents brought him appointment first as deacon, papal legate, abbot, and finally (against his will) pope.

Gregory is rightly known as the father of the medieval papacy. His noble Roman roots and training gave him a deeply embedded commitment to the prominence of Rome as well as the abilities and practical civil outlook of a Roman civil administrator. Working largely in isolation, Gregory effectively managed church estates (including the import and export of trade goods) to strengthen the church and serve the needs

333

of his flock. He took on negotiations and the defense of Rome from the Lombards in 592–593. Among the churches, he established a system of strong bishops with strong ties to Rome and promoted Rome's authority against attempts by the capital to intervene. Gregory was an influential teacher and theologian. His works on theology and liturgy firmly established him as a founding father of the western church, and his instructions to bishops, the *Regula Pastoralis,* served as an influential guide for ecclesiastics well into the Middle Ages.

Gregory is perhaps best known for sending St. Augustine and 40 monks to Britain in 597. He allowed a certain amount of flexibility in converting the Anglo-Saxons and other pagans to Christian practices in terms that they could understand and accept. Over 800 of Gregory's letters as well as other works survive. All in all, he achieved pretty impressive accomplishments for a man who thought that he was living in the last days and yet established the future of his office for centuries!

If I Had a Hammer: Clovis to Charles Martel

The popes were faced with a host of problems in the sixth and seventh centuries. As you read in Chapter 18, Arian missionaries had tremendous success among the Goths and Ostrogoths who eventually plundered their way to the west and settled in Italy, Gaul, and Spain. This left the orthodox papacy in a sea of Arian barbarians and without an army. What's more, a Germanic people known as the Lombards crossed the Alps and began to conquer northern Italy. The popes, cut off from the east, found an ally in the Frankish king Clovis (466–511), who converted to orthodoxy and established a vast kingdom centered on Paris. Although Clovis's Merovingian dynasty dissolved into anarchic infighting, his descendants continued to expand Frankish influence and domination over most of France and Germany.

The Franks became important allies to the popes and to the rebirth of Roman dreams in the west. They were directly linked with the "Roman" pope through orthodoxy and papal missions. Moreover, they were isolated from developments around the Mediterranean, such as the influence of either the eastern Empire or Islam. Frankish kings replaced the missing secular/military element for the western papacy that was present in the emperor/patriarch formula in the east and eventually gave the popes the power not only to establish their independence but to claim primacy over the east.

As the Merogingian dynasty disintegrated, their powerful "Mayors of the Palace" (commanders of the royal forces) at Paris became dominant in holding things together and in furnishing protection to

Great Caesar's Ghost!

Charles Martel's victory at Tours is charged with symbolism even today. Jean-Marie le Pen (the leader of the extreme right-wing party, le Front-Nationale) ignited a furor by appearing at Poitiers in recent years to deliver inflammatory speeches concerning Algerians and immigration from (Islamic) North Africa.

the popes. A major threat, not just to European stability, but to Frankish rule of Europe, was coming from the Muslims, who controlled Spain. As the Muslim army crossed the Pyranees into France under the Spanish governor Abd-er-Rahman, the Mayor of the Palace, Charles (688–741), brought Frankish forces against him. Charles had introduced a major innovation to his cavalry—the stirrup, against which a man could brace for using his sword or for striking with a lance (as in jousting) instead of throwing it. He routed the Muslims at Poitiers in 732, one of the history's decisive battles, and received the title *Martel*, or "The Hammer."

It wasn't long before history conceded to reality, and the Mayors of the Palace became the kings. Pepin the Short (714–768) was recognized by the pope in 749 and became the founder of the Carolingian dynasty. The popes appealed for his help against the Lombards, who were continually threatening their possessions in Italy. Pepin took care of the Lombards and formally recognized the pope's right as *ducatus Romanus* (Roman overlord) to central Italy. Evidence for the pope's claim to these lands was further established by the *Donation of Constantine,* an imperial decree in which Constantine the Great established papal possessions and rights in Italy.

When in Rome

The **Donation of Constantine** is one of the most famous forgeries in history. It was probably produced to bolster Pope Stephen II's claims on Italy with Pepin. The new king and pope each needed something from one another. Pepin needed to be recognized as king, and the pontiffs needed an enforcer to rid them of the Lombards *and* a recognized claim to their territories. Pope Stephen II made the journey over the Alps (he barely got through the Lombards) and crowned Pepin in 754; Pepin came back over the Alps and "restored" the papal lands to Rome in 756. In the Renaissance, Lorenzo Valla, using philological and historical analysis, proved that the Donation of Constantine was a forgery. We do not know if either Pepin or Pope Stephen knew this document was false.

The Empire Strikes Back

During the early *Middle Ages* (ca 500–1100), imperial Rome in the west lay dormant as a distant memory under the mantle of Middle Age feudalism. The Romance languages grew up, and Latin remained operant only as an ecclesiastical language of worship and study. Here, Rome's legacy remained discernable only in the use of Latin, in the structure of church hierarchy, and in the beginning formation of canon law, which took its model (though not its source) from the Theodosian Code. Later, when

When in Rome

The **Middle Ages** is the period between the fall of the Roman Empire in the west (470) and the beginning of the European Renaissance in the 1400s.
This period is also known as **Medieval** (which also means "pertaining to the Middle Ages"). The "early" Middle Ages run approximately 500–1100, the "high" Middle Ages from 1100–1500.

When in Rome

The term **Holy Roman Empire** refers to lands under the "Holy Roman Emperors" crowned by the pope. It had its beginnings in the crowning of Charlemagne (800) and then Otto I (962) as Roman Emperor. In spite of its beginnings with Charlemagne, the use of the name applies more to the twelfth century onward when the "Holy Roman Empire" was much more of a German phenomenon than French.

Justinian's works on civil law made it back into the west in the eleventh and twelfth centuries, ecclesiastical and civil law began to be studied and taught in a systematic fashion that was profoundly influenced by its Roman roots.

Still, the dream of universal political empire was there to be recalled. Although no military power would ever come again from Rome, a kind of central authority was developing in the increasing power of the papacy. When faced with Frankish power that was great enough to once again establish dominance over western Christendom (including Rome), an enterprising Pope Leo III turned the tables in 800 by legitimizing the Frankish empire as "Roman" and declaring victory. Thus were the beginnings of the *Holy Roman Empire*.

Great Big Caesar's Ghost! Charles the Great (Charlemagne)

The popes and eastern emperor had revived the title of Patrician for the Frankish kings, the title given to the military protector of the late western Roman Empire. This role was expanded by the greatest of the Carolingian monarchs, Charles the Great or Charlemagne (768–814). Charlemagne was an imposing figure (big, rough, and ruddy); he was also a remarkable general, administrator, and king. He united France, Germany, and Italy under his control by effective use of the Frankish army and by close cooperation with the church in Christianizing (by force when necessary) the Saxons.

Charlemagne came to Rome in 800 to see the holy sites and to settle the affairs of Pope Leo III, who was under attack from rival factions. At Christmas service, as he rose from prayer, the pope whipped out a crown, placed it on Charlemagne's head, and a well-rehearsed crowd proclaimed him emperor. Whether Charlemagne knew this Christmas present was coming or not is a matter of dispute. His court in Aachen had been talking about a "Christian Empire" previously, but Einhard, Charlemagne's biographer, said the king was angered by the surprise coronation. What probably surprised him was the pope's bold move, which gave the impression that the pope crowned the emperor. This precedent served the pope's interests when future kings sought to establish their own authority and legitimacy against the papacy in the Investiture Controversy (see "The Holy Roman Empire" later in this chapter) of the eleventh through fourteenth centuries.

The eastern emperor first understood Charlemagne to be an underling, but Charlemagne saw himself as an equal "Augustus." He had already begun construction of his capital at Aachen, which was called *Roma Secunda* (The Second Rome) and *Roma Ventura* (The Rome to Come) in direct contrast to Constantinople (*Nova Roma*, or New Rome). Charlemagne issued his own decrees, concluded alliances, and asserted imperial authority. Eventually, the east recognized Charlamagne. *Nova Roma* and *Roma Secunda* continued to claim the mantle of the old Rome, which had become an ecclesiastical center with the pope, the head of the "Holy Roman Republic" in central Italy.

The Carolingian Renaissance

Charlemagne wanted to reestablish Latin, whose use had nearly been forgotten except at the fringes of the Empire, particularly in the remote recesses of Britain and Ireland. Charlemagne ordered, in *De Litteris Colendis* (Concerning the Cultivation of Literary Studies), that Latin schools be set up at cathedrals and brought scholars, including Alcuin of York, to his court from all over the Empire to assist in reviving Latin education. Latin manuscripts were also sought out and recopied in the legible *Carolingian Miniscule* for study. This manuscript collection was crucial to the survival of Latin classical literature—nearly all that we have goes back to manuscripts copied in this period.

Roamin' the Romans

At Aachen (Aix la-Chapelle) in Germany, you can see the remains of *Roma Secunda*. Visit Charlemagne's unique octagonal cathedral and his chair, and—if you're there on one of the special festival days—some of the relics that he brought back from his coronation at Rome in 800.

When in Rome

One of the Carolingian Renaissance's great accomplishments was the development of a consistent, clear, and elegant style of lettering. This script, called **Carolingian Miniscule,** is the basis for modern typefaces. The serifs—the little feet at the beginnings and endings of vertical letters—imitate the beginnings and endings of hand-lettered strokes.

Charlamagne's octagonal cathedral (left portion) in Roma Secunda (Aachen, Germany).

Lend Me Your Ears

"We were seeing both proper sentiments and improper expressions in monastaries' compositions, which, though they tried, could not make clear what pious prayers the brethren were offering on our behalf. A neglect of learning had rendered pious devotion unable, in uneducated language, to express clearly in words without error what it was saying faithfully in the heart. And so we began to fear that this practical inability predicated less wisdom for understanding Holy Scripture than needs be. Errors of words are dangerous, errors of understanding more dangerous by far! And so do not neglect literary study but study diligently, with most humble and god-pleasing intent, so that you may fare well in penetrating the mysteries of the divine Scriptures."

—Charlemagne, from *De Litteris Colendis*

The Holy Roman Empire

Charlemagne's kingdom was split between his three sons. The middle kingdom ran along the Franco-German linguistic fault line, cutting a swath from the Netherlands to northern Italy between the vast regions on either side. I'm really tempted to say here that the continued splitting of Empires between sons is proof that people really don't learn anything from history. France and Germany have been at odds one way or the other over the territory of the middle kingdom ever since.

The mantle of "Emperor" was reinstated upon Otto I "the Great" (936–973) in 962. Otto established control of greater Germany and northern Italy. His empire, although it was made up largely of territory that never had been Roman, became known as the Holy Roman Empire in succeeding centuries. The Germanic emperors were chosen by the German nobility and confirmed (invested) by the pope. Disputes between emperors and popes as to who had ultimate authority became known as the Investiture Controversy. These tensions led not only to a sharper demarcation between church and state than either Islam or Byzantium, but to a climate that was ripe for Martin Luther's Reformation.

Great Caesar's Ghost!

Conflicts between church and state took, in the words of the singer-songwriter Warren Zevon, "lawyers, guns, and money." The popes and the Holy Roman Emperors had the medieval equivalent of the last two, but a few hundred years' lack of legal scholarship had left competent lawyers, amazingly, in short supply. This led to the resurrection of the study of both canon and Roman law codes among scholars in such centers as Bologna (eleventh century) and Naples (1212). The law schools in these cities grew into important medieval universities.

Onward Christian Soldier

As we've seen, the conquest under the banner of one god or the other has a long tradition. The eleventh through fifteenth centuries saw a variety of *crusades* to recapture lands for Christendom. Although you're probably most familiar with those to reconquer the Holy Lands, crusades for other territories, such as Muslim Spain, were also launched. The crusades began with an appeal from the Byzantine emperor Alexius Comnenus (father of the historian Anna Comnena) to Pope Gregory VII and Urban II

When in Rome

The **crusades** were holy wars (particularly of the eleventh through thirteenth centuries) in which Christians from Europe attempted to conquer territories (especially in the Middle East) that were held by Muslims or people holding beliefs that the crusaders considered heretical.

for help against the Turks. What Alexius got was not what he, or probably the pope, expected. Here's a chronology of some of the crusades that followed in the next centuries:

➤ **First Crusade** (1095). Pope Urban II called for this crusade and promised crusaders who died in battle the "immediate remission of sins."

➤ **People's Crusade** (1096). While the nobles assembled an army, peasants and poor knights marched off fervently to take the Holy Land. They massacred Jews in Germany along the way and were massacred in turn by the Turks near Antioch.

(1099). The better prepared army of nobles of the First Crusade reached the Holy Land, captured Jerusalem, and butchered its inhabitants. In 1144, a Muslim counter-crusade under Zengi retook the Crusader state of Edessa.

➤ **Second Crusade** (1147). In response the to the capture of Edessa, Pope Eugene II called for a crusade. This crusade ended in dismal failure and emboldened the Moslem states in their resistance to the Latins.

➤ **Third Crusade** (1189). Under Richard the Lion Heart, King Philip II of France, and the Holy Roman Emperor Fredrick, Barbarossa recaptured most of the Crusader states except Jerusalem.

➤ **Fourth Crusade** (1204). This campaign captured Constantinople and did serious damage to the Byzantine Empire (and its relations with the west).

➤ **Children's Crusade** (1212). Rallied by youth preachers in France and Germany, thousands of boys as young as six years old joined the march to the Holy Land. Many died en route, and those who reached Marseilles found that the sea didn't part for them as promised. Undaunted, the remainder set sail. Some died in shipwrecks, and the rest landed in Egypt instead of Palestine and were sold as slaves. Few returned to their homes.

➤ **Fifth Crusade** (1219). Preached by Pope Honorius III, this crusade set off to capture Jerusalem, but with this city so strongly defended by the Muslims, decided to try and conquer Egypt instead. Their attempt almost succeeded but bogged down at the city of Damietta, where internal dissention and bad leadership cost the crusaders Jerusalem and the Muslim's offer to return the True Cross, which then disappeared from history.

➤ **Sixth Crusade** (1228). The Muslim capture of Jerusalem in 1189 ignited great passions in Europe. The Holy Roman emperor Fredrick II recaptured the city in 1229, but he alienated the other crusader leaders and the pope.

340

➤ **Seventh Crusade** (1249). This Crusade was led by King Louis IX (St. Louis) of France, who had vowed to undertake it against the Muslims if he recovered from a serious illness. This crusade became great literature (such as the romanticized and chivalrous memoirs published between 1304 and 1309 by Louis's close advisor, Jean sire de Joinville) but failed to achieve its objectives. St. Louis and his army were captured by the Moslims in Egypt. He was ransomed and eventually returned to France.

The New Romans

The Holy Roman Empire continued in one form or the other up through Napoleon. Despite the name, it wasn't holy, Roman, or (if you research it) much of an empire most of the time. Nevertheless, Rome's name and legacy continue to be invoked for either reclaiming or establishing empires or republics. The empires of France, Britain, Russia, Spain, the Ottomans, and America have elicited comparisons intended as both praise and blame. As you can imagine, the legacy of imperialism and colonialism has shifted most toward the latter. Nevertheless, even current discussions of the European Union have brought Rome's legacy back as a historical shadow, along with all the possibilities, baggage, and barnacles that have adhered to it along the way.

Reichs and Rulers

Recent empires could hardly help but compare themselves to their Roman ancestors one way or the other. The Spaniards, in their conquest of the Americas in the sixteenth and seventeenth centuries, had an ambivalent attitude toward their Roman past. On the one hand, the Spanish had contributed greatly to Rome: Both Roman poets and emperors had come from Spain. On the other, the Spanish wanted to distinguish themselves in their own terms against other Europeans who had claim to the Roman legacy. The Spanish liked to portray their ancestors as being brutally subjugated by the Romans, but as having escaped that yoke to become the rulers of an even greater empire. Some Spanish missionaries, however, turned this argument on its head and maintained that the Spanish were in fact replicating Roman actions and attitudes in their brutal conquests, and warned that these would lead, as they had with Rome, to a Spanish fall.

Even though Napoleon put an end to the Holy Roman Empire in the treaty of Luneville (1801), that didn't stop him from playing off France's links with the Roman past. Like many great commanders, he appears to have personally favored Alexander the Great. But in becoming emperor of France (1804), Napoleon attempted to have the pope crown him as he had crowned Charlemagne and the Holy Roman emperors. Napoleon, however, had to take the crown from the pope and crown himself at the last minute. (Perhaps the pope was waiting for him to stand up?)

Roamin' the Romans

Napoleon, like many other European rulers, sought to emulate Roman grandeur and power in public architecture (French Empire style). The most famous example of this is the Arc de Triomphe through which he intended to march his army. He never got the chance, and it served as a bitter irony that Hitler was the first to use it.

Even the British played with comparisons to Romans, but like the Spanish, the British have had an ambivalent relationship with Rome. (Both are proud of having been a part of the Empire just as long as everyone bears in mind that they didn't become a part willingly and were hard to conquer.) Conquest from the continent was never something to validate. Closer to our own day, Hitler and Mussolini (Fascists, from *fasces*, the Roman symbol for authority) borrowed from Roman grandeur and promoted themselves and their conquests as new *Reichs* (reich means empire or kingdom) and Romes.

American Romans

Americans have their own Roman past, which anyone can read about in the works of the founders of the "Republic." Federalists like John Adams championed the idea of a state anchored by a strong executive and bicameral (having two legislative chambers) senate. Rome's legacy of tyranny was an uncomfortable subject, however, and so most of the references to Rome come from Rome's Republican past. Cicero, Livy, and Seneca feature heavily in the classical references penned during the lively correspondence leading to the formation of the United States Constitution. Democrats such as Jefferson championed more individualistic traditions, but in the end, the framers rested the American state solidly on a Roman foundation. That's why you'll find many statues of George Washington (who idealized Cato and Cincinnatus) and other framers wearing Roman togas, not Greek or Anglo-Saxon tunics.

Great Caesar's Ghost!

You probably have heard of the Third Reich of Nazi Germany under Adolph Hitler, but where did the other two Reichs go? The First Reich was the Holy Roman Empire, which came to Germany from Charlemagne through Otto I. This Reich lasted until Napoleon defeated the forces of the last Holy Roman emperor, Francis II (1768–1806). The Second Reich was founded by the first Imperial Chancellor Otto Von Bismarck (1815–1898) in 1871. WWI ended this Reich, and WWII ended the third.

Et Tu Brute: You're a Roman, Too

I said at the beginning of this book that whether you love them or hate them, there's no getting around the Romans. A sizable part of contemporary culture is wrapped around a Roman core. It's true that what was originally Roman has often changed and mutated to such a degree that it would be as unrecognizable to them as Manhattan Man would be to Lucy *Australopithecus.* But this is the nature of western classicism in which each generation finds (or even mistakes) something anew in its tradition and reinvents the past in its own image.

Nevertheless, so much of our tradition has been invented by, funneled through, or made in reaction to the Romans that they are culturally genetic to the west. While it's been impossible to create a complete "Roman genome project" in this (or any) book, I hope this one has helped you to better understand and appreciate some of Rome's fascinating story. I also hope that you'll want to unravel more of the story of Rome's evolving impact upon history while realizing that complexity and ambiguity are a part of the fruits of investigation.

We may not always know where we're going, but, like this car, the modern world still often travels on ways laid down by the Romans.

Back to Globalization

It may be time, for example, to return to a consideration of Rome's legacy concerning the relationship between individual and community and the interrelation of communities to a larger structure. In an age of tensions between global "community" and fragmentation of communities into ever-smaller niches (sometimes only connected by electrons and emotion), the Romans are worth revisiting both for cautions and for inspiration.

Just as the Greeks have been used as a potent model for the pursuit of individual human achievement, the Romans are the west's communitarian models. They, more than any culture since their time, attempted to negotiate practical differences in class, ethnicity, religion, legal status, and culture under the aegis of a common view of human order. Their achievements over the centuries, as well as their deficiencies, bear investigation and consideration.

The Living Latin Language

You already *comprehend* that many *intellectual concepts* and *traditions* were *created* or *survived* through *Rome*. But did you *realize* that you *communicate* in large *part* through dialects and *modes* of *Latin?* Although English is a Germanic *language*, it was heavily *influenced* by *French* (a *Latin derivative*) after the *invasions* of the Norman *Franks*. In *addition, Latin's influence* through *poetry, art, legal studies, sacred* and *secular literature* (*et cetera*) was so *profound* that *Latin* has both *inspired* and *infected* not only the *concepts,* but the very *terminology* that we use to *describe* and to *conceive* of our world. This *brief declaration provides* you a *minute picture* of how *pervasive Latin* is: *vocabulary* with *Latin origins* is *italicized.*

An American's Reflection

The Romans were essentially optimistic. They generally operated as if they could control the future by the choices they made in the present.

Romans suffered from many of the deficiencies, as well as from the advantages, of such an outlook. Optimists are always disappointed (because if you would just make the right choice everything would be fine, wouldn't it?), and the Romans were prone to blaming or doomsaying when things were not going their way. They tended to feel overly responsible to the god or gods that put them in charge of history. They often suffered the arrogance of thinking that they knew what was best for everyone, that they had everything under control, and that they could always figure it all out. Generally adverse to theory, they preferred the practical, the tried, and the real world of real life in Roman terms.

The Romans were, on the other hand, willing to take on the largest of challenges, persevere to the end of endeavors, and to doggedly insist that there was indeed no no-win scenario if one would just figure out how to go about things properly. Their history and legacy give good evidence that there was, indeed, something to it.

Veto!

Of course, you can't press an analogy between U.S. and Roman cultural attitudes to their historical role too far. Still, when you consider Jupiter's proclamation for Rome in Virgil's Aeneid *("For these people I place no boundaries of space or time: I have given them empire without end") and John O'Sullivan's* Manifest Destiny *("The far-reaching, the boundless future will be the era of American greatness. In its magnificent domain of space and time, the nation of many nations is destined to manifest to mankind the excellence of divine principles"), it gives you pause.*

At the risk of making overly broad proclamations, people living in the United States can learn a lot about U.S. political history from a consideration of Rome. The United States has a remarkably Roman attitude toward its place in history, progress, and the possibilities of the future. (It's probably not an accident that the United States' major contribution to the philosophical tradition is pragmatism, with its emphasis on practical results rather than on theory.) In looking back over the long history of U.S. traditions, citizens of the United States (and other Romans) might come to a better understanding of where we are, how we got here, and where we can go.

The Least You Need to Know

➤ The legacy of Rome continued to influence empires and imperial ambitions from Charlemagne to the Third Reich.

➤ The growth of papal power was rooted in filling spiritual and physical needs of central Italy in the fifth and sixth centuries and grew through an alliance with the Franks.

➤ European and American languages, history, and thought have been indelibly marked by the legacy of Latin and Rome.

➤ The study of Roman history and culture still has a lot to offer a multicultural and global world.

Timeline

800 B.C.E.	Rome in huts and villages on the hills.	Pre-Roman Italy; Royal Period
	Beginnings of cooperation and kingship.	
753	Rome founded on April 21, 753 B.C.E.	
700	Early Roman Kings.	Homer, Hesiod
	Etruscans come to Rome; Tarquinius Priscus.	
600	Servius Tullius; creation of *comitia centuriata* and other reforms.	Archaic Greek City-States, Literature
	Tarquinius Superbus; the *cloaca maxima* and the beginnings of Rome as an urban center.	
500	Roman Revolution and the beginning of the Republic. First treaty with Carthage.	The Republic / Golden Age of Classical Greece
	Rome defeats Etruscans and Latins.	
	Patrician/Plebian tensions. Succession of the Plebs.	
	Twelve Tables.	Athens and Sparta at War
	Rome expands territory; siege of Veii.	
400	Capture of Veii.	
	Latin League defeated; Rome creates *municipia* and begins foundation of *colonae* in Italy.	Rome Conquers Italy
	Campania added to Roman territory; Roman wars with Samnites and Etruscans.	
	Appius Claudius is censor.	
300	Rome at war with Samnites and Etruscans.	
	Wars with Tarentum and Pyrrhus; Pyrrhus withdraws and Tarentum is defeated.	Literature brought to Rome: Livius Andronicus
	First Punic War; Sicily becomes a province.	
	Corsica and Sardinia become provinces; gladiators first appear at Rome.	
	Second Punic War with Hannibal.	Rome Conquers Mediterranean / Latin Literature Begins: Ennius and Plautus
	First Macedonian War with Philip V.	
	Rome conquers Cicalpine Gaul.	

200 B.C.E. Second Macedonian War.

Rome conquers Spain, Syria (Seleucid Empire), Macedon, and Greece.

Carthage and Corinth destroyed, Macedon and Africa become provinces.

Slave revolts begin in Sicily.

The Gracchae.

Gallia Narbonensis becomes a province.

Wars against Jugurtha.

Consulships of **Marius**, **Cicero** born.

100 **Caesar** born.

Social (Civil) War in Italy; allies get citizenship.

Sulla takes Rome and becomes Dictator.

Slave revolt of **Spartacus**; rise of **Pompey**.

Pompey and **Crassus** are consuls; **Cicero** tries **Verres**.

Rise of **Caesar** and **Cicero**.

Cicero's consulship; the Conspiracy of **Cataline**.

First Triumvirate; **Caesar** campaigns in Gaul and Britain.

50 Civil war between **Caesar** and **Pompey**; Caesar becomes Dictator and is assassinated.

Antony and the rise of **Octavian**. The **Second Triumvirate** and the Proscriptions.

Antony (in East) and **Octavian** (in West) expand their powers; **Antony** and **Cleopatra** form alliance.

Civil War between **Octavian** and **Antony**; suicides of **Antony** and **Cleopatra**; Egypt annexed.

27 **Octavian** settles affairs, "restores" the Republic and becomes "**Augustus**."

Augustan reforms, settling of powers, establishes borders in Spain and with Parthia; monumental building programs (e.g. *ara pacis*, *forum Augustum*).

0 **Agrippa** dies; **Tiberius** comes to the fore as an heir.

The Republic

Cultural tensions: Cato the Censor

The "Scipionic Circle," Polybius, Terence

Rome Conquers the East; Internal and Civil Wars; Golden Age of Latin Literature to Death of Augustus

Ciceronian Age of Literature: Lucretius, Nepos, Catullus, Cicero, Caesar, Sallust

Augustan Age of Literature: Virgil, Livy, Horace, Propertius, Tibullus, Ovid

The Principate of Augustus

349

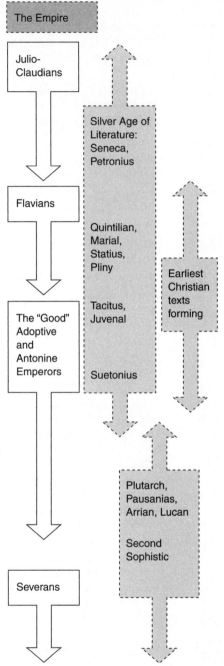

0 Jesus born; Ovid banished to Tomis.

Augustus dies; Germanicus and Drusus die.

Tiberius (14-37) and Sejanus; Jesus' crucifixion.

Gaius (Caligula) (37-41).

Invasion of Britain.

Claudius (41-54).

Nero (54-68); Seneca, Agrippina.

Rome burns; first persecution of Christians.

Jewish rebellion; suicides of Petronius, Seneca, Lucan; Nero's grand tour of Greece.

Year of Four Emperors: Galba, Otho, Vitellius, Vespasian (69); **Vespasian** (69-79).

Destruction of Temple in Jerusalem.

Titus (79-81).

Eruption of Vesuvius; destruction of Pompeii, Herculaneum and Pliny the Elder.

Domitian (81-96); persecution of Christians.

Nerva (96-98); historian Tacitus is consul.

100 C.E. **Trajan** (98-117); conquests of Dacia; conquests in the East; Pliny the Younger, Governor of Bythinia, writes to Trajan.

Hadrian (117-138).

Bar Kochba revolt.

Antonius Pius (138-161).

Marcus Aurelius (161-180); **Lucius Verus** (161-169); Germanic Wars, the *Meditations* composed.

Plagues at Rome; sporadic persecutions of Christians in provinces; Galen doctor at Rome.

Commodus (180-192); performances in the gladiatorial combats and hunts in Rome.

Pertinax and **Didius Julianus** (193) in turn become emperors and are assassinated.

Septimius Severus (193-211); Severus dies while campaigning in Britain.

200 C.E.

Caracalla (212-217); *Constitutio Antoniniana* grants citizenship to all.

Egalabalus (218-222); Eastern court rules at Rome; Julia Maesa and Julia Mamaea are influential.

Severus Alexander (222-235); wars against Persia and Germans.

Maximius Thrax (235-238).

Gordian I, II, Pupienus, Balbinus (238),

Gordian III (238-244), **Philip the Arab** (244-249), **Decius** (249-251), **Trebonianus Gallus** (251-253), **Aemilius Aemilianus** (253), **Valerian** (253-260), **Gallienus** (253-268).

Gallic Empire: Postumus (260-269), **Laelianus** (269), **Marius** (269), **Victorinus** (168-271), **Tetricus** (271-274).

Rise and fall of **Palmyra** (261-272).

Claudias II (268-270), **Quintillus** (270), **Aurelian** (270-275), **Tacitus** (275-276), **Florianus** (276), **Probus** (276-282), **Carus** (282-283), **Numerian** (283-284), **Carinus** (283-285).

300

Diocletian (284-305); **Maximian** (286-310); formation of Tetrarchy; major Christian persecutions.

Constantine the Great (306-337); Battle of Mulvian Bridge; Christianity becomes official religion; Council of Nicea.

Constantine II (337-340), **Constans I** (337-361), **Constantius II** (337-361), **Julian the Apostate** (360-363), **Jovian** (363-364).

West:

Valentinian I (364-375), **Gratian** (367-383), **Valentinian II** (375-392), **Eugenius** (392-394).

Visigoths invade East.

Honorius (395-423).

East:

Valens (364-378).

Theodosius I "The Great" (379-395).

Arcadius (395-408).

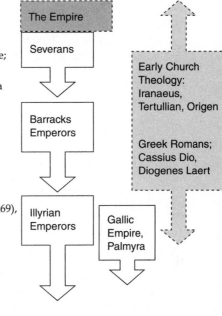

The Empire

Severans

Barracks Emperors

Illyrian Emperors

Gallic Empire, Palmyra

Early Church Theology: Iranaeus, Tertullian, Origen

Greek Romans; Cassius Dio, Diogenes Laert

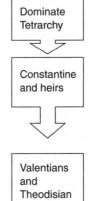

Dominate Tetrarchy

Constantine and heirs

Valentians and Theodisian

Christian Pagan conflict and synthesis

Ambrose, Eusebius, Marcellinus Porphyry, Symmachus

St. Augustine

351

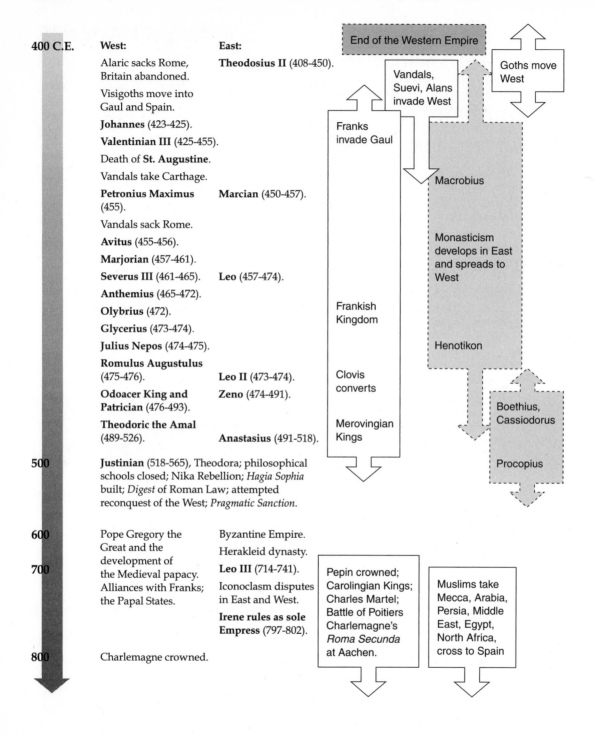

400 C.E.

West:

Alaric sacks Rome, Britain abandoned.

Visigoths move into Gaul and Spain.

Johannes (423-425).

Valentinian III (425-455).

Death of **St. Augustine**.

Vandals take Carthage.

Petronius Maximus (455).

Vandals sack Rome.

Avitus (455-456).

Marjorian (457-461).

Severus III (461-465).

Anthemius (465-472).

Olybrius (472).

Glycerius (473-474).

Julius Nepos (474-475).

Romulus Augustulus (475-476).

Odoacer King and Patrician (476-493).

Theodoric the Amal (489-526).

East:

Theodosius II (408-450).

Marcian (450-457).

Leo (457-474).

Leo II (473-474).

Zeno (474-491).

Anastasius (491-518).

500 **Justinian** (518-565), Theodora; philosophical schools closed; Nika Rebellion; *Hagia Sophia* built; *Digest* of Roman Law; attempted reconquest of the West; *Pragmatic Sanction*.

600 Pope Gregory the Great and the development of the Medieval papacy. Alliances with Franks; the Papal States.

700

Byzantine Empire. Herakleid dynasty.

Leo III (714-741). Iconoclasm disputes in East and West.

Irene rules as sole Empress (797-802).

800 Charlemagne crowned.

End of the Western Empire

Goths move West

Vandals, Suevi, Alans invade West

Franks invade Gaul

Macrobius

Monasticism develops in East and spreads to West

Frankish Kingdom

Henotikon

Boethius, Cassiodorus

Clovis converts

Merovingian Kings

Procopius

Pepin crowned; Carolingian Kings; Charles Martel; Battle of Poitiers Charlemagne's *Roma Secunda* at Aachen.

Muslims take Mecca, Arabia, Persia, Middle East, Egypt, North Africa, cross to Spain

Finding the Romans on Earth and in Cyberspace

Now that you've gotten a broad overview of the history of Rome, you probably have areas you'd like to learn more about. To that end, I've put together a selected list of resources in print and online for your further conquests.

Books

Good books on the Romans are legion. I've listed a few by category below, but by all means, head to your local library and bookstore and browse the stacks! For translations of ancient authors, the budget-conscious Penguin Classics feature good introductions and translations, and are usually available for a great price. Here are some books that you should be able to find in bookstores.

General Rome

Ancient Romans
by Chester G. Starr Jr.
Paperback—262 pages (November 1971)
Oxford University Press
ISBN: 0195014545

The Oxford History of the Classical World. Vol. II: The Roman World
by John Boardman, Jasper Griffin, and Oswyn Murray, Editors
Paperback—455 pages, Reprint edition (July 1997)
Oxford University Press
ISBN: 0192821660

The Roman Way
by Edith Hamilton
Paperback—Reissue edition (August 1993)
W.W. Norton & Company
ISBN: 0393310787

As the Romans Did: A Sourcebook in Roman Social History
Paperback—512 Pages, 2nd Edition (September 1997)
Oxford University Press
ISBN: 019508974X

The Republic

The Roman Republic
by Andrew Lintott
Paperback—116 pages (March 1, 2001)
Sutton Publishing
ISBN: 0750922230

The Making of the Roman Army: From Republic to Empire
by Lawrence Keppie
Paperback—272 pages (March 1998)
University of Oklahoma Press
ISBN: 0806130148

The Last Generation of the Roman Republic
by Erich S. Gruen
Paperback—Reprint edition (March 1995)
University of California Press
ISBN: 0520201531

Caesar

Caesar: A History of the Art of War Among the Romans Down to the End of the Roman Empire, with a Detailed Account of the Campaigns of Gaius Julius Caesar
by Theodore Ayrault Dodge
Paperback—816 pages, Reprint edition (October 1997)
Da Capo Press
ISBN: 0306807874

Caesar: Politician and Statesman
by Matthias Gelzer and Peter Needham (Translator)
Paperback—Reprint edition (October 1985)
Harvard University Press
ISBN: 0674090012

Caesar
by Christian Meier
Paperback—528 pages (February 1997)
HarperCollins
ISBN: 046500895X

The Augustan Age

Augustan Culture
by Karl Galinsky
Paperback—488 pages, Reprint edition (January 1998)
Princeton University Press
ISBN: 0691058903

The Urban Image of Augustan Rome
by Diane Favro
Paperback—368 pages (September 1998)
Cambridge University Press
ISBN: 0521646650

The Cambridge Ancient History: The Augustan Empire, 43 B.C.–A.D. 69
by Alan K. Bowman (Editor), et al.
Hardcover—2nd edition, Vol. 10 (May 1996)
Cambridge University Press
ISBN: 0521264308

Gladiators

Cruelty and Civilization: The Roman Games
by Roland August
Paperback—222 pages, Reprint edition (May 1994)
Routledge
ISBN: 041510453X

Gladiators and Caesars: The Power of Spectacle in Ancient Rome
by Eckart Kohne (Editor), et al.
Paperback—160 pages (December 2000)
University of California Press
ISBN: 0520227980

Emperors and Gladiators
by Thomas Wiedemann
Paperback—232 pages, Reprint edition (August 1995)
Routledge
ISBN: 0415121647

Women

Agrippina: Sex, Power, and Politics in the Early Empire
by Anthony A. Barrett
Paperback—320 pages (July 1999)
Yale University Press
ISBN: 0300078560

I Claudia: Women in Ancient Rome
by Diana E. E. Kleiner (Editor), et al.
Paperback—228 pages (October 1996)
Yale University Art Gallery
ISBN: 0894670751

I Claudia II: Women in Roman Art and Society
by Diana E. E. Kleiner (Editor) and Susan B. Matheson (Editor)
Paperback—224 pages (July 2000)
University of Texas Press
ISBN: 0292743408

Women in the Classical World: Image & Text
by Elaine Fantham, Sarah B Pomeroy, Natalie B. Kampen,
Helene P. Foley, and H. A. Shapiro
Paperback—448 Pages (March 1995)
Oxford University Press
ISBN: 0195098625

The Empire

*Chronicle of the Roman Emperors: The Reign-By-Reign Record of the
Rulers of Imperial Rome*
by Christopher Scarre
Hardcover (October 1995)
Thames & Hudson
ISBN: 0500050775

The Decline and Fall of the Roman Empire/Volumes 1, 2, & 3
by Edward Gibbon and Hugh Trevor-Roper (Introduction)
Hardcover—Boxed edition, Vol. 1–3 of a 6-volume set (October 1993)
Knopf
ISBN: 0679423087

The Decline and Fall of the Roman Empire: Boxed Volumes 4–6 (Everyman's Library)
by Edward Gibbon and Hugh Trevor-Roper (Introduction)
Hardcover—Boxed edition, Vol. 4–6 (October 1994)
Knopf
ISBN: 067943593X

Grand Strategy of the Roman Empire: From the First Century A.D. *to the Third*
by Edward N. Luttwak and J. F. Gilliam
Paperback—255 pages (February 1979)
Johns Hopkins University Press
ISBN: 0801821584

The Roman Empire
by C. M. Wells
Paperback—2nd Reprint edition (October 1995)
Harvard University Press
ISBN: 0674777700

The Roman Circus

Life, Death, and Entertainment in the Roman Empire
by D. S. Potter (Editor)
Paperback—280 pages (February 1999)
University of Michigan Press
ISBN: 0472085689

Roman Circuses: Arenas for Chariot Racing
by John H. Humphre
Hardcover (January 1986)
University of California Press
ISBN: 0520049217

Roman Warfare

Warfare in the Classical World: An Illustrated Encyclopedia of Weapons, Warriors and Warfare in the Ancient Civilizations of Greece and Rome
by John Gibson Warry
Paperback—224 pages (October 1995)
University of Oklahoma Press (Trd)
ISBN: 0806127945

Roman Warfare (History of Warfare)
by Adrian Goldsworthy and John Keegan (Editor)
Hardcover—224 pages (April 2000)
Cassell Academic
ISBN: 0304352659

The Roman Imperial Army: Of the First and Second Centuries A.D: *3rd Edition*
by Graham Webster and Hugh Elton (Introduction)
Paperback—400 pages, Reprint edition (March 1998)
University of Oklahoma Press
ISBN: 0806130008

Warfare in Roman Europe, Ad 350–425 (Oxford Classical Monographs)
Paperback—328 pages, Reprint edition (February 1998)
Oxford University Press
ISBN: 0198152418

Roman Architecture

Principles of Roman Architecture
by Mark Wilson Jones, et al.
Hardcover—280 pages (March 2001)
Yale University Press
ISBN: 0300081383

The Architecture of Rome: An Architectural History in 400 Individual Presentations
by Stefan Grundmann (Editor)
Paperback—350 pages (October 1998)
Edition Axel Menges
ISBN: 3930698609

The Story of the Roman Amphitheatre
by David Bomgardner
Hardback—304 pages (October 2000)
Routledge
ISBN: 0415165938

Roman Art

Roman Art
by Eve D'Ambra
Paperback—176 pages (November 1998)
Cambridge University Press
ISBN: 0521644631

Imperial Rome and Christian Triumph: The Art of the Roman Empire Ad 100–450
(Oxford History of Art)
by J. R. Elsner
Paperback—320 pages (November 1998)
Oxford University Press
ISBN: 0192842013

Roman Painting
by Roger Ling
Paperback (March 1991)
Cambridge University Press
ISBN: 0521315956

Early Church

The Christians as the Romans Saw Them
by Robert L. Wilken
Paperback—Reprint edition (February 1986)
Yale University Press
ISBN: 0300036272

Chronicle of the Popes: The Reign-by-Reign Record of the Papacy over 2000 Years
by P. G. Maxwell-Stuart
Hardcover—224 pages (November 1997)
Thames & Hudson
ISBN: 0500017980

Society and the Holy in Late Antiquity
by Peter Brown
Paperback—Reprint edition (December 1989)
University of California Press
ISBN: 0520068009

Pagans and Christians in Late Antiquity: A Sourcebook
by A. D. Lee
Library Binding—352 pages (October 2000)
Routledge
ISBN: 0415138922

The Formation of Christendom
by Judith Herrin
Paperback—544 pages, Reprint edition (August 1989)
Princeton University Press
ISBN: 0691008310

Byzantium

A History of the Byzantine State and Society
by Warren Treadgold
Paperback—874 pages (November 1997)
Stanford University Press
ISBN: 0804726302

Byzantium: the Early Centuries (see also *Byzantium: the Apogee* and *Byzantium: the Decline and Fall*)
by John Julius Norwish and Elizabeth Sifton
Hardcover—408 pages (March 1989)
Knopf
ISBN: 0394537785 (*Apogee*, 0394537793, *Decline and Fall*, 0679416501)

The Fall of Constantinople, 1453
by Steven Runciman
Paperback—270 pages, Reprint edition (February 1991)
Cambridge University Press
ISBN: 0521398320

Western Roman Empire to Charlemagne

Barbarians & Romans: The Birth Struggle of Europe A.D. 400–700
by Justine D. Randers-Pehrson
Paperback—400 Pages (March 1993)
University of Oklahoma Press
ISBN: 080612511X

Charlemagne
by Roger Collins
Paperback—292 pages (September 1998)
University of Toronto Press
ISBN: 0802082181

Daily Life in the World of Charlemagne (Middle Ages)
by Pierre Riche and Jo Ann McNamara (Translator)
Paperback—336 pages, Reprint edition (March 1988)
University of Pennsylvania Press
ISBN: 0812210964

Bulfinch's Mythology: The Age of Fable, The Age of Chivalry:
Legends of Charlemagne
by Thomas Bulfinch
Hardcover (March 1993)
Modern Library
ISBN: 0679600469

Roman Influence on the Modern West

The Founders and the Classics: Greece, Rome, and the American Enlightenment
by Carl J. Richard
Oxford, 1995
ISBN: 0-674-31426-3

The Pythia on Ellis Island
by Nancy Kassell
Oxford, 1998
ISBN: 0-7618-0942-2

The End of the Past. Ancient Rome and the Modern West (*Revealing Antiquity* 13)
by Aldo Schiavone, trans. by Margery J. Schneider
Paperback (2000)
Harvard University Press
ISBN: 0674000625

Cyber-Romans

The Romans have an empire in cyberspace. It may surprise you, but Classicists (scholars who study ancient Greece and Rome) were some of the first to venture into this territory to exploit its archival and educational opportunities.

As you know, the Web is full of both diamonds and Zircons, and it's hard at times to tell between them. So let me share with you a few wonderful places to start before you type "Rome" into that shop-vac of a search engine and suck in 19 million URLs. Before I do, however, my profound apologies to all my colleagues across the world, whose sites are truly worth citing and to whom I can only say, "*mea culpa, mea culpa*"—I just don't have room to cite them all. To you, the reader, I encourage you to take a moment to notice the people who maintain these sites, whose efforts at bringing you the past are truly Herculean.

Think Roman, Think Big

If you want to find reliable information about Rome and the Romans, it's best to begin with sites hosted by educational institutions. There are many wonderful sites on Roman civilization and culture. If you're looking in general, however, I suggest starting first with these two sites from which you can get to practically everything else:

➤ **ROMARCH** (acad1.depauw.edu/romarch/index.html). The ROMARCH site provides a central location from which to access a wealth of Web resources concerning the Roman world from the late Bronze Age to Late Antiquity. Moreover, the linked resources are rated, which makes it easier to find good information. ROMARCH originated at the University of Michigan, grew at the University of Cincinnati and at Stanford University, and is presently hosted by DePauw University.

➤ **Bill Thayer's Roman Sites** (www.ukans.edu/history/index/europe/ ancient_rome/E/Roman/RomanSites*/home.html). It is a gateway to over 2,150 Web sites, broken down by category, and linked with its parent site, LacusCurius (www.ukans.edu/history/index/europe/ ancient_rome/E/Roman/home.htm).

Other Gateways

You can find additional information concerning Rome and the Romans on sites that are geared more toward Ancient, Classical (Greek and Roman), Medieval, and Ecclesiastical topics. Here are some suggestions:

➤ **Perseus** (www.perseus.tufts.edu/). Perseus is "The Mother of All Classics Web Sites" and more than lives up to its goal of being "an evolving digital library of the ancient world and beyond." There are interconnected encyclopedias and overviews, texts in both original languages and translations, archeological sites, catalogues of vases and sculpture, maps of nearly every description, search tools, Latin texts, and more and more and more. If you're interested in the ancient world, you gotta go there. Perseus is housed at Tufts University.

➤ **Exploring Ancient World Cultures (EAWC)** (eawc.evansville.edu/ eawcindex.htm). I recently discovered this site and highly recommend it. The EAWC is part of a project to produce a high-quality textbook on the Internet. The Index contains linked resources for the Near East, India, Egypt, China, Greece, Rome, Early Islam, and Medieval Europe. You can investigate these cultures through an Internet Index, which points you to a chronology, essay, image, and primary text index for each of these cultures.

➤ **Maria Pantelia's Electronic Resources for Classicists: The Second Generation** (www.tlg.uci.edu/~tlg/index/resources.html). This site is geared primarily for people in the field, but you'll find links to everything you need for first-rate information. It covers most aspects of learning, teaching, and encoding the ancient world. ERC2 is housed at the University of California at Irvine.

➤ **University of Michigan Classics and Mediterranean Archeology Links** (rome.classics.lsa.umich.edu/welcome.html). Maintained by Sebastian Heath, this is a searchable (good thing, because it's l-o-n-g) list of links to almost every imaginable area of general and specific interest.

➤ **The Stoa** (www.stoa.org). The Stoa is a consortium of forward-minded academics and other individuals who are dedicated to fostering both academic and broader publications and information in the age of the Internet. You'll find links to many interesting projects concerning the ancient world, including an ongoing translation of the Suda, the enormous tenth century Byzantine Encyclopedia. (For the Suda-On-Line, go to www.stoa.org/sol).

If You Know What You Want

If you know what you want to find, there are quick ways to get to good information about the Romans and the ancient world. These include ancient world–specific search engines and topical sites. A few to mention are …

➤ **Argos** (argos.evansville.edu). Argos is a search engine limited to the ancient and medieval world. If you know specifically what you want, and it's about the Romans, start here. This search engine will not give you personal and promotional Web pages, but it will give you solid access to what you want to know. Argos is housed at the University of Evansville.

➤ **Diotima.** Materials for the Study of Women and Gender in the Ancient World (www.stoa.org/diotima). Diotima offers enormous access to information concerning women in the ancient world. Diotima is edited by Suzanne Bonefas (Associated Colleges of the South/Miami University) and Ross Scaife (University of Kentucky).

➤ **Hippias** (hippias.evansville.edu/). Hippias is a search engine limited to philosophy housed (like its parent, Argos) at the University of Evansville.

➤ **The Labyrinth** (labyrinth.georgetown.edu). The Labyrinth is the primary starting point for resources for Medieval study sponsored by Georgetown University.

➤ **Ancient Medicine/Medica Antiqua** (www.ea.pvt.k12.pa.us/medant). If you're interested in ancient medicine, this is the place to go. It features texts, research, and links relating to medicine from Bronze Age Greece through the end of the Roman Empire. AM/MA is sponsored by The Episcopal Academy and maintained by Lee T. Pearcy.

Special Topics: Latin Language, Roman Dates, Law, and Finding Other Amici

➤ The **Latin Language and Literature** (www.csbsju.edu/library/internet/latin.html) page housed at the College of St. Benedict and St. John is a terrific place to start. You can find dictionaries, texts, language aids, even Latin for Travelers!

➤ For Latin texts (in Latin), be sure to visit the enormous resources of the **Latin Library** (patriot.net/~lillard/cp/latlib), housed at Ad Fontes Academy.

➤ *Wheelock's Latin* is one of the standby texts for learning Latin, and has a number of resources to accompany the book. One of the best is **Paul Barrette's Electronic Resources for Wheelock's Latin** (cheiron.mcmaster.ca/latin/).

➤ Need to look up a Latin word? You can do this online at **Perseus** (www.perseus.tufts.edu/cgi-bin/resolveform?lang=la). Need the Latin for an English word? You can do this at Perseus as well (www.perseus.tufts.edu/cgi-bin/enggreek?lang=la).

➤ Figuring out Roman dates is a pain. If you need to know what your birthday (or any date) is on the Roman calendar or what MMDCIV times MMCCCVIII is, you can find handy conversion programs on **Steven Gibb's Roman Numeral and Date Conversion** page (www.guernsey.net/~sgibbs/roman.html).

➤ **Roman Law Resources** (iuscivile.com) is an informative and comprehensive site for the study of Roman law.

➤ If you're looking for other people interested in the Romans, check out the **TheVines** Ancient History site (ancient.thevines.com/). This is a terrific site for Rome and the Romans, which is well laid out and geared to engage a community of people with interests in Rome.

For a list of professional organizations and associations, check the list on **Maria Pantelia**'s page (www.tlg.uci.edu/~tlg/index/organizations.html).

The Medieval and Byzantine

Many books on the Romans end with the fall of the western Empire. We've continued into Byzantine and Medieval history. If you're interested in these areas, I can suggest two sources with which to begin, besides the ones mentioned above:

➤ **ORB: The On Line Reference Book for Medieval Studies** (orb.rhodes.edu/default.html) is a super-site of interrelated texts and other resources. It's incredibly impressive.

➤ How does he do this? I mean the sites maintained by **Hal Halsall** (www.fordham.edu/halsall/sbook1.html). His history *Sourcebooks* (includes Ancient, Medieval, Byzantine, Modern, and a number of regional "sourcebooks") are exceptionally well done. The *Sourcebooks* will put you in touch with a remarkable array of well-explained and interesting primary sources for the study of history (as well as movie reviews, historical outlines, and discussions of methodology). He also has one of the best **Byzantine Studies** pages (www.bway.net/~halsall/byzantium.html) that I've seen.

Lights, Camera, *Actio!* A Short List of Rome and Romans in Film

You'd be amazed at the number of films in which Rome or Romans play a direct or indirect role. I've included a short list of some of the more famous here for your next trip to the video store. For a more complete list, including foreign titles, check out Hal Halsall's *Ancient History in the Movies* (www.fordham.edu/halsall/ancient/asbookmovies.html) and his *Medieval History in the Movies* (www.fordham.edu/halsall/medfilms.html). Both of these sites feature descriptions and links to the *Internet Movie Database* (us.imdb.com/).

Roman Epics

The Sign of the Cross (Cecil B. DeMille, 1932; with Fredric March, Elissa Landi, Claudette Colbert, and Charles Laughton). Not as famous of a Nero as the *Robe*, but the uncut version is *spectacula*.

Quo Vadis (Mervin Leroy, 1951; with Robert Taylor, Deborah Kerr, and Peter Ustinov). This "Christians vs. the Evil Empire" epic features Peter Ustinov's famous portrayal of the dilettante Nero as the anti-Christ.

The Robe (Henry Koster, 1953; with Richard Burton). The soldier who wins Christ's garment at the crucifixion is transformed by his acquisition.

Sign of the Pagan (Douglas Sirk, 1955; with Jeff Chandler and Jack Palance.) Rome, love, and Christianity fend off Atilla the Hun.

Ben-Hur (William Wyler, 1959; with Charlton Heston). The cinematic epic of a Jewish prince who is sold into slavery and comes back to Rome for revenge. Some of the most famous chariot-racing scenes in cinema!

Spartacus (Stanley Kubrick, 1960; with Kirk Douglas and Laurence Olivier). A star-studded Cold War epic about Spartacus's slave rebellion.

The Fall of the Roman Empire (Anthony Mann, 1964; with Sophia Loren, Stephen Boyd, Alec Guinness, James Mason, and Christopher Plummer). Roman general tries to follow Marcus Aurelius only to be faced with Commodus; a precursor to *Gladiator.*

Gladiator (Ridley Scott, 2000; with Russell Crowe). A Roman general sold into slavery becomes a gladiator and keeps the Empire from going into the Commodus. Both praised and condemned, this movie has rekindled interest in Rome as spectacle.

Comedy and Such

Carry on Cleo (Gerald Thomas, 1964; with Kenneth Williams, Sid James, and Amanda Barrie). Two captured Britons become slaves and caught in a comic love triangle between Caesar, Antony, and Cleopatra.

A Funny Thing Happened on the Way to the Forum (Richard Lester, 1966; with Zero Mostel and Phil Silvers). This movie is based on the musical, which was in turn based on Plautus's play *Miles Gloriosus.*

Satyricon (Federico Fellini, 1969; with Martin Potter, Hiram Keller, Max Born, Salvo Randone, and Mario Romagnoli). Dark humor, brooding satire, and rich cinema mark Fellini's version of Petronius's picaresque novel.

Up Pompeii (1971). A slave comes into possession of a document giving the names of Nero's proposed assassins. You'll note that Pompeii blew up well *after* Nero's death and that the jokes predate Rome itself, but then this is *that* sort of British comedy.

The Life of Brian (Graham Chapman, 1979; with John Cleese and Graham Chapman). Monty Python's send-up of messianic hysteria. One particular scene, in which a centurion teaches the Jewish rebel Brian how to paint a protest sign in proper Latin, is a favorite with Latin students everywhere.

The Famous and the Infamous

Cleopatra (Cecil B. DeMille, 1934; with Claudette Colbert). A rich DeMille portrayal of Cleopatra as seductress of Roman men. The dialogue isn't Ciceronian (Caesar responds "nope" to the senators), but fun to watch.

Julius Caesar (Joseph L. Mankiewicz, 1953; with Marlon Brando, James Mason, John Gielgud, and Louis Calhern). A terrific adaptation of Shakespeare's classic drama.

Cleopatra (Joseph L. Mankiewicz, 1963; with Elizabeth Taylor and Richard Burton). A star-studded poetic drama featuring the dynamic duo of the silver screen of the time.

I, Claudius (Herbert Wise, 1976; with Derek Jacobi, Siân Phillips, Brian Blessed, and John Hurt). Ten-episode BBC television series based on the novels of Robert Graves (and Suetonius). One of the best you'll find.

Caligula (Tinto Brass and Bob Guccione, 1980; with Malcolm McDowell, Helen Mirren, Peter O'Toole, and John Gielgud). A big-budget and big-name rendition of Caligula's rise and fall that has some pornographic sequences.

Chi-Rho A Christian symbol made up of a combination of the Greek letters *Chi* and *Rho*.

Christendom The collected lands ruled by Christians or in which Christianity prevails.

client A person of inferior standing who officially engages a patron (a person of superior standing) for a mutual relation of support and protection.

coloni Tenant farmers who lived on the lands of the rich and worked them for a share of their crops.

comedy A genre of Greek drama that came into full development in fifth century B.C.E. Athens. A play about the humorous interaction of people, events, and ideas.

comitia centuriata (centuriate assembly) This assembly was created by the kings and organized originally by fighting units of 100 men (hence, a "centuriate" organization). It developed into the general assembly in the Republic, electing magistrates and hearing appeals. The centuries were organized according to property classification, and the classes voted as a block. Unfortunately for the lower classes, the voting was such that if the two richest property classes voted in agreement (which they often did), the vote was decided.

Concilium Plebis Plebeian assembly. This was the assembly that the plebs set up for themselves as a part of their succession in the "Conflict of the Orders." Only plebeians participated although patricians often influenced it through its ties with the wealthy plebeians and the tribunes. Occasionally, a patrician had himself adopted by a pleb to become eligible. The *comitia plebis* operated on the principle of "one man, one vote." It passed legislation, called *plebescita* (plebiscites), and elected officials (aediles) and their powerful representatives, the tribunes. The validity of plebiscites waxed and waned through the Republic depending on the strength of the senatorial party and the cohesion of the *nobiles*.

concordia ordinum ("the harmony of the orders") Cicero's phrase for the ideal co-operation between political and economic orders (nobles, equites, and so on) for the good of the state.

Constitutio Antoniniana In C.E. 212, all Roman citizens regardless of birth, economic status, or ethnic background, had equal civic status.

consul The chief executive official of the Roman Republic. Consuls held *imperium*.

crusades Holy wars (particularly of the eleventh through the thirteenth centuries) in which Christians from Europe attempted to conquer territories (especially in the Middle East) that were held by Muslims or people holding beliefs that the crusaders considered heretical.

cursus honorum Young aristocrats sought to follow a career path from quaestor to consul that was, in fact, called the "path of offices," or the *cursus honorum*.

cynics   Emphasized a frank practical morality which confronted pretentious shallow morality and custom. The most famous Cynic, Diogenes (ca 340 B.C.E.), lived in a dog house to repudiate the "civilized" customs for which he had contempt. (*Cyn* is the root for "dog" in Greek, and Diogenes's famous home may be what gave the Cynics their name.)

Dark Ages   C.E. 476–1000.

Delatores   Informers who accused others of treason or other offenses against the state. By law, *delatores* received one quarter of the property of the accused upon conviction (kind of like turning someone in for tax evasion today). Tiberius, contrary to some accounts, did not institute a reign of terror with this law, but his precedent-setting uses of it and the *delatores* became infamous.

Diaspora   "Dispersal." At times it refers to groups of people living outside of the homeland, at others it refers to the forced displacement of people from their lands. I refer to the period after 135, when Rome banned the Jews from living in Jerusalem or Judaea.

dictator   A supreme commander. Dictators were nominated by a consul and approved by the senate for a set period of time. The dictator was the chief official under a state of emergency and military law. He had complete control of all civil and military affairs.

dominate   From Latin *dominus*, "lord and master." The dominate covers the period from Diocletian (293) forward.

Donation of Constantine   One of the most famous forgeries in history. It was probably produced to bolster Pope Stephen II's claims on Italy with Pepin. The new king and pope each needed something from one another. Pepin needed to be recognized as king, and the pontiffs needed an enforcer to rid them of the Lombards *and* a recognized claim to their territories. Pope Stephen II made the journey over the Alps (he barely got through the Lombards) and crowned Pepin in 754; Pepin came back over the Alps and "restored" the papal lands to Rome in 756. In the Renaissance, Lorenzo Valla, using philological and historical analysis, proved that the Donation of Constantine was a forgery. We do not know if either Pepin or Pope Stephen knew this document was false.

ecstatic   Greek for "being stood outside of one's self." It refers to the experience of emotions or sensations so strong that they overwhelm and drive out one's normal faculties and self-possession.

Edict of Maximum Prices and Wages   In 302, Diocletian set price ceilings on over 1,000 goods and services. But prices continued to rise to the point where official production became unprofitable. In the face of declining production and a growing black market, the law was relaxed and finally canceled by Constantine, who nevertheless increased the burden of some of Diocletian's economic reforms.

Edict of Toleration   Allowed Christians to practice their faith and for their churches to operate legally.

369

Empire   Generally refers to the period after the Principate of Augustus (C.E. 14) when it is clear (at least to us) that the Roman empire was ruled by an emperor, whether he was officially recognized as a *princeps* or *dominus*.

fasces   When looking at things Roman, you might spot the fasces—bundles of wooden rods bound around a double axe with a red ribbon. Fasces were symbols of command authority, or *imperium,* which included punishment (rods) and execution (the axe). Mussolini, who hoped to establish a new Roman Empire, chose this symbol to express his political philosophy. He called his party fascist (but he apparently forgot the bit about being subject to the law).

fides   Means "faith" or "trust" and indicated living according to one's responsibilities, agreements, and pledges.

Gaul   The term "Gaul" is a catchall term for the Celtic and Germanic tribes that fought and migrated their way back and forth over Europe for centuries. In other places, you will find some of these people differentiated as Celts, Germans, or by their specific tribal names.

gnostic   A term that applies to sects that believe in a kind of secret knowledge (Greek *gnosis*) that depends on revelation. There were gnostic aspects to many Hellenistic religions and philosophies, and gnostic sects were an influential element of early Christianity. The gospel of John appears to have been written, in part, to contradict some of their claims.

Golden Age   The Golden Age is a period of Roman Literature roughly from 100 B.C.E to C.E. 14.

Gracchi   Refers to the brothers Tiberius (d. 133) and Gaius (d. 121) Gracchus, the tribunes who promoted land and voting reform in opposition to the senate. You can read more about them in Chapter 7.

Hellenistic   Refers to Greek civilization and culture throughout the Mediterranean and Asia Minor after the death of Alexander the Great in 323 B.C.E. to the Roman conquest of Egypt in 31 B.C.E.

hypostasis   The condition wherein Christ's two natures (human and divine) remained separate and distinct in the substance of one person.

Imperium   Latin for "power of command," which included the power of life and death.

keystone arch   The Romans' primary load-bearing architectural form. The keystone, which was shaped like a "V," was set at the top of an arch, banded, and cemented into place.

Latin League   A confederation of Latin cities neighboring Rome; each member held equal rights in the coalition. Rome conquered the Latins, broke up the League, and federated individual towns with itself.

liquid fire   More commonly known as Greek Fire, it was the secret weapon of the Byzantine Empire that turned the tide of battle for Byzantium against the Muslim fleets in 678 and 718. A Syrian refugee to Constantinople, Calinicus, created a chemical mixture that could be shot from a tube on a boat at an enemy warship. The gelatinous mixture would burst into flames like napalm, stick to boat and enemy, and burn fiercely even in water. The recipe was a state secret—so secret that the formula was eventually lost and never recovered. We still don't know what it was made of or how it was ignited when deployed.

Lombards   A Germanic people from west-central Germany who invaded over the Alps in the sixth century, settled, and established a kingdom along the northern part of modern Italy (still called Lombardy).

Magister Militum   "Master of the Soldiers," this was the military title for a supreme commander (under the emperor) of both infantry and cavalry.

Maiestas   Prosecutable treason, it came to include, by Julius Caesar's time, affronts to the dignity of the state. This law could become a capricious and dangerous political weapon in the hands of emperors (who were the state) and in the hands of un-scrupulous accusers called *delatores*.

megalomaniac   Greek for "huge madness." A megalomaniac has delusions of grandeur and conceives of himself as a person or divinity of enormous power and prestige.

metalling   Does not refer to "metal" (as in iron or bronze) in this context, but to the top surface of the road (such as the pavement) which bears the wear and tear of use and weather.

Middle Ages   The period between the fall of the Roman empire in the west (470) and the beginning of the European Renaissance in the 1400s. This period is also known as Medieval (which also means "pertaining to the Middle Ages"). The "early" Middle Ages run approximately 500–1100, the "high" Middle Ages from 1100–1500.

Mithridates VI (134–63 B.C.E.)   The powerful king of Pontus (on the Black Sea). Forty years of Roman oppression made the east ripe for rebellion against Rome and pro-Roman governments. When Mithridates invaded the province of Asia and then Greece in 88 B.C.E., these areas welcomed him as a liberator and attacked Roman citizens and interests. Sulla was appointed commander against Mithridates that same year.

Monasticism   The practice of living as a monk (from the Greek *monachos*, "hermit") usually according practices prescribed by tradition and rules handed on by other monks of a certain order.

Monophysitism   Holds that Christ's two natures (human and divine) had become one (divine absorbing human) in the substance of one person.

Montanism   Developed from the apocalyptic prophesies of Monatanus (ca 172), a charismatic Phrygian priest and preacher. His followers (Tertullian was the most prominent) treated his writings as scripture in their fervor for the end times. The sect was suppressed quickly, but continued in remote parts of Phrygia into the seventh century.

mystery religions   Contain secret forms of religious practice and doctrine, which are revealed only to initiated members and which usually involve beliefs about the afterlife. Initiates generally must undergo trials and oaths of secrecy before being allowed the revelations that admit them into the circle of believers.

neoplatonism   The most influential pagan philosophy of late antiquity, it was a complicated synthesis of philosophic and spiritual teachings. It not only influenced early Christian theologians (like Augustine), but also Medieval and Renaissance thinkers and writers.

Nicene Creed   "Nicene" from the Council of Nicea, "Creed" from the Latin *credo*, "I believe." A fundamental declaration and definition of what (orthodox) Christians believe. It lays out the basic tenants of faith regarding the nature of God, the trinity (God the Father, God the Son [Jesus], God the Holy Spirit) and the church.

Octavian   Historians and Classicists refer to Gaius Julius Caesar Octavianus as "Octavian" in his Republican days before 27 B.C.E. and as Augustus for the period after he was given this title.

Optimates   Favored the ultimate power of the senate and pursued their ambitions by traditional means.

pagan   From the Latin *paganus*, meaning "country peasant," it stems from Christianity being mostly an urban phenomenon in which the county dwellers (the *pagani*) were the last to convert. The same is true of the term "heathen," which refers to the primitive dwellers who lived in the wild "heaths" of Europe and England.

Panathenaic festival   A yearly civic and religious festival held in Athens in honor of the city's patron goddess, Athena.

Pater Patriae   Means "the Father of his country," the title Cicero (and later Augustus) was given by the senate.

patrician   An honorary title bestowed by the emperor, not an official office.

pax Romana   Means "the Roman Peace" and is the term that refers to the peace and stability that Rome maintained (within its borders) during the early empire.

periodic style   Refers to a style of composing complex sentences to contain clauses and subordinate constructions within the structure of the main sentence. These sentences have a form that goes somewhat like A-b-c-c*-b*-A* (if a letter indicates the beginning of a grammatical construction and the letter* indicates its completion). For example: "Periodic sentences are, for students who study Latin, the language of Cicero, or any language, very tedious to read."

philhellene   A lover of Greek culture and arts.

pontifex maximus   The high priest of Rome, the head of Roman state religion, and the head of the college of pontiffs. He appointed and oversaw the vestal virgins. Julius Caesar, all emperors, and finally the popes had this position and title.

Populares   Promoted their interests through the popular assembly and protected (when it suited their interests) the rights of the tribunes such as *intercessio* and *veto*.

post hoc propter hoc   One of many informal logic fallacies that still bear Latin names. In English, it translates as "after this (then) because of this" and describes the fallacy of claiming a cause and effect between two events based on their succession in time.

Praetorian Guard   Evolved from the bodyguards that protected a general. Augustus established several units from his own troops, and they became the later emperors's personal elite force.

Praetors   Second to consuls. They were primarily judicial officials (judges) and could have the power of *imperium*. They had to be at least 39 years old.

Principate   From *princeps*, "first citizen," it covers the period from Augustus (27 B.C.E.) to the emperor Diocletian (C.E. 293).

proscriptions   Published lists of names. A man on the list was declared a public outlaw and could be hunted down and killed for a reward. His sons lost their citizenship, and his property was confiscated and given to Sulla's friends or sold to pay his veterans. Many of the proscribed were guilty of nothing more than being rich.

Provincia   Originally meant an area within which military *imperium* could be exercised; provincial governors were, in effect, military commanders in occupation of conquered territory.

Punic   Derived from the Latin *Punici,* which the Romans called the Carthaginians. The word comes from their origin as Phoenicians. Classicists and historians therefore refer to the Roman wars with Carthage as the Punic, not Carthaginian, Wars.

pyrrhic victory   The cost of a "pyrrhic victory" is so great that it brings eventual defeat. In other words, you win the battle but (because of the cost of the battle) lose the war.

Quaestors   Public finance and record officials (roughly a Purser or Treasurer). They had to be at least 25 years old.

Republic   Refers to the period of Roman history from the overthrow of the monarchy (509 B.C.E.) to the Principate of Augustus (27 B.C.E.).

Romance languages   Those European languages descended from Latin, namely French, Italian, Portuguese, and Spanish.

Romanitas   The Latin term for "Roman-ness," it refers to the Roman way or manner of doing things.

Rostra   The speaker's platform in the forum from which orators such as Cicero delivered orations (public addresses). It was named for the Carthaginian ramming prows or "beaks" (*rostrae*) put on display there after the First Punic War (264–241 B.C.E.).

satire   A Latin poetic form that addresses any subject of life. The Romans were very proud of satire, which was completely their genre, or as the poet Horace put it, *satura tota nostra est* ("Satire is completely our own").

The **Second Sophistic**   A period of renaissance in Greek oratory and rhetoric in the late second and third centuries.

senatus consultum ultimum   Allowed the consul to take any steps he saw fit for protecting the Republic.

sesterce   A primary coin of the realm. It was worth 2½ of the main small coins, asses (no relation to the animal), and four sesterces made up a denarius, the principal large coin. A Roman soldier made about 900 sesterces a year, so Vitellius's banquets could have funded the legions for about a millennium!

Silver Age   A period of Latin Literature from 14 C.E. to roughly the death of Marcus Aurelius in 180.

standards   The banners and/or emblems carried before the troops. It was Marius who introduced the silver eagle on the standard of the legion.

Stoics   Named the *Stoa* (public colonnade) in Athens where they taught, they were founded in 315 B.C.E. by Zeno. Stoics emphasized self-control, detachment, and independence from the world, which they nevertheless believed was regulated by a divine reason for the common good. They recognized a common nature for all humanity. The Cynics originated with Antisthenes (ca 450 B.C.E.).

syncretism   Greek "blended together." The blending of different beliefs and customs into a synthesis that accommodates elements of each.

theocracy   When the state is ruled by a god or by an authority thought to be divinely guided and ruling in the god's name.

tragedy   A play about inescapable and inordinate suffering brought on by the human condition.

tribute   *Tributum*, it was the yearly assessment of taxes. Provinces and conquered peoples also paid installments as a part of treaties to cover the costs of conquest (yes, conquered people paid for their own subjugation).

vestal virgins   An ancient line of priestesses of the goddess of the hearth, Vesta. A vestal entered service at about six to ten years old and served for 30 years. After 30 years, a vestal was free to marry—though few did. Vestals oversaw a number of rituals and objects thought vital to the preservation of the Roman State.

Index

A

Accius, Lucius, 144
aediles, 70, 122
Aemilianus, 143
Aetius, 255-256
Afer, Publius Terentius (Terence), 144
Africa
    cultures, 45-46
        Carthaginians, 46-47
        Egyptians, 46
        Libyans and North Africans, 47
    Rome conquers Carthage (270–133
        B.C.E.), 81
        First Punic War (264–241
          B.C.E.), 82
        Second Punic War (218–202
          B.C.E.), 83-85
        Third Punic War and the
          destruction of Carthage
          (151–146 B.C.E.), 85
Agrippa, 183
Agrippina, 187, 193-195
Alans, 254
Alaric, 250-252
Alemanni tribes, 51
Alexander Severus, 224
Alexander the Great, 48-49, 80-81
American Romans, 342
amphitheaters, 166-167
Anastasius, 320
ancestor worship, 112-114
ancient Greek city-states, 48
Ancient History in the Movies (Halsall),
    Web site, 365
ancient Italy (pre-Roman times), 52
    central Italy, 54
    Etruscans, 52-53
    northern Italy, 53
    Samnites and Sabines, 54
    southern Italy, 54
Ancient Medicine/Medica Antiqua,
    Web site, 363
ancilla, 26
Ancus Marcius, 62
Andabatae gladiators, 311
Andronicus, Livius, 141
Angles, 254
animal contests, 20-22
Annales Maximi, 38
antiquarians, Latin, 295
Antoninus Pius, 210-211
Antony, Mark, 102-104
arch of Titus, 40-41
archeological sites. *See* remains
architecture, resource books, 358
Argos, Web site, 363
aristocrats
    aristocratic Republic, 67-68
    cursus honorum, 123-124

art, resource books, 358
assemblies, 121
    centuriate (*comitia centuriata*), 121
    plebeian (*concilium plebis*), 121
    senate, 121
    ward (*comitia curiata*), 121
Augustan period (Latin literature), 150
    authors
        Horace, 151
        Livy, 151-152
        Ovid, 152-153
        Propertius, 151
        Tibullus, 151
        Virgil, 150
    resource books, 355
Augustus, 9, 102-104, 175-176.
See also Octavian; Principate
    19 B.C.E. to C.E. 14, 177-178
    27 to 19 B.C.E., 177
    29 B.C.E., return to Rome, 174
    Actium until 27 B.C.E., 176
    other names and titles
        Octavian, 174-175
        Principate, 174-175
    power summation, 178-179
    Rome's transformation, 179
        "back to traditional values"
          program, 179-180
        borders, 180-181
        city changes, 180
        "Era of Big Government," 182
    succession, 182-183
        Agrippa, 183
        ramifications, 183-184
        Tiberius, 183
authors
    Christian
        early writers, 297-298
        late writers, 300-301
    Greek, 296
        romance novels, 296
        "Second Sophistic" period,
          296-297
    Latin
        antiquarians and encyclope-
          dists, 295
        history and biographies, 292-293
        medicine and science, 295
        novels and satire, 293
        philosophy, rhetoric, and
          letters, 294
        poetry and epics, 292
        technical subjects, 294-295
    Marcus Aurelius through the Fall
        of Rome, 298-299
        Christian literature, 300-301
        Latin west, 301
        pagan authors, 299-300
        Roman Greek authors, 299
autocracy, 176

B

B.C.E. (Before the Common Era), 4
barbarians, 30, 50, 253-254
    Angles, Saxons, and Jutes, 254
    Franks and Burgundians, 254
    Gauls, 50-51
        Alemanni tribes, 51
        Belgae tribes, 51
        Germani tribes, 51
    Huns, 254
    invasions, 253
    kingdom of Epirus, 51-52
    Vandals, Alans, and Suevi, 254
"Barracks Emperors," 224-227
Barrette, Paul, Wheelock's Latin Web
    site, 363
Before the Common Era (B.C.E.), 4
Belgae tribes, 51
Bill Thayer's Roman Web sites, 361
biographies, Silver Age of Latin
    literature, 292-293
Black Stone, 37
books, 353-365
    architecture, 358
    art, 358
    Augustan Age, 355
    Byzantium, 359-360
    Caesar, 354-355
    circus, 357
    early churches, 359
    historical representation in the
        movies, 365
    general Rome, 353-354
    gladiators, 355
    Roman Empire, 356-357
    Roman influence on the modern
        west, 360-361
    Roman Republic, 354
    warfare, 357-358
    western Roman Empire to
        Charlemagne, 360
    women, 356
"Boy Emperors," 248-249
Britain, imperial culture, 273-274
Burgundians, 254
Byzantium, 11, 238-239, 318. *See also*
    Constantinople; *Nova Roma*
    Byzantine history, 323
        1200–1453, 326-329
        717–867, 324-325
        867–1200, 325-327
        C.E. 610–711, 323-324
    Halsall's Sourcebooks Web site, 364
    influence of Byzantium, 327-329
    Justinian, 320-322
    origination events, 318-320
    resource books, 359-360

C

C.E. (of the Common Era), 4
ca (circa), 4
Caesar, Julius, 97-100
    literary accomplishments, 149
    resource books, 354-355
calendar dates, Steven Gibb's Roman Numeral and Date Conversion Web site, 364
Caligula, 189
    end of reign, 190-191
    erratic behavior, 190-191
    post-recovery, 190
Caracalla, 221-223
Carolingian Renaissance, 337-338
Carthage
    Carthaginian culture, 46-47
    Rome conquers Carthage (270–133 B.C.E.), 81
        First Punic War (264–241 B.C.E.), 82
        Second Punic War (218–202 B.C.E.), 83-85
        Third Punic War and the destruction of Carthage (151–146 B.C.E.), 85
Carus, Titus Lucretius (Lucretius), 148
Cassius Dio, 40
Cato, Marcus Porcius, 98, 144-145
Catullus, Gaius Valerius, 149
censors, 122
centuriate assembly, 121
centurions, 138
character films, resource list, 366
chariot racing (circus), 305-307, 357
charismatic cults, 278-279
Charlemagne, 336-338, 360
Christian culture
    Christianity, 286
    Crusades, 289-290
    Empire, 239-240
    literature
        early writers, 297-298
        late writers, 300-301
    persecutions, 287-289
churches, resource books, 359
Cicero, Marcus Tullius, 98, 134, 145
    orations, 147-148
        In Catalinam [Against Catiline], 1–4, 147
        In Verrem [Against Verres], Actio 1–2, 147
        Philippica, 148
        Pro Archia, 147
        Pro Caelio, 148
    pater patriae, 146-147
Cincinnatus, 78
circa (ca), 4
circus (chariot racing), 305-307, 357
citizens, 264-265
    Latin Empire, 270
        Britain, 273-274
        Gaul, 272-273
        Germany, 274-275
        North Africa, 271
        Spain, 272

Roman citizenship, 129-130
    foreign clients, 132
    Italy, 130-131
    Latin rights, 130
    rights abroad, 131-132
slaves and freedmen, 269
social classes, 265
    lower classes, 266
    middle classes, 267-268
    upper classes, 266
soldiers, 270
women, 268-269
"City of Rome," concept, 6-7
civil rights, origination, 5
Civil War, 100-102
clarissimi, 265
class divisions. *See* social organization
Claudius, 191
    conflicting character views, 191-192
    political accomplishments, 192-193
    wives, 193
Cleander, 218
Cleopatra, 102-104
clients (patrons and the patronized), 119-120
Cloelia, 76
Clovis, 334-335
Codex Sinaiticus, 300
collegia, 126-127
    flamen dialis, 127
    pontifex maximus, 126
    rex sacrorum, 127
colonae, 77
coloni, 268
Colosseum, 20
comedy films, resource list, 366
comitia centuriata, 67, 121
comitia curiata, 121
comitia tribunis, 70
Commodus, 216-218
commoners, 68
conceptual definitions of Rome, 6-8
    "Rome the City," 6-7
    "Rome the Concept," 8
    "Rome the Empire," 7-8
    "Rome the Religious Center," 8
    "Rome the State," 7
concilium plebis, 121
concordia ordinum, 146
concrete, 156
Conflict of the Orders, 68
    secession, 69-70
    tribunes, 70
    Twelve Tables, 68-69
conquest
    economics and administration power, 132-133
        abuse of power, 133
        banking and finance, 133-134
        lobbyists, 135
        public-private partnerships, 134
    reasons for Roman dominance, 17-19
Constantine the Great, 230, 235-238
    Byzantium rebuilding program (Constantinople), 238-239
    Christian Empire, 239-240
    love and loss, 241
    Maxentius conflicts, 235-236
    Mulvian Bridge and Daza, 236
    showdown versus Maxentius, 237

Constantinople, 238-239, 318. *See also* Byzantium; *Nova Roma*
    Byzantine history, 323
        1200–1453, 326-329
        717–867, 324-325
        867–1200, 325-327
        C.E. 610–711, 323-324
    influence of Byzantium, 327-329
    Justinian, 320-322
    origination events, 318-320
Constitutio Antoniniana, 222, 267
consuls, 122
contemporary influences, 343
    America, 344-345
    globalization, 344
    Latin language, 344
corporate farms, 136-137
Crassus, Marcus Licinius, 98
Crispus, Gaius Sallustius (Sallust), 149
crusades, 339-341
cults
    charismatic cults, 278-279
    cult of Isis, 282-283
    cult of Mithras, 283-284
    ecstatic cults, 278-279
culture, 262. *See also* literature; values
    art, resource books, 358
    east versus west, 262-263
    family dynamics, 107, 278-280
        education, 109
        household member names, 107-108
        pater familias, 107-109
        slaves, 115-116
        urban and rural distinctions, 111
        women, 110-111
    literature, 11-12
        early Latin literature (ca 300–100 B.C.E.), 12
        Golden Age (ca 100 B.C.E.–death of Augustus in C.E. 14), 13
        late Empire (ca 180–565), 13-14
        Silver Age (ca 41–180), 13
    major cities and capitals, 263-264
    public entertainment, 303-304
        chariot racing (circus), 305-307
        gladiators, 307-314
        history, 304-305
    religion, 112, 278-280
        ancestor worship, 112-114
        gods and goddesses, 113-115
        "old time" religion, 112-113
    self-image, 105
        dignity and authority, 106-107
        discipline and practicality, 106
        farmer-soldier ideal, 106
    social organization, 265
        lower classes, 266
        middle classes, 267-268
        slaves and freedmen, 269
        soldiers, 270
        upper classes, 266
        women, 268-269
    work life, 135
        corporate farms (*latifundia*), 136-137
        professional soldiers, 137-138
        trading luxury goods, 137
        work in the city, 135-136
        work in the country, 136

curiales, 267-268
cursus honorum, 123-124
cynic philosophies, 281

D

Daza, 236
delatores, 190
dictators, 123
Didius Julianus, 219
Dimachaeri gladiators, 311
Diocletian, 229-231
    dominate title, 230-231
    Edict of Maximum Prices and Wages, 234
    Maximian, 231-232
    reformation efforts, 232-234
    retirement, 234
    tetrarchy, 231-232
Diotima, Web site, 363
documents (evidence of Roman existence), 37-38
    Annales Maximi, 38
    Fasti, 37-38
    Lapis Niger, 37
    Twelve Tables, 37
Dominate, 175, 230-231
Domitian, 205-206
Donation of Constantine, 335
Druidism, 284-285
dynasties
    Flavian, 201-202
        Domitian, 205-206
        Titus, 204
        Vespasian, 202-204
    Julio-Claudian, 186
        Caligula, 189-191
        Claudius, 191-193
        Nero, 194-198
        Tiberius, 186-189
    Severan, 219-220
        Alexander Severus, 224
        Caracalla, 221-223
        Elagabalus (Hierogabalus), 223-224
        Macrinus, 223
        Septimius Severus, 220-222
    Theodosian
        Aetius and the end of the Theodosians, 255-256
        "Boy Emperors," 248-249
        Stilicho and Alaric, 250-252
        Theodosius the Great, 247-248
        women of influence, 249-251

E

early churches, resource books, 359
EAWC (Exploring Ancient World Cultures) Web site, 362
ecstatic cults, 278-279
Edict of Maximum Prices and Wages, 234
Edict of Toleration, 237
education, 109
Egyptians, 46
Elagabalus (Hierogabalus), 223-224
ementissimi, 265

emperors, 27
    "Barracks Emperors," 224-227
    "Boy Emperors," 248-249
    characteristics, 28
    Constantine the Great, 230, 237-238
        Byzantium rebuilding program (Constantinople), 238-239
        Christian Empire, 239-240
        love and loss, 241
    designation process, 28
    Diocletian, 229-231
        dominate title, 230-231
        Edict of Maximum Prices and Wages, 234
        Maximian, 231-232
        reformation efforts, 232-234
        retirement, 234
        tetrarchy, 231-232
    "Five Good Emperors," 206
        Antoninus Pius, 210-211
        Hadrian, 209-211
        Marcus Aurelius, 211-213
        Nerva, 206-207
        Trajan, 207-209
    Flavian dynasty, 201-202
        Domitian, 205-206
        Titus, 204
        Vespasian, 202-204
    Gallic empire, 225-226
    Illyrian emperors, 226-227
    Julian the Apostate, 245-246
    Julio-Claudian dynasty, 186
        Caligula, 189-191
        Claudius, 191-193
        Nero, 194-198
        Tiberius, 186-189
    Maxentius and Constantine, 235
        conflicts, 235-236
        Mulvian Bridge and Daza, 236
        showdown, 237
    Palmyrene empire, 225-226
    post-Constantine, 244
        three sons of Constantine, 244-245
    post-"good" emperors (Commodus to Aurelian period), 216
        Commodus, 216-218
        Didius Julianus, 219
        Pertinax, 218-219
    Severan dynasty, 219-220
        Alexander Severus, 224
        Caracalla, 221-223
        Elagabalus (Hierogabalus), 223-224
        Macrinus, 223
        Septimius Severus, 220-222
    Theodosius the Great, 247-248
    Theodosius to Alaric and the Sack of Rome, 246-252
    time frames of rule, 27-28
    "Year of Four Emperors" (68/69), 199-200
        Galba, 200
        Otho, 200
        Vitellius, 200-201
Empire (Roman)
    "Empire of Rome" concept, 7-8
    "Fall of Rome," 28-29
        Aetius and the end of the Theodosians, 255-256

after the "fall," 331-335
        barbarians, 30, 253-254
        causes, 256-257
        economic factors, 29-30
        global climate changes and ecological effects, 30
        lead content in water supply, 29
        Rimicer, 256
    legacy of Rome, 341
        American Romans, 342
        contemporary influences, 343-345
        reichs and rulers, 341-342
    resource books, 356-357
encyclopedists, Latin, 295
engineering, 168
    concrete usage, 156
    military camps, 168
    road systems, 157-158
        bridges, 160-161
        building process, 159
        elevated roadways, 161
        major highways, 161-163
        major road projects of the Republic, 157-158
        tunnels, 160
    siege equipment, 169
    theaters and amphitheaters, 166-167
    urban planning, 167-168
    water planning, 163-164
        getting water to the city, 164
        water distribution, 165-166
Ennius, Quintus, 142
entertainment (public), 20-21, 303-304
    animal and human contests and combat, 20-22
    chariot racing (circus), 305-307
    fascination explanation, 314
    gladiators, 307-309
        dwarfs, amazones, and amateurs, 311-312
        end of the games, 314
        event reenactments, 312
        game-day description, 312-313
        specialists, 309-311
        who they were, 309-310
    history, 304-305
epics
    films, resource list, 365-366
    Silver Age of Latin literature, 292
Epirus, 51-52
equipment (military), engineering plans, 169
equites, 118-119
"Era of Big Government," 182
Essedarii gladiators, 311
Etruscans, 52-53
Eudocia, 250
Eusebius, 41
evidence of Roman existence
    early church sources, 41-42
        Eusebius, 41
        St. Augustine, 41
    outside sources, 39
        Cassius Dio, 40
        Flavius Josephus, 40
        Plutarch, 40
        Polybius, 39

remains, 32-33
　　frontiers and provinces, 34
　　Herculaneum, 34-36
　　Pompeii, 34-36
　　Rome, 32-33
　　throughout Italy, 33-34
　　under water, 36
　textual evidence, 37
　　graffiti and other unofficial
　　　remains, 39
　　official documents, 37-38
　　Roman literature, 38
Exploring Ancient World Cultures
　(EAWC) Web site, 362

F

Fabian tactics, 84
"Fall of Rome," 28-29
　Aetius and the end of the
　　Theodosians, 255-256
　after the "fall," 331-332
　　popes, 332-335
　barbarians, 30, 253-254
　causes, 256-257
　economic factors, 29-30
　global climate changes and ecolog-
　　ical effects, 30
　lead content in water supply, 29
　Rimicer, 256
family dynamics, 107
　education, 109
　household member names, 107-108
　pater familias, 107-109
　slaves, 115-116
　urban and rural distinctions, 111
　women, 110-111
Fasti, 37-38
festivals, history, 304-305
films
　resource list
　　character films, 366
　　comedies, 366
　　epics, 365-366
　Web sites
　　Ancient History in the Movies
　　　(Halsall), 365
　　Internet Movie Database, 365
　　Medieval History in the Movies
　　　(Halsall), 365
First Punic War (264–241 B.C.E.), 82
"Five Good Emperors," 206
　Antoninus Pius, 210-211
　Hadrian, 209-211
　Marcus Aurelius, 211-213
　Nerva, 206-207
　Trajan, 207-209
Flaccus, Quintus Horatius (Horace), 151
flamen dialis, 127
Flavian dynasty, 201-202
　Domitian, 205-206
　Titus, 204
　Vespasian, 202-204
Flavius Josephus, 40
foedus Cassianum, 76
Franks, 254
freedmen, imperial culture, 269

G

Gaius (Caligula), 189
　end of reign, 190-191
　erratic behavior, 190-191
　post-recovery, 190
Galba, 200
Gallia Placidia, 249, 251
Gallic empire, 225-226
games, 20-21, 303-304
　animal and human contests and
　　combat, 20-22
　chariot racing (circus), 305-307
　fascination explanation, 314
　gladiators, 307-309
　　dwarfs, amazones, and amateurs,
　　　311-312
　　end of the games, 314
　　event reenactments, 312
　　game-day description, 312-313
　　specialists, 309-311
　　who they were, 309-310
　history, 304-305
Gauls, 50-51, 78-79
　Alemanni tribes, 51
　Belgae tribes, 51
　Germani tribes, 51
　imperial culture, 272-273
　northern Italy (197–170 B.C.E.), 88
Germani tribes, 51
Germanicus, 187
Germany, imperial culture, 274-275
gladiators, 22, 307-309
　dwarfs, amazones, and amateurs,
　　311-312
　end of the games, 314
　event reenactments, 312
　game-day description, 312-313
　resource books, 355
　specialists, 309-310
　　Andabatae, 311
　　Dimachaeri, 311
　　Essedarii, 311
　　Laquearii, 311
　　Myrmillones, 310
　　Provocatores, 311
　　Retiarii, 310
　　Sagittarii, 311
　　Scissores, 311
　　Secutores, 310
　　Thraeces, 310
　who they were, 309-310
gnostics, 298
gods/goddesses, 113-115
Golden Age (Latin literature), 13, 148
　Caesar, 149
　Catullus, 149
　Lucretius, 148
　Sallust, 149
　Varro, 148
"Good Emperors," 206
　Antoninus Pius, 210-211
　Hadrian, 209-211
　Marcus Aurelius, 211-213
　Nerva, 206-207
　Trajan, 207-209
government
　political structure, 120-123
　　centuriate assembly, 121
　　cursus honorum, 123-124

　　magistrates, 122-123
　　plebeian assembly, 121
　　senate, 121
　　ward assembly, 121
　Roman Republic, 70-71
　　aristocrats, 67-68
　　Conflict of the Orders, 68
　　legislative bodies, 71
　　secession, 69-70
　　tribunes, 70
　　Twelve Tables, 68-69
Gracchus brothers, 92-93
　Gracchus, Gaius (d. 121 B.C.E.),
　　93-94
　Gracchus, Tiberius (d. 133 B.C.E.), 93
graffiti, evidence of existence, 39
Greece
　culture, 48
　　Alexander's Empire, 48-49
　　ancient Greek city-states, 48
　　Magna Graecia, 50
　literature, 296
　　romance novels, 296
　　"Second Sophistic" period,
　　　296-297
　Rome conquers the Mediterranean
　　(270–133 B.C.E.), 86
　　conquering the east, 87-88
　　Illyrian Wars (229–228,
　　　220–219 B.C.E.), 86
　　Macedonian Wars, 86-87

H

Hadrian, 209-211
Halsall, Hal
　Ancient History in the Movies Web
　　site, 365
　Medieval History in the Movies Web
　　site, 365
　Sourcebooks Web site, 364
Hannibal, 83-85
Herculaneum, 34-36
Hierogabalus (Elagabalus), 223-224
Hippias, Web site, 363
historical literature, Silver Age of Latin
　literature, 292-293
history
　aristocratic Republic, 67-68
　city location, 54-55
　comparative timeline of Roman
　　history and literature, 12
　"Fall of Rome," 28-29
　　Aetius and the end of the
　　　Theodosians, 255-256
　　after the "fall," 331-335
　　barbarians, 30
　　causes, 256-257
　　economic factors, 29-30
　　global climate changes and
　　　ecological effects, 30
　　lead content in water supply, 29
　　Rimicer, 256
　general facts, 4-5
　　civil rights origination, 5
　　historical cycles, 5
　　Latin language influence, 5-6
　　multicultural background, 4

kings, 61, 63
    Ancus Marcius, 62
    Numa Pompilius, 62
    Romulus, 62
    Servius Tullius, 62-63
    Tarquinius Priscus, 62
    Titus Tatius, 62
    Tullus Hostilius, 62
legislative bodies, 66-71
myths (Rome's foundation), 58-61
period framework, 8-9
    Byzantine Period (565–1453), 11
    Imperial Age (traditionally C.E. 14–476), 10
    Principate of Augustus (27 B.C.E.– C.E. 14), 9
    Republican Period (ca 509–27 B.C.E.), 9
    Royal Period (ca 800–509 B.C.E.), 9
pre-Roman ancient Italy, 52
    central Italy, 54
    Etruscans, 52-53
    northern Italy, 53
    Samnites and Sabines, 54
    southern Italy, 54
world domination, 17-19
Holy Roman Empire, 336-341
honestiores, 265
Horace, 151
Horatius Cocles, 76
human contests and combat, 20-22, 307-317, 355
humiliors, 265
Huns, 254
hypostasis, 319

I

Ides of March, 101-102
Illyrian emperors, 226-227
Illyrian Wars (229–228, 220–219 B.C.E.), 86
Imperial age, 10, 67-68, 262
    east versus west, 262-263
    Latin Empire, 270
        Britain, 273-274
        Gaul, 272-273
        Germany, 274-275
        North Africa, 271
        Spain, 272
    major cities and capitals, 263-264
    Roman citizens, 264-265
        slaves and freedmen, 269
        social classes, 265-268
        soldiers, 270
        women, 268-269
Internet Movie Database Web site, 365
Isis cult, 282-283
Italy
    pre-Roman ancient Italy, 52
        central Italy, 54
        Etruscans, 52-53
        northern Italy, 53
        Samnites and Sabines, 54
        southern Italy, 54
    Roman conquest, 75-82
        conquering Magna Graecia, 80-81
        division of power, 77-78

        Gallic tribes, 78-79
        Latin League, 76-77
        Samnites and central Italy, 79-80

J

Janus, 112
Judaism, 285-286
Julian the Apostate, 245-246
Julio-Claudian dynasty, 186
    Caligula, 189
        end of reign, 190-191
        erratic behavior, 190-191
        post-recovery, 190
    Claudius, 191
        conflicting character views, 191-192
        political accomplishments, 192-193
        wives, 193
    Nero, 194
        actions and behaviors, 195-196
        Agrippina, 194-195
        end of reign, 197-198
        Rome's fire, 195-197
    Tiberius, 186-187
        death circumstances, 189
        Germanicus and Agrippina, 187
        Sejanus, 188-189
        senatorial relations, 187-188
Justinian, 320-323
Jutes, 254

K–L

kings, 61-63
    Ancus Marcius, 62
    Numa Pompilius, 62
    Romulus, 62
    Servius Tullius, 62-63
    Tarquinius Priscus, 62
    Titus Tatius, 62
    Tullus Hostilius, 62

Labyrinth, Web site, 363
language, Latin
    contemporary influences, 344
    worldly influence, 5-6
    Web sites, 363
Lapis Niger, 37
Laquearii gladiators, 311
Lares, 112
late Empire literature, 13-14
latifundia, 136-137
Latin
    Empire, 270
        Britain, 273-274
        Gaul, 272-273
        Germany, 274-275
        North Africa, 271
        Spain, 272
    language
        contemporary influences, 344
        worldly influence, 5-6
    League, 66, 76-77
    literature, 294
        antiquarians and encyclopedists, 295
        Augustan period, 150-153

Cato and Catonism, 144-145
Cicero, 145-148
comparisons to Greek literature and culture, 140-142
Early period (ca 300–100 B.C.E.), 12
first century B.C.E., 145
history, 140-142
Golden Age, 148-149
medicine and science, 295
philosophy, rhetoric, and letters, 294
Scipionic Circle, 143-144
Silver Age, 291-295
technical subjects, 294-295
Web sites
    language and literature, 363
    library, 363
    Wheelock's Latin (Paul Barrette's Electronic Resources for Wheelock's Latin), 363
laws and legal structure, 124
    court proceedings, 125
    precedent principle, 125
    prosecution and defense, 124-125
    Web sites, 364
legislative bodies, 66-71
Libyans, 47
literature. *See also* culture
    Christian
        early writers, 297-298
        late writers, 300-301
    comparative timeline of Roman history and literature, 12
    evidence of Roman existence, 38
    Greek, 296
        romance novels, 296
        "Second Sophistic" period, 296-297
    Latin, 294
        antiquarians and encyclopedists, 295
        Augustan period, 150-153
        Cato and Catonism, 144-145
        Cicero, 145-148
        comparisons to Greek literature and culture, 140-142
        Early period (ca 300–100 B.C.E.), 12
        first century B.C.E., 145
        history, 140-142
        Golden Age, 148-149
        medicine and science, 295
        philosophy, rhetoric, and letters, 294
        Scipionic Circle, 143-144
        Silver Age, 291-293
        technical subjects, 294-295
    Marcus Aurelius through the Fall of Rome, 298-299
        Christian literature, 300-301
        Latin West, 301
        pagan authors, 299-300
        Roman Greek authors, 299
    period framework, 11-12
        Early Latin Literature (ca 300–100 B.C.E.), 12
        Golden Age (ca 100 B.C.E.–death of Augustus in C.E. 14), 13

late Empire (ca 180–565), 13-14
Silver Age (ca 41–180), 13
Livius, Titius (Livy), 151-152
Lombards, 332
lower-class Romans, 266
Lucilius, Gaius, 144
Lucretius, 148
Ludis
Apollinares, 304
Cereales, 304
Florales, 304
Megalenses, 304
Plebii, 304
Romani, 304

M

Macedonian Wars, 86-87
Macrinus, 223
Magister Militum, 250
magistrates, 122-123
aediles, 122
censors, 122
consuls, 122
dictators, 123
praetors, 122
pro-praetors, 123
quaestors, 122
Magna Graecia, 50, 80-81
maiestas, 188
Marcus Aurelius, 211-213
Marius, Gaius, 94-95
Maro, Publius Virgilius (Virgil), 150
Martel, Charles, 334-335
master titles
"Master of the Cavalry," 257
"Master of the Foot Soldiers," 257
"Master of the Soldiers," 257
matrona, 26
Maxentius, 235
conflicts, 235-236
Mulvian Bridge and Daza, 236
showdown versus Constantine, 237
Maximian, 231-232
Medica Antiqua, Web site, 363
medical literature, Latin, 295
Medieval history Web sites
ORB: The On Line Reference Book
for Medieval Studies, 364
Medieval History in the Movies
(Halsall), 365
Mediterranean cultures and civiliza-
tions, 44
African Continent, 45-46
Carthaginians, 46-47
Egyptians, 46
Libyans and North Africans, 47
barbarian tribes, 50
Gauls, 50-51
kingdom of Epirus, 51-52
Greece, 48
Alexander's Empire, 48-49
Ancient Greek city-states, 48
Magna Graecia, 50
Near East, 44
Persians, 44-45
Phoenicians, 45

Rome conquers the Mediterranean
(270–133 B.C.E.), 86
conquering the East, 87-88
Illyrian Wars (229–228,
220–219 B.C.E.), 86
Macedonian Wars, 86-87
"megalomaniac," 190
metalling, 159
Middle Ages, 335-336
Carolingian Renaissance, 337-338
Charlemagne, 336-338
crusades, 339-341
Holy Roman Empire, 339
middle-class Romans, 267-268
military camps, 128, 168
Mithras, 283-284
modern west (Roman influence),
resource books, 360-361
monasticism, 300
money, denominations, 201
monophysitism, 319
Montanism, 298
movies. *See* films
Mucius Scaevola, 76
Mulvian Bridge, 236
municipiae, 77
Myrmillones gladiators, 310
mystery religions, 280, 282
myths (Rome's foundation), 58
story of Romulus, 58-60
traditional story, 60-61

N

Naevius, Cornelius, 141
Naso, Publius Ovidius (Ovid), 152-153
near east cultures, 44
Persians, 44-45
Phoenicians, 45
Neoplatonism, 245-246
Nero, 194
actions and behaviors, 195-196
Agrippina, 194-195
end of reign, 197-198
Rome's fire, 195-197
Nerva, 206-207
Nicene Creed, 240
nobles, 68, 118-119
North Africans, 47, 271
Nova Roma, 318. *See also* Byzantium;
Constantinople
Byzantine history, 323
C.E. 610–711, 323-324
717–867, 324-325
867–1200, 325-327
1200–1453, 326-329
influence of Byzantium, 327-329
Justinian, 320-322
origination events, 318-320
novels
Greek romance, 296
Silver Age of Latin literature, 293
novus homo, 94-95
Numa Pompilius, 62
numbering systems, conversion
programs (Steven Gibb's Roman
Numeral and Date Conversion Web
site), 364

O

Octavian, 9, 102-104, 174-175. *See also*
Augustus; Principate
19 B.C.E. to C.E. 14, 177-178
27 to 19 B.C.E., 177
29 B.C.E. return to Rome, 174
Actium until 27 B.C.E., 176
other names and titles
Octavian, 174-175
Principate, 174-175
power summation, 178-179
Rome's transformation, 179
"back to traditional values"
program, 179-180
borders, 180-181
city changes, 180
"Era of Big Government," 182
succession, 182-183
Agrippa, 183
ramifications, 183-184
Tiberius, 183
Odoacer, 256-257
of the Common Era (C.E.), 4
optimates, 93-94
orations (Cicero), 147-148
In Catalinam [Against Catiline],
1–4, 147
In Verrem [Against Verres], Actio
1–2, 147
Philippica, 148
Pro Archia, 147
Pro Caelio, 148
ORB: The On Line Reference Book for
Medieval Studies Web site, 364
orders
beginning of the Roman Republic,
66-67
Conflict of the Orders, 68
secession, 69-70
Twelve Tables, 68-69
tribunes, 70
Orestes, 256-257
organizations, 364
Otho, 200

P

Pacuvius, Marcus, 143
paganism, 245-248, 299-300
Palmyrene empire, 225-226
Panaetius, 143
Panathenaic festival, 304
Panteleia, Maria, Electronic Resources
for Classicists Web site, 362
pater familias, 107-109
pater patriae, 146-147
patres, 66
patricians, 68, 118
patrons, 119-120
pax Romana, 267
Penates, 112
Perennis, 218
perfectissimi, 265
Pergamum, 87-88
periodic style, 147

periods
historical, 8-9
Byzantine Period (565–1453), 11
comparative timeline of Roman history and literature, 12
Imperial Age (traditionally C.E. 14–476), 10
Principate of Augustus (27 B.C.E.–C.E. 14), 9
Republican Period (ca 509–27 B.C.E.), 9
Royal Period (ca 800–509 B.C.E.), 9
literature, 11-12
comparative timeline of Roman history and literature, 12
Early Latin Literature (ca 300–100 B.C.E.), 12
Golden Age (ca 100 B.C.E.–Death of Augustus in C.E. 14), 13
Late Empire (ca 180–565), 13-14
Silver Age (ca 41–180), 13, 291-293
Perseus Web site, 362-363
Persians, 44-45
Pertinax, 218-219
philhellenes, 143
philosphical literature, Latin, 294
Phoenicians, 45
Plautus, Titus Maccus, 141
plebeians, 68, 118-121
Plutarch, 40
poetry, Silver Age of Latin literature, 292
political structure, 120-123
aristocrats
cursus honorum, 123-124
assemblies
centuriate (*comitia centuriata*), 121
plebeian (*concilium plebis*), 121
senate, 121
ward (*comitia curiata*), 121
magistrates, 122-123
aediles, 122
censors, 122
consuls, 122
dictators, 123
praetors, 122
pro-praetors, 123
quaestors, 122
Polybius, 39, 143
Pompey, Gnaius, 97-98
pontifex maximus, 67, 126
popes, 332-333
Clovis to Charles Martel, 334-335
Pope Gregory the Great, 333-334
populares, 93-94
populus, 66
post hoc propter hoc, 216-217
Praetorian Guard, 28
praetors, 122
precedent principle, 125
princeps, 9-10
Principate (Augustus), 9, 102-104, 174-175. *See also* Augustus, Octavian
19 B.C.E. to C.E. 14, 177-178
27 to 19 B.C.E., 177
29 B.C.E. return to Rome, 174
Actium until 27 B.C.E., 176

other names and titles
Octavian, 174-175
Principate, 174-175
power summation, 178-179
Rome's transformation, 179
"back to traditional values" program, 179-180
borders, 180-181
city changes, 180
"Era of Big Government," 182
succession, 182-183
Agrippa, 183
ramifications, 183-184
Tiberius, 183
pro-praetors, 123
professional organizations, Web sites, 364
Propertius, Sextus (Propertius), 151
proscriptions, 96
protected sects, 280
Cult of Isis, 282-283
Cult of Mithras, 283-284
mystery religions, 280, 282
religious philosophies, 281
Provocatores gladiators, 311
public entertainment, 20-22, 303-304
chariot racing (circus), 305-307
fascination explanation, 314
gladiators, 307-309
dwarfs, amazones, and amateurs, 311-312
end of the games, 314
event reenactments, 312
game-day description, 312-313
specialists, 309-311
who they were, 309-310
history, 304-305
publicani, 134
Pulcheria, 250
punic, 47, 271
Punic Wars
First Punic War (264–241 B.C.E.), 82
Second Punic War (218–202 B.C.E.), 83-85
Third Punic War and the destruction of Carthage (151–146 B.C.E.), 85
pyrrhic victory, 52
Pyrrhus, 80-81

Q–R

quaestors, 122
Quintus Fabius, 84

religion, 112
ancestor worship, 112-114
gods and goddesses, 113-115
"old time" religion, 112-113
philosophies, 280
cynic, 281
stoic, 281
protected sects
Cult of Isis, 282-283
Cult of Mithras, 283-284
mystery religions, 280, 282
religious philosophies, 280-281
resource books (early churches), 359
Roman attitudes, 278-280
structure (collegia), 126-127
flamen dialis, 127
pontifex maximus, 126
rex sacrorum, 127

unprotected sects, 284
Christianity, 286-290
Druidism, 284-285
Judaism, 285-286
"Religious Center of Rome" concept, 8
remains (evidence of Roman existence), 32-33
frontiers and provinces, 34
Herculaneum, 34-36
Pompeii, 34-36
Rome, 32-33
throughout Italy, 33-34
under water, 36
Republic (Roman), 9
aristocratic Republic, 67-68
breakdown factors
Anthony and Cleopatra, 102-104
Civil War, 100-102
Gracchus brothers, 92-94
internal struggles (146 B.C.E.), 91-92
Marius and Sulla, 94-97
Pompey and Caesar, 97-100
Carthage conquest (270–133 B.C.E.), 81
First Punic War (264–241 B.C.E.), 82
Second Punic War (218–202 B.C.E.), 83-85
Third Punic War and the destruction of Carthage (151–146 B.C.E.), 85
founding events, 63-65
royal growing pains, 65-66
social organization, 66-67
Italian conquer (500–270 B.C.E.), 75-76, 79, 82
conquering Magna Graecia, 80-81
division of power, 77-78
Gallic tribes, 78-79
Latin League, 76-77
Samnites and central Italy, 79-80
Mediterranean conquest (270–133 B.C.E.), 86
conquering the East, 87-88
Illyrian Wars (229–228, 220–219 B.C.E.), 86
Macedonian Wars, 86-87
Octavian
29 B.C.E. return to Rome, 174
renamed Augustus, 174-175
Principate transition, 175
resource books, 354
Western conquer (270–133 B.C.E.), 88-89
Gauls in northern Italy, 88
Spain, 88-89
resources
books, 353
Ancient History in the Movies (Halsall), 365
architecture, 358
art, 358
Augustan Age, 355
Byzantium, 359-360
Caesar, 354-355
circuses, 357
early churches, 359
general Rome, 353-354

gladiators, 355
Medieval History in the Movies (Halsall), 365
Roman Empire, 356-357
Roman influence on the modern west, 360-361
Roman Republic, 354
warfare, 357-358
western Roman Empire to Charlemagne, 360
women, 356
film titles
character films, 366
comedies, 366
epics, 365-366
Web sites, 361-364
Ancient Medicine/Medica Antiqua, 363
Argos, 363
Bill Thayer's Roman Sites, 361
Diotima, 363
Exploring Ancient World Cultures (EAWC), 362
films, 365
Halsall's Sourcebooks, 364
Hippias, 363
Labyrinth, 363
Latin Language and Literature, 363
Latin Library, 363
Maria Pantelia's Electronic Resources for Classicists, 362
ORB: The On Line Reference Book for Medieval Studies, 364
Perseus, 362-363
professional organizations and associations (Maria Pantelia's page), 364
Roman law, 364
Roman numeral and date conversion (Steven Gibb's Roman Numeral and Date Conversion), 364
ROMARCH, 361
Stoa, The, 362
TheVines, 364
University of Michigan Classics and Mediterranean Archeology Links, 362
Wheelock's Latin (Paul Barrette's Electronic Resources for Wheelock's Latin), 363
Retiarii gladiators, 310
Revolution, 63-67
rexes, 66, 127
rhetorical literature, Latin, 294
Rimicer, 256
road systems, 157-158
bridges, 160-161
building process, 159
elevated roadways, 161
major highways, 161-163
major road projects of the Republic, 157-158
tunnels, 160
Roman numerals (Steven Gibb's Roman Numeral and Date Conversion Web site), 364

romance novels, Greek, 296
Romanitas, 272
Romans
family values, 107
education, 109
household member names, 107-108
pater familias, 107-109
slaves, 115-116
urban and rural distinctions, 111
women, 110-111
religion, 112
ancestor worship, 112-114
gods and goddesses, 113-115
"old time" religion, 112-113
self-image, 105
dignity and authority, 106-107
discipline and practicality, 106
farmer-soldier ideal, 106
work life, 135
corporate farms (*latifundia*), 136-137
professional soldiers, 137-138
trading luxury goods, 137
work in the city, 135-136
work in the country, 136
ROMARCH Web site, 361
Rome
city development, myths, 58-61
conceptual definitions, 6
"Rome the City," 6-7
"Rome the Concept," 8
"Rome the Empire," 7-8
"Rome the Religious Center," 8
"Rome the State," 7
Romulus, 58-62
Etruscan story, 59-60
Greek story, 59
Latin story, 58-59
Rostra, 146
Royal Period, 9
ruins. *See* remains

S

Sabines, 54
Sagittarii gladiators, 311
Samnites, 54, 79-80
Saoterus, 217
satire, Silver Age of Latin literature, 293
Saxons, 254
scientific literature, Latin, 295
Scipionic Circle, 143-144
Accius, 144
Aemilianus, 143
Lucilius, 144
Pacuvius, Marcus, 143
Panaetius, 143
Polybius, 143
Terence, 144
Scissores gladiators, 311
secession, 69-70
Second Punic War (218–202 B.C.E.), 83-85
"Second Sophistic" period, 296-297
Second Triumvirate, 102-103
Secutores gladiators, 310
Sejanus, 188-189
senate, 66, 121

Septimius Severus, 220-222
Servian Wall, 62-63
Servius Tullius, 62-63
Severan dynasty, 219-220
Alexander Severus, 224
Caracalla, 221-223
Elagabalus (Hierogabalus), 223-224
Macrinus, 223
Septimius Severus, 220-222
Silver Age of Latin literature, 13, 291
history and biographies, 292-293
novels and satire, 293
poetry and epics, 292
slavery, 23, 115-116
attaining freedom, 24
imperial culture, 269
ironies, 25
slave status, 23-24
sources of origin, 24
status, 23-24
types of slaves, 23
social organization, 117
beginning of the Roman Republic, 66-67
classes of Roman citizens, 265
lower classes, 266
middle classes, 267-268
slaves and freedmen, 269
soldiers, 270
upper classes, 266
women, 268-269
Conflict of the Orders, 68
secession, 69-70
tribunes, 70
Twelve Tables, 68-69
Latin Empire, 270
Britain, 273-274
Gaul, 272-273
Germany, 274-275
North Africa, 271
Spain, 272
nobiles and equites, 118-119
patricians, 118
patrons and clients, 119-120
plebs, 118
Social Wars (90–88 B.C.E.), 95
soldiers, 137-138, 270
soror, 26
Spain
imperial culture, 272
Rome conquers the West (270–133 B.C.E.), 88-89
specialists (gladiators), 309-310
Andabatae, 311
Dimachaeri, 311
Essedarii, 311
Laquearii, 311
Myrmillones, 310
Provocatores, 311
Retiarii, 310
Sagittarii, 311
Scissores, 311
Secutores, 310
Thraeces, 310
spectator sports, 303-304
chariot racing (circus), 305-307
fascination explanation, 314
gladiators, 307-309
dwarfs, amazones, and amateurs, 311-312

end of the games, 314
event reenactments, 312
game-day description, 312-313
specialists, 309-311
who they were, 309-310
history, 304-305
St. Augustine, 41
standards, 98
state games
Ludi Apollinares, 304
Ludi Cereales, 304
Ludi Florales, 304
Ludi Megalenses, 304
Ludi Plebii, 304
Ludi Romani, 304
"State of Rome" concept, 7
Stilicho, 250-251
Stoa, The, Web site, 362
stoic philosophies, 281
Suevi, 254
Sulla, Lucius, 94-97
syncretism, 279

T

Tarquin the Elder, 62
Tarquin the Proud, 62-63
Tarquinius Priscus, 62
Terence, 144
tetrarchy, 231-232
textual evidence of existence, 37
graffiti and other unofficial
remains, 39
official documents, 37-38
Annales Maximi, 38
Fasti, 37-38
Lapis Niger, 37
Twelve Tables, 37
Roman literature, 38
Thayer, Bill, Bill Thayer's Roman Sites, 361
theaters, 166-167
theocracy, 241
Theodoric the Amal, 257
Theodosian dynasty
Aetius and the end of the
Theodosians, 255-256
"Boy Emperors," 248-249
Stilicho and Alaric, 250-252
Theodosius the Great, 247-248
women of influence, 249-250
Eudocia, 250
Gallia Placidia, 249, 251
Pulcheria, 250
TheVines Web site, 364
Third Punic War and the destruction
of Carthage (151–146 B.C.E.), 85
Thraeces gladiators, 310
Tiberius, 183, 186-187
death circumstances, 189
Germanicus and Agrippina, 187
Sejanus, 188-189
senatorial relations, 187-188
Tibullus, Albius (Tibullus), 151
Titus, 41, 62, 204
Trajan, 207-209
tribunes, 70
tribuni plebis, 70
tributum, 87
Tullus Hostilius, 62
Twelve Tables, 37, 68-69

U

University of Michigan Classics and
Mediterranean Archeology Links, 362
unprotected sects, 284
Christianity, 286
Christian persecutions, 287-289
Christian versus Christian,
289-290
Druidism, 284-285
Judaism, 285-286
upper-class Romans, 266
urban planning, 167-168

V

values. See also culture
families, 107, 278-280
education, 109
household member names,
107-108
pater familias, 107-109
slaves, 115-116
urban and rural distinctions, 111
women, 110-111
religion, 112, 278-280
ancestor worship, 112-114
gods and goddesses, 113-115
"old time" religion, 112-113
self-image, 105
dignity and authority, 106-107
discipline and practicality, 106
farmer-soldier ideal, 106
work life, 135
corporate farms (latifundia),
136-137
professional soldiers, 137-138
trading luxury goods, 137
work in the city, 135-136
work in the country, 136
Vandals, 254
Varro, Marcus Terentius, 148
Vespasian, 202-204
Vesta, 112
vestal virgins, 59
Vesuvius, 34-36
Virgil, 150
virgo, 26
Vitellius, 200-201

W–X

ward assembly, 121
warfare, resource books, 357-358
water planning, 163-164
getting water to the city, 164
water distribution, 165-166
Web sites, 361-364
Ancient Medicine/Medica Antiqua,
363
Argos, 363
Bill Thayer's Roman Sites, 361
Diotima, 363
Exploring Ancient World Cultures
(EAWC), 362

films
Ancient History in the Movies
(Halsall), 365
Internet Movie Database, 365
Medieval History in the Movies
(Halsall), 365
Halsall's Sourcebooks, 364
Hippias, 363
Labyrinth, 363
Latin Language and Literature, 363
Latin Library, 363
Maria Pantelia's Electronic
Resources for Classicists, 362
ORB: The On Line Reference Book
for Medieval Studies, 364
Perseus, 362-363
professional organizations and
associations (Maria Pantelia's
page), 364
Roman law, 364
Roman numeral and date conversion
(Steven Gibb's Roman Numeral
and Date Conversion), 364
ROMARCH, 361
Stoa, The, 362
TheVines, 364
University of Michigan Classics
and Mediterranean Archeology
Links, 362
Wheelock's Latin (Paul Barrette's
Electronic Resources for
Wheelock's Latin), 363
Western civilzations, Roman conquest
(270–133 B.C.E.), 88-89
Gauls in northern Italy, 88
Spain, 88-89
Wheelock's Latin Web site, 363
women, 25
classifications, 25-26
cultural roles, 110-111
imperial culture, 268-269
ironies, 26
resource books, 356
status, 26
Theodosian dynasty influences,
249-250
Eudocia, 250
Gallia Placidia, 249, 251
Pulcheria, 250
work life, 135
corporate farms (latifundia), 136-137
professional soldiers, 137-138
trading luxury goods, 137
work in the city, 135-136
work in the country, 136
writers. See authors

Y–Z

Year of Four Emperors (68/69), 199-200
Galba, 200
Otho, 200
Vitellius, 200-201

Zeno, 256-257, 320

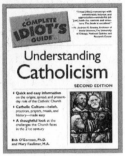

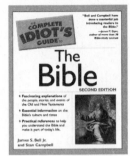

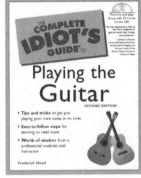

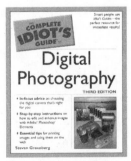
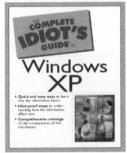